Protest Beyond Borders

Protest, Culture and Society

General editors:

Kathrin Fahlenbrach, Institute for Media and Communication, University of Hamburg.
Martin Klimke, New York University, Abu Dhabi.
Joachim Scharloth, Technical University Dresden, Germany.

Protest movements have been recognized as significant contributors to processes of political participation and transformations of culture and value systems, as well as to the development of both a national and transnational civil society.

This series brings together the various innovative approaches to phenomena of social change, protest and dissent which have emerged in recent years, from an interdisciplinary perspective. It contextualizes social protest and cultures of dissent in larger political processes and socio-cultural transformations by examining the influence of historical trajectories and the response of various segments of society, political and legal institutions on a national and international level. In doing so, the series offers a more comprehensive and multi-dimensional view of historical and cultural change in the twentieth and twenty-first century.

Protest Beyond Borders

Contentious Politics
in Europe since 1945

Edited by

Hara Kouki and Eduardo Romanos

berghahn
NEW YORK · OXFORD
www.berghahnbooks.com

First published in 2011 by
Berghahn Books
www.berghahnbooks.com

Library of Congress Cataloging-in-Publication Data

Protest beyond borders : contentious politics in Europe since 1945 / edited by
Hara Kouki and Eduardo Romanos.
    p. cm. — (Protest, culture and society ; v. 5)
    Includes bibliographical references and index.
    ISBN 978-1-84545-747-1 (hardback) — ISBN 978-1-84545-995-6
(institutional ebook) — ISBN 978-1-78238-117-4 (paperback) —
ISBN 978-1-78238-118-1 (retail ebook)
    1. Europe—Politics and government—1945- 2. Protest movements—
Europe—History. 3. Social movements—Europe—History. 4. Social
integration—Europe—History. 5. Transnationalism—Political aspects—
Europe—History. 6. Transnationalism—Social aspects—Europe—History.
I. Kouki, Hara. II. Romanos, Eduardo.
    D843.P75 2011
    940.55—dc22

2010024068

British Library Cataloguing in Publication Data

A catalogue record for this book is available from the British Library

Printed in the United States on acid-free paper

ISBN 978-1-78238-117-4 paperback
ISBN 978-1-78238-118-1 retail ebook

Contents

Figures

Preface

Kathrin Fahlenbrach, Martin Klimke,
and Joachim Scharloth

In recent years, the transnational dimension of protest movements has received attention from a wide audience outside of as well as within academic circles. However, the diverse historical roots of many of today's transnational activist networks or NGOs are still surprisingly unexplored by the research community. Although the turbulent social movements of 1960/70s are increasingly viewed as social and cultural responses to emerging patterns of an economic, technological, and political globalization, their European dimension has only been marginally analyzed.

This is all the more surprising given the fact that protest movements in Europe after the Second World War have increasingly acted within a transnational public sphere, particularly since the 1960s. On the one hand, their political, social, and cultural goals reflected international political developments (e.g., in their opposition to military intervention or their protest against global economic developments). On the other hand, national protest movements have strategically used transnational mass media effectively to mobilize and to address both a domestic and an international public, which they additionally tried to influence by creating alternative media networks. Yet, there seems to be a lack of international comparison that could not only systematically describe the similarities and differences between the single national movements, but also evaluate how they contributed to the evolution of a (trans-)national civil society in Europe. Especially during the Cold War, the (albeit difficult) diffusion of Western media, cultural items, and practices into Eastern Europe was an important interface across the ideological divide. After the collapse of the Soviet Union and the Warsaw bloc system, the various political, social, and cultural developments then provided vastly new possibilities for the evolution of a European public sphere.

To overcome this research deficit, an international research network on "European Protest Movements Since 1945" was established in 2006 with the support of the European Commission. By now, it boasts more than 250 affiliates from more than 30 countries and numerous disciplines, and it has established a permanent platform that fosters cross-disciplinary dialogue and exchange on the phenomena of dissent and social protest across the world. As is reflected in its publications, online guides, and conferences and workshops, one of the main areas of concentration of this network has been the impact that European protest movements had, not only in paving the way for a substantial change of the domestic systems, but also how they influenced the emergence of a (trans-)national civil society and the transformation of the public sphere after the Second World War.

Drawing on a conference at the Martin-Luther-University in Halle, Germany, this volume documents one of the first results of this network and its academic endeavor. The selected papers assembled in this book develop inspiring new perspectives on the transnational dimension of European protest movements today as well as on their transnational roots in recent history. The fact that many of the contributors approach the subject from various disciplinary backgrounds embodies the spirit of our research network, which is to advance the international and interdisciplinary dialogue on social movements. We firmly believe that only by bringing together different sociological, historical, cultural, and media perspectives on social movements, that the internal dynamics and external interactions of protest movements, whether domestic or transnational, can be adequately analyzed. This volume and its contributors are an important step in this direction.

Transnational Approaches to Contentious Politics

An Introduction

Hara Kouki and Eduardo Romanos

Emerging from an international workshop, this volume examines a variety of different aspects of social mobilization since 1945, while the contributors constitute an equally heterogeneous group of young political scientists and historians, anthropologists, as well as researchers on social movement and the media. Their research poses numerous questions covering a broad range of issues across time and space, looking retrospectively at global interactions during the Cold War, as well as looking forward at reconfigurations of protest politics in the twenty-first century, both in Western and Eastern Europe. Blurring chronological and geographical boundaries of study and merging strictly defined methods and disciplines, this volume, however, runs the risk of being nothing more than a list of fragmented and loosely arranged points and, as such, part of a burgeoning literature on the diversification of realities that has emerged as a result of the growing interconnectedness of the world in which we live. Are we, then, about to confirm once more the multiplicity of possible approaches on what is the living reality of our globalizing and globalized times?

All of the chapters, each in its very own different way, testify indeed to the tension between the local, national, and global that has become all the more ubiquitous in recent decades. In an effort to understand the changing constellations of contemporary Europe, the volume's contributors examine historical aspects of social and political movements or future perspectives of protest, while, at the same time, they look at social mobilization across countries in the East and West—it is precisely in this multiplicity and fluidity in terms of space and time that a common thread may be located in their research. No matter how diverse the focus and the methodology of each, they ultimately speak to one another. All seem to depart from the assumption that categories of analysis are not automatically attached to a specific territory or a particular time span. Within this context, scholars rely on contemporary theoretical analyses when revisiting collective action in communist countries or when attempting to integrate new historical studies on the Cold War into the exploration of contemporary activism in Europe. What seems to link the diverse contributions that follow, then, is that protest movements are examined from a *transnational* perspective and with the aid of *framing* processes. In this way, different instances of mobilization manage somehow to be creatively juxtaposed with one another.

David Snow and Robert Benford define a "frame" as "an interpretive schemata that signifies and condenses the 'world out there' by selectively punctuating and encoding objects, situations, events, experiences, and sequences of action in one's present or past environment."[1] First used in sociology in 1974 by Erving Goffman in order to make sense of the communicative acts of everyday interaction,[2] frames soon jumped into the study of social movements, where they have become one of the larger dominant areas of research (along with the study of political opportunities and organization resources). Framing refers here to the processes of cognition and interpretation intervening in social mobilization; acting as what surrounds (and marks out) a picture, frames focus attention to what is and what is not relevant for actors by defining what is going on in a situation in order to encourage protest and to involve people in mobilization.[3] Frame analysis, however, far from constitutes an exclusive methodological tool for sociologists and political scientists; indeed, it is employed by scholars from a broad array of disciplines within the social sciences and humanities, as this volume demonstrates.

The concept of 'transnationalism' represents another good example of interdisciplinary exchange (or, perhaps, interdisciplinary contamination and eventual generalization). Although earlier coined in international economics to describe flows of capital and labor across national borders, it became popular in the 1980s, when, in the field of international relations, the term was applied to grasp the increasing importance of non-state actors, in particular NGOs and multinational corporations, in the international arena. Since then, the use of 'transnationalism' or 'transnational' has mushroomed amazingly, being today at the crossroads of both academic research and public debates,[4] on the lips of scholars, political activists, journalists, and politicians. It is therefore not unusual to hear about transnational migration phenomena, transnational social spaces, transnational citizenship, and also transnational protest and social movements. The latter are best seen as networks of actors organized at local, national, and international levels, who mobilize people across national boundaries around a shared aim, very often toward the promotion of a global change.[5] Recent scholarship has finally come to describe transnationalism not only as the study of processes and relationships that have developed across or beyond the nation-state, but, furthermore, as a "gaze that begins with a world without borders."[6]

At this point, though, we do not intend either to reproduce the discussion on these definitions or to use them in order to denote a normative agenda for the book. Both of these terms imply a certain interactionist approach toward the study of social movements and, as such, they seem to provide us with an entry point into the particularity of this volume. To begin with, then, the individual entries of this volume travel across time and space in diverse ways, but, at the same time, they all approach social mobilization as an active and open-ended process.

Transnational Dimensions of Protest in Cold War Europe

The book is divided into four parts; the first section reveals ways in which protest activities in Europe were interconnected during the Cold War period. Even if the contentious politics of the 1960s and 1970s were the catalyst that led to the resurgence of social movement studies and to the development of new theories, historians have only very recently started to apply such approaches to the investigation of the protest activities that manifested themselves during those years. This kind of research leads to the merging of current movement theorems and analytical tools, such as *cross-national diffusion*[7] and *frame coding*, with the exploration of social structures and national traditions through time. It forms, hence, part of an attempt to explain the history of social interactions, of networks, ideas, and processes that merge and travel within or beyond the political borders of postwar Europe. It also forms part of an attempt to make sense, through a transnational narrative, of the contemporary world, not as a static and solid system, but something that at times comes together and at others moves apart. It is within this context that the first three chapters examine largely unexplored instances of protest activities and networks that developed in Europe from the end of the Second World War to the 1970s. Importantly enough, they all take into account the activists' relationship to worldwide realities, while also bringing into play Eastern European and Soviet perspectives.

In his chapter, Andrew Oppenheimer focuses on expressions of solidarity among West German protesters during the years 1945 until 1974. This piece of social movement history accounts, on the one hand, for the relationship of German pacifism with other national and international contexts, such as Cold War tactics, global anti-nuclear mobilization, Third World liberation movements, as well as Protestant and broader Christian currents; on the other hand, Oppenheimer also adopts a discourse-analytic approach in order to deal with the internal dynamics of expressions of peace and solidarity as developed within activist communities. In his analysis, these two perspectives are interwoven. The threat posed by nuclear weapons destabilized existing domestic pacifist arguments and simultaneously provided a new, supranational language in which pacifists could frame their claims, tactics, and motivations. Globally oriented expressions of anti-nuclear solidarity emerged, shaped by contemporary political events as well as available worldviews in West Germany, while also linking West German protesters with other mobilizations around the world during the 1960s. Oppenheimer analyzes the non-linear processes of rupture, formulation, adoption, and reproduction of mobilizing frames from a deeply informed historical perspective; his analysis being also sensitive to contingencies and ambivalences.

Celia Donert's contribution tackles the issue of historical struggles and movements of minorities in Europe by introducing a little-known chapter in the history of one of the most important protests of 1960s international mobilization: the "Gypsy" question in Czechoslovakia as developed in and around Prague in the spring of 1968. The struggle of Roma activists for recognition through transnational mobilization efforts are directly linked with general aspects of communist ideology, with changes in Czechoslovak socialism, as well as with the expanded social ferment of the 1960s. Developments at the international level altered the relationship between the activists and the power-holders: the minorities who lacked a territorial state interpreted the postwar international law on human rights as an opening in the structure of political opportunities through which they could defend their interests and, thus, they framed their protests accordingly; at the same time, this new reality was seen by states as a direct threat to the principle of sovereignty. Based on a great variety of previously unexplored archival material, the chapter examines how this diffusion of images, ideas, and networks shaped the movement by bringing to light both aspects of a shared, collective Roma identity, as well as tensions and differences between the various local communities. Donert delves into the particularities of the case study while paying great attention to the broader social, political, and intellectual contexts, thus integrating into the analysis broader interconnected phenomena, for instance, the way in which the broad issue of self-determination within multinational states was theorized at that time.

Similarly concerned with the new international human rights order is the final entry of this first section, which examines the campaign against the political abuse of psychiatry in the Soviet Union. The chapter focuses on the campaign for the release of the Ukrainian dissident Leonid Plyushch from a psychiatric hospital, which was mounted in 1975/1976 in both blocs by individual activists and nongovernmental groups, such as Amnesty International. Moreover, the author examines the discussions that were taking place in the West throughout the 1970s and 1980s concerning the motivations of the Soviet psychiatrists involved in the abuse; psychiatrists, journalists, and activists were debating the universality of those local and particular cases of mistreatment. Through the examination of these instances of mobilization in both the Western and the Eastern bloc and through the media, Hara Kouki follows the emergence of the human rights vocabulary in postwar Europe as a novel frame for citizens to communicate on issues of state repression and dissent at a transnational level and beyond Cold War politics. The contemporary human rights movement, thus, is not presented as the eventual triumph of a universal good; on the contrary, the author attempts to understand how it has been formed across countries and through instances of convergence as well as divergence, while producing its own narratives and ways of understanding the world.

Contentious Politics in a New Era of Transnationalism

The underlying idea of growing interconnectedness fashioning the above-mentioned texts is already an integral part of the second section, which deals with aspects of mobilization in contemporary Europe. Technical advances as well as "related economic, cultural and political developments have contributed to an intensification of both concrete global interdependence and consciousness of the global whole."[8] Globalization is difficult to define, but it is vaguely perceived as a constant process of the reconfiguration of the conditions of social life, as well as of the schemata necessary for its analysis. This global politics is shaped by relationships and struggles between states, non-state actors, international associations, and individuals across the world. And, in this sense, the social movements that take the form of transnational collective action reflect this kind of evolution and, thus, are the focus of much current writing and discussion. Forming part of this literature, the chapters in this section look at illustrative episodes of mobilization in contemporary Europe, as shaped both in relation to transnational contexts and within specific local communities. What is important is that all of the three contributions study globalization as an open-ended transformation full of heterogeneities and contradictions that have yet to be resolved.

Aron Buzogány's chapter represents a bridge, in many ways, between the study of current social movements and the historical essays that precede it. Buzogány persuasively draws a complex and dynamic picture of state–society relations in the new EU member states by examining the non-state actors, namely, the environmental and the Roma rights movement activism in Hungary and Romania in the pre- and post-accession periods. His approach is multileveled, and he looks at how the process of European integration altered at once the political and legal opportunities as well as the constraints for mobilization at the national level, the resources on which collective action is founded, and the processes of the attribution of meaning and motivation (*framing*) that facilitates the activation of protest mobilization in the new setting. Through this case study, Buzogány highlights the significant changes brought by the constitution of supranational authorities in the construction of domestic actors, providing protest movements with a new interlocutor and new goals. His chapter also draws a map of some long-term effects that Europeanization can generate, such as the professionalization, differentiation, and projectification of societal actors in Central and Eastern Europe.

In the next chapter, Simon Tenue surveys the anti-G8 coalitions in Germany. The research is built on participant observation conducted during the mobilization against the G8 summit in Heiligendamm in June 2007 and on an analysis of printed and online material produced during and after the protest event. Teune departs from the conviction that the transnational Global Justice Movement is a network of inherently differentiated networks. In order to grasp, thus, this plurality in the strategies and actions chosen by the movement groups and in their ideas for social change, he puts forward an interactionist perspective on ideology. The author, then, moves on to locate the underlying link between different actors, so as to reconstruct a coherent picture of a heterogeneous reality by applying the notion of communication repertoires, which enriches substantially our understanding of the symbolic construction of collective action. What is at stake, once again, is the cognitive level, here in the form of intra-movement differences, shaped by local traditions and particular historical references, and affecting strategic choices.

In the last chapter of this section, Johanna Niesyto follows up on the issue of communication of transnational collective action, with an investigation of the impact of new electronic technologies. The text focuses on anti-corporate European campaigns and explores the ways in which the internet is used in global justice contention. Defined as socio-technical networks, two of these campaigns are analyzed with the aid of framing concepts and the contextual dimensions introduced by Manuel Castells (the social, the technical, and the geographical contexts). The result is an ambitious comparison that reconstructs the master frames, the frame bridging, and the transnational dimensions of the campaigns, viewed as instances of mesomobilization. Bringing to the fore the dynamic interactions between the local, national, and European levels, Niesyto reveals the multiplicity of actors, issues, forms of organization, and tactics that are constantly emerging in the new era of transnational protest.

Broadening Theoretical Approaches

Until now, we have touched upon several aspects of transnational mobilization as revealed both in unknown episodes of the Cold War era and in currently unfolding forms of protest. But interconnectedness changes not only the relations between and beyond nation-states and societies in the past, present, and future, but also the inner quality of the social interaction and political culture itself. Globalization affects the ways we interpret the local when viewed within the global and, as a result, leads to a redefining of the categories and analytical tools we use to explain the world around us. When social interaction is examined as part of complex and open networks across territory and time and not as integrated within the defined and rational world of a nation-state, then social movement research cannot but adjust and combine theoretical perspectives. The endless effort of updating the lenses and tools aiming to grasp the changing, complex dimensions and new dynamics of the post-1945 transnational civil society often collides with persistent "black boxes" in which the various dominant approaches have shown sustained disagreement, as, for instance, the "missing" link still to be found between structure and agency,[9] or the "dizzying array of empirical findings" regarding the relationship between repression and mobilization.[10] The three contributions that follow testify to these and other emerging research challenges to social movement theory; while focusing on micro and local levels of protest, they bring into play broader processes of contention and, in this way, demonstrate that a revisiting of dissent analysis in new terms is something unavoidable.

In his chapter, Lorenzo Bosi examines the development of the Northern Ireland Civil Rights Movement from the 1960s to 1972. Combining aspects of the political opportunity structure and the master frames approach, he persuasively argues for the need to look at collective action beyond the confines of unconventional political behavior, and situates it instead within a complex but real network of power relations over time. This interactionist approach adopted by Bosi leads him to study how mobilization in Northern Ireland gradually acquired an ethnonationalist character, which he does by looking both at broader historical and political settings and within the internal dynamics of the movement itself. Departing from a variety of qualitative sources, he traces the evolution of the competitions among different organizations and groups within the movement, the process in which the mobilizing message that aligns with the dominant representation of the political environment succeeds. In doing so, Bosi injects a clear and dynamic element of agency into previous scholarly understandings of the Northern Ireland movement, but also in the study of social movements in general.

In the following chapter, Eduardo Romanos proceeds to the analysis of Spanish anarchism from 1939 to the 1950s within a similar contextual perspective. After the Spanish Civil War (1936–1939), the once-powerful Spanish movement suffered a strong decline. An extended version within the literature on the anti-Franco opposition talks about the anarchists' inability to adapt to the highly repressive domestic context and the changing international scenario as a main cause of this decline. Challenging this motionless picture by means of new archive material, Romanos first surveys the evolution of the ideological positions of its participants and then surveys how they were influenced by international political and intellectual postwar environments. Toward the end, the author moves on to a reconsideration of the interplay between repression and mobilization, putting forward a theoretical perspective grounded in both frame-coding and identity-building processes. Through this case study, he discusses the problems that the political opportunity approach presents in the understanding of the emergence of sustained collective action in highly repressive settings, and he advocates the formulation of a multi-factor hypothesis, which includes strong subjective variables.

This section comes to an end with Dominik Lachenmeier's contribution, which treats a wholly different subject: the current (re)organization of communication strategies of European trade unions. The chapter concentrates on a comparative study of Swiss, German, and Austrian trade unions, and looks at reforms in their external and internal environments brought about by the mass media and by processes of transnationalization and Europeanization, as well as by changes in their social basis. What seems to be of interest is the theoretical framework of the research—the author grounds this original piece on Niklas Luhmann's theory of "autopoietic organizational systems," by combining the constructivist systems theory approach along with the conception of intermediary organizations, which are seen as formal structures interacting with internal and external environments: their social basis (members, supporters, sympathizers, etc.) and the institutional environment shaped by the political system.

Outlook for Research

The texts presented so far have engaged in a variety of themes from a variety of perspectives, while being organized around three sections. But a closer look at the separate contributions reveals that even this broad categorization is rather artificial. The first section engages in Cold War histories, which, however, could hardly be inscribed into a single nation-state frame; the authors, equipped with analytical tools from social movement scholarship, (re-)visit little-researched episodes of collective protest of the postwar decades. Within the same context, the contributions of the second part treat various forms of mobilization in the era of globalization, which developed at a transnational level through the global diffusion of ideas and images; they, however, constantly bring into play the continuities and ambiguities inherent in local communities throughout history. In the third part, as well, the contributors believe that existing disciplinary theories fall short of examining single issues within broader chronological and spatial contexts, and, as a result, they argue for the importance of amplifying and merging approaches in order to comprehend multi-faceted realities. The fourth section concludes this volume; its two brief chapters respectively conclude the abovementioned categories, but move a step forward by posing outlooks for further research.

Mariya Ivancheva's contribution focuses on the role of the dissident intellectuals in the formation of civil society in Eastern European countries, both in the pre- and the post-communist periods. While going beyond a simplified interpretation of the events in 1989, the author makes nice use of the master frames approach so as to critically examine the active interplay between civic activism in both blocs. As such, this study compels us to rethink Soviet and Eastern European dissent activities, while the second text, by Swen Hutter, poses a similar challenge in the field of current transnational mobilization. The author moves beyond normative assumptions related to the effects of globalization on national contexts by looking at the ways national party and protest politics are affected by the emergence of new structural cleavages. Viewed from this perspective, globalization and transnationalization surface as multi-leveled and dynamic processes that shape our view of past and present collective action, as well as the research designs we use for such analysis.

Following this overall line of reasoning, Donatella della Porta, in the After-word, nicely summarizes and brings together all of the contributions by locating the present book within the study of transnationalization in social movement analysis. Due to recent transnational social mobilizations as well as academic en-counters between social movement and international relations scholars, this field of research is constantly expanding and being enriched; to this development, this volume brings further innovation by embracing multi-disciplinary approaches and research in both the West and the East.

Conclusion

As mentioned at the beginning and subsequently verified, this is a collection on aspects of social mobilization in Europe, which contains contributions from across the disciplines, with the aid of diverse methodologies and concerning different questions. However, the answers provided have something in com-mon. Researchers have dwelled on aspects of social mobilization both in East-ern and Western European countries, and have challenged the idea that there are simple continuities between 1968 and 1989 and normative transitions from the pre- to the post-communist periods. They provide us with pictures of the anti-globalization movement not as stemming from a universal spirit prevailing among the myriads of activists, but as negotiated within heterogeneous groups and across the world. They integrate into their research formal politics, the role of the media, the cross-cultural exchange of people, images, and ideas, as well the particularities of localities in order to examine the boundaries and attrac-tions that emerge at various moments of collective action. In other words, the authors approach social movements in an interconnected world from a *framing* perspective that allows their object of research to take shape in a contextual manner. Throughout this frame-negotiation process that permeates the texts that follow, the binary dichotomies between East and West, local and global, resistance and domination, national and international, are dismantled. They are instead integrated into a dialectic interplay between individuals, international structures, and local cultures. Within this multi-polar context of multiple actors, thus, there is no sense in locating "evil" in external factors, such as the "West," "globalization" or "capitalism," or in allowing room for teleological versions and assumptions concerning social struggles. Instead of rationalizing or controlling the extent of ambiguities and tensions, the approach we have adopted thus stems from, and further produces, complexities. Social movements are non-linear phe-nomena and involve dynamic social relations, and this book attends to their formation and evolution.

Researchers drawn from various backgrounds and driven by different as-sumptions study collective action in various contexts and with diverse expec-tations: what seems to link all of the texts is exactly their liquidity across the disciplines, objects of research, and methodologies used. Interdisciplinarity, multiplicity, and heterogeneity, then, are not a product but an integral part of each of the individual contributions of the book. And we tend to believe that this is the only way to escape from territorially and chronologically bounded explanations and to understand not just the current effects of globalization, but also how borders and attractions have been emerging throughout history. That means that we approach transnational dynamics not as an exception of our times that compels a reframing of answers, but as an underlying reality that conditions the questions we pose and the categories we use to experience the world. The book is not, thus, about social interactions that surface in transitional moments of postwar European history across or beyond borders; on the contrary, it assumes that these transnational episodes between East and West and the points of continuum between the local and the global are the norm. Their analysis will bring us closer to an understanding of complex realities both of the past and the future of social phenomena. To conclude, then, we wish to clarify that the diversity of approaches and the different themes we are about to present are not something *against which* we have managed to find a common thread in this volume, but *through and as a result of which* individual pieces have been brought into dialogue with each other. And once we have established that diversity and fragmentation are *a priori* basic dynamics in the coming together of (this volume on) social mobilization, then we can find a common platform so as to (research) protest.

This volume would not have been possible without the continuous support by the organizers of the international workshop and editors of the series. Martin Klimke, Joachim Scharloth, and Kathrin Fahlenbrach helped us during the long process of production by being a permanent source of inspiration and learning. At Berghahn Books, Noa Vázquez and Ann Przyzycki offered useful assistance, and Marion Berghahn has proved a patient and supportive editor. Two anonymous colleagues reviewed a first draft, providing valuable insight and advice. We gratefully acknowledge them all, along with the contributors to the volume and Professor Donatella della Porta, who gave us the best conclusion we could ever have had as well as helpful remarks during the process of its completion.

Notes

1. R.D. Benford and D. Snow, "Framing Processes and Social Movements: An Overview and Assessment," *Annual Review of Sociology* 26(1)(2000): 614.
2. E. Goffman, *Frame Analysis: An Essay on the Organization of the Experience* (New York: Harper Colophon, 1974).
3. J.A. Noakes and H. Johnston, "Frames of Protest: A Road Map to a Perspective," in *Frames of Protest: Social Movements and the Framing Perspective,* eds. H. Johnston and J.A. Noakes (Lanham, MD and Oxford: Rowman & Littlefield, 2005), 1–29. Recent, broad accounts on frames and social movements, also in F. Polletta and M.K.

Ho, "Frames and Their Consequences," in *The Oxford Handbook of Contextual Political Studies,* eds. R.E. Gooden and C. Tilly (Oxford: Oxford University Press, 2006), 187–209; and D.A. Snow, "Framing Processes, Ideology and Discursive Fields," in *The Blackwell Companion to Social Movements,* eds. D.A. Snow, S.A. Soule, and H. Kriesi (Oxford: Blackwell, 2004), 380–412.

4. R. Bauböck and T. Faist, eds, *Diaspora and Transnationalism. Concepts, Theories and Methods* (Amsterdam: IMISCOE – University of Amsterdam Press, 2010).

5. J. Smith, "Transnational Movements," in *The Blackwell Encyclopedia of Sociology,* ed. G. Ritzer (Malden, MA: Blackwell, 2007), x: 5060–5064.

6. P. Levitt and S. Khagram, eds, *The Transnational Studies Reader* (London: Routledge, 2007), 5. See also P. Clavin, "Defining Transnationalism," *Contemporary European History* 14(4), (2005): 421–439; R. Waldinger and D. Fitzgerald, "Transnationalism in Question," *American Journal of Sociology* 109 (2004): 1177–1195; B. Yeoh and K. Willis, eds., *State/Nation/Transnation: Perspectives on Transnationalism in the Asia-Pacific* (London: Routledge, 2003); M.P. Smith and L.E. Guarnizo, eds., *Transnationalism from Below* (New Brunswick: Transaction, 1998); J. Smith, C. Chatfield, and R. Pagnucco, eds., *Transnational Social Movements and Global Politics: Solidarity Beyond the State* (Syracuse, NY: Syracuse University Press, 1997); T. Risse-Kappen, ed., *Bringing Transnational Relations Back in: Non State Actors, Domestic Structures, and International Institutions* (Cambridge: Cambridge University Press, 1995); I. Grewal and C. Kaplan, *Scattered Hegemonies: Postmodernity and Transnational Feminist Practices* (Minneapolis: University of Minnesota Press, 1994).

7. D.A. Snow and R.D. Benford, "Alternative Types of Cross-national Diffusion in the Social Movement Arena," in *Social Movements in a Globalizing World,* eds. D. della Porta, H. Kriesi and D. Rucht (Basingstoke: Macmillan, 1999), 23–39; M.G. Giugni, "The Cross-National Diffusion of Protest," in *New Social Movements in Western Europe: A Comparative Analysis,* eds. H. Kriesi et al. (Minneapolis: University of Minnesota Press, 1995), 181–206; and D. McAdam and D. Rucht, "The Cross-National Diffusion of Movement Ideas," *The Annals of the American Academy of Political and Social Science* 528 (1993): 56–74.

8. D. della Porta and H. Kriesi, "Social Movements in a Globalizing World: an Introduction," in *Social Movements in a Globalizing World,* eds. D. della Porta, H. Kriesi, and D. Rucht (Basingstoke: Macmillan, 1999), 3.

9. R. Koopmans, "The Missing Link between Structure and Agency: Outline of an Evolutionary Approach to Social Movements," *Mobilization* 10 (1) (2005): 19–33.

10. J. Earl, "Introduction: Repression and the Social Control of Protest," *Mobilization* 11 (2) (2006): 129–143.

Transnational Dimensions
of Protest in Cold War Europe

Chapter 1

Extraparliamentary Entanglements
Framing Peace in the Federal Republic of Germany, 1945–1974

Andrew Oppenheimer

This chapter explores the role played by expressions of solidarity in the ethical and political economies of West German social movements.[1] Despite their prominence in postwar vocabularies of protest, expressions of solidarity have received little scholarly attention. What analysis there has been treats solidarity as a self-evident, stable term of analysis reflecting the common cause of activists internationally in supposedly related campaigns for liberation from structural forms of neocapitalist and neocolonial oppression.[2] Absent from this is any concern for the internal dynamics of these expressions—the claims they signify at given moments in time; the motivations that underlie them; and the manner in which different forms of expression either unite or divide protest communities.[3] By contrast, I attend to the internal, processual negotiation and (re)articulation of the terms of solidarity among West German protesters. My findings, specifically on pacifist expressions of solidarity, encourage an analysis of protest that considers the nature and limits of shared discursive resources and accounts for the relationship of West German protest to broader cultural economies, both within the Federal Republic and beyond its borders.

By tracing the shift from German pacifism's nationally oriented framework to its engagement with inter- and transnational political concerns, I account for the historical factors that motivated and structured the expressions of solidarity and, ultimately, forced activists to reassess the broad and encompassing definition of pacifism that had been accepted (though not universally) by German peace activists since the late nineteenth century. Paying particular attention to the *Deutsche Friedensgesellschaft* (DFG), I argue that the contingencies and ambivalences of expressing solidarity are crucial to the history of Germany's oldest and most venerable peace association and to West German peace activism in general. Furthermore, I highlight the ways in which expressions of solidarity signify moments of collective identification and the prospect of ethical, political, and cultural overlap between pacifist and non-pacifist protesters within West Germany's extraparliamentary opposition. Expressions of solidarity thus open a window onto the discursive mechanisms of group identity formation and patterns of cultural transfer within and between communities of protesters.

Specifically, I explain how the Cold War and the threat posed by nuclear weapons destabilized existing pacifist arguments and simultaneously provided a new, supranational language in which pacifists could formulate their cause. Highlighting the influence of Protestant criticisms of modern society, I describe the emergence of globally oriented expressions of anti-nuclear solidarity among pacifists that further enabled their identification with and support for national liberation movements around the world during the 1960s. I then explore the ensuing dilemma for pacifists caught between the conflicting implications of anti-nuclear and political solidarity. Finally, I call for greater attention to the common communicative forms and strategies employed by—indeed, the overlap in intellectual agendas between—protesters from different organizational, ideological, and demographic backgrounds.

(Re)Thinking Peace

While the Nazis dismantled peace associations and suppressed peace work, they did not annihilate the entire interwar community of German pacifists.[4] A considerable number of activists outlived the Thousand Year Reich, and it was pacifists from the cohorts active during the interwar years that initiated the process of rebuilding peace organizations after the Second World War. The DFG was reestablished in November 1946 under the direction of men from the interwar "Hagen circle," activists such as Fritz Küster, who had once promoted active struggle against entrenched martial values and interests. Küster and his fellow "radicals" had sought to build a centralized, disciplined movement set in opposition to a government that, in their eyes, furthered Germany's militarist traditions despite its parliamentary form.[5] They revived this agenda after the Second World War in a program that criticized the militarist spirit that had permeated—indeed, structured—German social and cultural life during the late nineteenth and early twentieth centuries.[6] As during the interwar era, DFG leaders approached militarism as a social problem that, in the form of specific material relationships and cultural assumptions, fostered a belief in the German right to dominate other peoples. Political renewal, they argued, first required the disarming of the German mind.[7]

The approach to militarism as a domestic social problem reflects the specific national orientation of peace activists in the immediate postwar years. The accusations of their interwar-era opponents notwithstanding, German pacifism was not (and had never been) a- or anti-national. To the contrary, pacifists had taken the existence and rights of nations for granted, and after the Second World War, they continued to regard militarism as a national problem.[8] National assumptions even oriented pacifist visions of world community, which maintained the integrity of member nations. DFG leaders envisioned a collective of discrete nations into which Germany would be integrated as an equal. There were other organizations, such as the West German branch of WOMAN (World Organization of Mothers of All Nations), which sought to transcend national distinctions, in this case through an essentialist vision of mothers as representatives of the human conscience.[9] And, of course, many pacifists thought wistfully of a future global community and world government.[10] They remind us that peace politics are not intrinsically bound to a national paradigm. Yet, as DFG Chairman Harald Abatz observed, people had not yet come so far as to consider themselves citizens of the world or to look at the earth as their "fatherland."[11]

It follows that national assumptions would inform pacifist responses to domestic and international concerns, including the Cold War. DFG leaders did not just advocate an independent middle path or neutral position for Germany between the US and Soviet camps; they conceived of the Cold War as a conflict motivated by the national-militarist interests of US and Soviet political elites. For them, both Truman's "dollar offensive" and Stalin's "imperialism" reflected domestic conditions within the United States and Soviet Union akin (though by no means identical) to those found in Germany.[12] In hindsight, the analysis seems quite anachronistic, as more a reflection of interwar concerns than an analysis of a geopolitical conflict premised upon mutually exclusive visions of sociopolitical order.[13] One thing is certain: with its emphasis on aberrant social structures and the need for cultural and political renewal, DFG rhetoric did not resonate with West Germans. They preferred Konrad Adenauer's strategy of *Westbindung*, which reflected popular fears of Soviet expansionism and—as even pacifists acknowledged—delivered substantive political gains that the people on the street could appreciate.[14]

It thus became clear that something was amiss with organized pacifism, its methods, and, indeed, its basic presumptions. Emerging threats, such as the Cold War and the deployment of nuclear weapons, demanded that pacifists formulate their positions anew.[15] Capitalizing on public fears of a third, catastrophic world war, pacifists reoriented their rhetoric from anti-nationalist-militarism to supranational themes of war and peace, portraying Germans largely as at the mercy of extranational decision-making. In this way, DFG leaders made its first meaningful inroads into West German public opinion and breathed new life into their organization.[16]

The first explicit indications of the new direction came in 1954 in response to US and Soviet tests of hydrogen bombs and the stationing of nuclear and other US weapons systems on West German soil. For pacifists, the hydrogen bomb represented a decisive juncture in human history. With its invention, mankind would live with the knowledge of its ability to end world history through a single act.[17] Heightening fears, the Cold War arms race gave people reason to believe that the prospect of global destruction initially evoked by Hiroshima would be realized sooner rather than later. It was in this context that pacifists turned to a supranational language of human suffering and global annihilation.

Poignant expressions of this turn came in speeches by then DFG President Martin Niemöller at rallies of "*Kampf dem Atomtod*" (KdA). KdA was the Social Democratic-led campaign against government efforts to establish a nuclear-capable West German army. During 1958, as many as 325,000 West Germans protested under its aegis against nuclear weapons and the estimates of 1.4 billion deaths worldwide (almost 50 million in the two German states) from a nuclear war.[18] Scholars agree that Social Democratic opposition to nuclear weapons was motivated more by power politics than principle.[19] This helps explain official KdA emphasis on nuclear weapons as a national issue threatening the prospects for national reunification and the fate of the German people.[20] Yet, the "imploring humanitarian pathos" of campaign speakers reminds us that participants sought to apply moral pressure on the western Allies.[21] It was in this vein that Niemöller expanded beyond national concerns and spoke of mass death in universal terms. "Atomic clouds," after all, "do not ask after friend or foe, rich or poor, white or black, western or eastern worldview; they turn against everything that lives, and they threaten everything with death."[22]

While similarly global in its orientation, anti-nuclear pacifism distinguished itself from established internationalist and "One World" arguments for peace by taking worldwide catastrophe as its starting point and, from there, reasoning through sustained social and political criticism toward a logic of renewal that corresponded to the prospect of human annihilation.[23] Like non-pacifist critics of nuclear weapons, such as Karl Jaspers, pacifists drew upon interwar discourses on cultural crisis to convey the disharmony of the nuclear age.[24] Nuclear weapons embodied the appropriation of inherently progressive technologies in the name of deviant—or at least incomplete—notions of freedom.[25] More than a threat in their own right, nuclear weapons evoked an uncanny sense of dislocation that critics attributed to an aberrant relationship between social values and technological change. Pacifists felt that man, living under these conditions, had been cut loose from his metaphysical moorings. The once clear distinction between the sacred and the profane had been blurred; the fruits of civilization—art and religion, science and technology—now served only to numb him to impending catastrophe.[26] Though lacking Jaspers's erudition, pacifist statements against the bomb conveyed general agreement with the logic of renewal formulated by the philosopher, namely, one that accepts the possibility—indeed, the probability—of catastrophe and on this basis leads toward a "reformation of political existence," from one premised upon conflict to one premised upon cooperation. If the bomb represented global suicide, its rejection would be the first step toward redressing the disharmony of the age.[27]

A key element in the global turn of pacifist criticism was the influence of the Protestants associated with the Dahlemite wing of the Confessing Church.

Dahlemites were perhaps the staunchest faction within the pastoral movement that protested Nazi interference in ecclesiastical matters during the Third Reich. After 1945, men such as Niemöller and Hans Iwand worked to establish a national church that conformed to the doctrinal revisions laid out in the Barmen Declaration and Dahlem resolutions of 1934. Challenging conservative Lutheran dogma, they called for a church active in public affairs, not in obedience to the state, but as a critic of government policies that did not conform to Christian principles.[28] While scholars have discussed official church forays into peace activism,[29] too little attention has been paid to the influence of reform-minded pastors and laymen within non-Christian peace organizations and the strong Christian currents that ran through pacifist thought in general beginning in the mid 1950s. Figures associated with the Dahlemites and the related councils of brethren (*Bruderräte*) were overrepresented in pacifist leadership circles, where they raised evangelical voices to address matters of secular governance.

In the hands of these pastors and laymen, anti-nuclear pacifism conveyed a Christian critique of West German public life. Niemöller and his associates rejected the formalist tendencies of West German democracy that, they believed, ran counter to the Christian foundations of democratic practice.[30] True democracy, they argued, reflected "reverence for the individual and respect for the decisions of conscience that fall to him … as a Christian and as a citizen." Furthermore, they claimed that the prophetic spirit nullified all friend-foe thinking and replaced it with "the message of godly, fatherly love that makes all men God's children and brothers."[31] The most explicit statements on the connections between Christianity, democracy, and peace came from Niemöller, who approached political discourse as a practical facet of moral discourse and, in this fashion, argued for the positive obligation of citizens *against* the state in the name of a supranational, Christian ethic of community.[32]

Given the prominence of Protestant pastors and laymen in anti-nuclear pacifism of the mid to late 1950s, it is hardly surprising that anti-nuclear rhetoric frequently drew upon Christian imagery. To quote Christian Geissler: "The highest goal of man is man himself, his self-realization in solidarity—or as the Christians say—together in love with all other human beings."[33] More prosaically, Fritz von Unruh envisioned a peace movement grounded in individual acts of conscience that, in concert, would forge a path toward human understanding. Evoking Beethoven's lyric "All men will be brothers," von Unruh specifically called upon European, Christian cultural traditions as the basis for a *Pax Anima*.[34] While it would be wrong to reduce all pacifist motivations to a specific ecumenical, reformist ethic, one cannot discount the distinctly Christian universalist overtones of the "*metaphysics* of anti-nuclearism" emerging in the Federal Republic at this time.[35]

These strong Christian overtones also speak to anti-nuclear pacifism's Eurocentrism. Far from thinking through practical acts of solidarity with Algerians, Egyptians, or Vietnamese, anti-nuclear pacifists of the late 1950s and early 1960s promoted European universalist cultural traditions as a global solution to the nuclear dilemma, offering them as a model—ethical, political, and cultural—for the world's "colored peoples."[36] In a different, though related, register, the characterization of Europe as both white and Christian raises questions about how pacifists—their critiques of National Socialism notwithstanding—understood and responded to Germany's recent genocidal past. At a minimum, West German pacifists embodied what Y. Michal Bodemann calls a "Christian initiated strand of memory," which generalized questions of racism and mass murder into universal themes of the human condition.[37] The mechanics of this process are evident in pacifist rhetorics of mass death that coupled Auschwitz and Hiroshima as moments in a teleology of destruction grounded in a dialectical relationship between technological progress and cultural crisis.[38] In this manner, pacifists tended to elevate the moral implications of global destruction over the fact of Judeocide. There was no deliberate attempt on the part of pacifists to relativize the genocide of European Jewry. However, the imperatives of the moment fostered a discourse on world and German suffering, akin to other prevalent West German discourses on victimization, which more or less supplanted earlier statements on German responsibility for the suffering of others and contemplated acts of violence more terrible than genocide.[39]

Peace, Pathos, and the Promise of Liberation

The humanitarian pathos of anti-nuclear pacifism, so evident in the morally and eschatologically charged remarks by DFG leaders and spokespersons, indicates several developments. First, pacifists had found an issue with broad public resonance on which they could capitalize. Second, having weathered intense anti-communist political pressures during the early and mid 1950s, DFG leaders had developed a more positive attitude toward large-scale protests involving non-peace groups. They began to encourage their members to participate in anti-nuclear protests in conjunction with non-pacifists, which were demonstrating against the general conservative political consolidation of the Adenauer era. In so doing, DFG leaders associated their organization with a burgeoning movement that criticized West German political practices and social norms. Third, the humanitarian pathos of peace rhetoric signals a substantive change in pacifist thought on the idea of community. Though the transition was by no means absolute, the trend was from considering the nation and the community of nations as the proper subjects of peace work toward thinking about humanity in general.

Scholars of extraparliamentary protest do not fully appreciate the significance of these expressions of humanitarian pathos. Take Karl A. Otto's seminal analysis of the "Ostermarsch der Atomwaffengegner," the Easter March campaign.[40] Inspired by the British Campaign for Nuclear Disarmament, it began in 1960 as a four-day series of silent marches held every Easter to bear witness to the human cost of nuclear warfare. Despite the many merits of Otto's analysis of this campaign, he gives the false impression that expressions of humanitarian pathos and politics were mutually exclusive propositions and that the anti-nuclear pacifism of the 1950s and early 1960s was thus fundamentally apolitical.[41] While the claim is valid for certain campaign organizers, Otto ascribes it to the campaign *in toto*. On this basis, he describes a process of politicization tied to generational change among Easter March participants that led teleologically to the protests connoted by "1968." Otto's analysis proceeds at the expense of a complete analysis of anti-nuclear activism that would account for the entire spectrum of motivations and interests of Easter Marchers. My research indicates that early campaign participants considered their actions to be fundamentally political. Demonstrating multiple and overlapping motivations in their exhortations against the global, human cost of nuclear war, protesters refused to distinguish moral exhortation from political action. Not only does this analysis belie Otto's systematic account of a transition from moral witness to political action,[42] it forces us to recognize that pacifists of the moment considered humanitarian and political aims to be co-constitutive. This matters because it is ultimately on this basis that we can situate pacifists in the extraparliamentary political campaigns of the 1960s.

Anti-nuclear activists sought to subordinate civic discourse to a moral one, leading them to embrace a language of global community, which in turn became the basis for a good deal of peace rhetoric during the 1960s, including (but not limited to) that rhetoric voiced during the Easter Marches and marshaled against both proposed emergency legislation and the Vietnam War. The latter case is particularly instructive. It offers a window onto how pacifists established global terms of solidarity that set the stage for expressions of solidarity with Third World liberation movements. At the same time, pacifist identifications with the South Vietnamese National Liberation Front (FNL) tested the very terms of the solidarity that had inspired it. Facing both the FNL's military actions and provocative acts of solidarity by members of the broader West German extraparliamentary opposition,[43] pacifists had to consider whether their vision of solidarity could be reconciled with the politics of non-pacifist forces committed to similar programs of progressive social change.

These issues evolved gradually over the course of a decade and came to a head only during the early 1970s. Initial pacifist responses to the Vietnam War remained wholly consistent with established tenets of both the DFG and the War Resisters' International (WRI). Responding to fears of a protracted military conflict that threatened to spill out over Vietnamese borders, DFG leaders pursued a two-pronged strategy of anti-war rhetoric and humanitarian relief coordination. One of the most successful humanitarian initiatives of the era was the *Hilfsaktion Vietnam* (HV), an independent relief fund founded in early 1966 by DFG leaders August Bangel, Niemöller, and Gottfried Wandersleb, in cooperation with Heinz Kloppenburg (*Versöhnungsbund*) and the trade unionist Walter Fabian.[44] However, as the US military effort escalated and politicians raised the prospect of direct West German involvement in the conflagration, peace activists adopted a new position that combined support for anti-colonial struggles with a critique of (supposedly) late capitalism.[45] And where they once emphasized war and peace between East and West, peace activists began to speak of the increasingly sharp and bitter antagonism between the world's "colored" and "white" peoples.[46]

An expanding horizon of pacifist concerns is evident. Activists saw in Vietnam an expression of inequalities in global wealth distribution, neocolonial empire, and race relations.[47] Attending to these underlying conditions, in 1968 the WRI declared that it opposed all forms of degradation and dehumanization.[48] Following the WRI's lead, West German pacifists began to speak of themselves as part of a "freedom movement" that opposed systemic forms of social violence. These sentiments were codified in the 1968 program of the newly merged *Deutsche Friedensgesellschaft-Internationale der Kriegsdienstgegner* (DFG-IdK), which committed the organization to democracy in government, economy, and society: "[The DFG-IdK] strives to help realize a social order founded upon social justice, in which the free development and full force of basic democratic rights are ensured."[49] While this statement offers no concrete vision of social reform, when read together with articles published in pacifist magazines on the dangers of sexual repression and the destructive impact of obedience on human dignity, one sees that pacifists had broadened their focus from the narrow confines of the violence of war to address a range of military, political, social, and cultural forms of violence and domination.[50]

The increasing attention paid by pacifists to systemic patterns of inequality and repression suggests parallels to the arguments of anti-authoritarian representatives of the student movement, activists who criticized the sociocultural alienation and repression of organized capitalist societies.[51] Pacifists certainly expressed agreement with and support for student activists of the New Left.[52] Their affinity found expression in both offers of and actual cooperation with non-pacifist and student activists within specific organizations and large-scale protest actions.[53]

Of course, such moments of cooperation raise questions about their extent and relevance to the histories of extraparliamentary protest and social movements. Existing scholarship suggests that what common ground there may have been in respective agendas was marginal and largely irrelevant to the history of the protests associated with "1968." Ingrid Gilcher-Holtey, for instance, argues that student identification with Third World liberation movements translated into a "cognitive orientation" toward a strategy for action in the western industrialized states that supported non-western liberation struggles and distinguished students from their pacifist counterparts.[54] Certainly, when seeing themselves as agents of global revolution, West German student activists discussed, justified, and, in some cases, pursued violent acts against what they saw as structural barriers to liberation in their own society and in solidarity with those groups and individuals whom they considered their Third World counterparts.[55] My research, however, indicates that identification with Third World liberation struggles per se did not distinguish students from their extraparliamentary collaborators. As elsewhere, West German pacifists read Frantz Fanon, supported Ho Chi Minh, and, again, came to see themselves as part of "a freedom movement" that opposed systemic forms of social violence made manifest in capitalist, colonial, and totalitarian regimes.[56] According to Jean van Lierde, Secretary of the Belgian WRI, peace work was a facet of the global struggle for liberation. Echoing Rudi Dutschke, van Lierde even encouraged acts of sabotage against capitalist and socialist states in support of Third World liberation struggles.[57]

The concern of peace activists for First World repression and their support for Third World liberation movements demonstrates openness to leftist criticisms of the "West." According to former DFG co-Chair Hannelis Schulte: "DFG people (and I) took the position that the financiers [that stood] behind the veil of fine speeches wanted neither democracy nor disarmament. Hence [we] hoped that socialism [as embodied by the FNL] pursued a more honest politics of peace."[58] Niemöller offered a more philosophical explanation of the interest in socialism. He had come to see the socialist project as "a rational … task of humanity." Severe economic disparities between the First and Third Worlds, as well as a global population explosion, made the planned regulation and division of material production a Christian obligation: "We know," he declared, "that *Mitmenschlichkeit* is and must be an unavoidable aspect of our [Christian] *Menschsein.*"[59]

I do not want to paint a rosy picture of unquestioned cooperation and fellowship among all groups within the extraparliamentary opposition. It is clear that anti-authoritarians, such as Dutschke, dismissed pacifism as an expression of repressive bourgeois humanism.[60] My point is simply that if there was an ideological divide separating pacifist and New Left activists, it did not center on identification with revolutionary movements, but rather on the means employed toward revolutionary ends. Van Lierde, for instance, argued for a radical anti-imperialism that maintained both practical and theoretical fidelity to the doctrine of non-violence. Similarly, the WRI insisted on non-violent revolutionary struggle, arguing that violent acts of revolution perpetuate the cycle of inhumanity that revolutionaries should seek to redress.[61] West German pacifists tended to agree. Niemöller, for one, insisted that the *Völkersolidarität* required to resist imperialist hegemony could not be established through violent means.[62]

Still, pacifists could not agree on where to draw the line between permissible and non-permissible acts of struggle and solidarity. West German pacifists were unwilling to denounce categorically other—particularly non-European—liberation movements for perpetrating violent acts.[63] In general, they refused to speak dogmatically on violence versus non-violence, choosing instead to consider and judge specific acts of "resistance" in context. According to Schulte: "[We] should ask of every situation whether the destruction of things and human life cannot be avoided. We may look at destructive violence only as an ultimo ratio—as the very last resort."[64] For his part, DFG-IdK co-Chair Helmut Michael Vogel resisted the WRI's stance against broadly conceived notions of violence (*Gewalt*), and argued for a narrow focus on the violence of war (*Kriegsgewalt*). This would simultaneously anchor pacifism and allow greater mobility for action/resistance against non-war related forms of oppression.[65] Vogel rejected dogmatic views of pacifism, which he described as expressions of irrational sentiment. He and his colleagues envisioned a pacifism that opposed warfare, but that supported those who fought "the same struggle" irrespective of their chosen means.[66] In short, DFG-IdK leaders expressed ambivalence over both the role of non-violence in liberation struggles and the prospects for non-violence in general as a means of sociopolitical change at their particular moment in history.

Conclusion: Solidarity as an Extraparliamentary Frame

Eventually, West German ambivalence clashed with the WRI leadership's insistence on non-violent means of action.[67] This set the stage for conflict during the early 1970s between the DFG-IdK and the WRI's Executive Committee that marked a turning point in the history of West German pacifism. This conflict, over whether pacifism is an absolute doctrine or a contextually specific practice, is the subject for another article. Here, I will say only that it led West Germans to significantly narrow the range of ideas and strategies that they associated with pacifism.[68]

As I have explained, the origins of this conflict lay in efforts to define pacifist solidarity. The twin environments of the Cold War and the nuclear age established new, supranational parameters for expressions of solidarity. Articulated from the standpoint of an evangelically inflected critique of modern society, anti-nuclear pacifism enabled identification with and support for liberation movements across the globe during the 1960s. Like their extraparliamentary counterparts at home and abroad, West German pacifists increasingly defined peace not as an absence of war, but in terms of social justice. With this shift came an opportunity for pacifists to consider the prospect of aggressive, even violent, means of action outside the realm of their traditional opposition to the violence of war. However, as solidarity movements became increasingly active at home, West German pacifists found themselves caught between conflicting inclinations. Their commitment to solidarity with humanity ultimately clashed with their desire to support liberation movements and the reality of Europeans and non-Europeans perpetrating acts of violence against other human beings.

It is important to place pacifist notions of solidarity in their overlapping organizational contexts, for they evolved as the DFG underwent competing processes of political consolidation and integration—processes that pulled the organization in diverging directions. On the one hand, the DFG brought itself into line with international pacifist doctrine as espoused by the WRI. This had become a prerequisite for the organizational merger of German peace associations, which, for the DFG, was a matter of survival.[69] Abandoning its traditional open door policy to all perspectives promoting peace, the DFG officially embraced the WRI's position on principled non-violence during the early 1960s and required its members to sign the WRI's pledge condemning war in all of its guises. In the future, the DFG would follow the WRI's lead, seeking to remake itself as part of a (vaguely defined) freedom movement.[70] On the other hand, West German pacifists were establishing a niche for themselves within domestic extraparliamentary opposition campaigns. Seeking allies against proposed emergency legislation as well as the Vietnam War, DFG members increased their activities with, and ties to, trade unions, civil rights organizations, and student groups.[71] During the 1960s, effective peace work meant participation in large-scale, coalition-based protest actions. In addition, DFG leaders hoped to attract younger activists from this engagement—activists who might formulate questions of peace anew from the perspective of contemporary economic and sociological analysis.[72] Whereas the consolidation of pacifist forces proceeded on the basis of WRI principles, domestic cooperation with non-pacifist activists led some members of the DFG in a countervailing direction that emphasized the critique of structural violence over and above exaltations of peace. So strong was the latter's influence that international observers began to question the sincerity of West German commitments to WRI doctrine.[73]

If the conflict among pacifists resulted in a reworking of the terms of West German pacifism, its analysis reveals considerably more. Pacifist expressions of solidarity indicate the intersection of and tensions between broader cultural economies within the West German extraparliamentary opposition. In the language of social movement theory, solidarity represents a "frame" that both assigned meaning to relevant acts and indicates overlapping and potentially conflicting cultural influences.[74] Put differently, there is an ambiguity inherent in framing devices that is central to their cohesive function, creating an opportunity for multiple constituents to find meaning in a core protest vocabulary. This ambiguity maintains the potential for disagreement, discontent, and division. As the history of West German pacifism demonstrates, it also provides a point of entry into the internal politics of extraparliamentary opposition and the process of (re)producing moral and protest economies that cuts against the grain of assumptions about organizational, ideological, and generational difference.

This type of discourse-analytic approach offers multiple advantages to the historian of social movements. The focus on the language of protest opens up aspects of social movement research that have been largely neglected by scholars who use the political "success" and "failure" of social movements as indices of their historical relevance.[75] Whether we are discussing the influence of Christian pastors within circles of peace activists; the importation and appropriation from England of protest techniques and symbols by the initiators of the West German Easter Marches;[76] an alliance of local activists in Darmstadt formed to protest national emergency legislation;[77] the support given by pacifists to African-American soldiers stationed in the Federal Republic who contemplated desertion;[78] or the self-identification of pacifists as participants in a global struggle for social liberation, we need to account for the constellation of entangled relationships and overlapping cultural economies signified by and out of which expressions of peace and solidarity emerged.[79]

This approach to social movement research also provides us with tools and an opportunity for thinking through the limits (or failures) of solidarity and community formation. I have alluded to pacifist Eurocentrism and the ways in which activists distinguished (white) Europeans from the world's "colored peoples."[80] How might the recourse to racial categories in expressions of solidarity have paradoxically re-inscribed boundaries of human difference in peace activism?[81] I cannot pursue this question here in detail. Rather, it must suffice to say that, at a minimum, the discursive approach to social movements enables scholars to consider pacifism as something more than the uncomfortable remainder of an extraparliamentary equation that associates motivations underlying the protests of the 1950s and 1960s with social standing and interest.[82] To the contrary, pacifism may now offer a view onto the constitution and delineation of protest communities; the ethical and political contestation at the heart of these processes; and the ways in which protesters drew upon, (re)articulated, and potentially contributed to the broad cultural and political constellations of the societies that produced them.

Notes

1. This is an abbreviated and revised version of A. Oppenheimer, "By Any Means Necessary? West German Pacifism and the Politics of Solidarity, 1945–1974," in *Peace Movements in Western Europe, Japan and the USA during the Cold War*, ed. B. Ziemann (Essen: Klartext Verlag, 2008), 41–60. It appears here with the permission of Klartext Verlag. Translations are by the author, unless otherwise noted.

2. See W. Balsen and K. Rössel, *Hoch die internationale Solidarität. Zur Geschichte der Dritte Welt-Bewegung in der Bundesrepublik* (Köln: Kölner Volksblatt Verlag, 1986), 22.

3. For an exception to the rule, see M. Klimke, "Black Panther, die RAF und die Rolle der Black Panther-Solidaritätskomitees," in *Die RAF und der linke Terrorismus*, ed. W. Kraushaar (Hamburg: Hamburger Edition, 2006), 562–582.

4. See "Aus der Friedensbewegung," *Die Friedens-Warte*, 1946: 120 and 155–159; "Die deutsche Pazifisten der Vorkriegszeit," *Die Friedens-Warte*, 1946: 392–393.

5. H. Donat, "Die radikalpazifistische Richtung in der Deutschen Friedensgesellschaft (1918–1933)," in *Pazifismus in der Weimarer Republik. Beiträge zur historischen Friedensforschung*, eds. K. Holl and W. Wette (Paderborn: F. Schöningh Verlag, 1981), 27–45.

6. *Programm und Aufgaben der Deutschen Friedensgesellschaft. Bericht über den Zonentag in Bielefeld am 8. November 1946* (Hannover: Verlag "Das Andere Deutschland", 1946).

7. *Programm und Aufgaben*, 3–5. Cf. W. Wette, "Befreiung vom 'Schwertglauben'—Pazifistische Offiziere in Deutschland 1871–1933," in *Pazifistische Offiziere in Deutschland 1871–1933*, ed. W. Wette (Bremen: Donat Verlag, 1999), 9–39; "Erste Tagung des Landesverbandes Schleswig-Holstein der Deutschen Friedensgesellschaft (24. bis 26. August 1946)," *Die Friedens-Warte*, 1946: 392.

8. For Weimar-era critics see K. Holl, "Pazifismus," in *Geschichtliche Grundbegriffe: Historisches Lexikon zur politisch-sozialen Sprache in Deutschland*, 8 vols, eds. O. Brunner, W. Conze, and R. Koselleck (Stuttgart: E. Klett Verlag, 1972–1977), 782–783.

9. *Welt-Organisation der Mütter aller Nationen. Appell der Mütter an das Weltgewissen: Ehrfurcht vor dem Leben!* (Hamburg, [1958]).

10. H. Abatz, "Was will die Deutsche Friedens-Gesellschaft?," *Welt-Spiegel*, December 1950.

11. Abatz quoted in S. Appelius, *Pazifismus in Westdeutschland. Die Deutsche Friedensgesellschaft 1945–1968* (Aachen: Verlag Mainz, 1999), 165.

12. See H. Kühn, "Deutschland zwischen Washington und Moskau," Hauptstaatsarchiv Nordrhein-Westfalen Düsseldorf (henceforth HStAD), RW 259 235/1–16.

13. On the early Cold War, see W. Loth, *The Division of the World, 1941–1955* (New York: St. Martin's Press, 1988), 51–100.

14. Circular from H. Abatz to DFG regional affiliates, 22 September 1953, HStAD, RW 115 263/176–7. On West German anticommunism, see D. Siegfried, "Stalin und Elvis. Antikommunismus zwischen Erfahrung, Ideologie und Eigensinn," *sowi* 28 (January–March) 1999: 27–35.

15. Appelius, *Pazifismus in Westdeutschland*, 394.

16. Letter from A. Bangel to C. Fautz, 11 November 1954, HStAD, RW 115 432/115; report on the first public meeting of the DFG-Bad Pyrmont, 18 November 1954, HStAD, RW 115 432/118–19.

17. See G. Heipp, ed., *Es geht ums Leben! Der Kampf gegen die Bombe 1945–1965. Eine Dokumentation* (Hamburg: H. Reich Verlag, 1965), 23; esp. M. Niemöller, "Die Hölle auf Erden," in Heipp, *Es geht ums Leben!*, 23–25.

18. H.K. Rupp, *Außerparlamentarische Opposition in der Ära Adenauer. Der Kampf gegen die Atombewaffnung in den fünfziger Jahren* (Köln: Pahl-Rugenstein Verlag, 1970).

19. Rupp, *Außerparlamentarische Opposition*, 127–129. Cf. M. Cioc, *Pax Atomica: The Nuclear Defense Debate in West Germany During the Adenauer Era* (New York: Columbia University Press, 1988), 116–133, 164–176.

20. Rupp, *Außerparlamentarische Opposition*, 154–156, 283–287.

21. Rupp, *Außerparlamentarische Opposition*, 127–128, 154.

22. M. Niemöller, "Wehrt euch gegen den Atomtod – Freiheit für die Volksbefragung!," in Niemöller, *Reden 1958–1961* (Frankfurt am Main: Stimme-Verlag, 1961), 22–30.

23. For a summary of internationalist and 'One World' arguments, see L. Wittner, *One World or None: A History of the World Nuclear Disarmament Movement Through 1953* (Stanford: Stanford University Press, 1993).

24. K. Jaspers, *Die Atombombe und die Zukunft des Menschen* (München: R. Piper Verlag, 1957), 7–27.

25. F. Burdecki, "Ordnungsprinzip wider Kampfprinzip," *Die Friedens-Warte*, 1946: 7–19. Cf. B. Manstein, "Mut zur moralischen Entscheidung," in Heipp, *Es geht ums Leben!*, 32–34.

26. O. Michel, "Sammlung der Geister. Gedanken zur Kulturkrise der Gegenwart," *DFG-Informationsdienst*, July, 1955: 1. For a different take on cultural pessimism and its role in nuclear discourse, see H. Nehring, "Cold War, Apocalypse and Peaceful Atoms. Interpretations of Nuclear Energy in the British and West German Anti-Nuclear Weapons Movements, 1955–1964," *Historical Social Research* 29(3)(2004): 150–170.

27. Jaspers was no pacifist. In fact, he derided their "outrage and appeals" that spoke to the symptoms of "the human disaster" but which failed to account for its underlying causes. Jaspers, *Die Atombombe und die Zukunft des Menschen*, 7–27, here 15. Cf. Michel, "Sammlung der Geister"; "Niederschrift über die Sitzung des Bundesvorstandes der Deutschen Friedensgesellschaft am 24.4.1954 in Hamburg," HStAD, RW 115 430; "Erklärung der Arbeitsgemeinschaft deutsche Friedensverbände (ADF), 23–24 April 1954," Evangelisches Zentralarchiv in Berlin (henceforth EZAB), 51/Q/II/b/3 bis 5; "Entschliessung der ADF," 23 July 1955, EZAB, 51/Q/II/a; "Programm beschlossen auf dem Bundestag der DFG in Heidelberg vom 5.–7. Oktober 1956," HStAD, RW 259 488/4.

28. On the role of Dahlemites in postwar church history, see M. Greschat, *Die evangelische Christenheit und die deutsche Geschichte nach 1945. Weichenstellungen in der Nachkriegszeit* (Stuttgart: Kohlhammer Verlag, 2002); M. Hockenos, *A Church Divided: German Protestants Confront the Nazi Past* (Bloomington: Indiana University Press, 2004); F.W. Kantzenbach, *Politischer Protestantismus. Von den Freiheitskriegen bis zur Ära Adenauer* (Saarbrücken-Scheidt: Dadder Verlag, 1993), 241–245.

29. Rupp, *Außerparlamentarische Opposition*, 56–64; Cioc, *Pax Atomica*, 92–115; A. Cooper, *Paradoxes of Peace: German Peace Movements since 1945* (Ann Arbor: University of Michigan Press, 1996), 39–48.

30. J. Harder, "Demokratie und Krieg. Vortrag vor der Deutschen Friedensgesellschaft in Duisburg," *Stimme der Gemeinde*, 1 September 1960: 525–532.

31. F. Wenzel, "Erneuerung aus Prophetischem Geist," *DFG-Informationsdienst*, December 1960: 1–3.

32. M. Niemöller, "Pazifistische Realpolitik," *DFG-Informationsdienst*, December 1960: 4–10.

33. C. Geissler, "Auschwitz, Hiroshima und die Hoffnungen des Menschen," *Deutsche Volkszeitung*, 4 August 1961: 13.

34. F. von Unruh, "Entscheiden wir uns für den Frieden, so wird Frieden sein!," in F. von Unruh, *Wir Wollen Frieden. Die Reden und Aufrufe 1960/61* (Düsseldorf: Monitor-Verlag, 1961), 11–24. On von Unruh, see H.J. Schröder, "Fritz von Unruh (1885–1970)—Kavallerieoffizier, Dichter und Pazifist," in Wette, *Pazifistische Offiziere in Deutschland 1871–1933*, 319–337.

35. The phrase is Michael Geyer's. See M. Geyer, "Cold War Angst: The Case of West-German Opposition to Rearmament and Nuclear Weapons," in *The Miracle Years: A Cultural History of West Germany, 1949–1968*, ed. Hanna Schissler (Princeton: Princeton University Press, 2001), 376–408, here 396; author's emphasis.

36. See "'Spaltung nur unter der weißen Rasse'. Kirchenpräsident Dr. Niemöller bei der Deutschen Friedensgesellschaft," *Generalanzeiger für Bonn*, 23 March 1962, HStAD, RW 115 224/4. Cf. von Unruh, "Entscheiden wir uns für den Frieden." For a critical account of Eurocentrism in the anti-nuclear movement, see Balsen and Rössel, *Hoch die internationale Solidarität*, 56–60.

37. Y.M. Bodemann, "Eclipse of Memory: German Representations of Auschwitz in the Early Postwar Period," *New German Critique* 75 (Fall)(1998): 57–89.

38. Geissler, "Auschwitz, Hiroshima und die Hoffnungen des Menschen," 13.

39. Consider Heinrich Vogel's claim that "Hiroshima is more than a gas chamber, it is Hell!" Quoted in Appelius, *Pazifismus in Westdeutschland,* 430. On the German victim of war, see R. Moeller, *War Stories: The Search for a Usable Past in the Federal Republic of Germany* (Berkeley: University of California Press, 2001).

40. K.A. Otto, *Vom Ostermarsch zur APO. Geschichte der ausserparlamentarischen Opposition in der Bundesrepublik 1960–1970* (Frankfurt am Main: Campus-Verlag, 1982).

41. Otto, *Vom Ostermarsch zur APO,* 65–77.

42. Otto, *Vom Ostermarsch zur APO,* 65–67 and 180–84.

43. P. Richter, "Die Außerparlamentarische Opposition in der Bundesrepublik Deutschland 1966 bis 1968," in *1968. Vom Ereignis zum Gegenstand der Geschichtswissenschaft,* ed. I. Gilcher-Holtey (Göttingen: Vandenhoeck und Ruprecht Verlag, 1998), 35–55.

44. W. Fabian and H. Kloppenburg, "Die Hilfsaktion Vietnam, ihre Entstehung und Entwicklung," HStAD, RW 338 340; M. Klein, G. Müller, and R. Schlaga, *Politische Strömungen in der Friedensbewegung 1966–1974. Diskussionen, Auseinandersetzungen und Veränderungen in der Deutschen Friedensgesellschaft (DFG), der Internationale der Kriegsdienstgegner (IDK) und dem Verband der Kriegsdienstverweigerer (VK) bis zu deren Vereinheitlichung zur Deutschen Friedensgesellschaft/ Vereinigte Kriegsdienstgegner (DFG/VK)* (Frankfurt am Main: Verein zur Förderung Friedenspolitischer Ideen und Initiativen e.V., 1978), 38–40; F. Werkmeister, "Die Protestbewegung gegen den Vietnamkrieg in der Bundesrepublik Deutschland 1965–1973," D. Phil. diss., Philipps-Universität Marburg/Lahn, 1975, 35–38.

45. "Erklärung der Deutschen Friedensgesellschaft zur Forderung amerikanischer Politiker deutsche Truppen nach Vietnam zu senden," *DFG-Informationsdienst,* March 1966: 2–3. Cf. letter from H. Schulte to Le Tuy Van, Au Comité de la Paix de la République Démocratique du Viet Nam, 6 September 1969, HStAD, RW 338 469.

46. "Friede als Idee und reale Aufgabe," *DFG-Informationsdienst,* March 1966: 8–9.

47. R. Opitz, "Arbeitstagung der DFG," *DFG-Informationsdienst,* November 1965: 6.

48. "Freiheit—Revolution—Gewalt—Gewaltlosigkeit. Arbeitspapier des Internationalen Rates der War Resisters' International (WRI) vom 12.–17. August 1968," HStAD, RW 115 443/75-7.

49. "Programm der DFG/IdK," *Courage,* July/August 1968: 4–5.

50. For examples, see H. Stubenrauch, "Sittlichkeit—Gewalt—Sexualität," *Zivil,* November1966: 118–119; R. Seewann, "Christian Anders verweigert den Kriegsdienst," *Courage,* December 1968: 3.

51. For a succinct statement by anti-authoritarians on social domination, see R. Dutschke et al., "Gewalt," *Konkret,* no. 6, 1968: 25–26. For evidence of common ground between pacifist and student activists in the broader realm of cultural and especially sexual politics, compare the articles cited in the previous note to D. Herzog, *Sex After Fascism: Memory and Morality in Twentieth-Century Germany* (Princeton: Princeton University Press, 2005), esp. 141–183.

52. See [PS], "Die Studenten," *Arbeitskreises Hannoverischer Kriegsdienstverweigerer DFG IDK VK,* August 1967: 1–2; M. Niemöller, "Der Tod Martin Luther Kings ist eine

Frage an die ganze Menschheit," in *Martin Niemöller. Reden, Predigten, Denkanstöße 1964–1976*, ed. H.J. Oeffler (Köln: Pahl-Rugenstein Verlag, 1977), 145–147.

53. See letter from A. Bangel to Sozialistischer Deutscher Studentenbund, 25 November 1965, HStAD, RW 115 200/52; the latter's reply, 12 December 1965, HStAD, RW 115 200/16; leaflet of the Darmstädter Aktionsgemeinschaft gegen die Notstandsgesetze (1966), reprinted in K.A. Otto, *APO. Die außerparlamentarische Opposition in Quellen und Dokumenten (1960–1970)* (Köln: Pahl-Rugenstein Verlag, 1989), 305–306.

54. I. Gilcher-Holtey, *Die 68er Bewegung. Deutschland, Westeuropa, USA* (München: Verlag C.H. Beck, 2001), 45–49.

55. Gilcher-Holtey, *Die 68er Bewegung*, 37–49; B. Rabehl, "Repressive Toleranz. Der SDS und das Problem der Gewaltfreiheit," in *Gewaltfreiheit. Pazifistische Konzepte im 19. und 20. Jahrhundert*, eds. A. Gestrich, G. Niedhart, and B. Ulrich (Münster: LIT Verlag, 1996), 133–150.

56. "Freiheit—Revolution—Gewalt—Gewaltlosigkeit." Cf. "Was ist die Nationale Befreiungsfront (FNL)?," *DFG-Informationsdienst*, June/July 1965: 7–8; G. Brinkmann, "Ho Tschi Minh ist kein Fanatiker," *DFG-Informationsdienst*, February 1967: 6–7.

57. J. van Lierde, "Sind Pazifismus und Revolution vereinbar?," *Der Kriegsdienstgegner. Le Résistance à la guerre. Bulletin der Schweizer Sektion der Internationale der Kriegsdienstgegner*, December 1971: 1–2. Cf. R. Dutschke, "Die geschichtlichen Bedingungen für den internationalen Emanzipationskampf," in *Rebellion der Studenten oder die neue Opposition*, eds. U. Bergmann, et al. (Reinbeck bei Hamburg: Rowohlt Verlag, 1968), 85–93.

58. Letter from H. Schulte to the author, 13 December 2004.

59. Niemöller quoted in Niemöller et al., *Junge Christen befragen die Kirchen. Zwei Gespräche* (München: K. Desch Verlag, 1968), 60–61.

60. W. Mausbach, "The Present's Past: Perspectives on Peace and Protest in Germany, 1945–1973," *Mitteilungsblatt des Instituts für soziale Bewegungen* 32(2004): 67–98, here 92–93; Dutschke et al., "Gewalt."

61. "Freiheit—Revolution—Gewalt—Gewaltlosigkeit."

62. M. Niemöller, "Die Bedeutung des Widerstandes in der heutigen Zeit. Rede auf dem Bundeskongreß der VVN in Frankfurt/Main 5. Mai 1967," in *Martin Niemöller. Reden, Predigten, Denkanstöße*, 110–113.

63. Letter from H. Schulte to the author, 13 December 2004.

64. H. Schulte, "Über die Bedingungen des Friedens: Gerechtigkeit und Demokratie," *Courage*, July/August 1968: 6–7; R. Riemeck, "Gewalt und Gewaltlosigkeit," *Courage*, January 1970: 4–5.

65. H.M. Vogel, "Pazifismus kennt keine moralische Neutralität," in *Widerstand gegen den Krieg. Beiträge zur Geschichte der War Resisters' International/Internationale der KriegsdienstgegnerInnen*, ed. W. Beyer (Kassel: Weber-Zucht-Verlag, 1989), 60–63.

66. Vogel, "Pazifismus kennt keine moralische Neutralität."

67. See U. Davis, "DFG/IDK and the WRI—Background Paper (1973)," International Institute of Social History (henceforth IISH), WRI 55; Minutes of WRI Council meeting, 16–17 December 1972, IISH, WRI 51.

68. I discuss this conflict at length in "Conflicts of Solidarity: Nuclear Weapons, National Liberation Movements, and the Politics of Peace in the Federal Republic of Germany, 1945–1975," Ph.D. diss., University of Chicago, 2010.

69. Letter from M. Stierwaldt and A. Bangel to A. Tatum, 17 May 1959, IISH, WRI 227.
70. Letter from M. Stierwaldt and A. Bangel to S. Morris, 11 February 1959, IISH, WRI 227; letter from A. Bangel to A. Tatum, 8 April 1960, IISH, WRI 227.
71. See, for example, the leaflet of the Darmstadt Aktionsgemeinschaft gegen die Notstandsgesetze (October 1961), reprinted in Otto, *APO*, 305–306.
72. Letter from A. Bangel to H. Spielmann, 8 February 1968, HStAD, RW 115 207/124.
73. See Davis, "DFG/IDK and the WRI—Background Paper (1973)."
74. As elaborated by sociologists of protest, framing is the discursive effort by activists to "assign meaning to and interpret relevant events and conditions in ways that are intended to mobilize potential adherents and constituents, to garner bystander support, and to demobilize antagonists." D.A. Snow and R.D. Benford, "Ideology, Frame Resonance and Participant Mobilization," in *From Structure to Action: Comparing Social Movement Research Across Cultures*, eds. B. Klandermans, H. Kriesi. and S. Tarrow (London: JAI Press, 1988), 197–218, here 198. For a succinct statement on new social movements and an overview of social movement theory, see T. Bonacker and L. Schmitt, "Politischer Protest zwischen latenten Strukturen und manifesten Konflikten. Perspektiven soziologischer Protestforschung am Beispiel der (neuen) Friedensbewegung," *Mitteilungsblatt des Instituts für soziale Bewegungen* 32 (2004): 193–213. For the turn by historians to social movement theory, see B. Ziemann, "Peace Movements in Western Europe, Japan and USA since 1945: An Introduction," *Mitteilungsblatt des Instituts für soziale Bewegungen* 32, 2004: 5–19; also B. Ziemann, "Situating Peace Movements in the Political Culture of the Cold War. Introduction," in Ziemann, *Peace Movements in Western Europe, Japan and the USA during the Cold War,* 11–38.
75. Bonacker and Schmitt, "Politischer Protest zwischen latenten Strukturen und manifesten Konflikten."
76. H. Nehring, "National Internationalists: British and West German Protests against Nuclear Weapons, the Politics of Transnational Communications and the Social History of the Cold War, 1957–1964," *Contemporary European History* 14(4), (2005): 559–582.
77. Leaflet of the Darmstadt Aktionsgemeinschaft gegen die Notstandsgesetze (October 1961), reprinted in Otto, *APO*, 305–306.
78. See the leaflet "Uncle Sam wants <u>You</u> nigger," IISH, Neue Linke (BRD) 2745. Published by the SDS-Frankfurt, it lists the IdK as the first of several organizations for deserters to contact.
79. Ziemann, "Situating Peace Movements,"
80. Balsen and Rössel, *Hoch die internationale Solidarität,* 56–60.
81. For instance, there is evidence that activists envisioned differentiated fields of revolutionary action with correspondingly differentiated terms of revolutionary subjectivity in which acts of violence were only permissible outside of Europe among non-Christian, "colored peoples." See M. Niemöller, "Wir und die farbige Welt (Unsere Verantwortung vor der farbigen Welt)," in *Reden 1958–1961,* 62–70. Cf. "Black Power und was weiter?," *zivil*, December 1967: 125–130, 134.
82. Bonacker and Schmitt, "Politischer Protest zwischen latenten Strukturen und manifesten Konflikten."

Chapter 2

The Prague Spring and the "Gypsy Question"

A Transnational Challenge to the Socialist State

Celia Donert

Few episodes in the postwar history of Czechoslovakia have received greater attention than the Prague Spring, when reformers in the Czechoslovak Communist Party (KSČ) attempted to create a democratic socialism in the heart of the Soviet bloc, creating unprecedented opportunities for political liberalization, social mobilization, and internationalism in a Stalinist regime that had previously been one of the most conservative in Eastern Europe. The subsequent invasion of Czechoslovakia by Warsaw Pact troops contributed to the commemoration of the Prague Spring as a national rebellion against Soviet hegemony, a myth that Czech and Slovak historians have been laboring to confront since the collapse of communism opened up a greater range of archives and conceptual paradigms to historical scrutiny. Attempts to interpret the events that took place in Czechoslovakia during those heady, exciting months within a broader transnational history of "1968" raise more questions than can be answered comfortably by recourse to such myths of national resistance, or by the focus on heroic political reformers striving to create "socialism with a human face" that dominated many histories of the Prague Spring during the Cold War.

Turning the spotlight away from KSČ First Secretary Alexander Dubček and other famous political figures, this chapter illuminates a little-known episode in the history of the Prague Spring: the short-lived efforts of a small group of Roma (Gypsy) activists protesting communist assimilation policies aimed at the so-called "Gypsy population" and gaining collective representation for the Czechoslovak Roma by claiming recognition as a nationality, establishing an official Association of Gypsies-Roma, and subsequently attending the First World Romani Congress in London in 1971, a founding event for the fledgling international Romani movement that brought together activists from Eastern and Western Europe for the first time in the postwar era. As members of a generation of working-class youth who had benefited from unprecedented opportunities for upward social mobility after the KSČ seized power in February 1948, however, these Roma activists were reluctant rebels whose pursuit of an ambiguous national identity forced them, often unwillingly, to confront the limitations of membership in the socialist state.

Drawing on communist party archives, government reports, newspapers, and activists' private papers, this chapter shows how the "Gypsy Question" was redefined in Czechoslovakia during the Prague Spring, not only through the prism of national history or the contradictions of "Marxist-Leninist nationality policy," but also as part of a wave of popular challenges to the nation-state that seemed to cut across ideological, geographical, and economic borders in the 1960s. Although the transnational diffusion of images and ideas through the mass media and personal networks played an important role in changing the nature of Roma activism in 1968, this chapter concludes that the misunderstandings or disputes that frequently resulted from such connections were as influential as activists' perceptions of a shared or collective identity.

Nationalism and Social Revolution in the Prague Spring

Only weeks after the resignation of Antonín Novotný as KSČ first secretary in early 1968, a small group of Slovak Roma activists established an informal preparatory committee for an Association of Gypsies-Roma, which declared in its first bulletin: "The Gypsies-Roma in the Czechoslovak Socialist Republic (ČSSR) should be recognized legally (de jure) as a minority nationality."[1] Anton Facuna, an architect from Bratislava who had fought as a partisan in the wartime Slovak National Uprising, and Ján Cibula, a medical doctor from a Hungarian (Ungrika) Roma village in southern Slovakia, had already submitted a similar request to the KSČ over a decade earlier, only to be rejected. At that time, the Politburo had been adamant that the "Gypsy population" should be assimilated into socialist society using measures that oscillated between coercion and persuasion, such as forced settlement, segregating Roma children in "special schools" for children with special needs, and special programs of civic education and cultural enlightenment. At the same time, the lives of the Roma were transformed by communist programs of rapid industrialization introduced in Eastern Europe after the Second World War. Joined by educated activists from two well-known families of Moravian Roma—the Holomeks and the Daniels—the Slovak Roma continued to petition the Communist Party and the government during the turbulent months of 1968 for permission to set up social organizations that would represent the interests of the "Gypsies-Roma" within the communist-controlled National Front.

The Roma were not, however, awarded legal recognition as a nationality, even when the Czechoslovak parliament, after the federalization of the republic in October 1968, adopted a new constitutional law on the rights of nationalities. Unlike most of the other national minorities in central Europe, the Roma had no kin-state to defend their interests, nor did they possess a national territory, which was one of the main conditions for recognition as a nation in Stalin's famous essay on "Marxism and the Nationalities Question."[2] In requesting legal recognition as a nationality, the Roma were forced to confront the limitations of Soviet nationality policy, which was the model for policy toward national minorities in the Czechoslovak Socialist Republic.

In order to understand the historical context in which Roma activists such as Anton Facuna were operating, a few words on the importance of nationalism in the Prague Spring are needed. After the Second World War and the recent horrors of Nazi expansionism and occupation, the Czech-dominated political leadership saw minority nationalisms as a direct threat to state sovereignty. As a result, the reconstructed Czechoslovak state was highly centralized, with limited cultural rights granted to national minorities, such as the substantial Hungarian population of southern Slovakia, and an "asymmetric" institutional structure in which the Czechoslovak legislature and government were balanced by Slovak ones.[3] Economic development was, meanwhile, supposed to erase the causes of national conflicts, while civic education and a form of "socialist patriotism" would create a political community from the mass of producer-citizens, as the whole of society advanced toward socialism under the leadership of the Czecho-slovak Communist Party.

"Socialist industrialization" in Slovakia had the opposite effect, however, especially when the belated process of de-Stalinization was launched in Czecho-slovakia in the early 1960s.[4] The rehabilitation of prominent Slovak communists previously criminalized as "bourgeois nationalists" helped to channel dissatis-faction with centralized rule from Prague among Slovak politicians and intel-lectuals, for whom federalization was inseparable from democratization, into an important factor in the reform movement. Federalization was given prominence in the reformers' blueprint for political change, the KSČ Action Program of April 1968, and in turn provoked demands for expanded cultural rights from national minorities such as the Germans, Poles, Hungarians, Rusyns, and Ukrainians.[5]

Lacking a national territory, or more concretely a national state, to defend their interests, the Roma had little hope of gaining recognition as a national minority in Czechoslovakia. A government report justifying the new constitu-tional law on the position of nationalities in the ČSSR stated that only the Hun-garians, Germans, Poles, and Ukrainians were to be recognized as nationalities because only these groups were "homogeneous, and culturally and ethnically conscious."[6]

However, developments in international law meant that new political op-portunities were slowly opening up for minorities lacking a territorial state to defend their interests. Although the postwar international human rights order had privileged the universal protection of individual human rights and the prin-ciple of non-discrimination, the UN Covenant on Civil and Political Rights included a reference to the right of "peoples" to self-determination. In 1967, the United Nations launched an investigation into the concept of minorities in international law, "taking into account ethnic, religious and linguistic factors and considering the position of ethnic, religious and linguistic groups in the multi-national society."[7] The deeply contested concept of minority rights was seen by many states as a direct threat to the principle of state sovereignty. At stake was the growing tension between the territorial integrity of states, and the ambiguous right of peoples to internal and external self-determination, previously a political principle associated with Wilsonian idealism that had been elevated to the status of an international legal norm through the struggles of postwar decolonization.[8]

These developments, precipitated by a dramatic increase in secessionist movements, provoked political scientists to revive debates about the relationship between democracy and multi-nationalism. Postwar modernization theorists—particularly in the United States—had optimistically predicted that market economies and increased communications would create robust civic cultures within the borders of nation-states, particularly in the post-colonial world.[9] Less than twenty years later, however, political scientists were reaching for theories of "ethnic consciousness" or "culture-groups" to explain the explosion of political resistance to assimilation in multi-national states, not only in Africa and Asia, but also in industrialized or industrializing European economies with diverse political systems, such as Spain, Belgium, and Yugoslavia.[10]

From Nationalist Movements to Transnational History?

The crisis of self-determination, which threw into question the usefulness of the "nation" as a category of historical analysis, highlights the importance of studying the events of 1968 in a comparative or transnational perspective. The dramatic events of 1968 continue to capture the interest of historians, popular as well as academic, seeking to explain the significance of the "year that rocked the world."[11] For scholars interested in the interaction between internationalist ideologies and national contexts, the importance of locating 1968 in a global context, or studying the role of personal networks and the mass media in transmitting ideas and images across national borders, seems evident. However, the degree to which 1968 should be seen as either a turning point in global politics from an era of confrontation to an age of détente—as some scholars have claimed—or a precursor to the events of 1989, seems less clear.[12]

How "transnational" was social mobilization in 1960s Europe? Tony Judt has castigated the cultural revolution in Western Europe as "parochial," particularly for its blindness to contemporary developments in the East, arguing that "if Western youth looked beyond their borders at all, it was to exotic lands whose image floated free of the irritating constraints of familiarity or information."[13] The Soviet bloc meanwhile saw the emergence of Marxist revisionism, as artists, journalists, economists, and philosophers sought to create an alternative socialism after the terror of the recent Stalinist past.[14] Encounters between student protesters from Czechoslovakia and from western Europe highlighted the very different ideologies animating the rebellions on either side of the Iron Curtain, as exemplified by Czech students' critical responses to Rudi Dutschke's attacks on parliamentary democracy during his visit to Prague in early April 1968.[15]

The obsession among militant activists with "exotic lands" was symptomatic of the changing focus of postwar European social thought as the emancipatory potential of the working class seemed to plunge into inexorable decline. New agents of social change were needed, whether embodied in the "Third World," students or marginalized racial minorities.[16] Even as the revolt in Paris was reaching its climax, the *engagé* sociologist Alain Touraine had described the 1960s protestors as a new social movement and thus distinct from older mass movements distinguished by economic and class differences.[17] Only recently, however, have historians turned to sociological theories of social movements in order to explain the ideologies, identities, and practices that shaped protests during the 1960s.[18] If many such histories tend to be skewed in favor of the left-wing activists who were the self-styled heroes of the rebellions, more recent research has also focused on 1968 as an important moment in the rise of the "New Right."[19] Considering the "proletarian" dimension of the 1968 revolts, Gerd-Rainer Horn has noted striking parallels in the role played by the "new working class" during the 1968 revolts in France, Italy, and Czechoslovakia, particularly through demands voiced by technical personnel and middle management, but nevertheless concludes that "in assessing 1968 globally, elements of cultural revolution far outweigh instances of a genuine workers' revolution."[20]

Countering these ideological clashes were the startling new currents in music, art, and fashion that offered an opportunity to identify with an emerging youth culture that was itself transnational. An increasing number of young Czechoslovaks were able to travel to the West for work and study in the 1960s.[21] Counter-cultural lifestyles were emerging in Czechoslovakia; as an example, in 1965, Czech students elected the Beat poet Alan Ginsberg as King of the Majales, the annual student festival.[22] Finally, the Prague Spring (and its failure) did influence the shape of politics across the Iron Curtain, especially among the West European Left and, in particular, the communist parties of western Europe.[23]

Redefining the "Gypsy Question" under Reform Communism

The politics of the "Gypsy Question" reflected the changing dynamics of class, race, and culture as agents of social change in postwar Europe. Official policy toward the Roma at the time of the Prague Spring was still guided by principles adopted by the KSČ in a secret political resolution in 1958, which had declared the complete assimilation of the "Gypsy population" into socialist society as its goal. This resolution was one of a raft of measures adopted by the KSČ under the leadership of Antonín Novotný in preparation for Czechoslovakia's planned liquidation of the "old way of life," given normative form in a new "socialist" Constitution of 1960. The teleological narrative of assimilation, from "backwards" Gypsy origin to socialist citizen, mirrored the path toward socialism that was supposed to be followed by society as a whole. By 1968, however, the contradictions and limitations of this socialist ideology of integration were becoming ever more apparent. Economic growth, a precondition for the promised transition to communism, had ground to a halt in the early 1960s. Over-investment into heavy industry, inefficiencies in collectivized agriculture, and declining demand for Czechoslovak exports from Comecon trading partners resulted in a recession that kick-started the reform process.

During these years, discussions about the "Gypsy Question" often appeared in the state-controlled media, partly at the instigation of communist party ideologists. The chief party ideologist, Jiří Hendrych, had been instructed by the KSČ Presidium to "use the press, radio and television in order to shape public opinion correctly regarding the ... solution of the gypsy question."[24] In fact, a survey of the central and regional press shows that many different interests influenced the representation of the Gypsy Question in the official press. While magazines such as *Kulturní tvorba*—which was published by the main KSČ daily newspaper *Rudé právo*—used language that mirrored party resolutions, the outspoken and increasingly critical Czech writers' journal *Literární noviny* published a number of pieces about the Roma, which challenged official representations of the Gypsy Question, in tone as well as content. When *Literární noviny* devoted an entire weekly issue to the Roma in October 1965, the latest government resolution on the Gypsy Question was reprinted alongside lengthy reportage about the Roma settlements of eastern Slovakia, deliberately contrasting the bureaucratic language with their own expressive style of journalism.

Rhetoric about the Gypsy Question reflected contemporary concerns about the influence of western popular culture on the young and social deviance among the working classes that were widespread during the 1960s throughout the socialist states. An article about the Roma in Ostrava, a sprawling industrial town in northern Moravia, reported that the city's Gypsy musicians had dropped traditional "gypsy melodies" in favor of "*big beat* [rock'n'roll] and jazz." Commenting approvingly on the upward social mobility of one Roma family in Ostrava, the journalist noted that the father of the house "already had hard hands" from factory work while his wife "kept an iron grip over the finances and order in the family." Their young sons were allowed to buy blue jeans—*texasky*—and boots with pointed toes, but otherwise they had to bring all of their earnings home. Notwithstanding the sarcastic tone of the article—the journalist reported that "Just like in the better families, the lady of the house asks her daughter to play piano for the guests"—this was the ideal Gypsy family of the new Czechoslovakia, as imagined in official party discourse. With an industrious male breadwinner, a wife and mother well-attuned to the mores of her milieu, and employable children satisfying their desire to participate in an international youth culture by limited consumption of a few material goods, this family was both a group of individuals fulfilling the economic functions demanded of them by the state and a unit reproducing the norms and values of socialist society.

In contrast, newspaper coverage of Roma living in rural eastern Slovakia, the poorest region of the republic, emphasized only the political and economic costs that were being generated by the inhabitants of "gypsy settlements." The president of the Government Committee for the Gypsy population in Košice, the provincial capital of eastern Slovakia, gave a number of interviews to the press in which he railed against the lifestyle of "unintegrated" Roma, whom he described to *Obrana lidu*—the newspaper of the armed forces—as "parasites, recidivists, vagrants and prostitutes." Alongside features on new types of tanks and big guns, photographs of Czechoslovakia's 22-year old Miss World candidate, this article painted the typical family of the Slovak gypsy settlements in sensationalist language, claiming that the average "hovel" housed 15 to 20 family members, that pre-marital or underage sex was common, and that incest was leading to "degenerate" offspring.[25]

Sensationalist press reports about poverty-stricken "Gypsy settlements" in rural Slovakia, or high crime rates within "Gypsy districts" of bigger cities, served a dual function, shifting the blame for social problems away from structural or political factors and onto "deviant" social groups, whilst providing the "better families" with a more secure sense of their newly gained social status.[26] As the social historian Sandor Horvath has observed of similarly sensationalist press coverage of urban slum-dwellers in Hungary, "Social mobility was a particularly important goal of state socialism, and people needed to know exactly where they stood. The discourse about barrack slums in Stalintown also encouraged all those living in planned apartments to feel fortunate for being spared the poverty that officially did not exist in socialism."[27] As communist parties, from the late 1950s, refocused their policies of economic and social development around higher living standards, the poverty and marginalization of the Roma or other excluded groups were represented as a "social" problem caused by "deviance" or "hooliganism," although a few critically minded journalists drew the occasional parallel between the lives of the Slovak Roma and racial segregation in the United States.

Reluctant Rebels. The Associations of Gypsies-Roma after the Prague Spring

On 5 April 1968, the day on which the KSČ adopted the Action Program that was supposed to serve as the blueprint for "socialism with a human face," the Slovak Roma activist Anton Facuna sent a formal request to the government for nationality recognition, stating: "Previous measures concerning the so-called

'Gypsy question,' even if they included well-meant proposals and regulations after 1945, have been for the most part implemented incorrectly. These measures have not fulfilled the conditions of social democracy for us Gypsies-Roma." The document also claimed that "administrative measures will not suffice to guarantee the rights of Gypsy-citizens." At the heart of the petition was an appeal for full citizenship for the Roma:

> We do not simply want to be citizens with formal state citizenship, we also want our ČSSR to become our homeland in every respect, we want to be proud of our socialist homeland. There are 250–300,000 of us in the ČSSR ..., mostly in Slovakia. Among our ranks we count intelligentsia, good workers, musicians, craftsmen—of course, there are also criminals and parasites, whose reeducation also concerns us.... Our history is spattered with the blood of our mothers and fathers. We are spread across the whole world. In some places we live better, in some worse, and in some really badly. We have our own ancient language, perhaps only in different dialects, but we understand each other across the whole world, we have our songs, our dances, our stories and our unwritten laws, even if not all of us still know them ... We demand that we Gypsies should be able to help other Gypsies to reach the level of the rest of the population, socially, culturally, and even politically.[28]

The activists who established the Associations of Gypsies-Roma in Czechoslovakia had entered into adulthood and professional life in the early 1950s. With personal memories of the persecution suffered by the Roma during the war, these activists belonged to the postwar generation that had benefited from new avenues for social mobility, guarantees of material security, and political stability provided by the authoritarian welfare state established under communist rule after 1948. At that time, a new ruling elite of around 250,000 people, mostly from the working classes, had hastily been created by the Communist Party, while the prewar middle classes had been all but extinguished by extensive nationalization of industry, the suppression of private commerce, and collectivization of agricultural land.[29] Twenty years later, this arriviste elite was facing pressure from the frustrations of a generation born after 1945.[30] By 1967, some 60 percent of the working population in Czechoslovakia was aged between fifteen and thirty-seven, less the children of Marx and Coca-Cola than of Gottwald and Kofola.[31] With no direct memory of the hardships of the 1930s, this generation had less reason than their parents to be grateful for the benefits of the communist welfare state. Rather than the friend-enemy dichotomies of the Stalinist era, the political scientist Kieran Williams has pointed out, the "salient cleavages were now those of education, nationality, and (non) membership in the party."[32]

The structure of Communist Party membership reflected these social and demographic changes. In 1967, some 19.2 percent of the adult population in the Czech lands and 11.5 percent in Slovakia were members of the party, although KSČ membership in Slovakia was increasing slightly as a result of the industrialization of this formerly agricultural region.[33] Fewer young people were entering the party, and the better educated (those with secondary and higher education) were joining party organizations in their workplace, which indicated that careerism was one of the most important motives in holding a party card. Moreover, the KSČ was no longer the party of the proletariat, as the proportion of the working class declined in relation to the new "technical" intelligentsia who had joined the party after 1948, or 1956.[34] The gathering storm clouds of the social revolution were heavy with the unfulfilled expectations—political and social, personal and material—of citizens under forty years of age, while the nomenklatura parachuted into power as young people between twenty-five and thirty years old in the early 1950s maintained their hold over the power structure. "In short," Kieran Williams writes, "half the population had no experience of the capitalist system but had not profited from the socialist one."[35]

The Roma activists seeking to establish Associations of Gypsies-Roma in Czechoslovakia during the Prague Spring represented a complex, and potentially contradictory, mixture of the ideological and sociological currents described above. Almost all were members of the new intelligentsia that had been pushed into positions of economic and social importance by the communist-controlled social revolution after 1948. The leadership of the Associations was drawn mainly from men who worked in the party apparatus or in the technical professions. Although the KSČ had initially tried to educate a cadre of Gypsy elites who would disseminate the goals of socialism among the rest of the population, official policy and rhetoric on the "Gypsy Question" never achieved its purported goal of eliminating racial discrimination against the Roma, instead assimilating older folk prejudices, stereotypes derived from criminal anthropology, and the primitivist paradigms of developmental anthropology to the discourse of scientific socialism.[36] In short, the term "Gypsy" [cikán] remained a highly pejorative label in official, semi-official, and unofficial discourses in Czechoslovakia, as elsewhere in Europe.[37]

Many "citizens of Gypsy origin"—to use the official communist terminology—who attained such positions tended either to renounce their Romani roots or confined this part of their identity to their private lives. Contemporary fieldwork by a Polish anthropologist suggested that "many 'hidden' Gypsies who were influential Party and Administrative officials suddenly 'appeared' to fill leadership positions in the regional and local Roma Associations in Slovakia." Despite having "passed" as non-Roma, these local elites were "very attractive as potential allies to many of the urban Gypsies whose positions in the community were ambiguous."[38] The concepts and vocabulary of identity politics may be partly useful in explaining the practices of the Czechoslovak Roma activists, but not entirely so. Being a "citizen of Gypsy origin" seems not to have been an "identity" in the sense of expressing an authentic, individual self, but was rather an aspect of an individual's public role as a socialist citizen, albeit one that was acknowledged—if often unwillingly—as inherently subversive or even shameful.

In early 1969, Czech and Slovak Roma activists were given permission to establish official Associations of Gypsies-Roma within the National Front, the umbrella organization for political parties and social organizations, which received hundreds of requests from groups seeking collective representation in 1968. The Roma Associations were established as "cultural-educational organisations" whose main task was to raise the living standards of their members through civic education and cultural activities. Written into the statutes of the Associations, therefore, was an assumption that the Roma were inherently "backward." Moreover, the organizations themselves lacked real political power. As contemporary internal government reports emphasized, these Associations were "social organizations which cannot, of course, take on the role of the state administration, and their membership in the National Front can only ensure their participation in the political life of society. Their participation in a complex solution [of the Gypsy Question] is not guaranteed."[39] Although the Roma leadership were subsequently allowed to participate in the Government Commission for the Gypsy Population, they had no decision-making power.

The Associations of Gypsies-Roma were closer to neocorporatist institutions than prototypes of a liberal civil society, and thus these "cultural-educational" organizations exemplified the ambiguities of the new political system designed by reformers such as Zdeněk Mlynář. The leadership of the Roma Associations was nominated by the party, rather than elected by the membership, and all meetings and congresses were carefully monitored by party and government officials. Rather than returning to prewar democracy, the Czechoslovak reformers were attempting to blend socialism with democracy. Promises in the Action Program that politics would be influenced by public opinion—whether through freedom of expression or the institutional representation of interest groups such as trade unions—were balanced by frequent references to the integration [sbližování] of social groups as the ultimate aim of politics.[40] By contrast, the young playwright Václav Havel argued that public opinion could not be truly free without the creation of an opposition party, while Petr Pithart argued that the National Front would be a superfluous counterpart to a functioning Parliament.[41] In fact, official plans for a reformed Parliament and National Front were closer to a corporatist model in which representation and state intervention would be fused, thus merging "the expression of group interests ... with channels of implementation of policy."[42]

Although bureaucratic, elite-led, and prevented by political pressure from expressing overtly political demands such as nationality recognition, the Associations of Gypsies-Roma marked a vital moment in the history of Romani activism in Czechoslovakia. For the first time, the Czechoslovak Roma were able to organize collectively in a formal institutional structure. The Unions also provided a future point of reference for a younger generation of Roma activists, who were often more critical of the communist regime than their elders. While seeking to support a Roma linguistic or cultural identity through attempts to standardize the Romani language, or to stage festivals of Roma music and dance, activists also attempted to act politically in the social sphere, for example, by attempting to establish all-Roma housing cooperatives. Although the fear of political repression undoubtedly influenced the work of the Associations, this does not exclude the possibility that many of their members were influenced as much by a desire for cultural recognition than a belief in the narrative of socialist integration.

East Meets West at the First World Romani Congress, April 1971

The final section of this chapter analyzes the internationalization of Roma activism during the Prague Spring and the way in which Cold War politics played out at the First World Romani Congress. This congress was the first official meeting of Romani activists from eastern and western Europe after the Second World War. Making contacts with activists living abroad had been a goal of the Associations of Gypsies-Roma, and one of these meetings was to have lasting effects. In 1968, a young British man named Grattan Puxon, who was active in the Gypsy pressure groups that sprang up in Great Britain, Ireland, and France during the 1960s, traveled to Bratislava "to discuss [with Czech and Slovak Roma] a link up with the emerging international movement."[43] As a result, the leadership of the Czech and Slovak Roma Associations were invited to attend the First World Romani Congress, an event organized by Puxon and his fellow activists, in April 1971. A small delegation of three Czech Roma activists was given official permission to attend the Congress as representatives of the Associations of Gypsies-Roma. The Congress adopted a blue and green flag—with the optional addition of a red wheel—and the anthem *Gelem, gelem* (with new words by the Yugoslav musician Jarko Jovanic and the Slovak medical doctor Ján Cibula), and closed with a festival on Hampstead Heath that participants claimed was attended by a thousand people.

The First World Romani Congress, though a less grand affair than its name suggested, was nonetheless a turning point in the history of international Romani activism. Attended by around twenty delegates from France, Finland, Great Britain, Germany, Ireland, Spain, and Yugoslavia, the Congress was held in the English village of Orpington in Kent. As well as discussions on war crimes, education, culture, language, and social affairs, the delegates staged a demonstration outside the police station in Walsall to protest the recent deaths of three Gypsy children who had perished in a fire after a police raid on a caravan site. "After having tea with some local Gypsies," a British activist later wrote, the delegates then "returned to Kent."[44]

The Czech delegates to the World Romani Congress were closely supervised by the Czechoslovak authorities during their visit to Britain.[45] Moreover, the delegates who attended with official permission from the Communist Party were visibly startled to see Ján Cibula, a Slovak Roma activist who had recently gone into exile in Switzerland, at the Congress. "Nonplussed ...," the British activist Grattan Puxon later recalled, "Tomas Holomek emphasized in a hesitant opening speech that the Czech Romani Union had full recognition ... He claimed that no discrimination existed like that in western Europe in the Czech provinces or Slovakia."[46] The Czech Roma, for their part, were obliged to report to the Czechoslovak authorities that they had successfully convinced the Congress of the benefits that socialism had brought to the Gypsies of Eastern Europe.

Upon their return to Brno, the Czech Roma compiled a suitable official report on their visit, which stated in a horrified tone that "the Roma, particularly in England, are nomadic. They have no employment whatsoever and are restricted to staying in a certain place in their *Karavany* (mobile homes connected to a car)." Elaborating further on the life of the English Roma, the report explained that: "They travel collectively—at least 15–20 *Karavany*. They can get material goods to a limited extent, typically for a capitalist system, but they can never get political rights and the other social achievements and advantages provided by a socialist state. They are not engaged in political and public life." Moreover, "most English Roma live in their caravans close to rubbish dumps and other waste, without social assistance, without any kind of communication with civilization." Only private associations provided any kind of social assistance: "Charity and again charity."[47]

Expressions of horror from the Czech Roma about the *Karavany* of the British Gypsies were clearly intended to placate the communist authorities, but they also symbolized a deeper divide within the international Romani movement about the nature of Roma identity. The British Caravan Sites Act, which required local governments to provide adequate numbers of licensed caravan sites for Gypsies and travelers, had been viewed as a triumph by British activists as it removed the restrictions on traveling imposed by previous British legislation.[48] For British Gypsies, traveling was an integral part of Gypsy identity. Self-identified Roma in Czechoslovakia and other central European countries, however, viewed "nomadism" very differently. The Czech delegates to the World Romani Congress noted in horror that, under the Caravan Sites Act, "the Roma should be restricted to certain places, reserved for their KARAVANY. Our delegation and the delegations from socialist states did not agree with this proposal, because it is clearly a case of overt discrimination against the Roma in England."[49] This attitude partly reflected recent social changes in Czechoslovakia, and partly reflected long-term historical trends. Vagrancy had been criminalized in Czechoslovakia in 1958, and the police, together with local governments, had waged an often-violent campaign against Roma who continued to travel in family groups.

However, many central European Roma—especially those in the Hungarian lands of the Habsburg Empire (contemporary Slovakia, Hungary, and Romania)—had been settled for centuries. Only certain Roma groups—notably the Vlach or Olah Roma—had traveled as a way of life.

Despite the lack of consensus about Roma identity and government policy, internal debates among the Czech Roma elite suggest that they viewed international contacts as a means of creating solidarity among the Roma at home. The Czech Roma leadership's report on the World Romani Congress must clearly be read with caution, given the tight restrictions imposed on Czechoslovak citizens allowed a rare trip to the West. If the sources do not provide a "true" picture of the Roma response to their visit to London, the records of a debate within the Roma Association at least indicate how the journey was discussed within the organization itself. Thus one delegate suggested that internationalism would provide a way of generating solidarity among the Roma across national boundaries. "It's necessary to understand the Roma on a broader level," one Czech Romani delegate argued, "From this international perspective, it's not simply a matter of indifference to me that the Roma in Slovakia live badly, for example." Another veteran Czech Romani activist, Tomáš Holomek, argued that "we must continue to make international contacts with Roma at various meetings in the socialist and the capitalist countries, and we must disseminate our progressive thinking in the capitalist states."[50]

Conclusion

After the closure of the Roma Unions in 1973, the Czech and Slovak Roma elites retreated from public life, while still maintaining sporadic personal contacts with activists abroad. As a result, the Czechoslovak Roma continued to receive invitations to participate in subsequent World Romani Congresses, although restrictions on foreign travel during the era of "normalization" from 1969–1989 made this increasingly difficult. The state-controlled media presented events such as the Second World Romani Congress, held in Geneva in 1978, as an instrument for the attempted overthrow of socialism, rather than as an opportunity to showcase socialist minority policies. At the same time, splits between Roma from Eastern and Western Europe continued to influence the direction of the international Romani movement.[51]

Reflecting the greater lobbying power of activists from Western Europe, the first resolutions adopted by international organizations on the Roma cemented this association between nomadism and Gypsy identity. In September 1969, the Parliamentary Assembly of the Council of Europe adopted a recommendation on the "situation of Gypsies and other travelers in Europe."[52] The recommendation noted that the "situation of the Gypsy population in Europe is severely affected by the rapid changes in modern society, which are depriving the Gypsies and other travelers of many opportunities to carry on with their traditional trades and professions, and worsening their handicaps with regard to literacy and educational and professional training." The recommendation also noted that "discrimination" against the Gypsies as "an ethnic group" was incompatible with the "ideals underlying the European Convention on Human Rights and the United Nations Declaration on Human Rights."[53]

Nevertheless, the example of socialist Eastern Europe continued to inspire activists in the West after 1968. Grattan Puxon, the British activist who visited Czechoslovakia in 1968, was commissioned by the British Minority Rights Group to write the first report on the European Roma in 1973.[54] Shortly afterward, he moved to Yugoslavia to live in the Romany district of Shuto Orizari on the outskirts of Skopje, where he wrote a polemical article—"Gypsies, Blacks of Eastern Europe"—published in *The Nation* in 1976, in which he claimed that the Eastern bloc system of minority rights offered the only guarantee of Romany cultural identity in Europe: "Yet, for all its shortcomings, Marxist socialism ultimately offers us a way forward. If we have the courage to speak out. I say this because in socialist Eastern Europe minorities that receive nationality status receive automatically specific constitutionally guaranteed rights, and state aid for their realization."[55]

In this essay, Puxon referred to his visit to Bratislava "in those uncertain weeks before the Russian intervention" as an example of the promise that "true" Marxism—identified with the Czechoslovak reform movement—offered to the Roma. Arguing that "Lenin's example is ignored and the postwar Socialist countries have … distorted Marxism to justify repression," Puxon claimed that Party workers in Czechoslovakia "were warned not to fraternize with those Gypsies 'who are attempting to make an issue out of nationality.' They feared trouble, not from patriarchal headmen who might resist innovation but from younger *Roma* who, under the influence of Communist ideology, were *demanding* change."[56] The aim of this article is not, however, to present a hagiography of Roma activists during the Prague Spring, nor a celebration of internationalist solidarity during a "transnational moment of change," but to use these multiple perspectives on the Gypsy Question in socialist Czechoslovakia as a starting point for reflecting on the importance of transnational flows of images and ideas when writing a new history of social mobilization in postwar Eastern Europe.

Notes

1. SNA Bratislava, f. ÚV KSS—Predsedníctvo—č. krabice 1341, j. 720 / 13 Zásadnutie Predsedníctva 3.1.1973 (21.12.1972) *Správa o situácii a činnosti Zväzu Cigánov-Romov na Slovensku a jeho účelového zariadenia Bútiker* (Annex III).
2. On Soviet nationality policy see T. Martin, *The Affirmative Action Empire: Nations and Nationalism in the Soviet Union 1923–1939* (Ithaca: Cornell University Press, 2001), 32; F. Hirsch, *Empire of Nations: Ethnographic Knowledge and the Making of*

the Soviet Union (Ithaca: Cornell University Press, 2005); Y. Slezkine, *Arctic Mirrors: Russia and the Small Peoples of the North* (Ithaca: Cornell University Press, 1994); R. Suny and T. Martin, eds., *A State of Nations. Empire and Nation-Making in the Age of Lenin and Stalin* (Oxford: Oxford University Press, 2001).

3. C. Skalnik Leff, *National Conflict in Czechoslovakia. The Making and Unmaking of a State* (Princeton: Princeton University Press, 1988).

4. J. Rychlík, *Češi a Slováci ve 20. století. Česko-slovenské vztahy 1945–1992* (Bratislava: Academic Electronic Press, 1998).

5. J. Žatkuliak, *Federalizácia československého štátu 1968–1970: vznik česko-slovenskej federácie roku 1968* (Brno: Doplněk, 1996).

6. Žatkuliak, *Federalizácia československého,* 273–275: Dôvodová správa vlády ČSSR k návrhu ústavného zákona o postavení národností v ČSSR, 26.9.1968.

7. Cited in P. Thornberry, *International Law and the Rights of Minorities* (Oxford: Oxford University Press, 2001), 151.

8. A. Cassese, *Self-Determination of Peoples. A Legal Reappraisal* (Cambridge: Cambridge University Press, 1999).

9. K. Deutsch, *Nationalism and Social Communication: An Enquiry into the Foundations of Nationality* (Cambridge, MA: The MIT Press, 1953).

10. W. Connor, "Self-Determination: the New Phase," *World Politics* 20(1)(1967): 30–53.

11. M. Kurlansky, *1968: The Year that Rocked the World* (New York: Ballantine Books, 2004).

12. C. Fink, P. Gassert, and D. Junker, eds., *1968: The World Transformed* (New York: Cambridge University Press, 1998); see also G.-R. Horn and P. Kenney, eds., *Transnational Moments of Change: Europe 1945, 1968, 1989* (Lanham: Rowman and Littlefield, 2004); M. Klimke and J. Scharloth, eds., *1968 in Europe: A History of Protest and Activism, 1956–1977* (New York: Palgrave Macmillan, 2008).

13. T. Judt, *Postwar. A History of Europe since 1945* (London: Heineman, 2005), 421.

14. Judt, *Postwar,* 422–449.

15. J. Pažout, "Reakce československých studentů v době Pražského jara na protestní hnutí na Západě," in *Bolševismus, komunismus a radikální socialismus v Československu sv. II,* eds. Z. Karník and M. Kopeček (Praha: Dokořán, 2004); P. Bren, "1968 East and West. Visions of Political Change and Student Protest from across the Iron Curtain," in Horn and Kenney, *Transnational Moments of Change,* 119–136.

16. G.-R. Horn, "The Changing Nature of the European Working Class: The Rise and Fall of the 'New Working Class' (France, Italy, Spain, Czechoslovakia)," in Fink, Gassert, and Junker, *1968: The World Transformed,* 351–371.

17. A. Touraine, *Le Mouvement de Mai ou le Communisme Utopique* (Paris: Editions de Seuil, 1968).

18. See the review essay by W. Mausbach, "Historicizing '1968'," *Contemporary European History* 11(1)(2002): 177–187.

19. M. Kurlansky, *1968: The Year that Rocked the World* and the critical review by J. Suri, "Remembering the Images and Emotions of 1968," *H-Net Review,* 2004, retrieved 15 April 2008, from http://www.h-net.org/reviews/showrev.cgi?path=21333109949 3514; also J. Suri, *Power and Protest: Global Revolution and the Rise of Détente* (Cambridge, MA: Harvard University Press, 2003).

20. G.-R. Horn, "The Changing Nature of the European Working Class," 351–371.

21. J. Pažout, "Reakce československých studentů"; on travel restrictions see J. Rychlík, *Cestování do ciziny v habsburské monarchii a v Československu : pasová, vízová a vystěhovalecká politika 1848–1989* (USD: Praha, 2007).

22. F. Pospíšil, "Campaign against "Vlasatci" [long-haired youth] in Communist Czechoslovakia," conference paper presented at Marie Curie Conference on European Social Movements, Zurich, 2007.

23. M. Bracke, *Which Socialism, Whose Détente? West European Communism and the Czechoslovak Crisis of 1968* (Budapest: Central European University Press, 2007).

24. NA Praha, f. 02-1, sv. 110, a.j. 114-4, KSČ ÚV Předsednictvo, Kontrolní zpráva o plnění usnesení ÚV KSČ o práci mezi cikánským obyvatelstvem v ČSSR, 4 June 1965.

25. *Obrana lidu*, Interview with Juraj Špiner, tajomník Komisie pre riešenie cigánskej otázky pri Východoslovenskom KNV "O cigánoch s porozumením, ale nie sentimentálno," Roč. XXVI, 14. října 1967, č. 41, s. 9.

26. On the symbolic function of the "wild Gypsy" in legitimating upward social mobility in socialist Yugoslavia, see M. van der Port, *Gypsies, Wars and other Instances of the Wild. Civilization and its Discontents in a Serbian Town* (Amsterdam: University of Amsterdam, 1998).

27. S. Horváth. 2005. "Pubs and 'Hooligans' in a Socialist City in Hungary: the Public Sphere and Youth in Stalintown," in *European Cities, Youth and the Public Sphere in the Twentieth Century,* eds. A. Schildt and D. Siegfried (Aldershot: Ashgate, 2005), 88.

28. MRK Brno, f. Miroslava Holomka, *Návrh na zriadenie Zväzu čsl. Cigánov* (to Predsedníctvo vlády ČSSR, 5 April 1968) – opis.

29. K. Kaplan, *Kořeny československé reformy 1968 sv. III–IV* (Brno: Doplněk, 2002); K. Jech, *Soumrak selského stavu 1945–1960* (USD: Praha, 2001); L. Kalinová, *Společenské proměny v čase socialistického experimentu. K sociálním dějinám v letech 1945–1969* (Praha: Academia, 2007).

30. A. Marwick, *The Sixties: Cultural Transformation in Britain, France, Italy and the United States, c. 1958–c. 1974* (Oxford: Oxford University Press, 1998); A. Schildt and D. Siegfried, eds., *Between Marx and Coca-Cola. Youth Cultures in Changing European Societies, 1960–1980* (Oxford: Berghahn Books, 2006).

31. Klement Gottwald was the first President of Czechoslovakia after 1948. Kofola was a substitute cola drink produced in Czechoslovakia from the early 1960s.

32. K. Williams, *The Prague Spring and its Aftermath. Czechoslovak politics, 1968–1970* (Cambridge: Cambridge University Press, 1997), 5.

33. Kaplan, *Kořeny československé reformy 1968, vol. II*, 94.

34. Ibid., 97.

35. Williams, *The Prague Spring and its Aftermath*, 6; see also J. Pecka, J. Belda, and J. Hoppe, *Občanská společnost 1967–1970: emancipační hnutí uvnitř Národní fronty 1967–1970* (Brno: Doplněk, 1995), 51.

36. See M. Stewart, *The Time of the Gypsies* (Boulder: Westview Press, 1997).

37. For a penetrating critique of representations of "Gypsies" in Czech popular culture, see V. Sokolova, "A Matter of Speaking. Racism, Gender and Social Deviance in the Politics of the 'Gypsy Question' in Communist Czechoslovakia, 1945–1989," PhD diss., University of Washington, 2002.

38. I.-M. Kaminski, *The State of Ambiguity. Studies of Gypsy Refugees* (Gothenburg: University of Gothenburg, 1980), 220.

39. NA Praha, f. MPSV [uncatalogued], MPSV Zpráva o současném stava řešení otázek cikánského obyvatelstva v ČSR, 2 December 1969.
40. For a detailed discussion see K. Williams, *The Prague Spring and its Aftermath*.
41. V. Havel, "Na téma opozice" (1968), and P. Pithart, "Národní fronta nebo parlament?" (1968), in J. Hoppe, *Pražské jaro v médiích. Výběr z dobové publicistiky* (Brno: Doplněk, 2004).
42. Williams, *The Prague Spring and its Aftermath*, 18.
43. G. Puxon, "'The Romani Movement: Rebirth and the First World Romani Congress in Retrospect," in *Scholarship and the Gypsy Struggle: Commitment in Romani Studies*, eds. T. Acton and D. Kenrick (Hatfield: University of Hertfordshire Press, 2000), 92–113.
44. D.S. Kenrick. 1971. "The World Romani Congress," *Journal of the Gypsy Lore Society*, 101-108.
45. MZA Brno, f. SCR, kart. 2, Minutes of extraordinary meeting of the Czech Roma Union presidium, February 1972.
46. G. Puxon, "'The Romani Movement: Rebirth and the First World Romani Congress in Retrospect," 109.
47. MRK Brno, personal archive of Miroslav Holomek, "Report of Delegation of Central Committee of Czech Union of Gypsies-Roma to World Romani Congress," London, April 1971.
48. The Town and Country Planning Act 1947, the Highways Act 1959, and the Caravan Sites and Control of Development Act 1960, which had removed many of the stopping places available to previous generations.
49. MRK Brno, personal archive of Miroslav Holomek, "Report."
50. MZA Brno, f. SCR, kart. 2, Zápis z mimořádného zasedání před.UVSCR, 1.2.1972 v Praze.
51. T. Acton and I. Klimová, "The International Romani Union: An East European answer to West European questions? Shifts in the focus of World Romani Congresses 1971–2000," in *Between Past and Future: the Roma of Central and Eastern Europe*, ed. W. Guy (Hatfield: University of Hertfordshire Press, 2001), 157–226.
52. Council of Europe Parliamentary Assembly, *Recommendation 563 (1969) [1] on the situation of Gypsies and other travellers in Europe*.
53. Ibid.
54. Minority Rights Group report on the European Roma, London 1973.
55. G. Puxon, "Gypsies: Blacks of Eastern Europe," *The Nation*, 222 (17 April 1976): 461.
56. Ibid., 460–468.

Chapter 3

Human Rights as a Transnational Vocabulary of Protest

Campaigning against the Political Abuse
of Psychiatry in the Soviet Union

Hara Kouki

Introduction

In an article that appeared in an academic journal in February 2006 under the title "Human Rights Abuses in Mental Institutions Common Worldwide," we read: "Institutional psychiatry as a major tool of political suppression … may no longer be the problem that it was in the 1980s in the Soviet Union, but violation of international human rights law continue unabated … in China, Turkey, Nicaragua or Latvia." The "well-documented" story of psychiatric repression in the Soviet Union during the Cold War, when "a patient's conviction that the state must be changed was seen as indicia of mental illness,"[1] serves nowadays as a point of reference for political affairs and medical developments as well as for issues of dissent, state repression, and mental health reforms, within the Russian Federation and globally.

However, back in 1966, when various US and Western European scholars participated in an international medical congress in Moscow,[2] it seemed that there was nothing reproachable about Soviet psychiatry, neither in terms of medical or human rights standards. The official report and the media coverage of the event praised the achievements of the Soviet doctors and the international scientific exchange. All of this changed when, in February 1983, the USSR resigned its membership of the World Psychiatric Association's Congress due to mounted criticism coming from national psychiatric associations, human rights activists, and governmental organs. Public opinion was blaming Soviet psychiatry for suppressing political dissent following state and KGB directives.

What had happened in those few years that led to the public exposure of the political abuse of psychiatry in the USSR and then subsequently led to its universal condemnation? The present chapter seeks to trace the creation of a transnational campaign revolving around this delicate issue as developed beyond state initiatives during the Cold War, in an attempt to understand how human rights have been shaped and used as a vocabulary of protest in the postwar world.

And the Story Goes Like This...

The well known story of psychiatric abuse in the USSR has been written according to the memoirs of the dissidents and the activists, as these are recorded mostly, if not exclusively, in the writings of Peter Reddaway and Sidney Bloch: the two scholars compiled in 1977 *Russia's Political Hospitals: the Abuse of Psychiatry in the Soviet Union,* and, some years later, *Soviet Psychiatric Abuse: the Shadow over World Psychiatry* (1984). Those two publications are considered to be the principal textbooks on the issue, presenting the entire series of actions in great detail. Reddaway and Bloch, along with the other authors,[3] depart from the conviction that "the Soviet authorities" had "for many years systematically used psychiatry to suppress dissent by confining sane, non-violent citizens in mental hospitals until drug treatment [taught] them to conform to the dictates of the state."[4] The chronicle of the campaign has been incorporated in a storyline that may be summarized as following:[5] the first recorded case of labeling dissent as mental illness in Russia occurred in 1836, when the philosopher Pyotr Chaadayev was declared to be suffering from "derangement and insanity" after he had published a letter critical of Czar Nicholas I. However, psychiatric diagnosis was seldom used to deal with opposition until the late 1950s, when Khrushchev announced that, "there are no political prisoners, only persons of unsound mind." From this point, the Soviets started to rely extensively on "tame psychiatrists to label troublemakers insane,"[6] in order to avoid public trials and to silence dissent. Awareness of this kind of political abuse outside of the USSR began to develop in 1971, following accounts of the treatment of General Piotr Grigorenko and Vladimir Bukovsky, as well as the compulsory hospitalization of the well-known biologist Zhores Medvedev. While the allegations concerning those cases of abuse did not become an issue during the 1971 World Psychiatric Association (WPA) conference, some years later, the attitude of public opinion completely would change. For the next decade and a half, an international campaign developed against the issue of "psychiatric terror," which was based on the accusation that the KGB security organs were regularly referring citizens to psychiatrists due to their political ideas and activities on the basis of false diagnoses of "sluggish schizophrenia." According to an increasing number of allegations clandestinely disseminated to the West by a handful of Soviet human rights activists, dissidents were committed to mental asylums, such as the Serbsky Institute, where they were treated with particular cruelty.

In opposition to this state violation of human rights, national psychiatric associations became active and committees against political abuse of psychiatry were created, while groups and individual activists tackled the issue through contacts with USSR, press articles, and public protests. Due to increasing mobilization and extensive media coverage of the facts, the All-Union Society of Neuropathologists and Psychiatrists withdrew from the World Psychiatric Association in 1983. It was not readmitted until 1989, after Soviet officials had agreed to negotiate their rigid standpoint by publicly admitting errors in the realm of psychiatry; the Gorbachev reforms seemed to have brought an end to corruption among medical personnel and to the systematic mistreatment of mentally healthy people in the USSR. And, indeed, a report published in 1991 by the WPA claimed that, after what was then almost fifteen years of international campaigning, the practice appeared to have ceased in the Russian Federation.[7] What is more—the narrative continues—the Soviet experience during the Cold War years proved to be influential also in the long run, both inside and outside of the USSR. As a result of the campaign, "human rights and psychiatry" became the core issue of concern for several NGOs, and medical ethics were adopted worldwide; for instance, injunctions against basing diagnoses on political values or religious beliefs and against using psychiatric interventions for non-medical purposes have been codified by the WPA or the World Medical Association.[8] In 1991, the United Nations General Assembly approved the "Principles for the Protection of Persons with Mental Illness and for the Improvement of Mental Health Care" and the Council of Europe Recommendation 1235 on "Psychiatry and Human Rights" (1994). The story of the psychiatric abuse in the Soviet Union came full circle in 1992, when norms and ethics regarding professional independence in the sphere of psychiatry were codified in Russia's new mental health law.[9]

All in all, the campaign against the abuse of psychiatry in the Soviet Union that escalated in the 1970s has been both domestically and globally successful, in terms of bringing together unanimously dissenting voices against injustice, both at the time and in the years that followed. The emerging human rights movement, as reflected in the campaign, would finally triumph in introducing in both blocs and across the world central concepts such as legality, freedom of conscience, and respect for individuality. This human rights story has been turned into history and serves as a paradigm in postwar global affairs.

"History's Carnival": Framing the Campaign for the Release of Leonid Plyushch

One of the most publicized and successful instances of this movement was the international campaign for the release of Leonid Plyushch that was mounted during 1975/76.

The Ukrainian mathematician of Jewish origin, born in 1939, was a convinced Marxist according to his memoirs[10] and worked at the Institute of Cybernetics of the Ukrainian Academy of Sciences. After being arrested for "anti-Soviet propaganda and agitation" in January 1972,[11] he was confined to the Dnepropetrovsk psychiatric hospital in July 1973, where he was found to be suffering from "creeping schizophrenia with messianic and reformist ideas." In the following months, a large quantity of information reached the West suggesting that he had been detained in the asylum not on medical grounds, but for writing samizdat[12] on human rights-related themes; what is more, it was reported that his health had been seriously undermined after he was mistreated with drugs. The prisoner was finally released in January 1976 amidst a broad worldwide campaign, in which even the French Communist Party had issued a public statement of concern.[13] Immediately afterwards, Plyushch fled to the West, while psychiatrists, who examined the former patient, confirmed his allegations about the punitive nature of Soviet psychiatry.[14]

Leonid Plyushch was a human rights activist and a founding member of the "Initiative Group for the Defense of Human Rights," which was established in 1969 in order to protest against the violations of the Soviet constitution and the UN Declaration of Human Rights in the USSR. This was immediately followed by a proliferation of similar non-governmental organizations in the country, which rallied for the respect of human dignity regardless of nationality, religion or ideology by means of non-violent and public activities, such as the dissemination of non-political samizdat.[15] When Plyushch was arrested, a vast amount of material highlighting his case reached the West: his own writings, protests of his wife and friends, and statements and articles by fellow dissidents and academics addressed both to the Soviet authorities and to media and associations abroad.[16] Moreover, other Soviet citizens such as Sergei Kovalev or Andrei Sakharov were convicted and tried on charges including that of protesting against the violations of Plyushch's rights. All of those appeals rested on the accusation that during the activist's arrest, detention, and trial the Ukrainian criminal code had been violated. Relevant documentation on the dissident circulated in samizdat form mainly via the major human rights publication of the USSR, the *Chronicle of Current Events*,[17] which regularly reported on cases of violations of Soviet citizens' rights. Another important samizdat publication concerning psychiatric abuse was the "Manual on Psychiatry for Dissenters," which was compiled by Vladimir Bukovksy and Dr. Semyon Gluzman—this was dedicated to "Lenya Plyushch, a victim of psychiatric terror."[18] In the years to come, the majority of information emanated mostly from the "Working Commission for the Investigation of the Use of Psychiatry for Political Purposes," a committee founded in 1977 by the Podrabinek brothers in Moscow.[19] All of those actions and statements were articulated in terms of the so-called "strategy of legality," in which emphasis was put on the accepting the language of the law at face value and on calling the government to task whenever it ignored its own laws[20]—a tactic which Plyushch had also adopted.

On the other side of the Iron Curtain, it was mainly Amnesty International (AI) that, based on this information, became the first organization to launch a campaign defending Leonid Plyushch. This was boosted by an AI symposium organized in April 1975 in Geneva on the use of psychiatry for political purposes; during that meeting, psychiatrists along with activists adopted a declaration on ethical and legal aspects of the issue.[21] The mobilization for the mathematician departed from a pattern of research and actions that had already been invented and developed by Amnesty since 1971; this moved from research on mental health torture to publications in academic medical and popular journals, from lobbying medical associations to contacting dissidents and emigrants, while at the same time psychiatric groups were elaborating and disseminating information on individual cases of psychiatric abuse.[22] The Plyushch campaign gradually took a life of its own, as numerous individuals across Europe became involved, such as Dr. Low-Beer of the Royal College of Psychiatrists or the academic Peter Reddaway, co-founder of the "Working Group on the Internment of Dissenters in Mental Hospitals" established in 1971 in London, and also organizations, such as the "Comité des Psychiatres Francais contre l' Utilisation de la Psychiatrie a des Fins Politiques" in Paris, the International Commission of Jurists, the "League for the Rights of Man," the "International Federation for the Rights of Man," the Bertrand Russell Foundation, or the "Young Friends of the Ukraine." Academics, jurists, and doctors were mobilized to the cause through scientific and medical associations, which all encouraged research on theoretical aspects of the case, letter writing to the press, and the directing of appeals to the Soviet authorities.[23] These and other initiatives contributed to the formation of the ad hoc group "Comité International des mathématiciens pour la defense de Leonid Plyushch" in January 1974, which grew rapidly and attracted members in thirteen countries. Numerous articles and readers' letters about Plyushch appeared, press releases were issued, and appeals to "jurists and psychiatrists" were launched, meetings were held and a book on his case was published.[24] Due to an initiative by the French section of AI and supported by many human rights bodies, a Plyushch "Journée internationale" was arranged, in order to bring all of these voices together and make the protest even more vociferous, and another meeting for his liberation was held on 23 October 1975 in the Mutualité in Paris. Under the slogan "liberty is to be defended everywhere," the initiative in fact gathered the unanimous support of human rights, Jewish, and religious groups, national organizations, socialist coalitions, scientific associations, intellectuals, students, and mass media coverage, and was, thus, a great success in all respects.[25] A message addressed to campaigners by Igor Safarevich, a Soviet mathematician and member of the Human Rights Committee, resonates with the spirit of this entire mobilization:

All of you who are concerned with Plyushch's fate are united not by parties, class or national interest, but solely by the desire to save a human life. You are defending much more than a person. You are defending all those who are in the same plight ... which can help you to better comprehend your own life, and to evaluate your future, the future of your country and all the human race.[26]

A vital part of this campaign, as well as of all of the similar activities taking place throughout those years, was the attempt to make every step of it publicly known. Amnesty became acquainted of the unlawful arrest and detention of Leonid Plyushch when this was documented in samizdat form in the *Chronicle of Current Events;* the Research Department informed other activists and groups by disseminating the documents from the USSR and by coordinating actions through its *News Releases* and in relation with other human rights publications, such as the *Chronicle of Human Rights in the USSR;* letters and appeals concerning the mathematician were published in *Le Monde,* in *The Observer,* and in *The New York Times,*[27] while *The Lancet,* the *British Medical Journal,* and the *Bulletin of the Commission of Mathematicians for the Release of Plyushch* circulated essays once they became available and coordinated protests. Letters were also addressed to the BBC, the Voice of America, Radio Liberty, and Deutsche Welle that further informed people on the Plyushch case and, as a result, on the issue of psychiatric internment for political reasons in the Soviet Union. The regular exposure of all of those facts to the mass media was not a tactical choice for activists but an integral part of the whole process: news dispatches and articles were both the object and the subject of the human rights network.[28] In the years to come, this transnational and mediated network of communication would become all the more extended and evident and its actors more conscious of their role in it.[29]

The Plyushch case embodies the way the issue of confinement in psychiatric hospitals in the USSR came to be tackled: activists received, organized, and generated data in an effort to mobilize public opinion and influence scientific communities and government policy. A campaign was built on legal and medical grounds based on and attached to factual information distributed by the media; at the same time, there was a pervasive effort to avoid political implications at any cost, so as to work for the rights of suppressed individuals in the country while moving beyond Cold War tactics. As a result, this whole idea of legality, impartiality, and universal rights was embodied in individual and local cases of abuse: these cases escaped the anonymity of abuse and managed to get heard, and were treated in isolation to the social and political groups to which they belonged. The abstract idea of human rights was personified.

The philosophy of human rights has a long intellectual background; in this specific contemporary connotation, however, related with information gathering, international mobilization, civil and political rights, non-politicization, and the search for legal guarantees, it has been an invention of the recent postwar era.[30] While in 1953 the term did not mean much and in 1968 it was just a noble expression, it was not actually until the 1970s that a movement started to take shape and expand, when activists and nongovernmental organizations, drawing on legal provisions, invented a human rights language of global justice offering, thus, an alternative perspective to global politics. The campaign for the release of Leonid Plyushch gives us a hint of the exchange launched across the Iron Curtain throughout the 1970s; in the Soviet Union, a rather small but active group of activists produced samizdat publications, formed independent rights organizations, and initiated letter writing campaigns against censorship and the arbitrary repression exercised by the regime, as well as the inertia of Soviet citizens; in the West, groups and individuals—often disillusioned with official Marxism—were mobilized around the cause, and activists translated documents, edited appeals, and took initiatives against the Cold War ideological fronts and the apathy of their capitalist societies.[31] This chain of events reveals an emerging transnational network of information and protest that was trying to communicate local concerns, which, when articulated in terms of human rights, were perceived as global problems and desires. It was this strategic use of a human rights frame by diverse groups of people across a divided continent, thus, that transformed the fate of Plyushch into a symbol of victims of repression first in the USSR and, then, in every part of the world.

"Diagnosing Soviet Dissidence": Debating the Universality of a Local Case of Abuse

Using new conceptual terms, the nascent human rights culture managed to link people from various national, sociopolitical, and religious backgrounds in the campaign against state abuses—in our case, against psychiatric mistreatment in the Soviet Union. However, this transnational approach did not suffice per se to provide these people with an unambiguous perception of the event or on how to narrate it. On the other side of the spectrum, there were internal debates taking place during those years in the Western bloc among activists, doctors, and journalists concerning the confinement of dissidents in mental hospitals; those discussions reveal the complexity of conceptualizing human rights abuses on a universal level. No one seemed to deny that many dissidents had for a long time ended up in special hospitals after an obviously wrong diagnosis, due to their unacceptable political ideas and against legal provisions; however, what was rather controversial, for example, was the extent to which this reality was systematic and state directed.

For instance, it was the psychiatrist Dr. W. Lawrence Tonge, who, when asked to comment on the use of mental hospitals in the USSR in the control of political dissent, introduced to the discussion the motivations of the Soviet psychiatrists involved in the abuses. In the report he sent to AI in 1973, what seemed to trouble him is that, "the practice of psychiatry cannot be evaluated outside the context of the society to which it belongs." Without denying that in some cases the treatment of prisoners seemed to be totally inadequate, he argued that "in the same way as an English psychiatrist may have to labor the point in a matrimonial case that sexual perversion is not synonymous with mental disorder, so the Soviet psychiatrist has the task of demonstrating that reformist political ideas are not the same as paranoid illusions." Tonge understood mental disease and psychiatric services as being entangled in the ideological and socio-political functions of each society and, thus, "the task of the forensic psychiatry is the same in both countries." What Dr. Tonge called for was a better under-standing of cultural particularities in each country, since "in both instances, the psychiatrist is struggling against a cultural current which assumes that a taboo activity stems from a mental disorder."[32]

Dr. Tonge's critique echoes theories and activities concerning psychiatry that were widespread throughout the 1960s and 1970s. In 1961, Thomas Szasz's *The Myth of Mental Illness* was printed and Michel Foucault published his pioneering work *Naissance de la clinique: une archéologie du regard médical*, while the "Anti-Psychiatry Movement" in England and the "Democratic Movement" in Italy[33] were moving in parallel with the creation of patients' associations worldwide demanding their rights.[34] This turmoil was directed against established psychi-atric ethics and stemmed from an idea also permeating Tonge's text: throughout human history, systems of power have used "scientific psychiatric categories" and institutionalization as a tool in order to control the populace.

In any case, this document was not distributed within activists' circles and the debate started taking shape mainly in the writings of the psychiatrist Dr. Walter Reich. He suggested that the Soviet diagnostic framework was such as it tended to direct psychiatrists into making diagnoses that were in effect abu-sive—in other words, the psychiatrists believed their diagnoses. Reich was, since 1971, one of the first psychiatrists in the West who became actively engaged in the denunciation of mistreatment of political prisoners in the Soviet Union, by writing in the daily press and professional journals and by conducting interviews with émigrés and research missions in the USSR.[35] However, his approach to the issue was rather different. Against the belief that Soviet doctors were conscious of the political purpose of the abuse, his initial point of criticism was that, in fact, the dissident diagnoses were consistent with the Soviet approach to mental illness: psychiatry in that country had been undergoing a revolution since the late 1950s, with the rise to power of the Moscow school, founded and headed by Andrei Snezhnevsky. The psychiatrist promulgated a theory of schizophrenia that attributed the illness primarily to genetic rather than environmental deficits: this had emerged during the 1940s and the 1950s,[36] well before the practice of committing dissidents to psychiatric wards had begun to take place with any frequency, and, thus, was not created deliberately in order to make these diagno-ses possible. This new classification system became the standard by which most patients in the Soviet Union were diagnosed and, thus, was not only affecting dissidents: "the system created a category in their minds which was eventually assumed to represent a real class of patients and which was inevitably filled with real persons."[37]

This broad definition of mental illness, when coupled with the nature of political life in the Soviet Union and the social perceptions that this fashioned, brought Reich to his line of reasoning: dissenting behavior did seem strange in that country, and due to the inclusive diagnostic system, this sometimes came to be called schizophrenia; "in many and perhaps most instances, not only the KGB and other responsible officials but the ordinary psychiatrists themselves really believed that the dissidents were ill." As unorthodox political conduct was likely to provoke public and professional scrutiny, "a dissident stands a substantial risk of being diagnosed and believed to be schizophrenic whether or not the state interferes."[38]

And he was not the only one to put forward such an approach to the issue. Many similar arguments appeared throughout the 1970s. Boris Segal, a psychiatrist who had emigrated from Moscow to Boston, believed that the average Soviet psychiatrist was little different to his foreign colleagues in his moral and professional values. Many ordinary people, as well as doctors and KGB officials, were convinced that "'thought-less activities' against a gigantic apparatus are indications of mental illness"[39] and, thus, only in rare cases could one speak of a conscious violation of medical ethics. Similarly, Professor F. Jenner, one of the first scientists to condemn publicly cases of psychiatric abuse in the country,[40] believed that many people in the Soviet Union would regard it as mad to do or say anything in opposition to Soviet policy. This, "plus a broad concept of schizophrenia, a faith in drugs, a mental health directive and an understandable desire to fit in, or fear of not fitting in, with the strong support of much of the society and the powerful police, leads to what seems to us outrageous behaviour by psychiatrists."[41] Or, as Dr. Field remarked at the 1977 Congress of the WPA, it was "at least conceivable" that "the average Soviet psychiatrist, brought up within the context of Soviet culture and values will assess the very idea of opposition to the regime as prima facie evidence of some kind of deep disturbance."[42]

Walter Reich, then, shared the same skepticism as other activists: Soviet psychiatrists were not merely following security officials' directives, but they were entangled within a different perception of reality. There were also other points of disagreement: that the serious lack of information prevented the forming of a comprehensive picture; that criticism should be addressed to the Soviet colleagues without excluding them from international scientific communities and obstructing scholarly exchange; that violations of the rights of people labeled as mentally ill occurred also in other parts of the world due to the lack of legal safeguards, but that these violations did not gain similar levels of public attention.

All of these arguments formed part of an ongoing discussion among people engaged in the campaign. Activists, scholars, and journalists from diverse backgrounds had come together on the basis of a common cause: to defend human rights in the Soviet Union in terms defined beyond their state borders; now, they had to negotiate and create the terms of communication, which were conditioned in respect to public opinion and the media, the medical establishment, academic communities, and official responses in different national contexts. In their attempt to redress a particular injustice as a "universal wrong," activists tried to locate this mistreatment in its domestic context while, at the same time, relating it with cases of abuse taking place around the globe. And this process surfaced as the other side of the same transnational encounter that had produced the campaign for Plyushch's release.

The debate was shaped by the broader cultural currents and historical factors and by the same globalizing reality that brought those people together in the first place. Activists could sidestep the level of national politics that had shaped Cold War ideologies and get themselves heard beyond their local borders in the name of such universal concerns as human rights. However, Tonge's and Reich's arguments show that speaking about rights and psychiatry, for instance, was a complex, dynamic, and totally unpredictable process: in the 1970s, clinical approaches to mental illness were experiencing radical change, cultural products were questioning the official health care system, transnational aspects of psychiatry were coming to the fore, and the media was resonating public concern over state abuses of patients' rights worldwide.[43] These tendencies were inscribed within a generalized revolt taking place throughout those years against existing structures of the world order: "new" social and radical theories were challenging authorities, grand ideologies, and conventional cultural practices.[44] Even if indifferent to, in opposition to or in support of it, citizens were in any case taking part in this worldwide "culture of dissent" via its ever-present media representations. And all of these were instances happening all over the world and at a threatening speed—that is, against the bizarre experience of globalization. Human rights mobilization was a reaction to the stories and images of suffering that started to vehemently surface from home and from faraway places. On the other hand, it was this same "globalization" that offered an alternative possibility of coming together in order to change the world. The global rights vocabulary of protest was formed in interaction with this broad restructuring of established orthodoxies and borders.

The examination of the campaign for Plyushch's release reveals the possibilities for alterative citizen organization that opened up due to a human rights discourse. Functioning as a platform for people from the left and the right, from the East and the West, and from radical social movements and religious groups communicating on issues of state repression and dissent, human rights changed the framework against which people learned to situate their life and, thus, to experience and change it. On the other hand, the discussions among activists taking place in parallel presents us with the new challenges encountered by this universal ideology when faced with national/cultural contexts. Allegations about the abuse of psychiatry provoked a transnational encounter in which information moved horizontally due to newly created networks; at the same time, information was negotiated vertically by these same networks. Activists from different contexts experienced moments of identification that dissolved national barriers; at the same time, they also went through moments of differentiation that created new kinds of dividing lines. There were instances of cultural and social overlap, and times when the common frame of universal rights was used to express divergent experiences and expectations. What was new about this global experience of the 1970s, then, was not its *a priori* progressive or cooperative character, but that it transpired in less than usual terms. Global ideas in local contexts, local ideas in global contexts: in a few words, this campaign represented a transnational contact that could unite or further divide protest communities. The mobilization against the confinement of Soviet dissidents in asylums, as part of the campaign against state abuses in the USSR, as part of the emerging human rights movement, actually formed part of a general transformation that was taking place at the time, in which new ideas and practices emerged within the Cold War context. And the task would be to explore this combination of events and processes that led to the formation of human rights culture in order to comprehend the period under question, as well as the origins of our contemporary reality.

Human Rights beyond Left and Right or within Wrongs and Rights? A Conclusion

So far, we have attempted to move toward a transnational historicization of human rights during the Cold War years, one that would comprise the study of convergences/divergences created in relation to broader historical processes.[45]

According to this perspective, human rights culture has been presented not as a closed and established entity founded on eternal and moral categories waiting to be materialized, but as formed according to concrete temporal and local processes and multiplicities of relations. During the 1970s, activists across both blocs invented the human rights framework so as to break away from polarized politics and—what they perceived as—dried ideologies and instead to engage in issues of global injustice. The new politics as articulated in the Plyushch campaign formed part of a revolutionary project that brought to the fore suppressed voices, while responding to a historically determined conception of world affairs and resistance to state repression. Representing not the eventual triumph of a universal good, but a purely political choice against a Cold War background, this human rights movement started to produce its own narratives and structures of understanding the world. As evident in the debate concerning the diagnosis of Soviet dissidents, tensions between the local and the global throughout those years gave birth to new modes of explaining reality by means of negotiating established criteria of right and wrong, illegal and legal, normal and abnormal. The contemporary rights culture, hence, emerges precisely from this debate between the particular characteristics of a culture and universal claims[46] and within a context of Cold War politics, disappointment with ideologies, and social tension.

And the Story becomes History…

However, this attempt to historicize the emergence of the movement would be incomplete if it were not accompanied by a presentation of how this story has been written as history and how it is told and remembered, in other words, of how human rights discourses and struggles have been legitimized and have served as a point of reference.

As outlined at the beginning, the story of the campaign has taken concrete shape mainly in the texts edited by Reddaway and Bloch, who rely for information on ex-patients and émigré psychiatrists. The researchers attempt to present a factual picture of what happened without suggesting that the USSR was the only country in which psychiatry was abused, or that huge numbers of people were involved. However, along with the other authors, they divide Soviet psychiatry into a large body of passive medical personnel, into innocent/dissenting psychiatrists, and into a few "bad and corrupted" doctors; the latter were consciously following KGB directives when abusing the dissidents—victims of punitive psychiatry, some of whom heroically managed to transmit their experiences from this "increasingly paranoid regime" to the West. "Average doctors" were "too conformist to refuse," while "hundreds of cynical doctors cooperate[d] fully;" these followed the paradigm set by their Nazi colleagues[47] in an attempt to "extract recantations with the aid of drugs" from "honest, idealistic, dedicated defenders of human rights" for whom the prospect of betraying their beliefs seemed "abhorrent." On the one hand, there was simple evil, the KGB issuing orders and psychiatrists obeying them, and, on the other, pure good embodied in the heroic figures of human rights activists on both sides of the Iron Curtain. However, some individuals, at first, and society and state as a whole, later, moved unavoidably toward the realization of global rights that ultimately managed to familiarize the authoritarian and bleak Soviet reality with concepts such as freedom of conscience and human dignity. This pattern would be followed by other repressive regimes reflecting the eventual triumph of rights philosophy in a postwar world. Within this progressive narrative, this specific campaign is portrayed as part of a global moral struggle between wrong and right. The black and white lists of the protagonists subject all of the events to a moral classification of "the good activist versus corrupted power."[48] In this attempt to universalize the experiences of abuse in purely legalistic terms, the individuals and their actions are extracted from any historical-cultural background. This linear storyline goes on to narrate that, as a natural outcome of this story of abuse and its universal condemnation, international organizations adopted codes of psychiatric ethics: the case became an established point of reference in the field of psychiatry and human rights.[49] For instance, in the recent campaign mounted against the Chinese regime for punishing deviant citizens, human rights activists shaped their criticisms on the basis that, in this case, a "Soviet-style of political abuse of psychiatry has been adopted."[50] It is exactly in this monochromatic picture that the chronicle of psychiatric terror has become part of public knowledge.

The perspective adopted by the activists that took part in the events, then, became the approach used to make any reference to this campaign and shaped the categories in which similar stories are presented. However, a whole series of questions does not fit into this predictable narrative, such as the issue of the history of psychiatry in the Soviet Union and the debate presented above; the educational status of Soviet psychiatrists and their scientific relations with foreign colleagues; the conditions of incarceration not only of the political, but of all patients in Soviet psychiatric hospitals; the social prejudices accompanying mental health; the role of legal safeguards in the medical system and the possibilities/limits of international law toward this direction; and, how all of these issues relate to the political culture permeating life in the Soviet Union or with similar types of questions in other countries perhaps experiencing authoritarian rule.[51] The schematic representation of a complex reality, thus, obscures the existence of other colors, of complex historical roots, and sociopolitical circumstances. And as this approach to events becomes dominant, aspects of a specific living reality gradually vanish from the picture.

As a result, the way the story of the 1970s campaign has been incorporated into transnational postwar history seems to require further analysis. No one can deny the fact that there were numerous people who courageously resisted abuse, both in the Soviet Union and abroad: their stories should be told and remembered and their struggles, as well as the brutality of state abuses, should not be forgotten. Yet this approach fails to address our question, which is not to take a stand on those individuals according to our morality, but to examine how exactly we came to develop the criteria in order to classify them. In other words, to examine how the events and the people engaged in the campaign came to fit into the "good versus evil" moral scheme; how this new vocabulary of protest, which back in the 1970s was opening up space for a plurality of suppressed voices, has been crystallized into a monolithic pattern of normalcy according to which we interpret the past; how complex realities of suffering exposed in the postwar world have become rationalized in terms of "individual versus power" and according to a simplified "Resistance/Collaboration" interpretation; and how this approach to history has tended to produce an unrealistic, moral, and polarized view of people's behavior and of the choices they faced. The story of the campaign can help us to comprehend not only the culture of dissent that developed in the 1970s, but also its subsequent evolution.

Back in 1971, in the context of Cold War relations, human rights activists began to conceive a pattern of monitoring and protesting against the politically abusive use of psychiatry in the USSR. Within a few years, this human rights vocabulary became so influential so as to form part and to influence those relations. Writing the history of this campaign includes the examination of transnational alliances, as well as disputes, which, when examined in interaction within broader contexts and circumstances, shed light on human rights practices and ideas emerging at the time. But the campaigning against psychiatric repression in the USSR does not just illustrate the construction of the contemporary human rights regime; it has actually contributed to it. This story, which is narrated in terms of "good versus evil," functions nowadays as a tool for interpreting and responding to injustices around the world.

The question of our writing the transnational history of human rights is not to take a stand on the ideas and discussions implicated, but to examine how human rights concepts and regimes are structured throughout time and space and how they have been used in order to understand the world; and that also means examining when and how human rights can become as hegemonic and repressive as the violations against which they protest.

Notes

1. E. Katz, *Virginia Law Journal* (27 February 2006), retrieved 15 November 2007 from www.law.virginia.edu/html/news/2006_spr/perlin.htm.
2. D. Slobin, ed., *Handbook of Soviet Psychology: Prepared for the International Congress of Psychology, Moscow, USSR, August 4–11, 1966* (White Plains: International Arts and Science Press, 1966).
3. Also frequently cited and of the same rationale are the *White Book on the Interment of Dissenters in Soviet Mental Hospitals* (1974) by Anthony de Meeus, *Political Psychiatry in the USSR* by Robert Van Voren (Amsterdam, 1983), as well as Harvey Fireside's the *Soviet Psychoprisons* (1979).
4. International Association on the Political Use of Psychiatry (henceforth IAPUP), "Recent Publications on Soviet Psychiatric Abuse," *Information Bulletin* 12 (1982): 21.
5. As presented both in academic texts and media sources, as well as in human rights publications, such as Moscow Helsinki Group, *Human Rights and Psychiatry in the Russian Federation* (2004), retrieved 12 September 2007 from http://www.mhg.ru/english/3959925; Amnesty International, *Psychiatry: a Human Rights Perspective* (AI Index, ACT 75/003/95, 1995); R. Munro, *The Soviet Case: Prelude to a Global Consensus on Psychiatry and Human Rights* (2000), retrieved 23 November 2007 from the Human Rights Watch web site http://hrw.org/reports/2002/china02/china0802-02.htm.
6. "Censuring the Soviets," *The Times,* Monday, 11 September 1977.
7. WPA, *Report by the WPA Team of a Visit to the Soviet Union (9–29 June 1991)* (London: Royal College of Psychiatrists, 1991).
8. As the Declaration of Hawaii, approved by the General Assembly of the WPA in Vienna in 1983, or the Declaration of Tokyo approved by the World Medical Association in 1975.
9. R. Bonnie, "Introduction: the Evolution of the 1992 Law of the Russian Federation on Psychiatric Care," *Journal of Russian and Eurasian Psychiatry* 27 (1996): 69–96.

10. L. Plyushch, "Preliminary Declaration by Leonid Plyushch at the Press Conference held in Paris, 3 February 1976," in *The Case of Leonid Plyushch*, eds. M. Sapiets, P. Reddaway, and C. Emerson (London: C. Hurst, 1976), 143–151. This is the English translation of T. Khodorovitch, ed., *Istoryia Boleznyi Leonida Plyushcha* (Amsterdam: Fond imeni Gertsena, 1974). For more on his case see L. Plyushch, *History's Carnival, a Dissident's Autobiography* (London: Collins and Harvill Press, 1979); Amnesty International (henceforth AI), *The Case of Leonid Plyushch* (London: AI Publications, 1991); Y. Mathon and J.J. Marie, eds., *L'affaire Pliouchtch* (Paris: Éditions du Seuil, 1976).

11. According to Article 70 of the Criminal law of the Russian Soviet Federative Socialist Republic, "agitation or propaganda carried out with the purpose of subverting or weakening the Soviet regime or in order to commit particularly dangerous crimes against the state, the dissemination for the said purposes of slanderous inventions defamatory to the Soviet political and social system, as well as the dissemination or harboring for the said purpose of literature of similar content." cited in D. Barry, W. Butler, and G. Ginsburgs, eds., *Contemporary Soviet Law essays in Honor of John N. Hazard* (The Hague: M. Nijhoff, 1974), 32.

12. That is, "self-publication," a term used for unpublished manuscripts circulated privately.

13. Written by Rene Andrieu in the PCF's official newspaper *L'humanité*, 25 October 1975.

14. Reddaway and Bloch, *Soviet Psychiatric Abuse*, 65, and "*Arrival of Plyushch and family in Vienna, 12 January 1976*," AI, International Secretariat (henceforth IS) Archives, Campaign for the Abolition of Torture (henceforth CAT), Documents Concerning Torture in the USSR, folder 1229.

15. Among the groups formed were the Committee for Human Rights, Helsinki Monitoring groups, and groups for free emigration, for more see L. Alekseeva, *Soviet dissent: Contemporary Movements for National, Religious and Human Rights* (Connecticut: Wesleyan University Press, 1985); P. Boobbyer, *Conscience, Dissent and Reform in Soviet Russia* (London: Routledge, 2005), and V.A. Kozlova and S.V. Mironenko, eds., *Kramola: Inakomyslie v SSSR pri Khrushcheve i Brezhneve, 1953–1982 gg.: Rassekrechennye Dokumenty Verkhovnogo Suda i Prokuratury SSSR* (Moskva: Maternik, 2005).

16. T. Khodorovich and Y. Orlov, "They are Turning Leonid Plyushch into a Lunatic, Why?," *Russkaya Misl*, 15 May 1975; T. Zhitnikova, "Open letter to A. Snezhnevsky, 7 April 1975," *Cahiers de Samizdat* 24 (1975). See also articles in *Chronicle of Current Events* 32, 17 July 1974; 34, 21 December 1974; 35, 31 March 1975; or also the "*February Dossier concerning Documents about the Case of Plyushch,*" AI IS Archives, Index, Internal NS 189, 352/1975. For a detailed list of Plyushch's writings, see E. Driessen, S. de Boer, and H.L. Verhaar, eds., *Biographical Dictionary of the Dissidents in the Soviet Union, 1956–1975* (The Hague, Boston: M. Nijhoff, 1982), 438–439.

17. P. Reddaway, ed., *Uncensored Russia, the Human Rights Movement in the Soviet Union, the Annotated Text of the Unofficial Moscow Journal "a Chronicle of Current Events (nos 1–11)"* (New York: American Heritage Press, 1972); following volumes were published by AI in London and Khronika Press in New York.

18. *Cahiers du Samizdat* 13 (1975).

19. For more on the group, which was affiliated with the unofficial Moscow Helsinki group, see A. Podrabinek, *Punitive Medicine* (Ann Arbor: Karoma Publishers, 1979).

20. This was developed by the poet and mathematician Alexander Esenin Volpin, in works such as his famous *Juriditseskaia Pamiatka* (Judicial Memorandum), a broadly circulated samizdat in the Soviet Union in the late 1960s–1970s.

21. AI, IS Archives, CAT, Campaign and Membership Department, 1371/44/1975; AI, *Les abus de la psychiatre à des fins politiques: rapport sur le Symposium de Genève*, Genève AI (1975); *Guardian* and *The Times*, 21 April 1975, and *Le Monde*, 22 April 1975.

22. AI, IS Archives, Index NS/1971, *The Internment of Soviet Dissidents in Mental Hospitals*, and Clayton Yeo, *Psychiatry, Law and Dissent in the Soviet Union*, both internally distributed documents (NS/1975); AI, *Prisoners of Conscience in the USSR: Treatment and Conditions* (London: AI Publications, 1975), esp. the chapter on "Compulsory Detention in Psychiatric Hospitals," 101–137. For more on AI see S. Hopgood, *Keepers of the Flame: Understanding Amnesty International* (Ithaca, NY: Cornell University Press, 2006).

23. For instance, see letter to Prof Snezhnevsky by 88 Australian scientists in *Observer*, 20 August 1975.

24. See *Le Monde*, 12 December 1973; 2–3 February 1974; 25 April 1974; 7–8 July 1974; 6 September 1974.

25. Marco Carynnyk, in *History's Carnival*, xii; *New York Times*, 9 December 1975; and *Le Monde*, 25 October 1975.

26. Cited in International Commission of Jurists Bulletin 7, June 1975; and P. Reddaway, *The Times*, 24 April 1974.

27. *Observer*, 20 August 1975; *The Times*, 23 October 1975; *Sunday Times*, 16 March 1975; *New York Times*, 20 February 1974, 23 June 1974, 5 January 1976; *L'Humanité*, 25 October 1975; *Le Monde*, 24 and 25 July 1974, 3 February 1975; *Annales Medico Psychologiques* 4, 1976; and *Journal de Genève*, 13–14 October 1973.

28. Scientific journals, though, do not yet discuss cases of abuse, but instead deal with general aspects of medical ethics and psychiatry, G. Belkin, "Writing about their Science: American Interest in Soviet Psychiatry during the post Stalin Cold War," *Perspectives in Biology and Medicine*, 43(1), Autumn(1993): 34; M.G. Allen, Psychiatry in the United States and the USSR: a Comparison, *American Journal of Psychiatry* 130(12)(1973): 1333–1337.

29. For instance, Alexander Podrabinek, while confined to an asylum in 1979, petitioned the Soviet authorities to be provided with copies of the *CCE*, Western publications on psychiatric hospitals in the Soviet Union, and the *SS Korsakov Journal of Neurology and Psychiatry* containing information on the Congress in Honolulu, see IAPUP, *Soviet Political Psychiatry: the Story of Opposition* (London: IAPUP, 1983), 32.

30. K. Cmiel, "The Emergence of Human Rights Politics in the United States," *The Journal of American History*, Special Issue: The Nation and Beyond: Transnational Perspectives on United States History, 86 (3)(1999): 1231–1250; S. Moyn, "The Genealogy of Morals," *The Nation*, 29 March 2007. For recent works on human rights history, see I. Micheline, *The History of Human Rights, From Ancient Times to Globalization* (Berkeley: University of California Press, 2004); L. Hunt, *Inventing Human Rights. A History* (New York: W.W. Norton & Company, 2007) and

S. Moyn, *The Last Utopia: Human Rights in History* (Cambridge: Belknap Press of Harvard University Press, 2010).

31. For an analysis of the engagement of the French left in the Soviet cause, see M.S. Christofferson, *French Intellectuals Against the Left, the Antitotalitarian Moment of the 1970s* (New York: Berghahn Books, 2006).

32. AI, IS Archives, CAT, Documents Concerning Torture in the USSR, letter from Erik Baker to the International Executive Committee, 14 October 1973.

33. The main proponent of "anti-psychiatry" is Dr. Laing, Z. Kotowicz, *Laing and the Paths of Anti Psychiatry* (London; New York: Routledge, 1997), while important in the Italian movement was Dr. Basaglia, N. Scheper-Hughes and A.M. Lovell, eds., *Psychiatry Inside Out: Selected Writings of Franco Basaglia* (New York: Columbia University Press, 1987).

34. N. Crossley, *Contesting Psychiatry: Social Movements in Mental Health* (London: Routledge, 2006).

35. "Diagnosing Soviet Dissidents," *Harper's*, August 1978: 31–37; "The Force of Diagnosis, Opportune Uses of Psychiatry," *Harper's*, May 1980: 20–32; "Soviet Psychiatry," *New York Times Magazine*, 30 January 1983, 22–30; and "The World of Soviet psychiatry," in *The Breaking of Bodies and Minds, Torture, Psychiatric Abuse and the Health Professions*, eds. E. Stover and E.-O. Nightingale (New York: Freeman, 1985), 206–222.

36. W. Reich, "Psychiatric Diagnosis as a Ethical Problem," in *Psychiatric Ethics*, eds. S. Bloch and P. Chodoff (Oxford: Oxford University Press, 1981), 69.

37. Reich, "Diagnosing Soviet Dissidents," 35.

38. Stover and Nightingale, *The Breaking of Bodies and Minds*, 220.

39. B. Segal, "Involuntary Hospitalization in the USSR," in *Psychiatry and Psychology in the USSR*, eds. S. Corson and E. Corson (New York: Plenum Press, 1976), 271.

40. F.-A. Jenner, "The Political Misuse of Psychiatry," *British Journal of Psychiatry* 123 (5)(1973): 528.

41. Cited in IAPUP, *Information Bulletin* 4, June 1982: 15.

42. Cited in J. Wortis, "Soviet Psychiatry," *Psychiatric News* 14(4)(1979): 14.

43. The most eloquent example of this current is, of course, the novel by Steir Charles, *One Flew over the Cuckoo's nest* (1962) and its film adaptation (1974).

44. C. Fink, P. Gassert, and D. Junker, eds., *1968: The World Transformed* (New York: Cambridge University Press, 1998); M. Klimke and J. Scharloth, eds., *1968 in Europe: A History of Protest and Activism, 1956–1977* (New York: Palgrave Macmillan, 2008).

45. For a useful methodological approach to transnational history see P. Calvin, "Defining Transnationalism," *Contemporary European History* 14(4)(2005): 421–439.

46. This frame of analysis shifts the attention away from the well-known Relativist/Universalist debate, in which the claims of cultural relativism, *which* draw attention to regional, religious, and historical particularities, clash with the idea that human rights are global and beyond space and time. Within this context, particularist arguments are not examined as conflicting with universal claims, and the validity of the concept does not depend on the outcome of such a debate. See A. Pollis and P. Schwab, "Human Rights: a Western Construct with Limited Applicability" in *Human Rights: Cultural and Ideological Perspectives*, eds. A. Pollis and P. Schwab (New

York: Praeger, 1979), 1–18; J. Donnelly, *Universal Human Rights in Theory and Practice* (Ithaca: Cornell University Press, 2002).

47. See Z. Medvedev, *Question of Madness* (London: McMillan, 1971), 202; Plyushch, *History's Carnival,* 363; R.V. Voren, ed., *Soviet Psychiatric Abuse in the Gorbachev Era* (Amsterdam: IAPUP, 1989), 8; Fireside, *Soviet Psychoprisons,* 11–12.

48. Podrabinek, *Punitive Medicine,* 155–185; Fireside, *Soviet Psychoprisons,* 15, 31, 64; IAPUP, *Political Abuse of Psychiatry, A List of Victims, 30 November 1975* (London: IAPUP, 1985).

49. M. Knapp and D. McDaid et al., eds., *Mental Health Policy and Practice across Europe: the Future Directions of Mental Health Care* (Maidenhead: Open University Press, 2007), 402–406.

50. R. Bonnie, "Political Abuse of Psychiatry in the Soviet Union and in China, Complexities and Controversies," *The Journal of the American Academy of Psychiatry and the Law,* 30 (2002): 136–142; Human Rights Watch and Geneva Initiative on Psychiatry, *Dangerous Minds: Political Psychiatry in China Today and its Origins in the Mao Era* (New York: Human Rights Watch, 2002).

51. For such an alternative approach, see D. Cohen, *Soviet Psychiatry* (London: Paladin, 1989).

Part II

Contentious Politics in a New Era of Transnationalism

Chapter 4

Stairway to Heaven or Highway to Hell?

Ambivalent Europeanization and Civil Society in Central and Eastern Europe

Aron Buzogány

The coming together of Europe has multiplied both opportunities and constraints for societal actors from the new member states to pursue their interests
within the multi-level settings of the European Union (EU). On the one hand,
European integration has seen as an essential factor affecting the structures,
strategies, and visibility of these actors by opening new opportunity structures
and providing supplementary access points that can be used in complementary
ways to the pre-existing national ones. At the same time, however, this process
is also creating new constraints for participation and collective mobilization and
is seen to favor some societal actors more than others. These opportunities and
constraints challenge the traditional state-society relations and lead to a differentiation of the repertoires of action used by societal actors both on the domestic
and the EU-level.[1] How this happens, however, is highly differential, since the
way domestic actors are able to turn their new opportunities into strategic opportunities is determined largely by their financial and organizational capacities
and their political allies, but also by the openness of political decision-making
structures. A central question concerning societal actors in this multi-level governance setting is whether the new level is accessible to those actors who already
have access at the national level, or whether it serves as a compensating function
for nationally peripheral societal actors.[2]

This chapter provides answers to this question by evaluating the differential
empowerment of domestic actors from the perspective of non-state actors from
the new EU member states. It focuses on Europeanization as a transformation of
domestic political and legal opportunity structures at the national level, a change
in the resources societal actors can mobilize, and the cognitive frames they use
for legitimizing their aims in the multi-level setting of the European Union. The
assessment of the impact of EU enlargement analyzes pre- and post-accession

experiences of societal organizations and draws mainly on research carried out in Hungary and Romania within two fields of activism: the environmental movement and the Roma rights movement.[3]

Transformation and Europeanization of Civil Society

A strong civil society has been often identified as necessary for successful democratic transitions.[4] The Eastern European experience, where the fall of communism was brought about by millions of people in the streets during the mostly peaceful revolutions of 1989–1991, seemed to offer obvious evidence for this. As reflected in the normative political writings of dissident *intelligentsia* from the region, civil society in Eastern Europe seemed to re-emerge from its ashes.[5] Compared to the expectations of the founding years, however, the following years of democratization and economic hardship, the development of new cleavages and inequalities, the shocks of transition to market capitalism led to a rapid decline in political participation. At the same time, contradicting most of the pessimistic augury of the early 1990s, most of the Central and Eastern European countries experienced a generally low level of public protest that was unexpected taking into account the severe socioeconomic transition crises most countries of the region went through after 1989.[6] Nevertheless, one of the most serious challenges for the consolidation of democracy remains the "functional deficit" of interest representation in the formerly state socialist countries,[7] together with a generally low level of social capital, a particularistic political culture,[8] and a weak third sector engagement that remains below the Western European average.[9]

Starting from the mid 1990s, the changes and challenges affecting civil society in Central and Eastern Europe have become increasingly affected by the ongoing EU accession process. Europeanization is usually conceptualized in two ways, according to the two causal mechanisms determining the "domestification" of European policies.[10] The first is based on the rationalist "logic of consequentiality" and points to the EU-induced changes affecting the domestic opportunity structure, such as the role of the redistribution of resources, the presence of veto points, and the formal institutions as central factors affecting institutional change on the domestic level. The second is based on insights derived from sociological institutionalism and relies on the "logic of appropriateness." Here, EU-related changes of domestic norms and collective understandings play a role, and social learning is regarded as a fundamental mechanism of institutional change, which is catalyzed by epistemic communities and informal institutions as promoters of a reconceptualization of identities and interests.

The analysis of the domestic impact of the EU along these lines can be easily brought together with the emerging theoretical synthesis of social movement research.[11] The contribution uses the three dominant analytical perspectives employed in social movement studies, which focus on the availability of political opportunity structures, societal actor's resources, and on their cognitive frames. First, *political opportunity structure*-related explanations of societal activism stress that political actors, such as interest groups or social movements, respond to opportunities as they arise. Thus, the structure of those opportunities massively determines group strategies.[12] Opportunity structures, such as additional political access points for civil society actors from Central and Eastern Europe on the EU-level, can encourage or discourage certain activities depending on how political processes function and which access points are available for specific political activities. Factors such as the openness of the political system, the stability of political alignments or the presence of elite allies might provide opportunities for the movements. The availability of open legal structures can become an influential asset for societal actors with weaker capacities.[13]

Second, the behavior of societal actors is also dependent on the quantity and quality of organizational resources that they can mobilize.[14] The *resource mobilization thesis* maintains that the more resources an organization acquires, the more active it will be in policy-making. This presumes that political action, both of a conventional type (such as lobbying) or an unconventional one (such as protest), is based on the coordinated efforts and capacities of organizations. Therefore, the level of organization, formalization, and professionalization and the available financial resources are crucial in determining the modes and possibilities of political action social movement actors engage in. Thus, this perspective would presume that the (material) influence of the EU on civil society actors from Central and Eastern Europe through funding or capacity-building measures would change their repertoires of action.

Third and finally, the *cognitive framing thesis* focuses on the sources and functions of meaning and identity within social movements and stresses the importance of cognitive and ideational dimension of collective action.[15] Framing refers here to inter-subjective processes through which social movement actors convince other actors and the public of the legitimacy of their issues. Of critical importance is thus the degree to which a "frame," such as shared European ideals and norms, resonates with the experiences and the empirical context of the targeted audience, since these are likely to be successful if they reflect opinions and values that are already endorsed by society.[16] The focus lies here on using different frames in order to mobilize and achieve movement aims. Framings can both occur intentionally and unintentionally, they can be strategic or merely legitimating in nature, and they can be extended to mobilize members as well as non-members. At the same time, framing processes are not structurally pre-determined, as actors often 'make use of Europe' and cognitively transform discourses through redefining, interpreting, coding, and decoding their contradictory and ambiguous meanings.[17]

The Politics of Conditionality and Traditions of Anti-politics

Eastern European EU candidate states were exposed to outside pressures well before accession, resulting in a unilateral adjustment and underpinned by accession conditionality.[18] Before joining the European Union, these countries had to fulfill the conditions defined by the Copenhagen criteria, which included the adoption of the *acquis* and the administrative and judicial capacity to apply it. This meant the transposition of more than 10,000 pieces of EU legislation into the candidate state's own national legislation, including the adaptation of existing national law to EU law and the building-up of administrative and judicial institutions (norms, rules, procedures) to practically apply and to enforce the *acquis*. At the same time, the EU accession process has generated its very own mode of governance,[19] characterized by hierarchy, asymmetry, and conditionality, and focusing quite strictly on "institution building" and the creation of institutions necessary for the adoption of the *acquis communautaire*. In general, the process has emphasized the unilateral, top-down aspect of enlargement and focused mostly on the role of public actors of enlargement.[20] At least theoretically, it inhibited also a quite revolutionary potential for developing bottom-up participation for non-state actors in the accession countries. Technical assistance programs of the EU as well as the funding lines especially set up for promoting civil society included extensive references to "participation" or "common ownership." The yearly Monitoring Reports issued by the Commission on the progress of accession preparations highlighted the necessity of including and consulting with societal actors; in many cases, information obtained from NGOs were informal and yet main information resources for drafting those reports. This development was not restricted to the field of enlargement. The "governance turn"[21] has reached the EU and the inclusion of civil society has emerged as a potentially far-leading project in order to solve problems stemming from the democratic deficit of the EU.

In the accession countries, the simultaneous top-down EU regulations and the increasing involvement opportunities for civil society actors have met with traditions of state society interaction that were often only partially compatible with the EU model. State administrations have mostly inherited a bureaucratic tradition that was alien to the very idea of partnership with civil society. In some countries of the region, such as Romania, the authoritarian regimes obstructed any previous development of a societal sector, which only started to recover after 1989 through mainly external aid. Other states, such as Poland, Hungary, and the Czech Republic, already had strong civil society traditions that played an important role in pushing toward regime change. Here, the "ideology of civil society" became an instrument of dissidents in the 1980s, which propagated an alternative both to state socialism and to western capitalism.[22] This political philosophy was built on the idea of "anti-politics," which was put forward by Eastern European dissidents such as Václav Havel or George Konrád, and it defined civil society in terms of resistance against an oppressive state.[23] Suspicion of close involvement of non-state actors into policy processes remained still prevalent in the years of transformation, making the participation of non-state organizations in policy-making a recurring critical issue.[24]

Adding to this, the rapidly burgeoning NGO sector in the Central and Eastern European countries has highly divergent backgrounds. Some were successor organizations of socialist state organizations; others have emerged out of the dissident movements and played important roles during the transition process. For instance, the environmental movement in Hungary has played a politically important role during the last years of the communist regime and served as a cradle for other civil society-related groups.[25] In the mid 1980s, mass demonstrations triggered by plans of the government for building the Gabcikovo-Nagymaros dam on the Danube became crystallization points for opposition groups, including not only environmentalists, but all forces of the opposition as well, reaching from new left philosophers to young liberals around the samizdat movement to conservative groups. Fighting simultaneously for basic values and democratic institutions in order to fulfill their objectives, the Danube Circle received strong grassroots support. Its success—after it was awarded the Alternative Nobel Prize and the government withdrew the Danube dam plans—was already the beginning of its agony.[26] Even if after the regime change the importance of the environmental movement has decreased permanently, it is probably still the most important and best organized segment of Hungarian civil society, with a considerable history and a relatively high number of professional groups actively engaging in policy-making. In contrast, the emergence of a Roma rights group is a rather new phenomenon. Its emergence was triggered by the effects of the transition period that led both to increasing hardships for the Roma population and opportunities to get politically organized.[27]

Political and Legal Opportunities: Allies, Institutions and Laws

The enlargement criteria set out in Copenhagen co-determined the political and economic development of the Central and Eastern Europe (CEE) states. While these criteria were loosely defined, the adoption of and adaptation to EU law as set out in the 31 chapters of the *acquis communautaire* became a real challenge for the political systems of the accession countries. The legal harmonization process granted the provision of transparent and participatory legislation and offered possibilities for civil society to get involved in the closed and secretive policy process. Domestic transformation and Europeanization have often complemented each other; Europeanization gave societal actors strong opportunities and strong allies, as it connected them to existing sectoral policy networks at the EU level. But it also made the actors' governments more accountable by upgrading participatory rights in national legislations and introducing issues into the public sphere that before had not received attention. Civil society groups have recognized the window of opportunity opened by the accession process, and have started putting pressure on governments to introduce and then enforce EU legislation. Connections with influential advocacy coalitions based in Brussels and having important ties with the policy community, such as the Green Ten or the European Network Against Racism (ENAR), provided societal actors with the opportunity to register complaints in Brussels and to put pressure on their governments both via European institutions and through mobilizing international public opinion. Wedged between top-down pressure from the European Commission and bottom-up demands from civil society, governments have responded to the challenges of Europeanization with the creation of a new set of institutions, such as anti-discrimination bodies or environmental protection agencies, which provided new access points for civil society or increased the enforcement and monitoring capacities within certain policy fields.

The "downloading" of EU legislation during the accession period did not only change quite thoroughly the public policies and institutional settings, but also made national jurisprudence the subject of the European Court of Justice (ECJ). This step holds far-reaching consequences for societal actors, as they can both litigate in front of domestic courts or turn to a higher judiciary instance, such as the ECJ.[28] Compared with the strongly legalistic culture of Central and Eastern European states, the harmonization with EU Law together with the development of public interest litigation encourages societal actors working in different policy fields to include judicial activism in their repertoires of action. For environmental groups, the horizontal legislation in this area is of particularly high relevance as it challenges the very logic of the non-transparent administrative state well-rooted across the region. EU Directives, such as the Access to Information and the Environmental Impact Assessment Directive—which provide for a system of assessments prior to the consent to projects having significant impacts upon the environment—have efficiently challenged both public administration and business. The new nature conservation legislation provides also important leverage for societal actors. One of the most prominent environmental issues in Hungary was the success of the "Civilians for the Zengő Coalition," where societal actors drew on new nature protection legislation.[29] The plan of installing a NATO radar facility on the Zengő hill was the target of regular protests by a broad coalition of local, national, and transnational groups of green activists and local inhabitants, who claimed that building the radar facility would damage precious wildlife and destroy a nature reserve.[30] The Zengő case led to a procedural victory after a protected plant—the banatian peony—was discovered on the Zengő hill, which fell under the "protection" of the Flora-Fauna-Habitat directive (92/43/EEC) of the EU and was part of the NATURA 2000 Network of protected conservation sites. A similar case, where the Romanian environmental movement is engaged, is the case of Rosia Montana Gold Mine in Western Romania. A wide international civil society coalition emerged to oppose the project of a Romanian-Canadian mining company trying to resettle the village of Rosia Montana, which has a mining tradition going back to Roman times. The case became a focal point of the nascent Romanian green civil society and illustrated the way of how the legal tools provided by EU legislation, such as the Environmental Impact Assessment (EIA) directive, can become an instrument of environmental activism.[31] Parallel to using extensive media campaigns and public protest, Alburnus Maior, the local NGO representing the citizens fighting to stay in their ancestral village, was also involved in several dozens of legal cases against the mining company. As the EIA directive provides the opportunity to participate in the process in states that also might be affected by the transboundary effects of the project, Hungarian NGOs were pushing the Minister of Environment to become active on this matter with his Romanian colleague.

The EU's influence was not only important in policy fields where the EU has a strong regulatory framework, such as environmental policy, but also in an area where it is largely lacking formal powers, such as minority policy.[32] The EU acted here on a "do as I say, not as I do" basis and was crucial in influencing the development of progressive minority rights policies in the candidate countries.[33] EU conditionality has specifically stimulated the acceding countries to promote better treatment of Roma as an accession precondition, by making their situation one of the elements in the EU's conditionality policy. While the lobbying of Roma groups on the national level in Hungary is highly secluded and polarized between different political fractions, during the accession process it was successful in canalizing its efforts both through national parliaments and in strengthening its voice by sending parliamentarians to the European Parliament, where they became active champions of Roma issues on the EU level. At the same time, the EU's influence contributed to the reorientation of Roma rights activism from minority policy toward social policy, which provided an increasingly strong legislative framework as well as financial possibilities for the movement. Paralleling the strategic litigation culture used by the US civil rights movement in the 1970s, the leading advocacy organization in this field, the European Roma Rights Centre (ERRC), is using EU anti-discrimination law as its main tool to reach progress in the field of Roma rights. ERRC's strategies were reshaped in 2000, when the European Union adopted the Race Equality Directive, as well as several other directives related to anti-discrimination.[34] Pressing for full transposition of the EU anti-discrimination directives, as well as the ratification of Protocol 12 to the European Convention on Human Rights, which provided for a comprehensive anti-discrimination law, the ERRC worked closely with partner NGOs and government officials to secure a strong anti-discrimination law and practice. For several Roma groups, such as the Romani Civil Rights Foundation and the Legal Defense Bureau for National and Ethnic Minorities

(*Nemzeti és Etnikai Kisebbségi Jogvédő Iroda*), which were already using legal action before accession as a tool for enforcing Roma rights (albeit with limited success), the new legislation clearly increased the possibility of litigations on Roma related issues. The most famous case, which is likely to create a precedent, is the Miskolc School Desegregation Case, brought in June 2005 by the Chance for Children Foundation (CFCF) and featuring an *actio popularis* claim against the local council of the Hungarian city of Miskolc. CFCF was claiming that the council was indirectly responsible for segregation of Roma children in primary education. Based on the new anti-discrimination legislation, it was ruled that the segregation of Roma children violated their right to equal treatment based on their ethnic origin, as the city did not prevent the redrawing of school zoning areas, thus passively breaching its obligation of equal treatment, especially the obligation to accord to all similar quality service in education. The Miskolc case was carefully planned by the claimant organization and is likely to be followed by several such cases as the school segregation issues are rather dominant in the Hungarian and other Central and Eastern European school systems.[35]

Mobilizing Resources: The Matthew Effect?

External influences on societal actors in the accession states in the last two decades were immensely varied both in sources and targeting.[36] Immediately after the democratic revolution in 1989, international donors, such as international organizations, western governments, and NGOs, set out to strengthen civil society. Besides providing political and legal opportunities, Europeanization also provided financial opportunities. These were channeled either through EU projects providing for non-state actor inclusion, special funds for civil societies or western organizations working in Central and Eastern Europe. One of the best examples for external capacity building in the field of environmental policy was the establishment of the Regional Environmental Centre network, funded by the EU and the US, which was highly effective in providing contacts, organizing funding and networks, and linking environmental groups with each other.

Capacity building measures, access to expertise, exchange programs or the possibility of establishing links with like-minded organizations and becoming part of transnational or EU-wide networks also had an impact on the resources of civil society. Funding opportunities for Roma rights issues were made available through US foundations, some of them related to the Civil Rights movements or the Open Society Foundation. Transnational advocacy groups, such as Amnesty International, the Helsinki Federation or Human Rights Watch, took up the cause of the Roma as did transgovernmental organizations, such as the Organization for Security and Cooperation in Europe (OSCE), the Council of Europe or the World Bank. EU accession and the growing interest of the EU in addressing Roma issues in the candidate states redirected toward Brussels the

NGOs seeking funding. In many cases, this has meant a process of renaming already existing domestic programs by using EU-related technical slang, which encouraged "innovative" and "participative" projects and led in some cases to the drying out of the funding channels of some established initiatives.[37] The high dependence of an usually weak societal sector on foreign funding has also caused several other issues. Increased financing possibilities from EU funds, for example, have led other international donors to leave the accession countries. At the same time, state funding has often diminished due to the reliance of EU-related possibilities of funding. However, EU funding possibilities have become serious challenges to deal with as only a few NGOs have the capacity and expertise to respond to calls for participation or to write successful grant proposals. More often than not, EU financing required matching funds and was usually re-funding expenses already paid out. This has hurt particularly small local NGOs lacking the necessary knowledge, experience, networks, and human resources. In contrast, it favored issue networks formed by strong NGOs, which often include international partners and consultancies, where local groups had few chances to become involved. Adding to this, frequent changes in definitions of eligibility criteria by the EU have also undermined the possibility of long-term planning.

In the case of Roma activism in Romania, the reliance on donor funding has led to a development that increasingly challenged traditional power structures.[38] Roma activism in Romania started when the Democratic Union of Roma was founded in February 1990 as a national political organization. In the following years, the Roma Party (Partida Romilor) has emerged as the main actor in Roma politics. It failed repeatedly, however, to reach the 3 percent electoral threshold, but it did receive the minority seat for the Roma, which has been assigned to historical minorities after 1990. While competition for the votes of the Roma increased with the appearance of the electoral platforms, such as the Roma Ethnic Community and the Alliance for Roma Unity, Partida Romilor (renamed Partida Romilor Pro Europa during the accession period) succeeded in establishing itself as the main partner of the government regarding Roma-related issues. It has effectively lobbied for positions in state level organizations (such as the Council for National Minorities and the National Office for Roma) and was involved in the work on the National Strategy for Improving the Situation of the Roma and the development of the anti-discrimination legislation. Due to its clientelistic network, which was based on the extraction and redistribution of government subsidies, Partida Romilor regularly supported the ruling party. At the same time, the limited electoral mobilization capacity of the Roma population, the high electoral threshold as well as frequent conflicts within the Roma political community made the limits posed to political participation in high politics more than obvious. External funding opportunities have made a departure from participation in mainstream politics an increasingly viable and promising way to make progress. For the mostly younger, well-trained, and well-traveled Roma elite, embracing the concept of Roma rights has become an opportunity to circumvent clientelistic structures and to tap directly into the funding schemes of internationally active donor organizations and NGOs in fields such as human rights, education, community development, gender issues or anti-discrimination. This partial "NGO-ization" of Roma politics led to conflicts between the traditional legitimacy of Roma leaders, the political oligarchy in state and local level politics, and the emerging new sector of the young managerial elite, which was in charge of funds that largely outpaced the resources that could be distributed through the networks of the Partida Romilor. Adding to this, successful Roma rights groups such as Aven Amentza and Romano Criss did not require political legitimacy through elections and were successful in securing foreign funding, which made them largely independent from national sources.

These examples tend also to illustrate that the effects of EU accession on the resources of civil society in the new member states are highly differential. Although in individual cases western donors tended to determine the activities of the NGOs, preventing local groups from developing their own agendas, large scale studies do not find sufficient proof of this.[39] It is necessary to separate out the weak societal groups that were becoming donor-driven, or were established in order to "milk" donor organizations from the other civil society groups having strong capacities, for which the EU-effect has led to a further professionalization and a deepening of their core activities. Overall, these developments suggest the validity of a "Matthew Effect"[40] regarding the EU influence on civil society that stipulates that the rich get richer at a rate that makes the poor become relatively poorer.[41]

Framing Europe: Vision or Colonialist?

In the accession countries, the enlargement process was embedded in a general discourse relating to national self-identification and the assessment of the EU enlargement. The initial perception of EU accession as a legitimate and historically deserved "Return to Europe" often contradicted the countries' subordinated position during the accession negotiations. At the same time, self-criticism and overly high expectations of benefits after the accession period have shaped the public debate occurring during the mid 1990s.[42] A more contentious discourse arose at a later stage when EU accession talks and first encounters with the more shaded reality of EU policy-making became a certainty. Increasingly, images of Europe included those critical of the over-bureaucratized and inefficient European administrative structure or issues threatening national identities of the new member states, where the EU was depicted as an aggressive intruder and colonizer. These discourses in the public sphere were paralleled by sub-discourses within the societal sector. During the last two decades, the main issues affecting the Hungarian environmental movement have triggered different interpretation frames and ascribed various meanings to Europe. Throughout the first major conflict around the Gabcikovo-Nagymaros dam on the Danube, 'Europe' was represented by European environmentalist groups who helped mobilize people and thus presented a possibility of the connecting to and the reaching of a wider audience for the aims of the protest movement. References to the high standards of European environmental policy as well as the common "European heritage" (the Danube) were common and contrasted with the destructive tendencies of the centrally planned spatial planning policies of the socialist state. But when, due to a cyanide spill from a gold mine in Romania, the river Tisza was seriously damaged at the end of the 1990s, environmentalist discourse was already shaped both in terms of the coming EU accession and the emerging frame of "eco-colonialism," since the (Western-owned) mining company was seen as destroying local natural heritage and setting low environmental standards it could not use at home.[43] At the same time, the high regulatory standards of the EU gave hope that this behavior will not be tolerated once the countries of the region became members of the Union. After accession, EU directives, such as the Flora Fauna Habitat and the EIA, did indeed increase the leverage of environmentalist groups in the policy process by providing them with legal tools they can use to effectively hinder business activities; however, other EU-induced changes within the environmental policy field are criticized by environmental groups. One such case is the "GMO Directive."[44] The adoption of this legal piece has put Hungary under pressure to change its old legislation—that deals with GMOs rather restric-tively—to a new one, which offers loopholes for multi-national agro-industrial companies to enter the Hungarian market with their genetically modified prod-ucts. While hopeful at the outset of the process of EU accession, environmental civil society grew increasingly realistic as to the amount of EU influence as the date of accession came close.[45]

The difficulty of framing Roma-related issues lies in an overlap between ethnic and social characteristics.[46] Roma frames of dealing with "Europe" are rather new and mainly attributed to the recent process of Europeanization.[47] The perceived salience of the Roma issue and the funding possibilities connected to it gave rapid rise to activism of Roma elites, which started to look for transnational allies, organized themselves transnationally, and "Europeanized" their discourses. Regarding the strategic frames used by the Roma movement, the two dialectically dominating the discourse are the one defining "Roma as a national minority" and the opposite one defining "Roma as a social group."[48] While in a domestic setting the two frames still prevail in parallel, the growing transnationalization of Roma elites has led to the emergence of a third master narrative—"Roma as the European nation"—which is directed more toward the transnational level, or for that matter, the European level. Initially, these activities were centered mainly on the international arena and oriented toward a transnational "nation-building without a state," but as the European Union overtook the lead in financing Roma issues, the discourse of leading Roma movement organizations could easily redefine the Roma as a "European nation," which nicely coincides with calls from the Commission toward a "European identity." The added value of this strategic frame directed toward Brussels is that it quite effectively blurs the line between the contradictions of the two previous frames. The possibility of acting both as a socially excluded and as a minority group allows tapping at different stages into different resources. While the ethnic definition makes sense on the national level, the social group definition resonates better in Brussels, where Roma rights activists could effectively join forces with other groups working in the anti-discrimination field. Being able to define the Roma issue as both one of all-European relevance (due to, e.g., migration problems), but also as "Roma as the truly European nation" (which does not stick to nation states) effectively presents itself an ideal subject of an emerging European state. One of the telling Hungarian public debates on this issue was triggered by the case of several Roma families from the Hungarian village of Zámoly seeking political asylum in France after having allegedly received death threats and having been forced to flee from their village. By protesting before the European institution in Strasbourg, these families and the activists advising them framed the issue as one of European importance and brought it literally 'before' the European Parliament. The case received great attention both in the national and the international press and was put into the context of the Hungarian accession negotiations.

Conclusions: State-society Relations in Central and Eastern Europe

Three dimensions of EU-induced domestic change in two Central and Eastern European new member states have been drawn up here. The first one focused on the political and legal opportunity structures, a second one dealt with the resources of civil society, and a final one captured the cognitive framing of political behavior within civil society groups from the accession countries. These three lenses show that while on the one hand, EU-induced changes in state-society relations were inhibiting political and financial opportunities, they also came with more ambivalent effects, such as the partial alienation of civil society from their initial constituencies and making them dependent on external resources. The windows of opportunity opened by the accession process have provided civil society with possibilities to target new access points both on the European and on the domestic level. New legal instruments, both by increasing the transparency of the overall political process and by providing comprehensive legislation in sectoral policies, have led civil society to use new strategies in order to achieve their aims. But at the same time, it highlights that the hierarchical administrative traditions of post-socialist states have often been re-enforced by the technocratic, elite-centered tradition of the EU, leading to a development that has been summarized by Kristi Raik as "civil society has acquired increasing power *in* the discourses of integration, power *over* these discourses is still predominantly exercised by civil servants and the government."[49] By framing, i.e., discursively constructing the meaning of the EU, non-state actors seek to combine interpretations of the process, which could build on existing narratives of their constituencies and at the same time mobilize internal or external support.

While a combination of influence tactics at different levels is the most promising strategy to influence European politics, only a few civil society groups from the new member states are able to use both insider and outsider strategies. The dependence on external support has been influential in shaping societal actor's political strategies, leading to a low occurrence of protest activities on the European level as well as on the domestic level. Even if formal mechanisms provide access for civil society in policy-making also on the EU level, their influence remains very limited, as EU officials tend to regard civil society rather as recipients of policy information than as potential sources of public opinion and knowledge.[50] This technocratic approach increases the gap between public and non-state actors, and has negative influence on public participation and legitimacy. While this is a problem concerning all civil society groups in EU policy-making, it is especially hard on NGOs from the new accession countries, where the societal sector is weaker and might easily get lost in the labyrinth of European multi-level politics.[51]

Professionalization, differentiation, and projectification can be regarded as three lasting effects of Europeanization on civil society in Central and Eastern Europe. Professionalization has developed both due to the increasing issue specific specialization of civil society and as an impact of the reliance on state subsidies and external funding. This process inhibits a differentiation within the societal sector regarding relevant specializations, skills, capacities, and ideologies of civil society. EU accession has further strengthened differentiation through what has been described above as the Matthew Effect, where already powerful actors get even more resources due to their superior access to EU funds. Differential inclusion is likely to trigger long-lasting divisions within those included and those who (choose to or have to) remain outside. Finally, projectification highlights the everyday practice of civil society, which are increasingly integrated into a professionalized managerial system that makes them dependent and is at the same time also dependent on their participation. The funding possibilities available are tied to the acceptance of a seemingly rationalized special thinking mode that is largely alien both to traditional public administration and civil society: the planning and control of activities through project management.[52] Induced by participation in EU financed programs, one segment of civil society is increasingly developing into consultancy-like companies with rather symbiotic relationships toward donor agencies.[53] At the same time, projectification is far from being only a technical process, but remains an essentially political one as it does in fact reconfigure domestic power structures by creating a new "project class"[54] that becomes a broker between the EU, the national administration, and civil society. While professionalization, differentiation, and projectification are likely to remain long-lasting developments affecting the societal sector in Central and Eastern Europe, the EU's influence on policy outcomes will lack the political clout it had in the pre-accession period due to its control of the decision to grant Union membership to the accession states.

Notes

1. D. della Porta and M. Caiani, "Europeanization From Below? Social Movements and Europe," *Mobilization: An International Quarterly* 12(1) (2007): 1–20; D. Imig and S. Tarrow, eds., *Contentious Europeans: Protest and Politics in an Emerging Polity* (Lanham: Rowman & Littlefield, 2000); H. Kriesi, A. Tresch, and M. Jochum, "Going Public in the European Union: Action Repertoires of Western European Collective Political Actors," *Comparative Political Studies* 40(1)(2007): 48–73.
2. J. Beyers, "Gaining and Seeking Access: The European Adaptation of Domestic Interest Associations," *European Journal of Political Research* 41(5)(2002): 585–612.
3. Research for this contribution was partially done within the project "Coping with Accession. New Modes of Governance and Eastern Enlargement at the Freie Universität Berlin." The project was part of the Integrated Project "New Modes of Governance in Europe." Funding through the 6th Framework Programme of the European Union (CIT1-CT-2004-506392) is gratefully acknowledged by the author.
4. W. Merkel and H.J. Lauth, "Systemwechsel und Zivilgesellschaft: Welche Zivilgesellschaft braucht die Demokratie?" *Aus Politik und Zeitgeschichte* 42(6–7)(1998): 3–12.
5. V. Tismăneanu, *Reinventing Politics: Eastern Europe from Stalin to Havel* (New York: Free Press, 1992).
6. B. Greskovits, *The Political Economy of Protest and Patience: East European and Latin American Transformations Compared* (New York: Central European University Press, 1998).
7. H. Wiesenthal, "Interessenverbände in Ostmitteleuropa. Startbedingungen und Entwicklungsprobleme," in *Systemwechsel 4. Die Rolle von Verbänden im Transformationsprozeß,* eds. W. Merkel and E. Sandschneider (Opladen: Leske + Budrich, 1998), 83–113.
8. G. Meyer, "Values, Small Life Worlds and Communitarian Orientations: Ambivalent Legacies and Democratic Potentials in Post-Communist Political Culture," in *Political Culture in Post-Communist Europe. Attitudes in New Democracies,* eds. D. Pollack et al. (Aldershot: Ashgate, 2003), 169–181.
9. M.M. Howard, *The Weakness of Civil Society in Post-Communist Europe* (Cambridge: Cambridge University Press, 2003); A. Zimmer and E. Priller, eds., *Future of Civil Society: Making Central European Nonprofit-Organizations Work* (Wiesbaden: VS Verlag für Sozialwissenschaften, 2004).
10. T.A. Börzel and T. Risse, "Conceptualising the Domestic Impact of Europe," in *The Politics of Europeanisation,* eds. K. Featherstone and C. Radaelli (Oxford: Oxford University Press, 2003), 54–70.
11. D. McAdam, J.D. McCarthy, and M.N. Zald, eds., *Comparative Perspectives on Social Movements: Political Opportunities, Mobilizing Structures, and Cultural Framings* (Cambridge: Cambridge University Press, 1996); B.C. Schaefer and J. Carmin,

"Scholarship on Social Movement Organizations: Classic Views and Emerging Trends," *Mobilization* 10(2) (2005): 201–212.

12. H. Kitschelt, "Political Opportunity Structures and Political Protest: Anti-Nuclear Movements in Four Democracies," *British Journal of Political Science* 16(1)(1986): 57–85.

13. T.A. Börzel, "Participation Through Law Enforcement: The Case of the European Union," *Comparative Political Studies* 39(1)(2006): 128–152; C. Hilson, "New Social Movements: The Role of Legal Opportunity," *Journal of European Public Policy* 9 (2)(2002): 238–255.

14. J.D. McCarthy and M.N. Zald, "Resource Mobilization and Social Movements: A Partial Theory," *The American Journal of Sociology* 82(1)(1977): 212–241.

15. R.D. Benford and D. Snow, "Framing Processes and Social Movements: An Overview and Assessment," *Annual Review of Sociology* 26(1)(2000): 611–639.

16. F. Polletta and J.M. Jasper, "Collective Identity and Social Movements," *Annual Review of Sociology* 27(1)(2001): 283–305.

17. S. Jacquot and C. Woll, "Usage of European Integration—Europeanisation from a Sociological Perspective," *European Integration online Papers (EIoP)* 7(12) (2003).

18. T.A. Börzel and U. Sedelmeier, "The EU Dimension in European Politics," in *Developments in European Politics,* eds. P.M. Heywood, E. Jones, M. Rhodes, and U. Sedelmeier (Houndmills, Basingstoke; New York: Palgrave Macmillan, 2006), 54–70.

19. A. Dimitrova, "Enlargement, Institution-building and the EU's Administrative Capacity Requirement," *West European Politics* 25(4)(2002): 171–190.

20. H. Grabbe, "How Does Europeanization Affect CEE Governance? Conditionality, Diffusion and Diversity," *Journal of European Public Policy* 8(6)(2001): 1013–1031.

21. B. Kohler-Koch and B. Rittberger, "Review Article: The 'Governance Turn' in EU Studies," *Journal of Common Market Studies* 44(1)(2006): 27–49.

22. J. L. Cohen and A. Arato, *Civil Society and Political Theory* (Cambridge, MA, London: MIT Press, 1992).

23. A. Bozóki, "Die Politik der Opposition im Ungarn der 1980er Jahre," in *Weltregionen im Wandel: Mittel- und Osteuropa,* eds. A. Buzogány and R. Frankenberger (Baden-Baden: Nomos, 2007), 261–275; B.J. Falk, *The Dilemmas of Dissidence in East-Central Europe: Citizen Intellectuals and Philosopher Kings* (Budapest; New York: Central European University Press, 2003); D. Pollack and J. Wielgohs, *Dissent and Opposition in Communist Eastern Europe: Origins of Civil Society and Democratic Transition* (Aldershot: Ashgate, 2004).

24. T. Mastnak, "The Reinvention of Civil Society: Trough the Looking Glass of Democracy," *European Journal of Sociology* 46(1)(2005): 323–355.

25. K. Pickvance, *Democracy and Environmental Movements in Eastern Europe: A Comparative Study of Hungary and Russia* (Boulder: Westview Press, 1998); S. Rose-Ackermann, *From Elections to Democracy. Building Accountable Government in Hungary and Poland* (Cambridge: Cambridge University Press, 2005).

26. E. Hajba, "The Rise and Fall of the Hungarian Greens," *The Journal of Communist Studies and Transitional Politics* 3(1994): 180–191.

27. Z.D. Barany, *The East European Gypsies: Regime Change, Marginality, and Ethnopolitics* (Cambridge; New York: Cambridge University Press, 2002).

28. R.A. Cichowski, *The European Court and Civil Society: Litigation, Mobilization and Governance* (Cambridge; New York: Cambridge University Press, 2007).

29. For more details, see S. Kerényi and M. Szabó, "Transnational Influences on Patterns of Mobilisation Within Environmental Movements in Hungary," *Environmental Politics* 15(5) (2006): 803–820.

30. M. Vay, ed., *Zengő - Ökológia, Politika és Társadalmi Mozgalmak a Zengő-konfliktusban. [Zengő: Ecology, Politics and Social Movements in the Zengő-conflict]* (Budapest: Védegylet, 2005).

31. For more details, see http://www.rosiamontana.org/ as well as A. Buzogány and E. Baga, "Europa und das Gold der Karpaten. Lokale, Nationale und Transnationale Dimensionen des Bergbaukonfliktes in Rosia Montana," in *Projekte der Europäisierung. Kulturanthropologische Forschungsperspektiven,* Kulturanthropologie Notizen Bd. 78, eds. G. Welz and A. Lottermann (Frankfurt am Main: Institut für Kulturanthropologie und Europäische Ethnologie, 2009), 43–61.

32. J. Kelley, "International Actors on the Domestic Scene: Membership Conditionality and Socialization by International Institutions," *International Organization* 58(3)(2004): 425–461; G. Schwellnus, "The Adoption of Nondiscrimination and Minority Protection Rules in Romania, Hungary, and Poland," in *The Europeanization of Central and Eastern Europe,* eds. F. Schimmelfennig and U. Sedelmeier (Ithaca: Cornell University Press, 2005), 51–70.

33. M. Johns, "'Do as I Say,' Not as I Do": The European Union, Eastern Europe and Minority Rights," *East European Politics and Societies* 17(4)(2007): 682–699.

34. EU Directive 43/2000, on "implementing the principle of equal treatment between persons irrespective of racial or ethnic origin."

35. "Pereskedő alapítvány - Cigány gyerekekre kapott pénzen tanítják a többségieket" [Litigious foundation – Majoritarians are taught on money received for Gipsy children], Interview with Lilla Farkas, in: Heti Világgazdaság, 7 August 2007.

36. S.E. Mendelson and J.K. Glenn, *The Power and Limits of NGOs: A Critical Look at Building Democracy in Eastern Europe and Eurasia* (New York: Columbia University Press, 2002).

37. B. Wizner, "Osztok, Keverek. Cigány Programok és Roma Szervezetek Finanszírozása a Rendszerváltás Után," in *Kisebbségek Kisebbsége,* eds. J. Szalai and M. Neményi (Budapest: Új Mandátum, 2005), 430–458.

38. S. Miscoiu, "Is There a Model for the Political Representation of the Romanian Roma?" *Sfera Politicii* (2006): 123–124, 78–89.

39. D. Stark, L. Bruszt, and B. Vedres, "Rooted Transnational Publics: Integrating Foreign Ties and Civic Activism," *Theory and Society* 35(3)(2006): 323–349.

40. R.K. Merton, "The Matthew Effect in Science: The Reward and Communication Systems of Science Are Considered," *Science* 159(3810) (1968): 56–63.

41. The "Matthew effect" refers to a quote from the Gospel of Matthew (25:29): "For unto every one that hath shall be given, and he shall have abundance: but from him that hath not shall be taken away even that which he hath." In his works on the sociology of knowledge, Robert Merton has used this term to describe how already well-established and famous scholars are becoming even more famous compared to rather unknown ones working on the same project.

42. A. Horolets, "Pulling Europe Closer: The Strategy of Shame in Polish Press Discourse on Europe," in *Das Erbe des Beitritts: Europäisierung in Mittel- und Osteuropa,* eds. A. Kutter and V. Trappmann (Baden-Baden: Nomos, 2005), 155–170.

43. K. Harper, "'Wild Capitalism' and 'Ecocolonialism': A Tale of Two Rivers," *American Anthropologist* 107(2) (2005): 221–233.
44. EU Directive 2001/18 on the deliberate release into the environment of genetically modified organisms.
45. This marks an interesting historical loop: whereas during the 1980s, the ideology of "civil society" became a main working formula for the opposition, the deliberative political ideals underlying the concept became consecutively used in the framework of an increasingly neo-liberal, "hollowed-out" state (see Mastnak, "The Reinvention of Civil Society").
46. W. Guy, ed., *Between Past and Future: The Roma of Central and Eastern Europe* (Hatfield: University of Hertfordshire Press, 2001).
47. K. Simhandl, "'Western Gypsies and Travellers'-'Eastern Roma': The Creation of Political Objects by the Institutions of the European Union," *Nations and Nationalism* 12(1)(2006): 97–115.
48. I. Klimova-Alexander, *The Romani Voice in World Politics: the United Nations and Non-state Actors* (Aldershot: Ashgate, 2005).
49. K. Raik, "Bureaucratization or Strengthening of the Political?: Estonian Institutions and Integration into the European Union," *Cooperation and Conflict* 37(2)(2002): 137–156.
50. L. Hallstrom, "Eurocratising Enlargement? EU Elites and NGO Participation in European Environmental Policy," *Environmental Politics* 13 (1)(2004): 175–196.
51. B. Hicks, "Setting Agendas and Shaping Activism: EU Influence on Central and Eastern European Environmental Movements," *Environmental Politics* 13 (1)(2004): 216–233.
52. S. Sampson. 1996. "The Social Life of Projects: Importing Civil Society to Albania," in *Civil Society: Challenging Western Models*, eds. C.M. Hann and E. Dunn (London: Routlege, 1996), 121–142.
53. R.G. Bell, "Further Up the Learning Curve: NGOs from Transition to Brussels," *Environmental Politics* 13 (1)(2004): 194–215; A. Buzogány, "Romania: Europeanization in the Shadow of Forms without Substance," in *Coping with Accession: New Modes of Environmental Governance,* ed. T. Börzel (Houndsmill: Palgrave/Macmillan, 2009), 169–181.
54. I. Kovach and E. Kucerova, "The Project Class in Central Europe: The Czech and Hungarian Cases," *Sociologia Ruralis* 46(1)(2006): 3–21.

Chapter 5

Communicating Dissent

Diversity of Expression in the Protest against the G8 Summit in Heiligendamm

Simon Teune

Introduction

Just as its forerunners were, the Group of Eight (G8) summit in Heiligendamm, Germany, was challenged by protests emerging from the global justice movements (GJMs). The images of protest were complementing and at times eclipsing the images of the official summit.[1] When we recall the events in June 2007, we think of colorful marches with thousands and tens of thousands of participants, clowns poking fun at the security forces, protesters in black disguises throwing stones, discussions at the alternative summit, or activists roaming the fields near Heiligendamm to blockade the access to the venue.

Contending that the demonstrations in Heiligendamm were organized by the GJMs is a common and proximate assertion. At a closer look, however, the notion of a unitary movement might be misleading. On the one side, social movements are publicly visible in joint mobilizations and manifestos, which suggest unity. On the other side, social movements are characterized by the opposite of this: differentiation. What we call a social movement is a network of networks comprising a variety of actors with goals and beliefs that only partially intersect. To make it even more complicated, these constellations of political actors prove to vary significantly on the local and national level. Local traditions and the related perception of problems are an important factor shaping the dynamics of movement networks.[2] Likewise, social movements go back to different national histories, which developed under idiosyncratic opportunities.[3]

Some of the most evident divisions between different movement sectors go back to cognitive differences. Movement activists are guided by different perceptions of the world around them, the ways social change should be brought forward, and their own role in the political process. These standpoints result in perceptions of proximity to other actors in the field and in options for collective action. The numerous forms of protest directed at the meeting of political lead-

ers at the Baltic Sea reveal different takes on the interpretation of political reality and according concepts of social change. In order to understand the GJMs
and their inherent ambiguity of diversity and unity, this chapter will interpret
the different ways to express dissent. The evidence presented here goes back
to participant observation during the anti-G8 mobilization and a preliminary
analysis of written documents. Most of them are mobilizing leaflets, webpages or
résumés published after the summit.[4]

G8 Summits: Magnets for Global Justice Activists
and Opportunities for Social Movement Scholars

While international summits and meetings of international organizations used
to be an issue for a small segment of social movements during the 1970s and
1980s,[5] broad counter-mobilizations gained momentum only in the last decade.[6]
The first transnational protests against international meetings were organized
even though the context was not favorable: repression was significant during
these events, the majority of the media coverage was hostile to the protests, and
there was virtually no chance of success. Despite these disincentives, coalitions
of social movement groups targeted more and more international events. The
growing importance of these protests goes back to the fact that international institutions and meetings had a growing influence on political decisions and thus
on the life of the people across the globe. In addition, the international summits
matched with the meta-frame of anti-neoliberalism connecting the different actors within the GJMs.[7] The summits and meetings of international institutions
are framed as a materialization of a wrong political program, in general, and
as the cause for the individual problems a group might deal with in particular. As a consequence, events countering such international meetings uncovered
similarities in national struggles and facilitated the transnational coordination of
social movements. Activists used these events to define common transnational
agendas, aims, and demands. Both the preparatory process and the counter-
events themselves established a shared stock of experiences and facilitated the
emergence of a common identity beyond borders.[8] Thus, international summits
became symbolic sites of contention about the future of the planet. This perception gained ground among social movement activists and extended media coverage strengthened it. Moreover, the protest coincided with the breakdown of the
World Trade Organization (WTO) negotiations that occurred in Seattle in 1999
and in Cancun in 2003. The symbolic load of counter-activities and prior vic-
tories mobilized a significant number of activists, who traveled to distant venues
of protest. However, most of the organizational work for anti-summit protests
is dealt with by domestic movement organizations. This is why the remainder of
this chapter will concentrate on the field of those German actors who prepared

the ground for the protests in 2007. It is important to note that cooperation with actors from abroad and transnational diffusion processes played an important role in the preparatory process. Also, the participation of international activists was high at the protest events. However, in terms of organization and in terms of numbers, mobilizations countering international summits have also been an indicator for the status quo of the GJM's national branches.

The protests against the G8 summit in Heiligendamm were organized by an alliance characterized by an unprecedented degree of coordination among groups from the radical and moderate strands. The group of politicians gathering in Heiligendamm caused activists throughout the German GJMs to deal with the impact of the G8 on the specific field in which they were engaged. Even those groups who rejected participation in the mobilizations for Heiligendamm were forced to position themselves vis-à-vis the summit and the counter-activities.

Given the salience of the summit for political groups in Germany and abroad, the campaign against the G8 meeting serves as an excellent basis to understand the complexity of the GJMs, their internal divisions and coalitions as well as the different forms of protest that are used to gain leverage. In a campaign, we find the complex movement activity condensed. It is here that social movement groups struggle for visibility and define lines of conflict. In campaigns, these groups go public, they usually aim at speaking with one voice, and they have a limited agenda in terms of goals and time frame. These characteristics and the ability to analyze social movements at an intermediary level—between detailed case studies and generalizing assumptions about social movements as alleged unities—made scholars suggest investing more energy in the analysis of protest campaigns.[9]

Who Are the Players?

The Heiligendamm summit and the related meetings associated with the German G8 presidency triggered mobilizations of four alliances in the national context. Three separate leftist coalitions and one NGO coalition brought up different issues, resorted to different action repertoires, and mobilized their own constituencies. The more or less independent mobilizing efforts of Block G8, a coalition that organized the blockade of the venue, as well as local alliances, Attac, faith groups, parties, and the trade unions' youth organizations made the situation even more complicated. In a long-lasting preparatory process, the different players managed to agree upon a common schedule for the protest and they collaborated on some of the events, namely, the main demonstration and (to some extent) the alternative summit. As indicated above, the attempts for collaboration between different segments of the GJMs were more successful than in previous mobilizations.[10] It is a question of interpretation, however, to what extent we can speak of a single campaign against the G8 meeting in Heiligendamm.[11] Producing different mobilization contexts, the GJMs prove to be a complex "multi-organizational field."[12]

This multi-organizational field can be structured along two major axes. They mark preferences that play an important role both in the self-perception of political actors and in the way they perceive their environment. The axes are defined by two poles: radical vs. moderate, and spontaneistic vs. organized.[13] Both axes describe a space in which every political group or tendency can be located. This allows for identifying the different perspectives present within the GJMs (see Figure 5.1). The horizontal axis distinguishes between organizational principles. Groups tending toward the right pole emphasize the efficacy of their organization. They favor representative structures, the division of labor, and clearly defined hierarchies. The achievement of goals is considered a priority to the chosen means. Summing up these characteristics, groups in this area are *organized*. At the opposite pole, the means-end relation is reversed. Groups leaning toward this pole reject all organizational structures that delimit the autonomy of the individual member. Accordingly, these groups are *spontaneistic*.

The second axis that spans the field differentiates the range of criticism. Either the groups' critique of the status quo is *reformist*, aiming at dysfunctions of the political and economic regime, or it is *radical*, focusing on the totality of social organization instead of on single problems. The latter axis refers to the

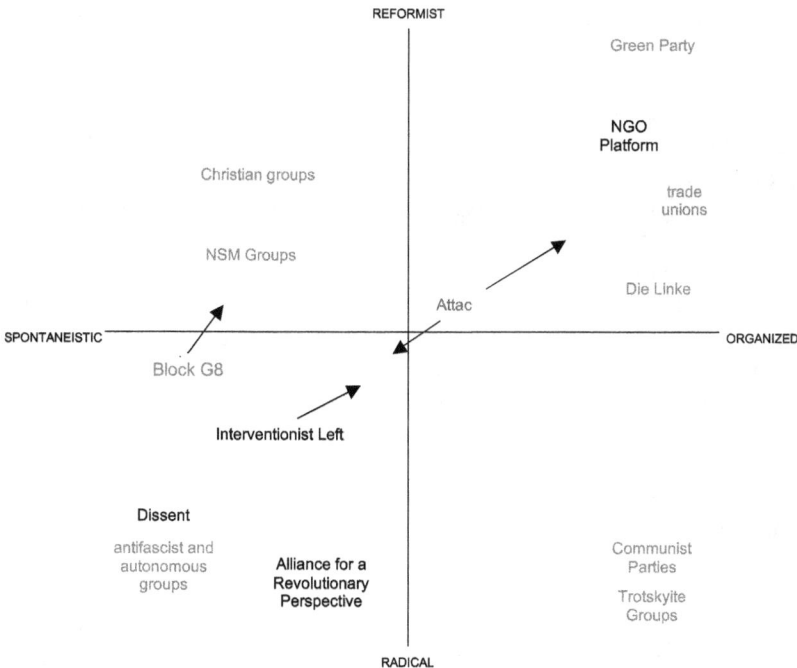

Figure 5.1. Field of Actors Challenging the G8 Summit.

dichotomy of radicals and moderates. However, both positions are considered as poles with the actors located somewhere in between. The axes also represent the main cleavages within the GJMs. The main conflicts in the field go back to the scope of criticism, hierarchies in self-organization (e.g., large organizations dominating small ones), and the choice of means.

The NGO platform, to begin with one of the anti-G8 coalitions, can be located in the section of the field where tempered criticism matches with an emphasis on organization. The coalition brought together several dozen NGOs, mainly from the environmental and development sector. Two parties that are established in the German party system add to the field: *Die Linke* and the Green party. Trade unions combine the same characteristics as the aforementioned actors. In contrast to Romanic countries where unions play a major role in the GJMs, they were of minor importance in the German mobilization.

In the subfield that combines the opposite attributes—grassroots democracy and anti-capitalism—there are three distinct coalitions challenging the G8. The *Interventionistische Linke* (Interventionist Left) was founded in 2005. It defined the upcoming summit as a focal point to enlarge the basis for criticism from the radical left. To reach this goal, the coalition collaborated intensely with moderate players, such as the NGO platform or *Die Linke* (this tendency is marked by an arrow). This cooperation was also manifest in the persons involved. Some activists within the Interventionist Left were at the same time working for NGOs or members of *Die Linke* and Attac. The other alliances in the radical left field kept at an arm's length from the moderate sector. Dissent, emerging from the mobilizations against the 2005 edition of the G8 summit in Gleneagles, is an autonomist network that embraces the hallmarks of Peoples Global Action. As far as the activists were concerned, there was hardly any overlap with moderate actors in the network. Separate from Dissent, the *Anti-G8-Bündnis für eine revolutionäre Perspektive* (Alliance for a Revolutionary Perspective) combined groups from an anti-imperialist and communist tradition. The coalition was small in number and virtually invisible as a collective actor.

Beyond these two subfields, there were groups that were guided by different principles. Moderate grassroots groups, taking a third sector, did not develop their own network. Groups in this subfield are typically grassroots groups rooted in new social movements (e.g., environmental, women's rights, and peace movements) or of the Christian faith. They tend toward the pole of moderate critique, but keep their distance from strict organizational principles. In the mobilization against the G8 summit, these groups either tended to collaborate with NGOs and parties or they found common ground with the radical camp. Block G8, an alliance that brought together groups experienced in the use of civil disobedience, represents the latter kind of merger.

Trotskyite and communist groups added to the actors in the field mobilizing for protest against the G8 summit. While they stick to a critique that transcends the given political and economic system, these groups underline the efficacy of firm organization. There are few formal ties with mobilizing actors from the other sectors. However, these groups tend to mobilize a large part of their constituencies for such events and they are very active in recruiting new members. As a consequence, they attained a high visibility in the protests relative to their actual weight.

Block G8 and the German offshoot of Attac are networks that are open to activists from the moderate and radical shore. In the preparation for the G8 protests, Attac members were part of both the NGO platform and radical alliances, such as the Interventionist Left. Even though there were quite a number of conflicts, Attac became a broker in the field. Without actually bringing together leftists and liberals, the network absorbed conflicts that would have been fierce in a direct confrontation between both sectors. Quite a lot of the organizational work for the G8 counter-activities was done collectively by activists from different strands of the GJMs. Christian activists and NGO representatives, trade unionists, and grassroot activists from anti-racist, feminist or autonomist groups planned and coordinated joint activities in three conferences in Rostock, a city close to the venue of the G8 summit. Eventually, most of the organization was done in working groups in between these conferences. The degree of cooperation was striking compared to the last G8 summit in Germany, in Cologne 1999. Although the quarrels were significant and at times the collaboration was close to being terminated, the inclusion of a broad array of actors was successful in the end. It is important, however, to remind the reader that most of the mobilization was done in the more homogeneous context of individual groups or local networks.

Bringing Ideology Back In

What defines the matrix structuring the field of G8 challengers presented above are different ideological poles. On the one axis, we find different positions about the range of social and political change that is considered necessary. The other axis confronts different ideas about the organization of dissent. The salience of shared beliefs used to be one of the major explanatory factors to collective action. However, this cognitive dimension has lost significance since resource mobilization theory focused on the organizational structures within social movements. Complementary approaches tended to focus on the conditions, dynamics, and impact of collective action. Accordingly, most of the research underemphasized ideological factors. However, the "cultural turn" in social movement theory has brought ideology back in. Defining the neglect of ideology as one of the shortcomings of a resource-oriented approach, Mayer Zald has invited social movement scholars to systematically include the ideological dimension in their analysis.[14] While Zald's ubiquitous concept of ideology has been contested,[15] a focus on shared beliefs seems particularly conductive to understanding movement groups' diverse approaches in communicating their dissent.

In his programmatic article, Zald pleads for understanding social movements as ideologically structured action (ISA), a notion that has been introduced by Russel Dalton in his quantitative analysis of European environmentalist groups.[16] Dalton's main finding is that ideology, rather than resources or forms of organization, is the explaining factor to understand the strategic choices social movement actors make. Using a qualitative method and focusing on two environmental groups, Carmin and Balser have strengthened Dalton's claim.[17] Dalton explains structure *and* action of social movement groups as dependent from a shared ideology.[18] According to the ISA model, forms of organization, the choice of issues, and action repertoires are influenced, but not determined, by a certain ideology.

This non-determinate relation is illustrated by the case of the mobilization against G8. Similar ideological positions resulted in diametric strategic decisions. Within the anti-capitalist sector of G8 challengers, for instance, there were several approaches to alliances. The Interventionist Left collaborated with liberals, NGO representatives, partisans, and Christian activists in order to increase the visibility of their stance. Vice versa, the Alliance for a Revolutionary Perspective and, to a certain extent, also Dissent rejected this kind of cooperation, assuming that radical critique is absorbed and powerless when brought into these contexts.

While Dalton's ISA model is certainly useful to understand political groups' strategic choices, the very core of the model, the concept of ideology, remains underspecified. In his study, Dalton does not go beyond the vague idea that ideology "provides a framework for organising and interpreting the political world."[19] A look back to the history of the notion of ideology shows that the discussion has long been dominated by a pejorative use of the term. In the tradition of critical theory (understood in the broad sense, from enlightenment to Marx to the Frankfurt School), ideology was perceived as a structure of deceit.[20] This tradition was challenged by the sociology of science and poststructuralist theories.[21]

Recently, approaches to integrate ideology into the analysis of social movements have come to the fore. Several social movement scholars implicitly underline the impact of a set of shared interpretative patterns.[22] They trace back decisions and actions that can be observed within social movement to experiences, values, and systems of reference. Fine and Sandstrom refer to ideology explicitly as a connection of interpretations of the world and the values that guide action.[23] In their definition, ideology has an interactionist origin and it is nothing with which people are overcome. Shared perceptions and evaluations emerge in group discussions and they guide collective action. However, not only the in-group produces coinciding patterns of interpretation; the cognitive common ground of a political group is also shaped by out-group ascriptions to the collective.

To strengthen this interactionist aspect, I define ideology as a largely shared system of interpretation that is reproduced in group processes and serves to construct and evaluate political reality. Understood this way, ideology is the cognitive basis for decisions and purposeful action. In the Dissent network, for instance, one of the most important objectives is grassroots democracy and the absence of hierarchy. Thus, joint attempts to minimize hierarchies in processes of organization are the touchstone for Dissent adherents in order to engage in networks or alliances. The rationale to choose these interactions can be understood only with reference to the underlying patterns of interpretation.

Of course, constructing a shared ideology is a dynamic process. Never will the interpretation of reality be identical for all members of a group, the less so in heterogeneous networks. If the intersecting set of perceptions is not considered satisfactory for collaboration, this will result either in controversies and ideological adjustments or in the exit of single activists or even a division of the group. This shows that part of a shared ideology is assumptions about the distance of a group vis-à-vis other actors. These assumptions motivate the association with one sector of the GJMs or the dissociation from another one. In the same vein, the decision to prefer one form of action to another will be guided by assumptions about the group's opportunities to affect the wider societal context.

The action performed by a group at the same time serves to reaffirm this perception. It defines the group's identity and its position in a political field. Being perceived by other players, the action is also an important reference point to classify the group from the outside perspective. Thus, out-group attributions reaffirm the construction of the group's position in the field. In a process that includes an action that goes back to the interpretation of the situation and an outward ascription, the position of G8 challengers is defined in an interactionist way.

A Universe of Expression and Subsets of Communication

To express and promote their ideas of social change, political groups communicate with the environments that surround them. They interact with other social movement groups, bystanders, mass media, and decision-makers using specific forms of communication. As indicated above, we distinguish between two levels of interaction. On the movement level, communication preferences can be observed in the way movement groups engage in joint campaigns and mobilizations. They consider certain groups as partners while they feel a distance to others and refrain from collaborating with them. On a more general level, GJM groups address other parts of the society beyond the movement context, and they choose different ways to do so.

Out of a multitude of possible modes of interaction that are available in a given cultural set, political groups choose only certain tactics while they refrain from using others. The classical account to understand sets of action that are used by social movements is the notion of repertoires. The term was coined by Charles Tilly to point out the historical conditionality of contentious action.[24] In a given period and a given space, citizens resort to a limited bundle of means with which to deal with a conflict. However, repertoires of action cannot only be defined for large social entities. As a subset of the means available, repertoires may be identified for individual groups that act in the larger societal framework. Political groups choose only certain forms of action from this tableau to reach their aims, namely, those they consider appropriate to express their political position.[25] While Tilly applied his concept of repertoires of action to conflicts between challengers and authorities, we will use the concept of communication repertoires to define the sets of action both within the movement and beyond. Communication repertoires focus at the basic constellation of an actor addressing (or ignoring) its environment. However, they are not limited to forms of protest, but include interactions within the field of challengers aiming at the display of a certain position.

The full spectrum of communication repertoires used in a social movement has hardly been subject to research. Although specific forms of communication have been ascribed to certain groups or parts of a movement, an analysis that explains communication strategies for groups or parts of a movement is yet pending. Having this as a goal, it is essential not to narrow the focus to goal-oriented communication, but to be aware of the fact that also the refusal of interactions and seemingly absurd communications have a purpose and are part of a communication repertoire.

The choice of certain forms of interaction and the rationale behind them brings us back to the G8 summit in Heiligendamm. The meeting was challenged by a variety of protest events that were carried by alliances with different ideological backgrounds. As developed above, the choices made to communicate their dissent were not by chance. They were made on the basis of a certain understanding of their own role in the political process and social change in general.

At the center of the analysis is the question as to which extent political groups get involved in different communicative contexts and how these are referred to. In this regard, the comparison of the movement level and the general political level should provide a deeper insight into the modality of strategic choices in two different systems of reference. The following section of the chapter is a first attempt to map the interrelations that characterize the field of G8 challengers and to map the spectrum of protest that is used to communicate dissent.

Identifying Communication Repertoires

In interactions with their environments, social movement groups express their ideas and offer frames to understand problems and possible solutions. By staging acts of protest, they might address a political institution, a large public or primarily their own community. Most of the attempts of communication are mediated by the coverage that occurs in mass media. In their organization of protests, social movement activists have to allow for this intermediate factor, which filters and amplifies the form and content of communication. Decisions about the addressee, however, mirror the position an actor has—or, more accurately, perceives to have—in a contentious political field. Thus, the choice of a certain communication repertoire allows for tracing the relationship between a political group and the environments it is facing—political institutions, elites, mass media, ad-hoc or alternative public spaces within the GJMs.

Communicating Public Dissent

A look at all of the protest events referring to the G8 summit in Heiligendamm reveals a grammar of protest that is spelled out. Out of the set of available forms of action, a movement group picks a limited subset that is perceived as an appropriate means of expression. Ranging from public appeals to arson attacks, for some of the forms of protest, we will now try to explain why their actors have chosen them.

The radical share of the GJMs does not consider the G8 a legitimate political actor. In this line of thought, the summit is an expression of the elitist hubris of the Global North claiming to make decisions that solve world problems. In fact, G8 members would continue policies to the advantage of their countries' economies. According to this perception, acts of protest would have to express the denial of legitimacy and the denial of the claim of world leadership. The consequences that are drawn from this analysis, however, differ considerably.

Some militant anti-imperialist activists committed arson attacks on targets allegedly responsible for neoliberal globalization, among others the private house of Thomas Mirow, Undersecretary of State at the Ministry of Finance and Economy. These attacks are considered as both noticeable damage done to political and economic leaders and as a signal to the majority of the people that do not profit from neoliberal globalization. While these activities took place in the run-up of the event, far away from the venue, less clandestine forms of violence were observable throughout the G8 summit. These other forms of action aimed at producing images of resistance against the G8 summit and the security apparatus protecting it.[26] Anarchists and autonomists took the mass rally in Rostock on 2 June 2007 as an occasion to attack the police and transport a message of dissent that was incommensurable within the media frame of both the protests and the summit aiming at benefiting the planet.

While violent forms of action where considered powerful means to promote a radical perspective on the G8 by only a small part of the radical movement sector, the lion share of radical activists refrained from this option. As long as violence against the police was not defensive, they considered attacks as detrimental to the communication of a radical critique. Instead, the alliance Block G8 favored blockades of the streets giving access to the venue of the summit, with a tactic that aimed at evading contact with the police. In this way, they hoped to circumvent images of violence and to obstruct the summit at the same time. Due to the nonviolent nature of the blockade, radical leftists could join forces with environmentalists and nonviolent groups, and they were attractive enough to non-experienced activists, who were needed to reach a critical mass.

However, activists of Block G8 and others who would not use violence offensively were aware of the trap of being embraced by the mass media and professional politicians. Thus, quite a number of them joined one of two Black Blocks in the Rostock rally. Named after the color that most people in the formation wear, the Black Block is a symbolic display of irreconcilable opposition. Activists wear black disguises to attain anonymity. Even though only a small part of the Black Block was involved in clashes with the police, the collective appearance aims at maintaining the image of unpredictability for the police.

The appearance of the Black Block and its association with violence also had an effect on other groups opposing the G8 summit. There are two reasons why the menace of violence is inacceptable for these players. On the one hand, they have learned through experience that violent clashes overshadow other forms of action, so that their messages cannot be heard in a mediated public sphere. On the other hand, they reject violence as an element of contention altogether. NGOs, parties, grassroots groups, and Attac had organized the demonstration in Rostock together with the Interventionist Left. They hoped to communicate the breadth of criticism of the G8 summit in peaceful images of protest. To reach this goal, journalists were important partners. However, as soon as violence seems to be possible, other forms of displaying dissent lose their attractiveness for correspondents. The content of the criticism that is directed at the G8 summit is hard to communicate on banners and posters during a demonstration. As a consequence, NGOs, Attac, and the Interventionist Left organized a countersummit to make clear that there were well-founded reasons to oppose the G8. Within the moderate sector of the GJMs, the alternative summit was considered important and was organized to offer alternatives to the policies that are made in international meetings. Beyond that, the Internventionist Left engaged in the event to increase the visibility of radical criticism and according concepts of change within the GJMs.

Most of the NGOs directly addressed the participants of the summit and called for fundamental changes in the policies of the G8. However, as this constellation presumes and confirms the summit as a legitimate actor in world politics, those appeals were unacceptable for all of those who denied the legitimation of the summit. Greenpeace, for instance, started two spectacular attempts to invade the red zone of Heiligendamm in order to hand over a petition to the assembled political leaders. Their activities were covered extensively by the media, but Greenpeace could not prevent them from interpreting the results of the summit as a step in the right direction. Greenpeace's message, that the summit had failed, did not receive the same attention as their daredevil operations. Addressing the G8 directly goes back to a *Realpolitik* that prefers short-term changes on the public agenda to radical criticism. In this line of thought, oppositional politics has to deal with the existing power constellations in order to reach short- and mid-term goals.

While challengers with a reformist concept of change address politicians directly, because they are in charge and are potential protagonists of change, radical opponents of the G8 summit consider the meeting itself part of the problem rather than part of the solution. The media are an important factor in communicating both messages. NGOs and parties have developed professional media relations to get their messages broadcasted. This applies also to most of the radical challengers. However, they did not try to influence the decisions in Heiligendamm. Rather, they hoped for a honest coverage of their activities that is not dominated by prejudices and ignorance. As they do not trust mass media to report on their motivations and the content of their critique, they develop alternative ways to communicate their messages to a larger public. Alternative media, most notably Indymedia, are one way to reach this goal. Another one is face-to-face contact with people outside of the movement. Dissent, for instance, organized an "info tour" with events all over Germany and Europe. Bringing information to the people was a way to convey a radical perspective on the G8 and to motivate participation in the protest.

Communicating within the Global Justice Movement

As a political field,[27] the GJMs are structured by the relationship of actors that are visible in the flows of communication. For example, a global justice group decides to join an anti-G8 coalition contingent on the perceived commonalities with other groups or organizations within this alliance. Among other factors, the density of communication is dependent on this perception of proximity. The arrangement of the actors in Figure 5.1 is constructed and mirrored in the communication flows between the groups active in the field.

A communist group that rejects the reformist agenda of a Christian solidarity group is unlikely to communicate directly with this group, to say nothing of a collaboration in a joint coalition. The same relationship holds for most of the autonomist groups and NGOs. Autonomists perceive the actions of the NGOs as grist to the mill of the G8 leaders, who stage the summit as an event that is decisive for the future of the planet. The agenda of the counter-summit, for instance, might be regarded as reformist in the radical movement sector because it refers to the agenda of the official summit. However, there were activists associated with Dissent who decided not to partake in the preparation of an event that reinforced the dominant discourse, while activists affiliated with the Interventionist Left held that more radical concerns could be disseminated only through participation in the counter-summit. The moderate organizers considered the latter group as (possibly difficult) partners, whereas the perception of the former group as irreconcilable hardliners might have been re-emphasized.

The interpretation of violence in the context of demonstrations is another cognitive element where divisions between the actors are visible. None of the radical alliances dissociated themselves from the violent protesters. This does not imply that these alliances supported violence. However, in public communications, they considered the violence of protesters as a minor issue compared with the state repression against leftist activists and the structural violence of global inequalities. Moreover, they underlined their acceptance of different forms of action. For most of the other actors in the field, namely, activists from moderate grassroots groups, parties, NGOs, and most of the activists in Attac, physical violence was not acceptable under the given circumstances. They delineated those activists who were involved in violent clashes from those who were peaceful, not only because it was their personal conviction to do so, but also because journalists forced them to draw a line and isolate those labeled as "violence prone." While prominent Attac members identified autonomist groups as those responsible for the violence and underlined Attac's distance to those groups, radical activists blamed the moderate camp following the agenda of journalists who were obsessed with violence. As a consequence, the cleavage between moderates and radicals was perceived as even more significant. The relationship between the Interventionist Left and their moderate partners was under scrutiny. The absence of violence on behalf of the protesters during the blockades certainly eased the tension as it showed that an alliance of groups with different ideological backgrounds could succeed in organizing an effective blockade.

Political Groups in a Contentious Field

In the interaction of movement groups, ideology obviously plays an important role. As the perception of reality is not shared, at least to a certain extent, this leads to conflict that impedes collaboration and fosters factionalism. Coalition and separation are processes that rest in interpretative frames and structure the multi-organizational field of the GJMs. In a larger context, different movement groups adopt different communication repertoires to influence target groups, such as political institutions, the mass media or a larger public. These communication repertoires are in turn evaluated and classified by target groups and other global justice activists.

If a group's perception of its environment is considered central to explain strategic decisions about acting, this environment has to be referred to more in detail. The political and economic regime marks the basic constants to which a political group relates. A movement group may be supportive or critical toward the basic societal features or it may reject it altogether. According to this basic position, the group can be analyzed with reference to its "membership in the polity."[28] The distinction between the "members" and the "challengers" of the polity was introduced by William Gamson in opposition to elitist and pluralist concepts of democracy. He confronted these theories with the fact that groups that may not play a role in the common process of negotiating could, under certain conditions, gain leverage. While Gamson initially drew the line between institutional political actors as members of the polity, on the one side, and social movements as challengers, on the other, the distinction is much harder to make when we look at the GJMs. Part of the actors engaged in the campaign against the G8 have to be considered as members of the polity. Apart from parties, trade unions, and charity organizations, which are important allies, several global justice movement organizations ceased to challenge the cornerstones of the regime.

The distinction between challengers and members of the polity is even more important when considering the discursive construction of a group's position. The perception to be a challenger, on the one hand, moulds the action of the group itself. But, on the other hand, the external ascription of the challenger role serves to reaffirm frontiers. What large parts of the society consider sayable in the context of legitimate criticism is subject to an ongoing process of self-ascertainment. Accordingly, a group that holds a certain position is either constructed as a legitimate speaker or is not. For instance, those groups that do not follow the moral imperative to dissociate from violent activists are excluded from the sphere of reasonable critics. This underlines that both the self-image of a political group and the reaction to the public construction of its political position (e.g., in press coverage or in judgments by politicians) are an integral part of the strategic determination of communicative repertoires.

This relational concept of the determinants for a communication repertoire aims at incorporating the context in which social movement groups interact. Thus, the interactionist concept of ideology allows for the knowledge that "the totality of a given empirical collective action is usually attributed a quasi-substantial unity, when it is instead the contingent outcome of the interaction of a multiple field of forces and analytically distinct processes."[29] The environment's political groups interact with are not extrinsic systems, but they are part of a political field that can be restructured in action. Thus, political constellations are both the starting point and the product of a group's interpreting reality.[30]

Conclusion

The images of protest connected to the G8 summit reveal part of the heterogeneity of the GJM. They reflect different ideas of how the need for change should be communicated. A group can decide to attack the fence that marks the red zone or it can fly giant balloons to symbolize the overcoming of security fences and borders. Both forms of action are chosen on purpose, because they imply a certain understanding of the summit and the protests against it. They are the carriers of two concepts of change.

Showing the acting of a group in its political context seems to be an important step in understanding the actors' motivation. The strategic choices of interacting with different environments reveal how reality is constructed in varying segments of the movement and which consequences for action result from these shared perceptions. Even though the set of opportunities available seems to be the same for the GJMs as a whole, the actors show very different reactions to them. Thus, the perspective on communication repertoires might help to show that opportunity structures are not universal frames, but are dynamic relations that are remodeled in contentious politics. Especially if the aspects of repression and access to the polity are considered, it is important to include processes of mutual construction between members and challengers of the polity in the analysis.

What does the notion of communication repertoires tell us about the initial problem of complexity in social movements? All forms of communication are selected on purpose, because they fit a certain notion of social change. Communication repertoires might help us to reconstruct the respective rationale behind actions that are obviously very different. Decisions about how to communicate with other social movement groups, bystanders, the mass media, and the political elite are shaped by a shared understanding of the group's position within the movement as a contentious political field.

Despite the differences in the field, unity is produced on a cognitive level. Activists use the notion of movement to underline the commonality of different actors. A shared perception of abstract problems and goals, the conviction that fundamental change is necessary, and the feeling of belonging are binding features of the topos "movement" that establish a delicate link between distant actors. Oftentimes, criticism is expressed with reference to an undetermined notion of a movement and its associated values. In the discussion that followed the violent clashes at the margins of the main demonstration in Rostock, activists evoked alleged traits of the GJM, such as "the movement does not support violence" or "the movement does not dissociate from any form of action."

When using the term "social movement," especially in the context of the diverse GJMs, scholars have to allow for the inherent plurality in their research. Analyzing the mobilization of large and resourceful actors, for instance, will result in specific findings that are distinct from processes and motivations in other parts of the movement. This demonstrates that there are good reasons not to infer assumptions about the movement as a whole from such a limited set of actors. If we take communication repertoires as an example, it seems inappropriate after what has been developed in this chapter to look only at those forms of action that (directly or indirectly) aim at influencing political leaders. In the case of the G8 summit, it might even be problematic to include in the analysis only those organizations that mobilize for protest at the Baltic shore. Certain parts of the GJMs are critical of the mobilizations targeting international summits or they prefer to organize local protests instead of traveling to the venue. If the plurality of positions is not represented in research, social movement analysis risks reproducing a reduced notion of reality.

Notes

1. The resistance against the meeting attracted enormous attention in the mass media, outnumbering the coverage of the event that triggered the protest. See D. Rucht and S. Teune, eds., *Nur Clowns und Chaoten? Die G8-Proteste in Heiligendamm im Spiegel der Massenmedien* (Frankfurt am Main and New York: Campus, 2008).
2. R. Roth, "Lokale Bewegungsnetzwerke und Institutionalisierung von neuen sozialen Bewegungen," in *Öffentlichkeit, öffentliche Meinung, soziale Bewegungen*, ed. F. Neidhardt (Opladen: Westdeutscher Verlag, 1994), 413–436.
3. For the GJMs, see D. della Porta, ed., *The Global Justice Movement: A Cross-National and Transnational Perspective* (Boulder: Paradigm, 2007); I. Sommier et al., eds., *La Généalogie des Mouvements Antiglobalisation en Europe. Une Perspective Compare* (Paris: Karthala, 2008).
4. For the purpose of my Ph.D. dissertation, of which this research is part, the material will be complemented by interviews and press articles.
5. For an exception, see J. Gerhards and D. Rucht, "Mesomobilization: Organizing and Framing in Two Protest Campaigns in West Germany," *The American Journal of Sociology* 98 (3)(1992): 555–596.
6. M. Holzapfel and K. König, "Chronik der Globalisierungsproteste," *Mittelweg 36* 6 (2001): 24–34; M. Pianta, "Democracy vs. Globalization. The Growth of Parallel Summits and Global Movements," in *Debating Cosmopolitics*, ed. D. Archibugi (London and New York: Verso, 2003), 232–256.
7. See M. Andretta et al., *Globalization from below. Transnational Activists and Protest Networks* (Minneapolis: University of Minnesota Press, 2006), ch. 3.
8. Even though the events might be perceived as transnational, Ariane Jossin has expressed doubts about the degree of blending among activists of different national descents. On the level of activist experiences, she prefers to speak of multi-national activism. See A. Jossin, "How Do Activists Experience Transnational Protest Events? The Case of Young Global Justice Activists from Germany and France," in *The Transnational Condition. Protest Dynamics in an Entangled Europe*, ed. Simon Teune (Oxford and New York: Berghahn Books, 2010), 42–63.
9. D. Rucht and D. della Porta, "The Dynamics of Environmental Campaigns," *Mobilization* 7(1)(2002): 1–14; G. Marwell and P. Oliver, "Collective Action Theory and Social Movements Research," In *Research in Social Movements, Conflict and Change* 7, ed. L. Kriesberg (Greenwich: JAI Press, 1984), 1–27.
10. As far as the duration is concerned, the coalitions challenge Tarrow's notion of short-term 'event coalitions' that he contrasts with enduring campaign coalitions (S. Tarrow, *The New Transnational Activism* (New York: Cambridge University Press, 2005), 171). Although the alliances did not continue and their work was unchanged after the event they were referring to, they worked together for up to two years. Adding

to this, attempts were made to maintain the connections beyond the G8 summit, in internal coalition meetings, in the context of the social forum process, in a congress, and a climate action camp.

11. S. Teune, "A Snap-shot of Movements. Assessing Social Movement Diversity through Campaign Analysis?," paper presented to the workshop *Campaign Analysis in a Globalizing World,* Evangelische Akademie Tutzing, 27–28 April 2007.
12. R.L. Curtis and L.A. Zurcher, "Stable Resources of Protest Movements: The Multi-Organizational Field," *Social Forces* 52 (1)(1973): 53–61.
13. See D. Rucht, S. Teune, and M. Yang, "Global Justice Movements in Germany," in *The Global Justice Movement: A Crossnational and Transnational Perspective,* ed. D. della Porta (Boulder: Paradigm, 2007), 157–183.
14. M.N. Zald, "Ideologically Structured Action: An Enlarged Agenda for Social Movement Research," *Mobilization* 5 (1)(2000): 1–16.
15. M. Diani, "The Relational Deficit of Ideologically Structured Action," *Mobilization* 5 (1)(2000): 17–24; B. Klandermans, "Must We Redefine Social Movements as Ideologically Structured Action?," *Mobilization* 5 (1)(2000): 25–30.
16. R.J. Dalton, *The Green Rainbow. Environmental Groups in Western Europe* (New Haven: Yale University Press, 1994).
17. J. Carmin and D.B. Balser, "Selecting Repertoires of Action in Environmental Movement Organizations: An Interpretive Approach," *Organization Environment* 15 (4)(2002): 365–388.
18. See Dalton, *The Green Rainbow,* 12.
19. Ibid.
20. Institut für Sozialforschung, "Ideologie," in *Soziologische Exkurse,* ed. Institut für Sozialforschung (Frankfurt am Main: Fischer, 1956), 162–181.
21. For an introduction see T. Eagleton, *Ideology. An Introduction* (London and New York: Verso, 1991).
22. E.g., Carmin and Balser, "Selecting Repertoires of Action in Environmental Movement Organizations," 365–388; J. Freeman, "A Model for Analyzing the Strategic Options of Social Movement Organizations," in *Waves of Protest: Social Movements since the Sixties,* eds. J. Freeman and V. Johnson (Lanham: Rowman & Littlefield, 1999), 221–240.
23. G.A. Fine and K. Sandstrom, "Ideology in Action: A Pragmatic Approach to a Contested Concept," *Sociological Theory* 11 (1)(1993): 24.
24. C. Tilly, "Getting It Together in Burgundy, 1675–1975," *Theory and Society* 4 (4)(1977): 479–504.
25. J.G. Ennis, "Fields of Action: Structure in Movements' Tactical Repertoires," *Sociological Forum* 2 (3)(1987): 520–533.
26. J.S. Juris, "Violence Performed and Imagined: Militant Action, the Black Bloc and the Mass Media in Genoa," *Critique of Anthropology* 25 (4)(2005): 413–432.
27. P. Bourdieu, *Das Politische Feld. Zur Kritik der Politischen Vernunft* (Konstanz: Universitätsverlag Konstanz, 2001).
28. W.A. Gamson, *The Strategy of Social Protest* (Homewood: Dorsey Press, 1975), 140.
29. A. Melucci, *Challenging Codes: Collective Action in the Information Age* (Cambridge: Cambridge University Press, 1996), 4.
30. N. Crossley, "From Reproduction to Transformation: Social Movement Fields and the Radical Habitus," *Theory Culture Society* 20 (6)(2003): 43–68.

Chapter 6

Digitalized Anti-Corporate Campaigns
Toward a New Era of Transnational Protest?

Johanna Niesyto

What is said to be new?

As mass media-communicated corporate public relations and product advertising form conditions for the distribution of product and corporate images, the transformation into a multimedia society and, in particular, the introduction and widespread appropriation of the Internet, enable the sociotechnical possibility of converting political protest in favor of anti-corporate campaigns using a consumerist repertoire. Appealing to citizens as "netizen consumers" creates new options for a politicization of market sphere-related activities.[1] Protest actors promoting consumer resistance use the Internet as a site of contestation: they use digital communication tools to deconstruct brand images and re-contextualize them against the backdrop of global justice. Moreover, they link up with the trend of what has been termed "lifestyle politics" (Bennett) by mixing popular culture, branding strategies, information technology, and protest messages. The new communication technology of the Internet, and other digital media as well, affects not only forms of social interaction, but also the way communication is expressed, e.g., via culture jamming.

Della Porta and Tarrow argue that anti-corporate campaigns represent new forms of transnational contention in three ways: with respect to organizational form they are characterized by weakly structured networks, in terms of repertoires of collective action they operate as consumerist (e.g., consumer boycotts), and with respect to identity they operate with "flexible identities"[2], the latter being commensurate with both heterogeneous networks and consumerist action. According to Bennett, two main types of transnational networks can be distinguished:[3]

> 1. *old era of transnational protest:* NGO advocacy networks, consisting of NGO-centered issue networks created by issue/goal framing; deploy-

ment of fracture lines along organization identity; restrictive agenda control for members; promotion of single issues; aimed at influencing governmental regulation; establishment of information regimes and maintaining organizational identity; establishment of strategic campaigns; unfolding the capacity of reform and crisis intervention; aimed at governments and some corporations; spread across homogeneous networks.[4]

2. *new era of transnational protest:* in contrast, Global Justice Movement (GJM) networks consist of loosely structured, polycentric, direct activist networks created by weak ties; that unfold a code of inclusive diversity, adopt self-organizing telecommunication technology; implement a collective agenda; advocate multiple issues; pursue goals of individual empowerment; establish permanent campaigns; extend the capacity of mass protest and value change; direct protest at corporations, industrial sectors, and economic blocs (G7, WEF, IMF, WTO); spread across diverse networks.

Figure 6.1. Corporate Flag.
Source: Adbusters Media Foundation.

Bennett describes intersections between the direct activist networks and networks of more established NGO-centered issue networks as being mutually embedded and acting together, as seen, for example, in the culture jamming campaign against Coca Cola. Here, Greenpeace and Adbusters joined forces to influence the corporation to change its coolants.[5] These conceived intersections will not be the focus of this chapter; rather, the shifts in the nature of civil society organizations networks toward direct activist networks are to be investigated here. Drawing from Bennett, I expect to find that: a) in contemporary transnational anti-corporate campaigns, individual direct activists, empowered by the Internet and consumerist protest repertoires form a rather informal, decentralized organizational backbone, and that b) these campaigns advocate multiple issues by criticizing corporations and/or entire industrial branches.

As Castells' theory of the network society regards social movements to be the cause and effect of the transformation of social, vertically integrated hierarchies into those of flexible networks and ascribing greater heterogeneity to social movements due to the development of the Internet, I resort to the three contextual dimensions introduced by Castells for the empirical analysis: firstly, the *social* context these networks are embedded in, in respect of the cultural questions they address; secondly, the *technical* context providing the real and digital dimension of social movement networks' communication; and thirdly, the *geographical* context, referring to the spatial nodes of a social movement network.[6]

Research Design

By this stage, it should have become clear that the basic unit of analysis for approaching the question of a new era for transnational protest is the campaign itself, understood as a communicative strategy with an outward orientation aimed at generating public attention. Concerning digitalized protest campaigns, I draw upon the notion of campaigns as sociotechnical networks, introduced by Foot and Schneider, in order to consider the various interconnections between the social and the technical.[7] Campaigns may be a suitable unit of analysis for approaching social movements, as here the actors define their frames and publicly participate in conflicts. One should, however, be aware of the limitations, as protest campaigns might not be "necessarily representative for the movement's general strategies, range of actors, action repertoires and the like."[8] Nevertheless, they present a good point of reference for investigating protest, as we are able to find a condensed form of social movement communication and action within them.[9]

Selecting two campaigns for the case study analysis, I refer to the data collected by the research project at the University of Siegen (Germany).[10] In order to answer the question as to whether a new era of transnational protest is on the rise, I have selected the "Clean Clothes Campaign" ("CCC") and the "*Kampagne Lidl ist nicht zu billigen*" (campaign to discount Lidl) ("KL")[11] from the abovementioned research project's sample of 109 anti-corporate campaigns, as both campaigns have set their thematic focus on human and labor rights, which has been done by every fifth campaign in the sample. In addition, these campaigns are organized by networks and network organizations, respectively, as are more than half of the campaigns found in the project's sample. Therefore, they are comparable and reflect to some extent the organizational type and issue focus of the biggest of the sample groups.

Regarding the *social dimension,* mainly cultural aspects will be discussed, because Castells stresses the production of cultural codes by social movements' communicative actions. On the world wide web, culture is seen by Castells as being a social medium: "[w]hile individual experiences may exist outside the hypertext, collective experiences and shared messages—that is culture as a social medium—are by and large captured in this hypertext."[12] The *technical dimension* explores whether, and if applicable to what extent, the Internet is used as part of the campaign's practices of framing, identity building, networking, and mobilizing.[13] In the case of networking, hyperlink analysis has also been carried out.[14] Finally, the *geographical dimension* is studied by applying the analytical differentiation introduced by Schriewer, who, on the one hand, distinguishes between the constructions of frames beyond the nation-state, and, on the other, distinguishes between the construction of social and institutional linkages beyond borders.[15] This can be integrated within the analytical grid offered by Castells, because visible and imagined spaces need to be considered, particularly against the backdrop of cyberspace. The latter emerges on the discursive level and comprehends practices of framing.

Concerning the social dimension as well as the geographical dimension, I will draw examples from framing concepts developed in social science.[16] By doing so, I therefore rely on the concept of mesomobilization,[17] because these campaigns are realized within networks. Common presentations of the collective campaign networks, such as conjointly published leaflets, brochures, and websites, are used here as data, as they represent a shared interpretation "that marks both an internal consensus and what is meant as a position to be presented to the external world."[18] With regard to the "CCC," the website of the European campaign is used as a source for analysis of the master frame, as it presents the overarching presentation of various "CCCs." These master frames are used as a reference in order to explore the discursively constructed geographical dimension of the campaigns. In the social context, it is examined as to how the national campaigns as well as different German network members semantically connect the "CCC" frame with their organization-specific, interpretative frameworks. In the case of "KL," the frame analysis will be restricted to the national level as the campaign's efforts to become a transnational protest campaign based on institutional ties has not been very successful. The reconstruction of the master frames and the frame bridging is conducted using examples from the campaigns. Information to the campaigns' technical dimension is gathered by website analysis. In addition, for the campaigns' contextual dimensions, various campaign artifacts, such as interviews, have been conducted with national organizers and, in the case of the "CCC," also with an initiator on the European level. In order to consider the local perspective, local organizers from both campaigns were interviewed and an online questionnaire was also developed and submitted to activists.[19] This information is reinterpreted against the backdrop of the research question. In each case, Germany represents the spatial analytical frame for the analysis of the national and local levels.

"Kampagne Lidl ist Nicht zu Billigen"

Social Dimension

The campaign against the German-based discounter Lidl was started in summer 2005 by the new social movement actor Attac Germany in cooperation with some of its members[20] and non-Attac members.[21] The campaign ended in the summer of 2006. Calling for social global rights and using the German based discounter Lidl as an example, the campaign criticized the negative consequences of the so-called dumping price strategies of the discounter on differently concerned groups in Germany and beyond. In the framework of the campaign "KL," concrete joint activities and information exchange were especially created, together with the farmer's organization AbL, Banafair (an organization that promotes fair banana trade), and Weed (a NGO endorsing global social justice and ecological sustainability). Furthermore, several references were made to the parallel campaign against Lidl by the trade union ver.di. Seeing itself as a decentralized campaign, Attac Germany felt the need for the implementation of a temporally limited, nationally operating coordination team that representatives of local groups could join. Aside from volunteers, this team was supported by a paid campaigner and a campaign consultant. According to the campaign's evaluation report, the status of the coordination team was critically perceived as implementing a top-down policy. All in all, the bottom line of the evaluation contained the rather sober statement that the self-imposed requirements were set too high, but that the coordination team sees a chance of success for the campaign by evolving it from being a pressure campaign to being a campaign with the character of permanence. For Attac itself, running a decentralized campaign constituted

6.2. Logo of the Attac Campaign Against Lidl.
Source: Used with permission of Kai Oliver Schulze, Attac.

an experiment that could be used to assess to what extent campaigns can be organized on a voluntary basis. In addition to what has been stated, the campaign called for a Europe-wide extension on its website and tried to mobilize other civil society actors outside of Germany.

The master frame of the German campaign combined a general criticism of globalization, including different issues, such as fair trade and global social rights, and prognostic frames,[22] such as a transparent product information policy and democratic control of Lidl's corporate practice:

> [w]ith this campaign *Attac criticises* the causes and disastrous consequences of this form of "Globalisation in the shopping trolley." We are acting against corporations because we believe that it's politically reasonable to stress a concrete phenomenon that can be experienced in everybody's daily life. With this campaign, we are criticizing globalization and consumerism in a way that—this shows us our experiences—is understood by the people easily. Therefore we have formulated demands that are aimed directly at the corporation Lidl, but still leave room for further considerations on a political level:
>
> *[1] Fair prices for bananas, water and milk! ...*
>
> *[2] Social rights for all – here and across the world! ...*
>
> *[3] Allow democratic controls! ...*
>
> *[4] Cards on the table, let's see where the products come from![23]*

Attac consciously recommended only rather vague remedies to the addressed problems, because they strove not to offer "ready-made solutions," but strove instead to launch a public discussion. The diagnostic frame formed a presentation of discounter policy as being a negative consequence of neoliberal globalization, as exemplified by the German-based discounter Lidl. Mobilization framing was achieved by direct calls of action to other organizations, by referencing both high media response and Lidl's reactions, and also by referring to a value-charged discussion in Germany about cutbacks in the social welfare system. This comprising frame offered alignments to the organization-specific framing of the core network members. As already mentioned in the above quotation, the trade union's demands of its autonomous campaign against Lidl were included within the prognostic framing. The other organizations did not make specific statements concerning the campaign on its website, but according to Attac, AbL had already called for protests against Lidl and other discounters since the beginning of 2004, as the discounted price of agricultural products, such as milk, had fallen below the cost of production and was therefore said to endanger the existence of dairy farmers. In the past, BanaFair e.V. and the development organization Weed had already indicated the existing connection between bargain prices in the North and poverty, lack of human rights, and environmental damage in the

South. Within this context, it becomes apparent that the anti-Lidl campaign's framing was strategically built upon frames developed earlier by the network members. Apart from one local Attac group, which, together with the local group "Aktion 3—Welt Saar," focused in its protest on working conditions, all other local groups had adopted the widespread master frame of Attac Germany without any modifications. This proves an internal consistency of Attac, based on decentralization, despite the above-mentioned complaints about a perceived top-down policy.

Technical Dimension

Attac Germany attempted to meet the demands of the campaign logic by attributing a crucial rule to the campaign website. Framing was achieved mainly by the presentation of information provided by the coordination team on the website. The achievement of identity building was attempted by making use of "we" references on the website as well as via the mailing list and email. In their responses to the aforementioned online questionnaire, the German activists confirmed that the website was highly significant and the most important campaign platform: about sixty percent of the activists were informed about the campaign via the website and ninety percent read the campaign's newsletter. Email and mailing lists were rated as the preferred means of communication. In addition, twenty percent stated that they had exchanges with at least ninety percent of their fellow activists only via the Internet. Furthermore, reports, picture galleries of previous actions, and a complete chronology were published online. The website was used to bundle and to merge activities occurring throughout the group, especially in regard to widespread activities of the small local groups. Hence, the campaign "KL" archived more than sixty local activities on the campaign website. Concerning networking activities, the website offset outgoing hyperlinks to all other campaign websites and received incoming hyperlinks from the entirety of the associated campaign websites; the centrality of this website was clearly apparent on the structural level. Whereas more than one-third of the cooperation partners referred to other cooperation partner's websites, virtual references among the local Attac groups' campaign sites were not found. With the campaign aware of its potential to be a European campaign, references to the broader network of promoting the negative consequences of a "globalization in the shopping trolley" were achieved by hyperlinking to similar European campaigns and civil society actors, such as the British campaign Tescopoly and the French NGO Action Consommation. Further references included the US campaigns of "Wake Up Walmart" and "Walmart Watch," but in this context, the national focus of the US-based campaigns were criticized. Additionally, hyperlinks with comments attached were set up to link to two other German campaigns that were active in the past and that were said to be successful historical examples of anti-corporate campaigning. Mobilization was primarily attempted via various calls for participation, such as calls of action on the website, downloadable campaign material, so-called mailomats, and so forth.

Geographical Dimension

The campaign "KL" aimed to become a European campaign. Attac Germany offered campaign descriptions and material in different languages on its website. By these means, Attac Germany firstly communicated its preference for looking for an exchange of information rather than for joint work. Later on, the campaign website called for a European anti-Lidl campaign based on a common strategy. Attac thereby referred to already existent protest actions in other European countries, such as Switzerland, France, Poland, or Sweden. Here, local groups operating close to the French border also played a crucial role, e.g., by maintaining contacts and by translating the campaign's critique into French. In addition, the campaign was presented on the European Attac Meeting in the spring of 2006. Attac saw the transnationalization of the campaign as a consequent continuation in becoming a GJM, operating on the international level. In this context, the call for cooperation connected the establishment of joint strategic campaigns directly to the transnationalization of the GJMs: "[i]nternational networking strengthens international co-operation and brings us closer to the aim of being a globally active anti-globalisation movement."[24] Despite all of these efforts, however, there was no visible European anti-Lidl campaign network. As already mentioned above, the campaign created a transnational dimension by promoting the negative consequences of "globalization in the shopping trolley" by means of hyperlinking to similar European campaigns and civil society organizations. Consequently, the transnational dimension of the campaign could be described as a very feebly structured network of similar campaigns.

As previously illustrated, the Attac campaign raised the issue of the Europewide expansion of Lidl as problematic and called for "global social rights." In addition, the frames of human rights and democracy criticized the international economic operations of Lidl. Attac extended its framing to the global scale, particularly by calling for fair prices for bananas and through the cooperation with the "Banana Campaign" based in Germany. As a result, the campaign's master frame placed emphasis on a truly global dimension by shedding light on the negative consequences of discounterization embedded in a global economic order.

"Clean Clothes Campaign"

Social Dimension

The incident that led to the founding of the "CCC" occurred in 1989. Women in a William Baird (UK) and C&A (NL) subcontracted clothing factory based in the Philippines were fired for demanding a minimum wage. Solidarity and women's organizations in Europe supported the female workers in the Philippines and started campaigning for "clean clothes" by calling for the improvement of working conditions in the textile industries. Following this, the "CCC" was founded in the Netherlands in 1990 and expanded into a Europe-wide network with joint strategies and principles. Six years later, as part of this process, the German "Kampagne für Saubere Kleidung" was established. The "CCC" is now run in ten European countries (Austria, Belgium, France, Germany, Holland, Italy, Spain, Sweden, Switzerland, and the United Kingdom). Although the campaign possesses an international secretariat, the organizers put emphasis on its rather loose structure on the transnational level.[25] However, each national campaign sends a representative to the European Coordination Meeting, which indicates a certain degree of formalization. The national campaigns consist of autonomous coalitions with NGOs (consumer, research, fair trade, youth, and women's organizations as well as solidarity groups), churches, and trade unions. Integration of the latter is of great importance, according to the interviewed research coordinator on the European level: "it is also essential that—if you work with worker organizations—you will also collaborate with organizations that represent workers."[26] Additionally, so-called "project groups" exist in several garment-producing countries, such as Bulgaria and India. Furthermore, the European campaign network is in turn part of a wider network of organizations or coalitions that run similar campaigns in other consumer countries (e.g., US groups, Fair Wear in Australia, Ethical Trade Action Group in Canada) and cooperates with international trade union organizations. In total, approximately two hundred civil society organizations participate in the campaign and in the corresponding sub-campaigns, such as the 2004 "Play Fair at the Olympics Campaign." The strategic character as a European campaign is also expressed in the names of the national campaigns: apart from the English and the French campaigns, all of the campaigns have completely adopted the term "Clean Clothes" or translated it into their national language.

The German "Kampagne für Saubere Kleidung" is currently comprised of eighteen civil society organizations (Christian, ecumenical, youth, and women's organizations, and trade unions). This core network is in charge of decisions and is also responsible for the financial and strategic planning as well as for the framing of the German campaign. Between network meetings, a managing committee supervises the network's affairs. Besides the core national network, a "circle of active members" exists that involves around 150 organizations, associations, groups, and individuals that participate continuously in the campaign on regional and local levels. All institutional bodies—"circle of active members," the managerial committee, and the national network—are managed by the coordination office, which forms the executive element of the German campaign and is in charge of public relations. This organizational structure indicates the character of a strategic campaign based upon professional and financial resources as well as on a joint strategy.

Figure 6.3. Logo of the Clean Clothes Campaign.
Source: Used with permission of Jeroen Merk, Clean Clothes Campaign.

On the European level, the master frame evolves around the issue of labor rights: "[t]he Clean Clothes Campaign aims to improve working conditions and to empower workers in the global garment industry, in order to end the oppression, exploitation and abuse of workers in this industry, most of whom are women."[27] Poor working conditions are defined as problematic by providing elaborate studies and statements concerning the worker's situation in various publications. The importance of the problem is illustrated in single cases through the urgent appeal system (diagnostic framing). The implementation of a code of labor practices by companies, empowerment of workers, ethical consumption, and lobbying for legislation are presented as concrete solutions (prognostic framing):

1. Putting pressure on companies to take responsibility in ensuring that their garments are produced in decent working conditions.

2. Supporting workers, trade unions and NGOs in producer countries.

3. Raising awareness amongst consumers by providing accurate information about working conditions in the global garment and sportswear industry, in order to mobilise citizens to utilise their power as consumers.

4. Exploring legal possibilities for the improvement of working conditions and lobbying for legislation to promote good working conditions and for laws that would compel governments and companies to become ethical consumers.[28]

Motivational framing is achieved by reporting the positive changes that resulted from Europe-wide campaign's actions: "[a]lso—after campaigns directed at their factories—workers have reported changes in the local health & safety circumstances. Especially in the first tier of the subcontracting chain, conditions might have become somewhat better."[29] Moreover, moralization through the use of value-laden terms, such as "responsibility," inherently implies a call to struggle for corporate accountability.

The German campaign—much like the other campaigns[30]—picks up the master frame's leverage points and links them to their networking campaign's members that are using broader frames. In doing so, the German campaign illustrates bridging to the issue of human rights, which is emphasized by the Christian groups: "[c]lean means worthy of a human being, socially clean."[31] Within the German network, further modifications are made by some network members: for instance, the Christliche Initiative Romero e.V. highlights the issue of poverty as a result of corporate policies in their diagnostic frame, whereas Inkota stresses the negative consequence of "free production zones" in producing and consuming countries. The trade union IG Metall underlines the issue of labor rights and Terres des Femmes runs their own sub-campaigns that focus on the issue of women's rights. As on the international level, the different network actors adopt the campaign master frame as an umbrella frame, but draw attention to other related issues.

Even though the European and the German campaigns on the national level offer a common framework for various actors due to their non-elaboration of an overarching frame in an ideological sense and their reference to generally recognized moral norms, contradictory developments exist in this collective network. The Austrian campaign, for example, offers a shopping guide that features a ranking of corporations that are producing more or less socially responsible products, whereas other campaigns such as the German campaign reject the tool of a corporation ranking and recommend a list of "alternative" garment sellers. In general, within the "CCC," the positions range from beliefs of being able to influence corporate and governmental policy by "politics with the basket of goods" to participation in social forums.[32]

Technical Dimension

The European as well as the German website of the "CCC" do not use the Internet to the same extent as the Attac campaign website targeting Lidl. First and foremost, the websites are used to communicate information on the campaign's framing. Besides the comprehensive information presented on the website and through the downloadable studies, there are attempts to accomplish identity building and mobilizing via a downloadable newsletter that also includes the protest activities of local groups and by the so-called urgent appeal system. The European website also offers to send protest emails, while most of the urgent appeals on the German site call for sending letters by mail. Regarding the German campaign, a mailing list does not exist in order to facilitate exchange with and amongst local activists. In contrast to the Internet-based "Attac community," face-to-face group meetings are the preferred platform of exchange, according to the activists. When looking at the campaign's networking structure, the hyperlink structure reflects the position of the European campaign website as a coordinating body, similar to the Attac campaign; the European campaign's online portal publishes a large amount of incoming and outgoing links. This centrality of the European campaign's website is also highlighted as half of the national sites do not include links to each other. Similar to the European level, the national site's centrality is obvious on an initial viewing owing to the many incoming and outgoing hyperlinks. In Germany, not all core network members provide information about the campaign on the Internet, and concerning the campaign itself, the "circle of active members" is not virtually present at all. Only a few hyperlinks can be found among the network members primarily involved in the campaign, but four out of the nine network member websites link to other national initiatives or to the European website. Hyperlinks to campaign projects in producing countries could not be found. In the case of non-members, the website of the "Kampagne für Saubere Kleidung" does not just provide links to external actors, but the European website and some of the other national websites also connect to the larger networks with which the protest campaign is involved. A few links to organizations and campaigns in garment producing countries, such as the "Thai Labour Campaign," are established on the European campaign website. These few North-South hyperlinks indicate a center-periphery structure in favor of a consumer-oriented campaign with a "corporate identity." Hyperlinks to similar campaigns and organizations in consuming countries addressing labor conditions and human rights are more widely available (e.g., to the "American Campaign for Labor Rights," the Canadian Maquila Solidarity Network, the California-based Sweatshop Watch, the British campaign "No Sweat," and the US-based news magazine "Corp Watch"). Thus, the "CCC" is characterized by central network organizations that ensure strategically planned and consistent communication on both European and national online levels, while at the same time the messages are spread across the online networks of diverse movements.

Geographical Dimension

Concerning the institutional dimension, the above-stated empirical insights have already revealed that the "CCC" can be depicted as a network of civil society organizations, which is set up on a European level based on a joint strategy and on rather formalized structures such as regular transnational meetings. Additionally, groups outside of Europe exist, such as in garment producing countries like India. Furthermore, the European campaign network is in turn part of a wider international network of organizations or coalitions. However, the campaign sees itself first and foremost as a European campaign. The position of non-Western members within the network seems to be rather ill-defined: "[o]rganizations who see themselves as partners in a specific CCC project or CCC activity …

find it strange to have the campaign referred to as European, thereby excluding them."[33] The absence of Southern NGOs and trade unions in the inner network circle follows a general trend in transnational civil society, suggesting underlying hierarchies.[34] As previously illustrated, in the context of the campaign's master frame of fair labor conditions as a universal human right links the campaign's demands to a transnational dimension. However, the campaign understands itself to be a European, and not a global, campaign, which focuses on the consumer aspect:

> [y]ou know, the reason why we have a European campaign and not a national or global one is that ... we are, of course, on the consuming side of the world. So that is probably one characteristic—although you have quite a lot of garment production in Eastern Europe, as well; consequently the eastern boundaries are not as sharp as they are in Germany or the Netherlands. I think part of the common identity is that we focus on brands, retailers and consumers on the retail end of the production and that we work with or support groups at the producing end of the chain. Our activities and actions thus are more focused on consumers and on the brands, whereas the trade unions in India focus, for instance, mostly on the manufacturers and the workers.[35]

This address to consumers is once more reflected in the current sub-campaign against the German and European discounter, Aldi, which is criticized for selling clothing produced and supplied by Chinese and Indonesian factories that violate labor laws. A study by the German civil society actor "Südwind" makes suggestions for consumer and trade unions to take action against the negative ends of discounterization.

Comparison

With regard to the *social dimension,* we find network structures in both campaigns, though the organizational structures indicate varying degrees of this. The "CCC" seems to be structured around organizational hubs, whereas the Attac campaign has at least tried to empower the individual also to take part in the campaign's decision-making processes. Likewise, "flexible identities" can be found in both campaigns evolving around Lidl's price dumping policy and working conditions in the garment industry respectively. This is established through cross-fertilization in order to integrate the diverse multiple issues relating to corporate practices that characterize new forms of transnational contention and that direct activist networks. In line with this approach, the civil society organizations' networking campaigns also refer to the consumerist forms of protest for ethical discursive consumption and fair trade respectively. Above all, the "KL" campaign's call for a Europe-wide expansion of the protest illustrates the organizing code based on meta frames, such as diversity and inclusiveness,[36] which allowed the involvement of various civil society organizations of new and old movements, as well as individuals with multiple identities: consumers, workers, and citizens. Moreover, this connection can be interpreted as a common master frame of both campaigns as their framing is:

> neither solely materialistic in the sense of Marxist nor anti-imperialistic or solely postmaterialistic in the sense of Ronald Inglehardt. It is rather a new synthesis of both: a reframing of working-class issues like workers" rights—fair pay, humane working conditions and the right to collectively organise—in a global dimension linked in with middle-class "lifestyle politics" (Bennett) of ethical consumption.[37]

While the analysis of the social dimension revealed that both campaigns are decentralized networking campaigns, address consumers as citizens, and raise multiple issues (even though at a varying extent, seeing as the master frame of the Attac campaign was larger), the *technical dimension* presents differences in web appropriation. The "CCCs" primarily provide the campaign's frames on the website in production mode. By contrast, the campaign by Attac invites co-production, predominantly through the mailing list, and tries to use a range of web applications in order to fulfill framing, identity building, and mobilizing practices. Both campaigns use hyperlinks for the purpose of networking within the campaigns. Moreover, the European "CCC" along with the Attac campaign uses hyperlinks to connect to civil society actors and campaigns outside of Germany and Europe respectively. This, however, already leads to another dimension.

Regarding the *geographical dimension,* both campaigns show that campaigns raising transnational issues are far from being exclusively organized around "transnational social movement organizations," (Smith) such as Greenpeace. Instead, they are mainly rooted at the local and national level. In particular, the Attac campaign has applied what Tarrow has termed as "transposition":

> first transposition allows a domestic movement to embrace transnational commitments without abandoning its domestic claims and those whose needs they try to represent; and, second, it allows a movement to spread through the impersonal ties of the media and the Internet or through weak ties of a brokerage chain, rather than depending on the more intense but narrower ties typical of relational diffusion.[38]

In terms of the integration of Southern actors in online protest work, I can state that the equity between North and South remains a challenge in both campaigns.

When the practice of framing is considered, both market-oriented campaigns inherently represent a form of transnationalism that attempts to incorporate the complex interdependencies of particularly economic globalization into a collective action framework, which is pursuing the goal of political and social change, on the one hand, and, on the other, lacking ideological elaboration. In particular in the case of the "CCC" system, conformity allows the proposal of solutions such as ethical consumption and the implementation and monitoring of codes of conduct and legislation to improve both consumers' rights and sustainable ecological and socially fair production. At this juncture, it is extraordinary but logical that neither campaigns have called for a boycott, standing in contrast to their historical precursors. Surprisingly, Southern groups of the "CCCs" have started to take an interest in extending the development of a consumer movement, which can be seen as an indication of the great mobilization potential of this master frame.

Conclusion: Toward a New Era?

Although both networking campaigns displayed elements of direct action, such as sending individual protest emails to the targeted corporations, the case studies showed that on all levels—European, national, and local—it was rather the stable organizational structures that remain the central hub around which protest action evolves. Likewise, the campaigns revealed "flexible identities" and consumerist repertoires, indicating a new era in transnational contention. However, the logic of campaigning demands characteristics such as centralization, establishment of information regimes, construction of consistent images, and strategic orientation typical for "first generation activism," which is carried out by the coordinating bodies. Altogether, the two campaigns employ a differently proportioned mixture of elements of NGO advocacy networks and of networks of GJM on the organizational level: the network of the "CCC" is characterized by centrality on both international and national levels, but it includes heterogeneous network members, is also rooted in a broader movement framework, and combines permanent and strategic campaigning. Due to the hybrid organizational character of Attac, the campaign "KL" consists of more attributes of a direct activist network, as it also has set up a collective agenda for national and local network members. Nevertheless, this campaign also aims at high media response in order to raise public awareness and discussion, and therefore also being restricted to the development of some kind of centrality that its initiators tried to achieve in the past with the help of a national campaigning team and its presence on the World Wide Web. On the national level, this campaign shows that balancing the inherent contradictions between strategic NGO-style mass media-oriented campaigning and rather decentralized networks seems unfeasible without the presence of a coordinating body. The fact that only a few local websites exist in both campaigns indicates the intention of the central national actors to integrate local activities into the public presentation of the campaign. With respect to the organizational structure, both campaigns confirm the hypothesis of della Porta and Tarrow that recent forms of transnational contention are mainly rooted at the local and national level.[39] Regarding transnationalism, both campaigns show that Europe forms an important context against which the framing strategies are set up. Furthermore, the technique of hyperlinking aids the formation of transnational ties based on ideas, at least in the sense of transposition, but here the rare references to Southern actors also demonstrates the continuing importance of places on the Internet. Regarding the technical dimension, it should be mentioned that both campaigns use the Internet intensively, though in different ways; however, both campaigns used the websites to offer large amounts of background information. Yet, providing information publicly on the Internet about the criticized corporations can be considered as the main "weapon." Power in the analyzed campaigns, as Castells puts it, is "primarily exercised around the production and diffusion of cultural codes and information content."[40] However, the web is a moving target, so the emerging adoption of Web 2.0 applications may open new channels for "second generation activism."

Notes

1. S. Baringhorst, "Political Empowerment of Citizen Consumers—Chances and Problems of Anti-corporate Campaigning on the Net," in *Net Working/Networking: Citizen Initiated Internet Politics,* eds. T. Häythtiö and J. Rinne (Tampere: Tampere University Press, 2008), 281–309.
2. The authors define "flexible identities" as "*identities characterized by inclusiveness and a positive emphasis upon diversity and cross-fertilization, with limited identifications that develop especially around common campaigns on objects perceived as "concrete" and nurtured by search for dialogue.*" S. Tarrow and D. della Porta, "Conclusion: 'Globalization,' Complex Internationalism and Transnational Contention," in *Transnational Protest and Global Activism,* eds. D. della Porta and S. Tarrow (Oxford: Rowman & Littlefield, 2005), 236; emphasis in original.
3. L.W. Bennett, "Social Movements beyond Borders: Understanding Two Eras of Transnational Activism," in della Porta and Tarrow, *Transnational Protest and Global Activism,* 213–216.
4. See also M.E. Keck and K. Sikkink, *Activists beyond Borders. Advocacy Networks in International Politics* (Ithaca and London: Cornell University Press, 1998).
5. Bennett, "Social Movements beyond Borders."
6. Manuel Castells, *The Rise of the Network Society. The information age. Economy, society and culture,* vol. 1 (Oxford: Blackwell, 1996).
7. K. Foot and S.M. Schneider, *Web campaigning* (Cambridge, MA: Massachusetts Institute of Technology, 2006), 14–15. This also stands in line with Castells' analysis, who also considers interrelations between technology and practices of social movements. Castells, *The Rise of the Network Society.*
8. D. Rucht and D. della Porta, "The Dynamics of Environmental Campaigns," *Mobilization* 7(1) (2002): 3.

9. S. Teune, "A Snap-shot of Movements. Assessing Social Movement Diversity through Campaign Analysis?," paper presented to the workshop *Campaign Analysis in a Globalizing World,* Evangelische Akademie Tutzing, 27–28 April 2007.

10. The following presented research design of the project "Changing Protest and Media Cultures" is based on the ideas and work of Prof. S. Baringhorst, V. Kneip, A. März, and J. Niesyto. For more details about the research design, see: http://www.protest-cultures.uni-siegen.de/engl/index.html.

11. In German, the campaign name and slogan consist of a wordplay comprising of the terms "*billig*" (cheap) and "*billigen*" (to approve), used in order to compress the campaign message of the scandalous price and social dumping policies of Lidl.

12. M. Castells, "Informationalism and the Network Society," Epilogue to Pekka Himanen, *The Hacker Ethic and the Spirit of Informationalism* (New York: Random House, 2001), 170.

13. S. Baringhorst, V. Kneip, and J. Niesyto, "Anti-Corporate Campaigns—Netzöffentlichkeit als Arena Politischen Protests," *Forschungsjournal Neue Soziale Bewegungen,* 3(2007): 49–60.

14. In the following, a detailed structural network analysis of the hyperlink structures is not carried out; rather, the presentation of the existence or non-existence of co-links is considered as sufficient in order to explore how technical devices in the World Wide Web are used by the campaigns.

15. Schriewer cited by H. Kaelble, M. Kirsch, and A. Schmidt-Gernig.. "Zur Entwicklung Transnationaler Öffentlichkeiten und Identitäten im 20. Jahrhundert. Eine Einleitung," in *Transnationale Öffentlichkeiten und Identitäten im 20. Jahrhundert,* eds. H. Kaelble, M. Kirsch, and A. Schmidt-Gernig (Frankfurt am Main: Campus, 2002), 10.

16. In a nutshell, the term "framing" is used to conceptualize this signifying work, which is one of the activities that social movements adherents and their leaders do on a regular basis. That is, "they frame, or assign meaning to and interpret relevant events and conditions in ways that are intended to mobilize potential adherents and con-stituents, to garner bystander support and to demobilize antagonists." D.A. Snow and R.D. Benford, "Ideology, Frame Resonance and Participant Mobilization," in *From Structure to Action: Comparing Social Movement Research Across Cultures,* eds. B. Klandermans, H. Kriesi, and S. Tarrow (London: JAI Press, 1988), 198. The resulting products of this framing activity within the social movement arena are referred to as "collective action frames." D.A. Snow, "Framing Processes, Ideology and Discursive Fields," in *The Blackwell Companion to Social Movements,* eds. D.A. Snow, S.A. Soule, and H. Kriesi (Oxford: Blackwell Publishing, 2004), 384.

17. J. Gerhards and D. Rucht, "Mesomobilization: Organizing and Framing in Two Protest Campaigns in West Germany," *The American Journal of Sociology,* 3(1992): 555–595.

18. Ibid., 574.

19. In the case of the Attac campaign, the link to the questionnaire was sent to 700 activists via the campaign's mailing list. The results referred to here include the answers of the seventy-six questionnaires completed between 4 and 25 August 2006. As the German "CCC" has no campaign mailing list, a link to the questionnaire was established on the German campaign website between 12 August and 12 October 2007. The results referred to here include the answers of the 30 completed questionnaires.

20. By name: Aktion Selbstbesteuerung e.V., Arbeitsgemeinschaft bäuerliche Landwirt-schaft e.V. (AbL), the trade union ver.di, and Weed.
21. By name: Banafair e.V. and Kampagne für Saubere Kleidung.
22. In social movement research, different types of frames have been distinguished: framing of identified problems (diagnostic framing), framing of action options and solutions (prognostic framing), and motivational framing, that is, the elaboration of motivational strategies by providing a rationale for action. See D.A. Snow and R.D. Benford, "Ideology, Frame Resonance and Participant Mobilization."
23. Attac, "The Anti-Lidl Campaign, Europe-wide!," retrieved 7 September 2006 from http://www.attac.de/lidl-kampagne/content/campaign/internat/engl/the_anti-lidl_campaign_europe-wide.doc, emphasis in original.
24. Attac, "The Anti-Lidl Campaign, Europe-wide!"
25. Clean Clothes Campaign, "Clean Clothes. International Meeting," 2001, retrieved 7 September 2006 from http://www.cleanclothes.org/ftp/SKO_bracelonadef.pdf.
26. Interview conducted with the research coordinator of the European "CCC" in Amsterdam by V. Kneip and J. Niesyto on 24 August 2007.
27. Clean Clothes Campaign, "FAQs. What does the Clean Clothes Campaign do?," retrieved 18 September 2006 from http://www.cleanclothes.org/faq/faq02.htm.
28. Ibid.
29. Clean Clothes Campaign, "FAQs. Has the Clean Clothes Campaign had any successes in improving working conditions?," retrieved 18 September 2006 from http://www.cleanclothes.org/faq/faq02.htm.
30. On the national level, campaigns such as the Spanish or the English campaign adopt the CCC's master frame in its entirety. Only one national campaign could be found in the framework of the analysis that extended the frame toward a strengthened consumer orientation. The French Campaign "De l'éthique sur l'étiquette" links labor rights to the consumers' rights to information: "De l'éthique sur l'étiquette acts in favour of the compliance of workers' rights in the world and the acceptance of the consumers' rights on information about the social quality of their purchases" (Collectif Ethique sur l'étiquette, "Pour le progrès social," retrieved 18 September 2006 from http://www.ethique-sur-etiquette.org/index.htm (author's translation)). In this manner, the French campaign also puts the issue of workers' rights in the wider context of global social justice: "Le collectif De l'éthique sur l'étiquette is [of] the opinion [that] social progress has to accompany economical progress and development" (Ibid.).
31. Kampagne für Saubere Kleidung, "Die Kampagne im Überblick," retrieved 19 September 2006 from http://www.saubere-kleidung.de/2-fs-wir.htm (author's translation).
32. S. Ferenschild, "Zwischen Konzernkritik und Unternehmensranking. Einflussmöglichkeiten auf Konzerne durch eine Kampagne—das Beispiel der Clean Clothes Campaign," *Inkota Brief,* 136(2006): 12–13.
33. Clean Clothes Campaign, "Clean Clothes. International Meeting."
34. H.K. Anheier and H. Katz, "Network Approaches to Global Civil Society," in *Global Civil Society 2004/5,* eds. H.K. Anheier, M. Glasius, and M. Kaldor (London: Sage, 2006), 220.
35. Interview conducted with the research coordinator of the European "CCC" in Amsterdam by V. Kneip and J. Niesyto on 24 August 2007.

36. Besides Attac, the French civil society organisation "De l'éthique sur l'etiquette" publishes a direct call of action on its website, which is also addressed to other civil society organizations. Collectif Ethique sur l'étiquette, "Pour le progrès social."

37. S. Baringhorst, "New Media and the Politics of Consumer Activism."

38. S. Tarrow, *The New Transnational Activism* (New York: Cambridge University Press, 2005), 139–140.

39. S. Tarrow and D. della Porta, "Transnational Processes and Social Activism: An Introduction," in S. Tarrow and D. della Porta, *Transnational Protest and Global Activism*, 11.

40. M. Castells, *The Internet Galaxy: Reflections on the Internet, Business and Society* (Oxford: Oxford University Press, 2001), 164.

Part III

Broadening
Theoretical Approaches

Chapter 7

From "British Rights for British Citizens" to "British Out"

Dynamic Social Movement Development
in the Northern Ireland Civil Rights Movement,
1960s to 1972

Lorenzo Bosi

The Northern Ireland Civil Rights Movement (hereafter, CRM) between the 1960s and early 1970s shifted from an inclusive, reformist movement to an exclusivist, ethnonationalist one.* What is the explanation for such a significant transformation? This chapter seeks to answer the question by looking at the complex interactions of political opportunities/threats and the internal dynamics and competitiveness between different organizations and groups within the movement. What I am suggesting in this work is that much of the process of social movement development is understandable only by looking at the broader political environment as well as by looking within the movement itself. Seeing social movements as heterogeneous networks that develop interactively over time and through different stages of mobilization, I will then show how shifting political opportunities influence the process of social movement development and how this process is led by the congruence of those mobilizing messages, which best align with the dominant representation of the political environment present at a given stage.

This work draws on a number of qualitative sources: archival materials, secondary sources, accounts of the Northern Ireland newspapers, semi-structured interviews, personal memoirs, and autobiographies. Archival research in several locations (the Special Political Collection at the Linen Hall Library and the Public Records Office of Northern Ireland both in Belfast; and the Conflict Archive on the internet (http://cain.ulst.ac.uk/)) supplied valuable documentation on the CRM. A qualitative examination of Northern Ireland daily newspapers of the time was conducted at the Newspaper Library in Belfast. Between January 2002 and October 2007, I also conducted 35 open-ended semi-structured interviews with former leaders and rank-and-file activists of the CRM.[1] In order to further comprehend participants' subjectivity and to further check the validity and reliability of the semi-structured interviews, I also used personal memoirs and autobiographies.[2]

An Interactive and Dynamic Framework for Assessing Social Movement Development

Collective action is not something outside of mainstream politics that must be studied on its own; on the contrary, "it is a complementary mode of political action"[3] embedded in a complex web of socio and political relations that reciprocally varies over time. Its analysis then must take account of the political historical settings and of other instances of political action in which contention is rooted. As political opportunities/threats change over time, they could favor the mobilizing message of some groups or organizations over others, depending on their congruence with the master frame dominant at that particular stage. For instance, different components of a social movement network will see a possible situation somewhat differently and will propose dissimilar mobilizing messages on what can and should be done in anticipating the next move or reaction of other actors in the political system in order to achieve particular goals.[4] Possible mobilizing messages are then the expression of different readings of what might be feasible in relation to certain sociopolitical situations, but they are also the outcome of ideologies, internal resources, and relevant purposes of determined cohorts. Competition as to what might happen when one is using a determinate repertoire of action, target or ideological frame instead of others is a constant process that takes place within social movements, in which groups and organizations battle to win ground from among the same support base and for similar sectors of public opinion whose interests they wish to represent.[5] Determinate organizations and groups in the movement's internal dynamic competition might also help through proactive processes to create political and cultural opportunities, which will favor their particular mobilizing message instead of others. In this sense, different mobilizing messages are not merely an instrument of competition with an enemy outside of the movement, but they are also a means of beating out political competitors within the movement itself.

Mario Diani[6] has developed a conceptual framework that allows the systematic analysis of how movement mobilizing messages align with the dominant representation of the political environment present at a given stage ("master frames")[7] and how this congruence is shaped by changing political opportunities. Initially, he proposes a combination of two variables: "the opportunities created by the crisis of the dominant cleavages" and "the opportunities for autonomous action within the polity,"[8] both of which depend on actors' subjective evaluations. How does one measure these two variables? Diani has reformulated Tarrow's work on political opportunities,[9] in which the first variable relies on the stability of the socio and political alignments that structure political participation and aggregation, and the second one relies on possible conflicts within the ruling elite, accessibility to participation in the political system, and the availability of influential allies. The way in which the state polices social protest is, in my research, a further component of the opportunities for autonomous action within the polity that determines the mobilization of social movements.[10] The cross-classification of these two variables results then, in Diani's work, in four possible representations of the political system in question, each of them related to a different master frame: "anti-system," "inclusion," "revitalization," and "realignment."[11]

Following Snow and his associates,[12] Diani concludes that for a mobilizing message to succeed, compared to others in a specific period, alignment with the dominant master frame configuration that is associated with the dominant political environment is a crucial determinant. Furthermore, the frame activities should be interpreted as "abstract forms of political rhetoric rather than as belief systems anchored to specific contents,"[13] and the frame alignment should be interpreted as "the integration of mobilizing messages with dominant representations of the political environment."[14] Although this framework helps to avoid "ad-hoc explanations" of social movement mobilization, it does not provide "explicit" dynamic and interactive scenes of collective action mobilization over time, which are essential in understanding changes in a movement development. My work, instead, intends to trace how the internal dynamic competitions between different organizations and groups within the movement are won by the mobilizing message that aligns with the dominant representation of the political environment present at that particular stage. In this way, sectors of a social movement can be in a privileged position to push forward their agendas and strategies over less resonant ones during the movement development. But, as I have said already, groups and organizations may try to formulate strategies

Opportunities for Autonomous
Action within the polity

		HIGH	LOW
Opportunities Created by a Crisis of the Dominant Cleavages	HIGH	Realignment Frames	Antisystem Frames
	LOW	Inclusion Frames	Revitalization Frames

Figure 7.1. Political Opportunities and Master Frames.
Source: M. Diani, "Linking Mobilization Frames and Political Opportunities: Insights from Regional Populism in Italy," *American Sociological Review,* 61 (6) (1996): 1056.

that alter the political environment and the internal composition of the movement and power in their favor. By tracing the activities of these social actors, a
clear and dynamic element of agency is injected into the determinism of Diani's
original schema.

Northern Ireland: An "Imperfect Two Party System"

Between 1921 and 1972, in the Northern Ireland socio and political system,
very little space existed for groups that did not align according to the region's
ethnonational cleavage. Fears of Irish recalcitrant and aggressive irredentism, of
an unreliable British government, and of northern nationalists' disloyal position
within the regime sufficed to keep intact the panclass Unionist alliance and to
justify socio and political domination in the region through an "unambiguously
and unashamedly sectarian" prevailing strategy.[15] The Unionist domination, from
the regime inception until its suspension by London in 1972, was also facilitated
by the ineffective attitude of most of the nationalist community and their refusal
to accept the legitimacy of the Stormont regime. The Nationalist Party's 'absten-
tionist defeatism'[16] never represented a real challenge to the Unionist establishment; its antagonism was taken for granted. Unionist leaders instead constantly
feared and regularly organized against any possible intraunionist class conflict
capable of splitting up the UUP (Ulster Unionist Party) vote support and of
jeopardizing the unionist interests.

The Emergence of the CRM Network
in the Post-Second World War Settlement

Northern Ireland assumed an important strategic international role, which was
of great advantage to the Allies throughout the Second World War and during the Cold War period for NATO; this was also as a result of the Free Irish
State's formal neutrality. The immediate outcomes of this were a reinforcement
in its relations with Britain and, then, a broadening of the social benefits of the
welfare state (result of the Attlee Labor government social welfare legislation),
with a subsequent substantial increase in both the size and role of the state. In
1949, with the Ireland Act, the British Labor government, which was sympathetic in the postwar era to the Northern Ireland elite, solidified the links with
the Stormont regime. This guaranteed that the region would remain part of the
UK unless its parliament decided otherwise. The strengthening of relations with
Westminster, which was also related to the welfare legislation that progressively
increased Stormont economic dependency on subsides from the British Exche-
quer, signified that the UK was to become the framework of comparison for the
Northern Ireland political system. The region was then no longer insulated from

the rest of the United Kingdom, and internationally, as it had been before the Second World War. "Deinsularization" meant progressive international pressure and influence on its home affairs, including the growth of new mass media, and the progressive change of the interpretative context of the sectarian balance of power and the actions that flowed from it. This helped to create a sense of optimism in the postwar environmental change processes among previous networks of affiliations—rooted in the socio and political opposition of the Unionist establishment—that a new political space had opened up on the streets.

The major policy issue in the British postwar era was the aim of a high employment rate, and Northern Ireland was well beyond achieving that. Economic conditions worsened during the late 1950s, setting off trade union demonstrations and deeply straining the interclass alliance that held the UUP together. This resulted in an initial period of instability in political alignments. Between 1949 and 1962, electoral support for political parties and groups that did not take a position on the "partition issue" (the Northern Ireland Labor Party, Independent Labor, and the Liberals) increased from 9.3 percent in 1949 to 23.7 percent in 1953, to 28.7 percent in 1958, and to 37 percent in 1962.[17] The isolated communal sub-cultures that up to this time structured people's daily lives and voting behavior were beginning to decline and these political realignments were instrumental in giving the early CRM activists visions of what might be possible. "Revisionist" constructive Nationalist reformers, "new look" republicans, trade unionists, and students drawing on "new leftist" ideology began to consider the costs and benefits of challenging the current political stalemate. Despite groups' and organizations' differences, they agreed at this point on the need to redress the grievances of discrimination, avoiding the partition issue, and provided the core of the movement with significant information, organizational settings, and material resources for recruitment and the successive visible mobilization. What matters for our purposes is that different cohorts of activists began to forge new ties and relationships spanning several groups, in order to "symbolically produce" a reformist mobilizing message of civil rights, social justice, and progressive politics, one that was capable of challenging the perceived second class citizenship status of the nationalist community in the socio and political context of the 1960s.

The fear of losing the urban working class unionist vote, because of the decline of the staple industries and the economic difficulties of the late 1950s and early 1960s, increased concerns among the establishment about the change in the UUP's political direction. Therefore, conscious that "banging the tribal drum was no longer sufficient"[18] in the new social and political conditions of the region, the Unionist establishment appointed Terence O'Neill as the new Prime Minister, on 25 March 1963. O'Neill opened a palliative process of "rhetorical" social reforms and better relations with the nationalist community. O'Neill's goals were, first, to regain the working class unionist vote, and, second, to relaunch unionism as a political project for the future of Northern Ireland. This was a political change that in the short-term gained success in the 1965 parliamentary elections, with a swing of 7 percent of the electorate to the Ulster Unionist Party, but one which frightened and alienated one part of the unionist community who thought O'Neill had gone too far. In particular, the western and border Unionist elites were opposed to O'Neill's modernism; they were afraid of losing control of their areas and ultimately of the ability of Northern Ireland to be governed.[19] But indecisiveness and a lack of courage to strike was dominant among mainstream Unionists; this in turn left room for action by the Reverend Ian Paisley, who promoted a Protestant Loyalist political agenda, suitable for that strata of the unionist community that "either experienced unemployment or faced the threat of it."[20]

The conflict division within the Unionist elite was perceived again as a favorable opportunity for launching a civil rights campaign in the region by pre-existing networks of affiliations.[21] The issues of civil rights, equality, and social democracy started to broaden across the region, and rapidly caused the creation of several groups and organizations with very different, frequently conflicting, aims, strategies, and ideas, a group which would later represent the organizational structure out of which the CRM was to develop in the late 1960s. The emerging latent CRM network united at this stage around a course of action, that of achieving full equal rights in Northern Ireland for everyone. As Fergus O'Hare, a radical activist from West Belfast, recalls:

> One of the arguments that some people would have been making at the time as part of the Civil Rights Movement was for "British Rights, for British Citizens." The argument was that while we might not particularly want to be British citizens, but if we were deemed to be British citizens then we wanted the same rights as other British citizen were entitled to.[22]

In working for reforms at this stage of the political development of Northern Ireland, different groups focused on very different things. There were those who looked at achieving socio and political inclusion in the Stormont regime (the "revisionist" constructive Nationalist reformers and the laborists), and those who sought to campaign for civil rights merely in order to undermine it. Among this latter strand of people, many thought that a civil rights agitation could be used to destabilize the Northern Ireland state and that, as a result, the future unification with the Republic of Ireland would come about much more quickly (a new anti-partitionist tactic coming from republican rethinking). But there was also a minority, caught up in the naivety of the international radicalism of the 1960s, who imagined the possibility of building a Socialist Republic capable of breaking down political divisions and rejecting both "green" and "orange" traditions (the "new" leftists).[23]

The Mass Mobilization of the CRM Network

The incapacity of Terence O'Neill to deliver the reforms promised by the regime, as he feared jeopardizing the UUP power in front of the emerging division inside Unionism, caused considerable frustration and resentment within the nationalist community. This immobility called into question whether indeed "opportunities for autonomous action by challengers"[24] were really available. Also, influenced by the international repertoire of direct action, some sections in the CRM network started then to believe that they had no alternative but to leave out legal tactics such as petitions, letter writing, leaflet production, and public meetings and instead started to take to the streets with marches and demonstrations.[25] Eamonn McCann, looking back in a recent interview, recalls:

> despite all the expectations of Terence O'Neill's alleged reforms, he was not delivering anything terribly meaningful, so the rising hope of the nationalist community was becoming frustrated and that created the situation on how people started to listen to suggestions such as: let's go on to the streets and start to push this process forward rather then depending on the good will of the UUP.[26]

The result was a new and innovative repertoire of contention that used a form of symbolic provocation inspired by the Northern Ireland tradition of communal marches and parades, combined with non-violent confrontational action that mimicked performances that had been seen on television in the US Black civil rights movement. Austin Currie, at the time a young Nationalist Party MP for East Tyrone and one of the initiators of the street campaign of the CRM, recalls in his autobiography:

> I had identified with the struggle of African-American for emancipation and equal treatment and had observed with keen interest the development of the civil rights campaign in America ... I was of the opinion that civil rights marches, if properly organized and controlled, could make a major contribution to publicising the true state of affairs in Northern Ireland, both in Britain and internationally and thereby result in the necessary British government pressure on the Stormont government.[27]

The competition between moderates and radicals within the movement was on the rise, when it had become apparent in many CRM activists' view that the reformist mobilizing message, with its legal tactics, would not bring about the expected changes in the region. It was then progressively, consciously, and strategically replaced by a more radical one, by one part of the movement, in order to disorientate the elites and attract media attention. The radical mobilizing message really challenged the legitimacy of the political system's rules of the region through new unconventional and confrontational disruptive forms of protest, but they were still non-violent. Strategically, they were meant to embarrass the Unionist establishment in front of the British public and Westminster at an international level. The radical mobilizing message successfully aligned at this stage with an emerging anti-system master frame, whose structural conditions included the crumbling of traditional alignments along with the perception of poor opportunities for autonomous action within the system. Put simply, a mobilizing message that reflected the anti-system master frame was better able to exploit the political opportunities of 1968. It should be remembered that the CRM network was not unanimous in such a radical shift. From within the CRM, the moderate component became exposed to the lack of effectiveness of their repertoire of action. Its reformist mobilizing message was less consistent with the anti-system frame of late 1968. Moderate leaders were afraid to use direct action tactics, which in their view would have led to widespread dangerous sectarian violence and communal conflict in the region as in the past (1930s), and as actually happened later. Radicals, instead, influenced by the international mood of the late 1960s, abandoned the moderate tactics and moved to their more familiar way of action in order to push the struggle forward. They were convinced that in raising a Civil Rights' struggle against the Northern Ireland regime, they would appeal to sections of the unionist working class, in the name of an abstract solidarity between the oppressed. The shift was also motivated in order to embarrass the moderate CRM leaders and establish a principal role for themselves within the movement. Radicals, in fact, became progressively impatient with the slow pace of opposition from the moderates, and thus they finally decided to find their legitimacy outside in the streets by radicalizing the conflict and hoping to move sections of Northern Ireland society toward their political aims. Moderate leaders, on the other side, who were afraid of losing the direction of the movement, then started to adopt unconventional tactics as well (such as squatting, sit-downs, strikes, protests, marches, and demonstrations). The complex reciprocal dynamic of the CRM's internal competition with the political opportunity changes of the late 1960s favored, at this stage, a radical mobilizing message.

The success of a mobilizing message in promoting and raising collective action mobilization is also contingent upon particular events and happenings that surround that particular social movement network. As a consequence of this tactical shift, a "transformative event" occurred in Londonderry on 5 October 1968. This was the second civil rights march that had been scheduled under the new tactical repertoire. The RUC (Royal Ulster Constabulary), the Northern Ireland police, responded violently to the march by beating unarmed demonstrators with batons and using potent water cannon even over bystanders. The violent images of police brutality were captured by a cameraman for Radio Telefís Eireann and shown throughout the world. The events of that day galvanized the movement and made it visible worldwide overnight. Fionnabarra O'Dochartaigh, at the time a radical member of the CRM, recalls: "If the State had ignored us, the Civil Rights Movement would have died in three or five months. The Unionists over reacted, I was the happiest man in the world, things would have never been the same again, they killed the apathy inside the Nationalist community. We got a mass movement almost overnight."[28] Images of the RUC's violence that day "inflamed and exacerbated feelings of resentment,"[29] and played "a significant role in fostering a sense of affective engagement, common identity and solidarity between the CRM and the wider Nationalist community."[30] Intense anger at the violence mobilized undergraduates, both unionist and nationalist, who framed the RUC's repressive tactics in terms of the events of May 1968 and the broader student movement around the world.

On the other side, the radical turn of the CRM alienated most of the moderate unionists who had had sympathy for the cause of civil rights at its beginning. The Unionist establishment framed the CRM challenge as a threat to the Northern Ireland's status quo and downplayed the violence used by the police in Londonderry. William Craig, Minister of Home Affairs at the time, branded the movement as a conspiracy to overthrow Northern Ireland's institutions.[31] We should remember that the UUP was also constrained to support the aggressive repression of the police if it was to hold power in front of a growing Loyalist countermovement inside of its own community. Nevertheless, pressed by Westminster, O'Neill announced a five-point program of reforms (22 November 1968) that dealt with most of the CRM's demands.[32] But it was too little, too late, for the nationalists.

Conflict and Decline in the CRM Network

While the moderate sectors of the CRM decided for a pause of agitation in order to give the reforms a chance and to allow the situation to normalize, radicals mocked the moderate's moratorium decision and announced on 20 December 1968 that they would stage a march between Belfast and Londonderry between 1–4 January 1969. It was a "calculated martyrdom," consciously organized in order to discredit the Unionist establishment and to challenge sectarianism.[33] Radicals intended to expose how far O'Neill was prepared to go in using the force of law in order to deny their right to demonstrate.[34] Using this strategy, radical activists attempted to transform a possible moment of mass anger into a political movement critical of the Northern Ireland legal system, for either socialist or republican purposes. Rory McShane recently remarked:

> The fact that this process started [O'Neill's reforms] was an encouragement rather than a disincentive; I think that because the process had

started it was showing that the political establishment was beginning to allow for some movement, it was a positive influence on us to continue to mobilize and campaign. Because we felt there was evidence of getting somewhere, we thought we should pressurize and mobilize further. That was the beginning, but it was not enough, but we kept pushing because the door was open.[35]

Moderates in the CRM strongly condemned the march, and regarded it as strategically ill advised. Paddy Joe McClean remembers how:

The Northern Ireland Civil Rights Association was particularly opposed to the PD march between Belfast and Derry, and I was one of the voices that opposed that. Because I knew from my background in rural districts the provocation that that would bring to the surface and the violence that would ensue, and heightening of sectarian tension, and that happened. But we opposed that.[36]

From the beginning, the march was characterized by violence and brutality. Loyalists saw it as a confrontational tactic. The worst came toward the end of the march, when two hundred Loyalists, with the collusion of the RUC, attacked about five hundred marchers in Burntollet, six miles from Londonderry. That night, widespread rioting broke out in Londonderry, and barricades went up for several days. Journalists had shadowed the march from start to finish, and the brutal incidents were once again given international media exposure. It was becoming clear that Northern Ireland was becoming more polarized along sectarian lines and falling into communal disorder. Mike Morrisey, a young activist of the Northern Ireland Communist Party, speaking after on the Belfast-Londonderry march, observed:

After the Burntollet ambush it was almost impossible to involve people in a non-violent strategy, there were just too many forces determined to engage in violence. This was almost the death of NICRA and its strategy, after that what I think is that the Civil Rights Movement became increasingly perceived as a Nationalist struggle as opposed to a Democratic struggle.[37]

Moderate activists in the CRM network started at this stage to pursue change through legislative arenas, progressively abandoning street politics and then the CRM. Denis Haughey recalled:

The march between Belfast and Derry was in my view an irresponsible exercise which would provoke political violence. And it was at that stage that I began to have concern that the sectarian violence, which was provoked by a minority of irresponsible students, was going to distract attention from the real problems of our society, and by the end of 1969 I began to be convinced that the only thing we needed was a coherent political approach, a coherent political party which would work on social justice issues.[38]

In February 1969, elections for the Stormont parliament showed that support for political parties that did not identify themselves on the partition issue dropped significantly to 11.7 percent. It appeared that the newly embraced Nationalist mobilizing message of the CRM network proved now to be the most realistic option. It better reflected changed political opportunities and successfully aligned with the revitalization master frame, that is, the restoration of the traditional, ethnonational political cleavage along with the perception of poor opportunities for autonomous action. The revitalization master frame at this stage resulted from the dynamic interplay of structural conditions, institutional and organizational constraints, individual actors, and transformative events.

While the radicals were able to draw the Unionist establishment and the Loyalist countermovement into overreacting against the CRM, they were incapable of directing the reaction of the movement and of the new waves of participants who entered at that stage, mainly because the changed political situation left an incongruence between their mobilizing message and the master frame that then became dominant.[39] Radicals, like moderates, were still partly involved in the campaign, but they lost the possibility of leading the people in the streets under their strategy and aims. Their old mobilizing messages had a lack of consistency with the new revitalization master frame. The inclusive, anti-sectarian, and polycentric collective identity of the CRM's first stage was now gradually replaced by an exclusive communal identity. The political issues at stake passed from civil rights reforms to the overthrow of the Unionist state and the subsequent unification of Ireland. The composition of the movement also changed. The new ethnonationalist message activated many participants from the Nationalist "ghettos," with a significant number of young working class activists and "rock throwers," whose backgrounds differed significantly from participants in the CRM's early stages of mobilization. Fergus O'Hare, at the time a young radical activist from West Belfast, attested to the intensified air of tension and feeling of threat in nationalist working class neighborhoods.

The police started to attack nationalist areas, and they attacked the Bogside at the beginning of 1969. Up until then we had been arguing for peaceful direct action, but when police started to attack people's homes it was no longer a question of sitting down peacefully, the question of defending your homes became a major issue for the movement. And then the question of defence of areas arose. When the police were using guns against people, the issue of military defence, and in the Irish context the issue of the IRA, came on the agenda. So the nature of the conflict and of the struggle began to change, the forces of the State became more hostile, more militarized and more directed on people's homes and the issue of defence and that sort of activity came onto the agenda. That's when IRA started reforming.[40]

Civil resistance (barricades, vigilantes, citizens' defense committees) replaced civil disobedience, and from then on the nonviolent and anti-sectarian strategies of the CRM network were progressively overtaken by violent communal conflicts. Sectarian disorder continued and on 12 August, the traditional Loyalist Apprentice Boys' march in Derry triggered three days of rioting between the Northern Ireland police and nationalist inhabitants in what became known as "The Battle of the Bogside."[41] Other demonstrations were organized across Northern Ireland in order to divert police resources away from Londonderry. This set in motion a chain of events where the ensuing rioting in Belfast resulted in the deaths of five nationalists and two unionists, 154 gunshot wounds, and 745 other injuries.[42] On 14 August, given the breakdown in relations between the regional authorities and the nationalist community, the British government reversed its standard policy of decades and agreed to send the British Army onto the streets to restore order. In a matter of days, they had deployed several thousand troops across the region, and an atmosphere of calm started to prevail. To the disgust of the Republicans, the Northern Ireland nationalist working class neighborhoods welcomed the British Army. But the honeymoon with the Army did not last long and a new Irish Republican armed campaign shortly reemerged, inflaming nationalist and republican sentiments. The initial CRM slogan of "British Rights, for British citizens" was now replaced by the cry of "Brits Out!"

Conclusions

Contentious scholars have predominantly treated social movements as invariant across time, leaving almost underdeveloped our knowledge of their development. The approach proposed in this chapter allows instead, for a long range, context sensitive analysis of the processes of movement development and moves away from the ahistorical nature of much of the literature, by assessing the dynamic process of social movement development over time and by looking at the intersection of political opportunities, master collective action frames, and mobilizing messages. This is an approach that highlights how the external political opportunities and internal competition interact to shape movement organization, composition, identity, and strategy.

Drawing on temporal changes in Mario Diani's schema, we saw how the Northern Ireland CRM changed from a peaceful and reformist movement to a militant insurgency, at least in part through the constraining force of dominant master frames. We saw that as political structures change, broad schemata of interpretation, or master frames, shape the perceptions of social movement participants so that some mobilizing messages and some collective identities are favored over others. Indeed, this means that some groups, some leaders, and some individuals within a diverse movement network will be privileged—some voices will be heard above others, and some actions will carry the day, while others will fall flat in the internal power struggle between different groups and organizations. Because all social movements are composed of a heterogeneous and emergent multi-actor dynamic, the CRM case points to processes that trace how social movements change more generally, highlighting the interplay among structure, culture, and agency.

Notes

* This chapter is a revised version of an article I published in 2006 on *Mobilization*. My thanks to Manlio Cinalli, Mario Diani, Richard English, Hank Johnston, and Chris Rootes for their comments on earlier versions of this argument. I want also to thank the ESRC (Economic and Social Research Council) for its support grant: PTA-026-27-1317.

1. I identified initial respondents from those who were prominent in the historical records of the movement and sampled names so as to achieve a representation of different background characteristics—political, ethnic, class, gender, forms of participation, and region. At the end of each interview, I asked for names of other possible respondents and proceeded to construct a snowball sample of ex-CRM participants from that pool.

2. D. della Porta, "Biographies of Social Movement Activists: State of the Art and Methodological Problems," in *Studying Social Movements,* eds. M. Diani and E. Eyerman (London: Sage, 1992), 168-193.

3. J. Goldstone, "More social movements or fewer? Beyond political opportunity structures to relational fields," *Theory and Society,* 33 (3/4)(2004): 337.

4. Different political actors, in trying to make sense of the mix of change processes that occur in the political system, simultaneously and interactively "engage in a series of actions in response to others, anticipating their reactions in turn," J. Jasper, *Getting Your Way* (Chicago: The University of Chicago Press, 2007), 6.

5. Competition within social movement is not only the result of power struggles and ideological disputes, but might be at the same time also provoked by external enemies in order to split the movement. Our effort should be, then, to explain how the external contexts and internal competition interacts and shapes each other in complex ways.

6. M. Diani, "Linking Mobilization Frames and Political Opportunities: Insights from Regional Populism in Italy," *American Sociological Review,* 61 (6)(1996): 1053–1069.

7. D.A. Snow and R.D. Benford, "Master Frames and Cycles of Protest," in *Frontiers in Social Movement Theory,* eds. A. Morris and C. Mueller (New Haven, CT: Yale University Press, 1992), 133–155.

8. Diani, "Linking Mobilization Frames and Political Opportunities," 1056.
9. S. Tarrow, *Power in Movement. Social Movements, Collective Action and Politics* (Cambridge: Cambridge University Press, 1994).
10. D. della Porta and H. Reiter, *The Policing of Protest* (Minneapolis: Minnesota University Press, 1998).
11. Diani, "Linking Mobilization Frames and Political Opportunities," 1056–1057.
12. D. Snow, B. Rochford, S. Worden, and R.D. Benford, "Frame Alignment Processes, Micromobilization, and Movement Participation," *American Sociological Review* 51 (4) (1986): 464–481.
13. Diani, "Linking Mobilization Frames and Political Opportunities," 1058.
14. Ibid., 1058.
15. J. Ruane and J. Todd, *The Dynamics of Conflict in Northern Ireland: Power Conflict and Emancipation* (Cambridge: Cambridge University Press, 1996), 121.
16. J. McGarry and B. O'Leary, *The Politics of Antagonism: Understanding Northern Ireland* (London: Athlone Press, 1996).
17. S. Elliott, *Northern Ireland Parliamentary Election Results 1921–1972* (Chichester: Political Reference Publications, 1973).
18. H. Patterson, *Ireland Since 1939* (Oxford: Oxford University Press, 2002), 183.
19. Close to the border with the Republic of Ireland and in the western part of the region, Unionists were a minority if compared with Nationalists. To maintain their power, the discrimination system was essential.
20. G. Walker, *A History of the Ulster Unionist Party: Protest, Pragmatism and Pessimism* (Manchester: Manchester University Press, 2004), 158.
21. *Tuairisc*, No. 7, August 1966.
22. L. Bosi's interview, 19 February 2004, with Fergus O'Hare, at the time a student at University College Dublin and a member of People's Democracy; he is now involved in social justice and cultural activities.
23. L. Baxter et al., "Discussion on the Strategy of Peoples Democracy," *New Left Review*, 55 (1969): 3–19.
24. Diani, "Linking Mobilization Frames and Political Opportunities," 1057.
25. The daily reports in the *Belfast Telegraph* and in the *Irish News* during June and July 1968 are excellent accounts that highlight the internal debate that took place within the Nationalist community, and more broadly in the CRM network, on the shifting of strategy toward civil disobedience and confrontational tactics. See also NICRA's (Northern Ireland Civil Rights Association) official history records: Northern Ireland Civil Right Association, *We Shall Overcome: The History of the Struggle for Civil Rights in Northern Ireland, 1968–1978* (Belfast: Northern Ireland Civil Right Association, 1978), 20.
26. L. Bosi's interview, 22 October 2003, with Eamonn McCann, at the time a journalist, active in the Londonderry branch of the NILP (Northern Ireland Labor Party) from the mid 1960s until the early 1970s, member of the Derry Housing Action Committee and the Derry Unemployment Action Committee; he is now a commentator and Civil Rights activist.
27. A. Currie, *All Hell Will Break Loose* (Dublin: O'Brien Press, 2004), 99.
28. L. Bosi's interview, 8 June 2004, with Fionnbarra O'Dochartaigh, at the time an unemployed, activist in the Republican movement in Londonderry during the

1960s, a member of the Derry Housing Action Committee and the Derry Citizens' Action Committee, founding member of the Irish Republican Socialist Party; now she is a Civil Rights activist.

29. Cameron Report, *Disturbances in Northern Ireland,* Cmd 532, HMSO, Belfast, 1969: 93.
30. E. Graham and M. Garry, "Policing, Collective Action and Social Movement Theory: The Case of the Northern Ireland Civil Rights Campaign," *British Journal of Sociology,* 51 (4) (2000): 681–699.
31. *Newsletter,* 7 and 17 October 1968.
32. Cabinet Conclusions, PRONI CAB/4/1412–1419.
33. M. Farrell, *Twenty Years On* (Co. Kerry Dingle: Brandon, 1988).
34. E. McCann, *War and an Irish Town* (Harmondsworth: Penguin Book, 1974).
35. L. Bosi's interview, 14 October 2003, with Rory McShane, at the time Students' Union president at Queen's University, having early involvement in the Irish Workers' Group, member of the NILP and active in People's Democracy; he is now a solicitor.
36. L. Bosi's interview, 28 October 2003, with Paddy Joe McClean, at the time a secondary school teacher, member of the NICRA. Today, he is involved in social justice activities.
37. L. Bosi's interview, 13 October 2003, with Mike Morrisey, at the time a student at Oxford University, member of the Communist Party of Northern Ireland and of the Northern Ireland Civil Rights Association. Today, he is a professor at Ulster University.
38. L. Bosi's interview, 10 October 2003, with Denis Haughey, at the time a secondary school teacher and member of NICRA, later a Stormont MP for the SDLP (Socialist and Democratic Labour Party). Today, he is active in social justice and political activities.
39. L. Bosi, "Social Movement Participation and the 'Timing' of Involvement: the Case of the Northern Ireland Civil Rights Movement," *Research in Social Movements, Conflicts and Change,* 27 (2007): 37–61.
40. L. Bosi's interview, 19 February 2004, with Fergus O'Hare, at the time a student at University College Dublin, member of PD; he is now involved in social justice and cultural activities.
41. N. O'Dochartaigh, *From Civil Rights to Armalites* (New York: Palgrave, 2005), 104–114.
42. Scarman Tribunal, *Report of Tribunal of Violence and Civil Disturbances in Northern Ireland,* Cmnd 566, HMSO, Belfast, 1969.

Chapter 8

Anarchism, Franco's Dictatorship, and Postwar Europe

High-Risk Mobilization and Ideological Change

Eduardo Romanos

Historians have traditionally considered Spanish anarchism to be the most suc-cessful variant of the international libertarian movement.[1] Most of them also believe that the terminal point of that variant came soon after the end of the Spanish Civil War (1936–1939) and Franco's dictatorship (1939–1975) came to power.[2] This chapter agrees with the first assumption, but considers the sec-ond to be open to question. Spanish anarchism indeed succeeded in creating a specific political culture and became a major political force in the first decades of the twentieth century. According to established opinion, harsh repression, familial rivalries, and the inability to bring ideology and tactics up-to-date have traditionally been considered the main explanations for the decline in 1939. However, this view corresponds with a lack of research on the post-Civil War pe-riod. I will critically confront the argument of ideological paralysis by analyzing the redefinition process of traditional "principles, tactics, and ends" carried out by the clandestine movement in the first years of dictatorship, and the relation of this ideological evolution to the repressive domestic and broader international contexts within which these ideas were formulated.

In the first part of the chapter, I will assess the political logic of those anar-chist activists who attempted to overcome traditional ideological positions. My attention then turns to the personalities and circumstances that influenced this ideological change from the outside, both in terms of the sociopolitical condi-tions of the international arena and the intellectual innovations advanced by left-libertarian thinkers in the aftermath of the Second World War. Finally, I underline the necessity for careful analysis when considering the relationship between Francoist repression and anarchist dissent, in terms of its evolution over time and taking into account how dictatorship and opposition dealt with the postwar international context after 1945. Thus, this chapter directly addresses what Loveman termed the "paucity of explicit attempts in the social movement literature to explain the emergence of sustained collective action in contexts of life-threatening risk."[3] According to a multi-factor explanation of the dynamics of high-risk activism,[4] I will discuss how opportunities, hope, and ideology converged in this particular case.

Fighting the Tyrant and Kropotkin's Beard

Once the Spanish Civil War was over, the defeated political forces began to question the reasons for failure. In the libertarian movement, these discussions were linked with other wartime debates about how to reinvigorate the war and the social revolution that the anarchists were organizing in the form of industrial and agrarian collectivization, and about how to manage to engage in both at the same time. In both the proceedings of meetings organized during wartime and the letters written by militants in postwar exile, we can identify the configuration of a strong trend toward the rectification of the traditional ideological background, which was defined in some occasions as "old procedures," "the Kropotkin's beard," or just a "burden" that was necessary to throw away.[5] Others opposed the evolution by mobilizing the "essence" and the "fundamental assumptions" of the historical movement against the "moral suicide" and "spiritual debacle" promoted by some of the reformers.[6] The National Meeting held in October 1938 in Barcelona offers a clear example of this confrontation. After thirteen sessions, the anarcho-syndicalist trade union Confederación Nacional del Trabajo (CNT), on the one side, and the anarchist organization Federación Anarquista Ibérica (FAI) and the youth organization Federación Ibérica de Juventudes Libertarias (FIJL), on the other, failed to reach a common agreement on tactics and their ideological progenitors and principles. The general secretary of the CNT defined some of the classical principles as a "literary and cultural heritage [that] have made the atmosphere tense and damaged us in the extreme." His counterpart in the FAI defended the same heritage and recommended that those who disagreed should "separate from them." At the end of the dispute, one of the delegates at the meeting pronounced a premonitory statement: "we are doomed to a rupture."[7]

The rupture finally came in 1945. The event that provoked this division was the decision of certain anarchists to join the republican government-in-exile, but many other causes were at stake: personal jealousies, accusations of negligence in war and exile, as well as ideological differences. It is not the aim of this chapter to detail the historical genealogy of this conflict. Rather, what is relevant here are subsequent events. From this point onward, those who aimed to collaborate with other political forces in the search for a diplomatic solution to Franco's dictatorship, and those who refused to compromise their traditional isolation from the political "game," moved into confrontation with one another. The clandestine committees in Spain, supported by an important group of exiles, adopted the former line, while the official CNT-in-exile adopted the latter. Two years after the rupture, the exiled maximalists underwent a process of radicalization or "ideological recovery," through which they came to define a Republic as a mere "transfiguration of the authority principle," and proposed traditional isolation from normative political process and insurrection as the sole revolutionary strategy, aiming for libertarian communism without transitional stages.[8] At the same time that they were defending these formulas, their rival group began to introduce new terms to the anarchist ideological vocabulary.

Existing work in the field has highlighted differences between the tactics and modes of organization of classical Spanish anarchism and republicanism, as well as noted some affinities in their ideological principles.[9] Evidence of such affinities can be found in some anarchists' biographies, whose political socialization began in local republican groups in the early 1930s.[10] Under Franco's dictatorship, these bonds grew stronger. Clandestine anarchists mobilized new principles and values in what may be termed the *classical republican image.* The anarchist press urged "the subjugated people," who lived under the threat of repressors who engaged in "armed violence with impunity," to put an end to "the tyrannical domination of the despot." The removal of the tyrant formed "the starting point for all liberties." New values entailed "the most elementary liberties" and "individual rights." The CNT substituted proletariat emancipation "for dignity and liberties for all levels of society, according to doctrines of equity."[11]

Under the postwar dictatorship, these new values and principles, which were mobilized by members of the clandestine movement, were translated into concrete proposals for political action that were bound up in a logical trajectory, which began with the defense of the Second Republic (in July 1945), continued with the promotion of a referendum once the dictatorship would be defeated (March 1946), and, for a brief period, would justify a monarchic coup d'etat (December 1949). All of them looked for the same end: liberation from Franco's dictatorship toward a regime where trade unions and the entire libertarian movement could freely develop. This objective recalls the *legalist* approach promulgated during the Primo de Rivera dictatorship (1923–1930), when the *possibilists* defended the "trade-union state" against the "anarchist utopia."[12] Nevertheless, the Spanish Civil War forced a strong rupture with the past. From July 1936, the CNT joined forces with the republicans against Franco, and transformed their previous anarcho-syndicalism into a more politically based approach, and remodeled past revolutionary alliances into a program geared toward national liberation rather than social revolution.

Although public liberties and rights were elements of anarchist ideology in the past, they worked in different ways from the 1940s onward. The classic defense of personal freedom in spheres such as culture and sexual behavior was embodied in a nineteenth-century discourse directed toward a total revolution, which was conceived in terms of the emancipation of the proletariat. In contrast, the postwar period saw the replacement of revolution and emancipation with more concrete mobilization principles, which were linked to the image of the republican struggle against tyrannical power.[13] Over time, the emphasis on the restoration of the Republic would shift to "democracy," rhetoric that had been previously mentioned only when clandestine press attempted to engage an allied commitment to topple Franco. Formal, and even capitalist, democracy would then facilitate the development of a new "humanist and revolutionary syndicalism," which appeared in the mid 1960s as an alternative to both capitalism and communism. This new syndicalism aimed to substitute the class struggle with global emancipation as well as to replace the violence linked to spontaneous insurrections with non-violent, everyday methods.[14]

In 1946, when the clandestine CNT press called for the "tyrant's removal," the organization specified the way in which this tyrannicide should be effected: not by "sporadic acts and useless sacrifices," but by "decisive acts" within political and diplomatic processes.[15] The same actors continued to hope for "an end to the oppressive regime without pointless violence" throughout the following decades.[16] Many of the organization's members had been involved in the "revolutionary gymnastics" of the 1930s, when collective violence had been described as the "fires of purification flame" or "the holy wrath of the people," but post-Civil War anarchists did not want to return to these scenes of hardship.[17] They came to reject violence as a means of reaching a better society. A source for this new strategy was the lived experiences of these anarchists who had performed action in the streets, or in the trenches, or in jails. As we will see below, a further factor was intellectuals' criticism of the supposed regenerative violence of "a certain idea of revolution."

Before turning to analyze some of the sources for anarchism's ideological shift, I would like to pose briefly some preliminary points of discussion on clandestine organizing. First, it is important to note that after their defeat in the war, the member organizations of the Movimiento Libertario got together around the remains of the CNT.[18] The clandestine trade union was led by a highly politicized and committed minority that aimed to maintain the historical force of the CNT by reproducing classical confederation-style structures under extreme persecution and repression. They failed, and the Francoist forces of repression won out. The confederation-style structure and process of open recruitment—both being elements of libertarian organizational identity—caused a domino effect. Until 1952, fifteen national committees of the CNT, the top level of the organization, fell and dragged down numerous of their regional and local counterparts with them.[19] Increasingly, these committees became affinity groups with little representation, nominally replacing one another after one of them fell.[20]

Regarding finances, the traditional autonomy of the Spanish libertarian movement was rooted in internal modes of financing, and Franco's dictatorship did not alter that. The main source of money was clandestine union dues, which was collected by local committees. This small amount of money was used to finance propaganda and other clandestine activities, to help companions in prison, and to pay general secretariats. Apart from union dues, money came from outside, either from anarchists in exile or from foreign organizations, for example, the Swedish anarcho-syndicalist trade union Sveriges Arbetares Centralorganisation (SAC), which provided the only effective international support.[21] In any case, these external sources did not constitute the larger share of finances. It is therefore important to underline that during the period when new political alliances were formulated, clandestine groups did not receive any economic help that might have conditioned their political criteria. One important example of this is given by the CNT's refusal in September 1946 of the help offered by the republican government-in-exile.[22] In their own words, these external sources of income might have damaged "the health and life of our Organization."[23]

New Horizons for Anarchism in Europe and Beyond

International contexts during and after the Second World War conditioned politics and the intensity of repression in Franco's Spain, but they also influenced opposition to the regime, including from the anarchists. Exogenous factors shaped anarchism both inside and outside of the peninsula, as exiles struggled to maintain their organization in multiple centers. For example, in France, the legal situation conditioned the attitude of the official CNT-in-exile. On the level of discourse, committees defended revolutionary and armed insurrection: however, at the practical level, after several closures of anarchist papers and the imprisonment of leaders, radical action in Spain was ultimately discouraged.

According to the supporters of the political alliances in Spain, the international community exerted significant pressure on their decision-making, functioning "as gigantic and inexorable pliers."[24] From 1945 to 1947, changes in the anarchists' ideology and tactics paid increasing heed to the new sociopolitical map of Europe. After 1945, the revival of political and economic life took place in terms of stability and then integration. Remembering the previous social confrontation that devastated the continent, consensus, moderation, and welfare were defined and defended as new democratic virtues.[25] With the advent of the Cold War came new alliances, and the new democracies finally backed away from any offers of help or support to the Spanish opposition.[26]

Postwar Europe did not provide the anarchist revolutionary movement with the optimal conditions for recovery. Anarchist organizations under fascist regimes prior to and during the Second World War had been massively persecuted and repressed; the Spanish movement, which had carried out the anarchist revolution in 1936, suffered acute hardships during that period. With distinguishing features in each case, the French, Italian, and British anarchist federations suffered deep crises soon after 1945.[27] The revision of tactics, bureaucratic forms of organization, anarchist isolation, and rapprochements with communist dissidents were stumbling blocks that eroded consensus within the movements, along with the generational problem, which became epidemic in postwar European revolutionary movements.

Whereas formal anarchist organizations had many problems recovering amidst postwar confusion, some thinkers brought new ideas that, to a certain extent, constituted a renovation of anarchist ideology. Although this is not the place to reconstruct the historical genealogy of this "new anarchism," some of its ideological contours will be examined, particularly those that influenced underground activity in Spain. Existentialism, or more concretely "the Paris School of Existentialism," was one notable influence. Within that group, the figure of Albert Camus stood out in terms of his contact with Spanish exiles, and in particular, the anarchists.[28] He made international denunciations of Franco's criminal regime (e.g., in the play *L'État de Siège* in 1948), and participated in several committees of support for refugees and exiles. Furthermore, Camus attended numerous conferences and produced newspaper articles for friends who hailed from different groups among the Spanish anarchist exiles, whose internal struggles he did not always fully understand.[29]

Camus, and more generally "the Paris School of Existentialism," refuted two principles of the anarchist tradition of political thought: first, its understanding of human nature, and, second, the necessary advent of a total revolution. The two elements were linked: total revolution would satisfy the desire to fulfill the potential of human nature.[30] Existentialism criticized this transcendental essence.[31] In addition, Camus distinguished between a "certain idea of revolution," that entailed violence, and which he denounced, and conscious rebellion. According to Marshall, "[where] the former often ends in the sacrifice of the individual, the latter involves an instinctive refusal to obey authority and an affirmation of personal identity."[32] Camus dealt with those issues in diverse works, particularly in *L'Homme Révolté* (1951). This book provoked mixed reviews among anarchists: André Breton, the surrealist and anarchist who was close to "the Paris School," refuted Camus' arguments, while, elsewhere, the Spanish exiled press praised the work.[33]

Camus' criticism focused on the abstract, foundational philosophy that lay at the core of nineteenth-century revolutionary thought, elements of which had been imported by the Spanish anarchists. In Camus' view, this approach created space for conceit and blanket justifications for any "revolutionary" act. However, his works took time to arrive in Spain. Hélène Rufat described how her father Ramón read *L'Homme Révolté* in prison in 1957.[34] His copy was probably sent by the Subcomité Regional de CNT de Asturias in France, whose members wrote in November of the same year to their collaborators in Spain:

Camus has written many good books. His masterpiece is *L'Homme Révolté*, a wonderful philosophical essay whose conclusions are close to us ... As you show a legitimate interest in knowing his work, tell us if you can read in French. We would send it to you as soon as possible with priority. For the moment, we will try to know whether it has been published in any American country in Spanish and whether it is possible for us to get it.[35]

Indeed, Losada had published it in Buenos Aires in 1953. However, Rufat's daughter says that the copy her father read was in French. It could have been bought by the Asturias exiles in France and sent to Spain using "the journey of non-committed people."[36]

In his comprehensive history of anarchism, Marshall considers Camus as one of the "modern libertarians," who, together with some other "modern anarchists," identified more closely with an ideology that renewed itself in the central decades of the twentieth century through dialogue and confrontation with socialism and liberalism.[37] Although many works by these "moderns" influenced young libertarians in the 1960s and 1970s, some of their contributions were already in circulation in the early postwar period and had become new sources for rethinking old anarchist principles. These moderns helped to divert attention away from the State, God, and socialist Revolution, and shifted the focus toward other forms of coercion and liberation. Using Koch's terminology, they started to configure a sort of poststructuralist anarchism, showing up "how political oppression is linked to the larger cultural processes of knowledge production and cultural representation," and leaving aside the "ontological approach," which had determined the relation between the individual and the structures of social life as conflict.[38]

Postwar authors located coercion as such in the control exercised by modern technologies (Aldous Huxley's *Science, Liberty and Peace*, 1946) and psychological patterns (Alex Comfort's *Barbarism and Sexual Freedom*, 1948). Regarding liberation, they proposed social change as organized around new aesthetics (wartime Herbert Read's *Education through Art*, 1943; Paul Goodman's *Art and Social Nature*, 1946), a new form of face-to-face urbanism (Paul Goodman's *Communitas: Means of Livelihood and Ways of Life*, 1947; influenced by Lewis Mumford's *The Culture of Cities*, 1938), and a more general moral and spiritual turn (Martin Buber's *Paths of Utopia*, 1949; Paul Goodman's *Gestalt Therapy*, 1951).

In Great Britain, some of these ideas were distributed by the Freedom Press group, which was set up in London in October 1886 with Peter Kropotkin's help, and was revitalized during the Spanish Civil War. Comfort and Read worked there, producing materials both for the *Freedom* newspaper and for other publications. In the 1940s, both authors criticized the insurrectional trend in anarchism and the "anarchist free society" utopia. Instead, they suggested a "genuine social change [that] has to grow out of prior changes in personality and concrete, social relationships, something which cannot be mandated by a 'political' act of revolution."[39] An art specialist, Read hoped to create a new aesthetic form of education that would liberate people from authoritarian ways of seeing and being. John Moore underlines how Read, rather than rehearsing "Bakuninist theses about the revolutionary potential of the lumpenproletariat ... directs attention away from the economic toward the cultural sphere."[40] He called for "a Black Market in culture," where art-as-commodity was bunk and a new covert culture of dissent challenged the hegemonies of "current art and literature." This market, as Moore describes, was a theoretical prelude to the underground culture and counterculture movement of the 1960s.[41]

As *Freedom* diffused Read and Comfort's ideas throughout postwar Great Britain, *Politics* magazine did the same with Paul Goodman in the US. The publication was set up in 1944 by the ex-trotskyist Dwight Macdonald, who opened it to communist dissidents, among them, Louis Clair, Bruno Bettelheim, Victor Serge, and C. Wright Mills. Referring to his political thought, Glazer underlines how Macdonald "came to believe [after the Second World War] that a new socialism required a search for ethical and humanitarian ideals rather than reliance on changing economic institutions."[42]

In Italy, *Volontà* magazine introduced Anglo-Saxon authors (e.g., Mumford, Read, and Goodman in 1946, 1947, and 1948, respectively) and French existentialists (Breton and Camus in 1949; Jean-Paul Sartre in 1952) to libertarian readers, as well as published articles of Spanish anarchists in exile. At the same time, articles of Italian authors appearing in the magazine were translated into English by people linked to *Freedom,* e.g., the anarchist thinker Colin Ward.[43] Latin-American publishing houses translated the work of some of these authors into Spanish in the late 1950s and the 1960s.[44] Previously, groups of exiled Spanish anarchists had come in contact with these new ideological trends and attempted to introduce them among the illegal organizations in Spain, as we have seen with Camus' book. Elsewhere, the works of new authors were imported into the exiled anarchist groups by Civil War veterans who functioned as mediators, such as Gaston Leval and Louis Mercier Vega—the former had been writing for *Volontà* since 1947, while the latter was editor of the journal from late 1950s and founded diverse periodicals among the exiled Spanish anarchists.

The intersection of multiple contexts—that of the illegal anarchist movement in Franco's Spain with the postwar anarchisms of Europe and the US—produced interesting results. Despite facing severe problems in circulating new ideas due to official repression, Spanish anarchism nonetheless adopted elements of new intellectual trends in different countries. By critically confronting the anarchist tradition, both shared a: (1) similar rejection of violence; (2) willingness to overcome proletarian exclusivism as well as the longing for total revolution; and (3) searching for pragmatic solutions to concrete problems.

Repression and Mobilization in Franco's Spain

According to Jennifer Earl's "theoretically driven typology of repression," control of the anarchists during Franco's dictatorship would have been an "observable, coercive repression by state agents tightly connected with national political elites."[45] Francoist elites designed and directed repression in postwar Spain in the pursuit of a general extermination of subversive ideologies. Along with other political dissidents, anarchists configured what Loveman called "high-risk collective actors" in a context where the potential consequences for opposing the dictatorship included "arrest, torture, disappearance, or murder of participants, their friends, and their family members."[46] Franco's dictatorship repressed without concealing its use of torture, murder, or imprisonment, especially in the postwar period. Repression was observable because it was intended to be exemplary. It sought to paralyze any opposition by threat. However, repression did not employ large-scale public massacres that might have facilitated a backlash.[47] Instead, it used bureaucratic and inclusive procedures legitimized by the New State law, involving a large part of the population in the persecution of their neighbors.

Apart from the above-mentioned typology, Earl reorganized existing literature by mapping research, representing the six dominant approaches, onto different types of repression.[48] According to that map, the "political opportunity approach" finds strong support in research literature on observable, tightly connected, coercion. This approach considers the timing of repression and mobilization in larger protest cycles and suggests that protest will experience less repression when both stable political opportunity structures (POS) and volatile political opportunities (PO) are opened, and vice versa. POS traditionally refer to "consistent—but not necessarily formal or permanent—dimensions of the political environment that provide incentives for people to undertake collective action by affecting their expectations for success or failure."[49] In contrast, more volatile PO are linked to short-term shifts in protest and repression.

The references used by Earl to establish the strong support given by research literature are Tarrow's work in the late 1960s and early 1970s in Italy, Della Porta's comparative research in Italy and Germany from the 1960s to the 1990s, and Brockett's analysis of the effects of violent repression in El Salvador and Guatemala in the early 1980s.[50] Although repression in all three cases displayed high levels of violence, neither the European democracies, nor the Central American regimes were authoritarian regimes as was Franco's dictatorship. In my opinion, differences between them are important. In those political contexts, the use of great physical force, although present, was considered illegitimate in the dominant political culture at that time, whereas political violence constitutes one of the foundational elements of Franco's dictatorship. In this case, where high repression meant the absence or scarcity of opportunity, mobilization needs strong subjective factors to emerge and to be sustained.[51]

According to POS definition, the most notable features of Franco's dictatorship that impinged on the character of both claims and contention were its immense executive power, essentially undemocratic nature, and its strongly centralized institutions led by closed minorities fighting each other for control. As a result, official repression forcefully targeted political opposition groups, who were extremely weak due to wartime fighting. Among them were the anarchist committees and groups that had not found any effective support among Franco's officers or from sources outside of Spain. Although in general terms these features remained stable over the years, some short-term shifts motivated by changing international contexts can be considered as more volatile PO. At the end of the Second World War, and more precisely after the fall of fascism in Italy (September 1943), state repression diminished, albeit it never disappeared. This relative relaxation lasted until 1947, once Franco's "waiting tactic" succeeded and the international community welcomed the dictatorship, which was finally acquitted by the UN in November 1950.[52]

Relative openness of PO in postwar Spain amplified anarchist mobilization in volume and visibility, that is to say, more propaganda was printed and distributed, more members were recruited, and stronger contacts with other opposition forces were established. However, they do not serve as plausible explanations for movement emergence and continuity in a context where dissident action still implied high risks, including possible death. Between 1943 and 1947, when the opposition waited for allied assistance to help bring an end to Franco's regime, hope in change grew and the opposition aimed to speed changes up through higher levels of mobilization. The idea of collaborating in a plausible solution to end the dictatorship helped to sustain mobilization and its high costs. However, PO and hope mediating in the perception of these opportunities required a motivational frame that gave sense and continuity to mobilization: ideology.

Social movement scholars have theoretically distinguished between ideology and frame. Zald established a first gradation partly between the two in terms of complexity and broadness, where "ideologies tend to be more complex and logical systems of beliefs than frames, though frames may be embedded in ideologies."[53] Oliver and Johnston have, however, recently shown to what extent the relationship between ideology and frame is still unclear, criticizing those works within the frame theory perspective that use them as synonyms.[54] Without leaving aside the debate, I will argue that anarchist ideology in Franco's Spain *acted* as an interpretative frame for a specific social and political situation, which embraced context (the Francoist dictatorship) and collective action (resistance). That frame was derived from a set of principles and theoretical assumptions linked to a particular ideology.[55] This does not mean that the interpretation and legitimation process of strategic choices in mobilization reproduced an enclosed, coherent worldview,[56] but, on the contrary, it was updated while questioning the political tradition to which actors were attached.[57] Spanish anarchists made sense of their situation by invoking some concepts that belonged to a distinctive vocabulary: political concepts whose meanings were revised through the contact with other political traditions and the political language of public discourse, and subject to negotiation and eventual modification in underground debates.

Spanish anarchists combated Franco's regime by denouncing and dismantling the appropriation and denaturalization that official discourse made of some social and political principles and values, e.g., democracy and welfare. In the 1940s, the first clandestine generation mobilized principles and values traditionally linked to the republican vocabulary, e.g., the idea of freedom as the absence of domination or by framing the clandestine fight as the defense of citizen's rights and liberties against *the tyrant*. Outside of the national context, ideological materials formulated by foreign authors fed the anarchists' discourse, although as mentioned above, censorship and filters imposed harsh limits to circulation and translation.

Ideology was not only an interpretative frame for resistance, but it was also a motivational one. It provided motives for clandestine mobilization. Anarchist ideas, beliefs, and values provided the individual with an identity (not only political) and configured a cognitive orientation that permitted a global interpretation of the social, political, and historical context.[58] Identity connected the individual with a community of *compañeros* with whom to share principles and assumptions and with whom to be linked through a strong sense of solidarity.[59] Moreover, identity had what we can call retroactive effects. Ideology attached the anarchist to a broad history of political struggle that, on the other hand, had recently found a devastating scenario in Spain. As the experience of belonging to a (political) group, identity reinforced the rhetorical link that the group maintained with such a tragic past. In short, ideology provided anarchists with interpretative tools that allowed them to understand the social and political world in political terms and at the same time *armed* them with values and principles that propelled their intervention in order to change that world.

Frame coding and identity building are dynamic and almost recurrent processes.[60] According to the "frame dispute coding categories," the conflictual relationship that is a distinctive element of social movements should be categorized in the diagnosis: the first stage of interpretative frame coding that "involves the identification of a problem and the attribution of blame or casualty";[61] namely, where agents responsible for conflict are selected and titled as opponents. If identity is simply the experience of a social relationship coupled with public representation of that experience,[62] social movement identity should be the experience of the conflictual relationship whose representation stands on shared and exclusive group stories about the we-they boundaries. Cleavage configures a mirror, where the group defines the values to share, and, at the same time, it configures a wall that contributes to group consistency and protects it from identity crisis.[63] According to this picture, repression should influence mobilization in two ways: a material one, decreasing mobilization resources; and a symbolic one, reinforcing the conflictual relationship between repression agents and social movement, and therefore the mobilizing actors' political identity (as an experience of that relationship). Repression, and its perception, strengthens the symbolic foundations of the wall that divides the agents and the targets of repression, thus reinforcing the bonds between victims. Narrative constructions of boundaries achieve extra plausibility in repressive contexts, as do the conflictual relationship they legitimize, corroborating the frames created around the representation of the social problem.[64]

Conclusion

This chapter gives a picture of anarchism in postwar Spain that underlines the errors of viewing the movement as simply inexistent or as a rigid, traditional group that was anchored in the past. Rather, clandestine anarchists sustained high-risk activism over time and undertook a difficult process of ideological evolution that was tied to the experience of exile. In parallel to that process, intellectuals appeared in the postwar international stage to bring new libertarian concepts and ideas. Despite the different contexts where new proposals were formulated, actors in and out of Spain moved toward the effective emancipation from out-of-date nineteenth-century hindrances that burdened anarchist political thought.

Franco's dictatorship repressed the clandestine CNT committees with the same virulence it employed against groups who opposed the regime by means other than diplomacy and political alliances, e.g., the anarchist urban and rural guerrilla. The regime was never threatened in a serious way, despite official conjuncture that linked anti-Francoist opposition with the victorious nations of the Second World War. Nevertheless, anarchists were prominent among the enemies who fought Franco's followers during the Spanish Civil War, and anarchism was among the diverse political "diseases" that, according to official propaganda, came from abroad and infected the *Patria*.[65] Hence, anarchists were important targets due to their historical mobilizing capacity and radical discourse.

Under these extreme circumstances, anarchist mobilization during the dictatorship required a confluence of multiple factors to emerge and to be sustained over time: firstly, temporary openings in the political opportunity structure, i.e., the relative relaxation of the repression that was facilitated by international politics; secondly, strong expectations of a regime breakdown, and consequently a strong perception of moving in this direction; and finally, ideology, which constituted an interpretative as well as a motivational frame for clandestine mobilization.

This chapter holds the 1950s as its terminal point. Further research could analyze subsequent changes, and provide elements for a historical understanding of the complete evolution of clandestine anarchism during the dictatorship. In the development of such a research project, the political opportunities opened by the Collective Bargains Law in 1958 and the new hopes and political horizons of the youth would be key elements to take into account.

Notes

1. The anarcho-syndicalist trade union Confederación Nacional del Trabajo (CNT), the "specific" anarchist organization Federación Anarquista Ibérica (FAI) and the youth organization Federación Ibérica de Juventudes Libertarias (FIJL), set up in 1910, 1927, and 1932 respectively, were the main organizations of the Span-

ish libertarian movement, which itself became a formal organization in wartime (Movimiento Libertario, set up in October 1938). An additional organization was the female branch of the movement Free Women, founded in 1936, although the National Federation was created only in August 1937. CNT's anarcho-syndicalism can be seen as a particular branch of anarchism, in which during its historical development, some elements merged with revolutionary syndicalism. I will use here the terms "anarchist" and "anarchism" in a broad sense to refer to the above-mentioned organizations and their members. I would like to thank Niall Whelehan and Tom Gilmour for their help with the English language.

2. E.g., J. Casanova, *Anarquismo y Violencia Política en la España del Siglo XX* (Zaragoza: Institución Fernando el Católico, 2007); J. Casanova, *Anarchism, the Republic, and Civil War in Spain: 1931–1939* (London: Routledge, 2004; org. ed. in Spanish, 1997); C. Molinero and P. Ysàs, "La Historia Social de la Época Franquista. Una Aproximación," *Historia Social* 30 (1998): 153; G. Woodcock, "Anarchism: A Historical Introduction," in *The Anarchist Reader*, ed. G. Woodcock (Hassocks: The Harvester Press Limited, 1977), 44–45; and J. Romero Maura, "The Spanish Case," in *Anarchism Today* (London, MacMillan, 1971), 60; and the work of the political theorist D. Miller, *Anarchism* (London: J.M. Dent & Sons Ltd, 1984), 141.

3. M. Loveman, "High-Risk Collective Action: Defending Human Rights in Chile, Uruguay, and Argentina," *The American Journal of Sociology* 104(2)(1998): 478.

4. See R.L. Einwohner, "Opportunity, Honor, and Action in the Warsaw Ghetto Uprising of 1943," *The American Journal of Sociology* 109(3)(2003): 650–675.

5. Letters of Spanish exile (Cipriano Mera from Boghari in Argelia, Juan García Oliver from Sweden, and Miguel García Vivancos and Gregorio Jover from France), Summer 1939, International Institute of Social History, Amsterdam (henceforth IISH), Fernando Gómez Peláez Papers (FGP), 255. This and further translations from Spanish into English are the author's.

6. Unsigned letter [Consejo General del Movimiento Libertario -CGML], 17 February 1941 (IISH, FGP). Also in the letter signed by G.E. [Germinal Esgleas, general secretary of the CGML], 4 December 1940, replying to that of Jover, Vivancos, and Juan Domenech sent on 20 August 1939; both in IISH, José Peirats Valls (JVP), 498.

7. Minutes of the *Pleno Nacional Conjunto CNT-FIJL-FAI,* October 1938, Barcelona, 23–55, IISH, Federación Anarquista Ibérica—Comité Peninsular (FAI-CP), 23A.1. These debates and controversies did not just take place in wartime and during the postwar Spanish anarchism. For example, some young French anarchists, influenced by the Spanish Civil War and popular front experiences, created a group in 1938, where members shared a common opposition to "official tendencies," "credos and catechisms," and a common commitment to a search for new methods and revolutionary tactics through "a fresh study of the reality of yesterday and of today." They set up a publication, *Révision, Revue d'Etudes Révolutionnaires,* Paris, February 1938–August 1939. See D. Berry, *A History of the French Anarchist Movement, 1917–1945* (Westport, CT, London: Greenwood Press, 2002), 294–297.

8. MLE-CNT. 1947. *Dictámenes y Resoluciones del II Congreso del MLE-CNT en Francia,* Toulouse: MLE-CNT en Francia. The term "ideological recovery" appears in F. Montseny, *Seis Años de Mi Vida, 1939–1945* (Barcelona: Galba, 1978), 231. The author was one of the main characters of Spanish anarchism in postwar exile.

9. A. Elorza, "Utopía y Revolución en el Movimiento Anarquista Español," in *El Anarquismo Español y Sus Tradiciones Culturales,* eds. B. Hofmann, P. Joan i Tours, and M. Tietz (Madrid: Iberoamericana, 1995), 79–108. One of the elements in common was anti-clericalism, which occupied a primordial level on the cultural and theoretical building of both ideologies. A recent work on republican anti-clericalism appears in D. Castro Alfín, "Palabras de Fuego. El Anticlericalismo Republicano," *Journal of Spanish Cultural Studies* 6(2)(2005): 205–225.

10. See E. Romanos, "Fernando Gómez Peláez: Crítica y Disidencia en el Movimiento Libertario en el Exilio," *Ayer* 67(3)(2007): 235–254.

11. *Juventud Libre* (March 1947), *Solidaridad Obrera* (July 1945), *Cultura y Acción* (May 1947), *La Voz Confederal* (August 1946), *Solidaridad Obrera* (April 1946), *CNT* (June 1947), *La Voz Confederal* (August 1946).

12. A. Bar, *La CNT en los Años Rojos. Del Sindicalismo Revolucionario al Anarcosindicalismo (1910–1926)* (Madrid: Akal, 1981); T. Abelló and E. Olivé, "El Conflicto entre la CNT y la Familia Urales-Montseny en 1928. La Lucha por el Mantenimiento del Anarquismo Puro," *Estudios de Historial Social* 32–33 (1981): 317–332; E. Vega, "Anarquismo y Sindicalismo durante la Dictadura y la República," *Historia Social* 1(1988): 55–62; A. Elorza, "La Utopía Anarquista bajo la II República," in *La Utopía Anarquista bajo la II República,* ed. A. Elorza (Madrid: Ayuso, 1973 [1971]), 351–468; Elorza. "Utopía y Revolución en el Movimiento Anarquista Español"; S. Tavera, *Federica Montseny* (Madrid: Temas de Hoy, 2005); C. Ealham, *Class, Culture and Conflict in Barcelona, 1898–1937* (London: Routledge, 2005); and Casanova, *Anarchism, the Republic and Civil War in Spain.*

13. Cf. Á. Herrerín López, *La CNT Durante el Franquismo. Clandestinidad y Exilio (1939–1975)* (Madrid: Siglo XXI, 2004).

14. CNT-UGT, "Vigencia y proyección del sindicalismo humanista," Spain, April 1960, Biblioteca Arús, Barcelona, Diego Abad de Santillán, 2.1.1.D.4; Dossier *Proyección del sindicalismo español,* n.d., Fundación Salvador Seguí (FSS), Madrid, CNT-interior (CNT-I), 165; L. Íñigo, *Los Cinco Puntos,* unpublished work, FSS, Lorenzo Íñigo.

15. *Fraternidad* (September 1946).

16. National Committee CNT, "Mensaje de la CNT de España," January 1963, FSS, CNT-I, 165.

17. See J.L. Ledesma, "La 'Santa Ira Popular' del 36: la Violencia en Guerra Civil y Revolución, entre Cultura y Política," in *Culturas y Políticas de la Violencia: España siglo XX,* eds. R. Cruz et al. (Madrid: Siete Mares, 2005), 147–192. For a theoretical discussion on the "strategic paradox" of the revolutionary process, see A. Chan, "Violence, Non-violence, and the Concept of Revolution in Anarchist Thought," *Anarchist Studies* 12(2)(2004): 103–123.

18. For the structure of the Movimiento Libertario, see note 1.

19. For quantitative analysis on repression, see Herrerín López. *La CNT Durante el Franquismo,* 145–167.

20. Affinity groups were an old mode of organizations, which were mainly and historically directed to subversive action, and maintained the movement in a latent state during clandestine periods. These groups also acted in Franco's Spain outside of the clandestine union structure, for example, in the guerrillas groups and inside prisons.

21. Letter of the National Committee, CNT in Spain, to the SAC, Spain, 14 April 1947, IISH, Ramón Álvarez Palomo.

22. National Committee, CNT in Spain, September 1946, FSS, Angel Marcos papers (AM), 6. Although the clandestine CNT did not receive any direct financial support from the Spanish republican government-in-exile, it is necessary to underline here that some of the opposition platforms the anarchist joined in Spain did receive financial support, such as, for example, the Alianza Nacional de Fuerzas Democráticas (ANFD). See also E. Marco Nadal, *Todos Contra Franco. La Alianza Nacional de Fuerzas Democráticas, 1944/1947* (Madrid: Queimada, 1982), 138.

23. National Subcommittee, CNT in France, Circular 37, Toulouse, 29 August 1946, FSS, CNT-MLE-E, 6.

24. Juan Manuel Molina, Letter to R. Álvarez, Alcalá (prison), 30 January 1947, IISH, Ramón Álvarez Palomo papers (RAP).

25. N. O'Sullivan, *European Political Thought Since 1945* (Basingstoke, New York: Palgrave Macmillan, 2004); and M. Mazower, *Dark Continent. Europe's Twentieth Century* (New York: Vintage Books, 2000).

26. See D.A. Messenger, "'Our Spanish Brothers' or 'As at Plombieres'? France, the Legacy of Resistance and the Spanish Opposition to Franco, 1945–1948," *French History* 20(1)(2006): 52–74; and J. Edwards, *Anglo-American Relations and the Franco Question in the Early Cold War, 1945–1955* (Oxford: Clarendon Press, 1999).

27. G. Cerrito, *Il Ruolo della Organizzazione Anarchica* (Catania: RL, 1973); U. Fedeli and G. Sacchetti, eds., *Congressi e Convegni della Federazione Anarchica Italiana. Atti e documenti (1944–1995)* (Pescara: Samizdat, 2002); G. Fontenis, *L'autre Communisme: Histoire Subversive du Mouvement Libertaire* (Mauléon: Acratie, 1990); G. Fontenis, *Changer le Monde: Histoire du Mouvement Communiste Libertaire (1945–1977)* (Toulouse: Le Coquelicot, 2000); D. Goodway, *Anarchist Seeds Beneath Snow: Left-Libertarian Thought and British Writers from Willian Morris to Colin Ward* (Liverpool: Liverpool University Press, 2006); J. Maitron, *Le Mouvement Anarchiste en France*, vol. II (Paris: Gallimard, 1992); and E.A. Marsilii, *Il Movimento Anarchico a Genova, 1943–1950* (Genova: Annexia, 2004).

28. C. Delacampagne gave the school this title, see "The Paris School of Existentialism," in *The Columbia History of Twentieth-century French Thought*, eds. L.D. Kritzman, B.J. Reilly, and M.B. DeBevoise (New York: Columbia University Press, 2006), 81. He does not properly include Camus in the school, as Camus "was not a philosopher in the strict sense," although Delacampagne clearly considers him as an intellectual reference.

29. Romanos, "Fernando Gómez Peláez: Crítica y Disidencia en el Movimiento Libertario en el Exilio;" and H. Molina, "Ayer, Hoy y Mañana. Relaciones entre Camus y los Libertarios Españoles: una Gran Red de Ideas, Principios y Humanismo," *Anthropos* 199(2003): 150.

30. D. Morland, *Demanding the Impossible? Human Nature and Politics in Nineteenth-century Social Anarchism* (London, Washington: Cassell, 1997); G. Crowder, *Classical Anarchism: the Political Thought of Godwin, Proudhon, Bakunin and Kropotkin* (Oxford: Clarendon Press, 1991); and B. Yack, *The Longing for Total Revolution. Philosophic Sources of Social Discontent from Rousseau to Marx and Nietzsche* (Princeton: Princeton University Press, 1986).

31. S. Priest, ed., *Jean-Paul Sartre: Basic Writings* (London, New York: Routledge, 2001), 301–302; and R. Wolin, *The Terms of Cultural Criticism: the Frankfurt School, Existentialism, Poststructuralism* (New York: Columbia University Press, 1992), 135ff.

32. P.H. Marshall, *Demanding the Impossible: a History of Anarchism* (London: Harper-Collins, 1992), 581. See also R. Aronson, *Camus & Sartre: the Story of a Friendship and the Quarrel that Ended It* (Chicago: University of Chicago Press, 2004), ch. 6.
33. For more on the Camus-Breton controversy, see G. Bataille, *The Absence of Myth. Writings on Surrealism,* trans. M. Richardson (London, New York: Verso, 1994), 158–176. Camus' work was praised in a series of articles in the Spanish libertarian periodical *Solidaridad Obrera* (Paris), which was started in 16 February 1952 by Felipe Alaiz.
34. H. Rufat, "En Cachette avec *L'Homme Révolté*: les Anarchistes Espagnols," in *Albert Camus et les Écritures du XX siècle,* eds. S. Brodziak et al. (Arras: Artois Presses Université, 2003), 154–155. His father openly recognized his intellectual debt with Camus in a discourse in honor of the author; this text can be found in R. Rufat, "Homenaje en Memoria de Albert Camus (Miembro del Comité de Honor del Ateneo)," *Anthropos* 199(2003): 155–157.
35. National Subcommittee, Paris, 12 November 1957, IISH, RAP.
36. Ibid. The term "non-committed people" refers to individuals not actively involved in the anarchist movement, but close to it by other means. These were usually relatives or friends of actual members, and, as such, they could import prohibited books into Spain without attracting police forces' attention.
37. Marshall, *Demanding the Impossible: a History of Anarchism,* chs. 37–38.
38. A.M. Koch, "Poststructuralism and the Epistemological Basis of Anarchism," *Philosophy of the Social Sciences* 23(3)(1993): 327–351.
39. S. White, "Making Anarchism Respectable? The Social Philosophy of Colin Ward," *Journal of Political Ideologies* 12(1)(2007): 13.
40. J. Moore, "Composition and Decomposition: Contemporary Anarchist Aesthetics," *Anarchist Studies* 6(2)(1998): 113–122.
41. Apart from social and political movements, Read's anarchism also influenced new artistic expressions. One of them was embodied during and after the Second World War by the "Poets of the Apocalypse," highly influenced by Read's *Poetry and Anarchism* (1938). The main authors were Henry Treece, Nicholas Moore, J.F. Hendry, and G.S. Fraser. According to a contemporary observer, those poets wrote with "a mood of personal resignation to the brutality of modern life, combined with skepticism regarding any confident prophets of world order. The lesson of the Second World War seems to have discouraged any whole-hearted sympathy with large, impersonal dogmas." In F.J. Hoffmann, "From Surrealism to "The Apocalypse": A development in Twentieth Century Irrationalism," *ELH* 15(2)(1948): 147–165.
42. P.M. Glazer, "From the Old Left to the New: Radical Criticism in the 1940s," *American Quarterly* 24(5)(1972). See also G.D. Sumner, *Dwight Macdonald and the Politics Circle. The Challenge of Cosmopolitan Democracy* (Ithaca: Cornell University Press, 1996).
43. C. Ward and D. Goodway, *Talking Anarchy* (Nottingham: Five Leaves Press, 2003), 51–52.
44. The publishers were America Lee, Reconstruir, and Proyección in Argentina, and Editores Mexicanos Unidos in Mexico. Apart from them, it is necessary to mention translations and theoretical materials published and distributed by Ruedo Ibérico, created in 1961 in France (Paris), and ZYX, a Christian dissidents' enterprise developed in the late 1960s in Spain.

45. J. Earl, "Tanks, Tear Gas, and Taxes: Toward a Theory of Movement Repression," *Sociological Theory* 21(1)(2003): 44–68.
46. Loveman. "High-Risk Collective Action: Defending Human Rights in Chile, Uruguay, and Argentina," 478.
47. R.A. Francisco, "The Dictator's Dilemma," in *Repression and Mobilization*, eds. C. Davenport, H. Johnston, and C. M. Mueller (Minneapolis: University of Minnesota Press, 2005), 58–81.
48. Earl, "Tanks, Tear Gas, and Taxes: Toward a Theory of Movement Repression."
49. S. Tarrow, *Power in Movement. Social Movements, Collective Action and Politics* (Cambridge: Cambridge University Press, 1994), 85.
50. S. Tarrow, *Democracy and Disorder: Protest and Politics in Italy, 1965–1975* (Oxford: Oxford University Press, 1989); D. Della Porta, *Social Movements, Political Violence, and the State: a Comparative Analysis of Italy and Germany* (Cambridge: Cambridge University Press, 1995); C. Brockett, "A Protest-Cycle Resolution of the Repression/Popular Protest Paradox," in *Repertoires and Cycles of Collective Action*, ed. M. Traugott (Durham: Duke University Press, 1995), 117–144.
51. See C. Kurzman, "Structural Opportunities and Perceived Opportunities in Social-Movement Theory: Evidence from the Iranian Revolution of 1979," *American Sociological Review* 61(1)(1996): 153–170; Loveman, "High-Risk Collective Action: Defending Human Rights in Chile, Uruguay, and Argentina"; and J.A. Goldstone and C. Tilly, "Threat (and Opportunity): Popular Action and State Response in the Dynamics of Contentious Action," in *Silence and Voice in the Study of Contentious Politics*, eds. R.R. Aminzade et al. (Cambridge: Cambridge University Press, 2001), 179–194.
52. Resolution 386 (V) adopted by the General Assembly of the UN (4 November 1950) resolved to revoke the recommendation, previously adopted in 1946, for the withdrawal of Ambassadors and Ministers of the Member States from Madrid and the ban on the Spanish membership in international agencies established by or brought into relationship with the UN.
53. M.N. Zald, "Culture, Ideology, and Strategic Framing," in *Comparative Perspectives on Social Movements. Political Opportunities, Mobilizing Structures, and Cultural Framing*, eds. D. McAdam, J.D. McCarthy, and M.N. Zald (Cambridge: Cambridge University Press, 1996), 262.
54. P.E. Oliver and H. Johnston, "What a Good Idea! Ideologies and Frames in Social Movements Research," in *Frames of Protest: Social Movements and the Framing Perspective*, eds. H. Johnston and J.A. Noakes (Lanham, MD, Oxford: Rowman & Littlefield, 2005), 199.
55. D.L. Westby, "Strategic Imperative, Ideology, and Frame," *Mobilization* 7(3)(2002).
56. See M. Billing et al., *Ideological Dilemmas: A Social Psychology of Everyday Thinking* (London: Sage, 1988); and D.A. Snow, "Framing Processes, Ideology, and Discursive Fields," in *The Blackwell Companion to Social Movements*, eds. D.A. Snow, S.A. Soule, and H. Kriesi (Malden, MA: Blackwell, 2004).
57. F. Polleta, "Culture Is Not in Your Head," in *Rethinking Social Movements: Structure, Meaning, and Emotions*, eds. J. Goodwing and J.M. Jasper (Larham, MD: Rowman & Littlefield, 2004).
58. Cf. "multiple identities" in new social movements, in D. Della Porta and M. Diani, *Social Movements: an Introduction* (Malden, MA: Blackwell, 2006), 98–100.

59. According to Ricoeur, ideology has an integration function, which consists of protecting or preserving an identity, without which neither the individual nor the group can exist. See P. Ricoeur, *L'Idéologie et l'Utopie* (Paris: Éditions du Seuil, 1997).

60. S. Hunt, R.D. Benford, and D. Snow, "Marcos de Acción Colectiva y Campos de Identidad en la Construcción Social de los Movimientos," in *Los Nuevos Movimientos Sociales. De la Ideología a la Identidad,* eds. E. Laraña and J. Gusfield (Madrid: CIS, 1994), 224. Cf. M.P. Hanagan, L. Page Moch, and W.T. Brake, eds., *Challenging Authority: the Historical Study of Contentious Politics* (Minneapolis: University of Minnesota Press, 1998).

61. The other two frame coding stages are the "prognosis," when solutions to the problems are suggested through the identification of strategies, tactics, and goals, and the "motivation," which gives people a reason to join collective action. R.D. Benford, "Frame Disputes within the Nuclear Disarmament Movement," *Social Forces* 71(3)(1993): 699.

62. C. Tilly, "Political Identities in History," in *Stories, Identities, and Political Change,* ed. C. Tilly (Oxford: Rowman & Littlefield, 2002), 57–68.

63. F. Cerutti, "Political Identity and Conflict," in *Identities and Conflicts. The Mediterranean,* eds. F. Cerruti and R. Ragionieri (Basingstoke: Palgrave, 2001), 9–25.

64. R.V. Gould, *Insurgent Identities: Class, Community, and Protest in Paris from 1848 to the Commune* (Chicago: University of Chicago Press, 1995), 202.

65. M. Richards, *A Time of Silence: Civil War and the Culture of Repression in Franco's Spain* (Cambridge: Cambridge University Press, 1998), 46.

Chapter 9

Organizational Communication of Intermediaries in Flux

An Analytical Framework

Dominik Lachenmeier

Introduction

Until recently, social scientists who studied formal organizations and social scientists who studied social movements had little to do with each other. But as Gerald F. Davis and his co-authors observe "developments in the wider society and in scholarship have made it clear that the time is ripe to break down the barriers between these two fields."[1] Following this ambition, this chapter focuses on so-called "intermediary organizations," such as political parties, associations or nongovernmental organizations (NGOs), which often have their historical roots in social movements.

Social movements are networks of persons, groups, and organizations that want to induce, stop or reverse social change by protests.[2] That is to say, social movements are not formal organizations, but they can include formal organizations. In the course of their establishment, movement actors can develop formal structures, such as positions, divisions or hierarchies, and can become formal organizations. Examples of this are the green parties or NGOs such as Greenpeace, which emanated from the environmental movement, or trade unions, which have their roots in the labor movement.

This chapter centers on formal structures of intermediary organizations that fulfill the function of organizational communication—i.e., communication of the organization as a social entity toward different internal and external environments, such as members, political decision-makers or the mass media (divisions or positions for public relations, marketing, member communication, etc.). Hereby, a special focus lies on the changes of the formal structures of organizational communication. In the following, a theoretical framework will be presented that enables an analysis of intermediaries' reforms of organizational communication—inter alia, in reaction to perceived changes in internal and external environments, such as losses of members, transnationalization, and

Europeanization processes concerning the political system, or a growing importance of the mass media for the mediation of political interests.

The theoretical conception is essentially based on Luhmann's theory of autopoietic organizational systems.[3] Systems theory seems to be fruitful for this purpose, because it focuses on the relationships and borders between organizations and their environments.[4] This "system-environment-thinking" is helpful in understanding organizational change as well as organizational communication toward different internal and external environments.[5] Furthermore, the theoretical conception resorts to Streeck's theory of intermediary organizations.[6] Streeck helps to specify the most important relations of intermediary organizations to internal and external environments as well as the corresponding main problems that have to be solved by organizational communication. On the basis of this theoretical framework, central environmental changes can be described that could have prompted intermediary organizations to reform their internal and external communication.

The theoretical framework that will be presented in this chapter shall be exemplified with the organizational communication of the Swiss, the German, and the Austrian trade union confederations (SGB, DGB, and ÖGB).[7] Numerous studies of European trade unions have been recently published.[8] Nevertheless, the organizational communication of trade union confederations still is a largely unexplored issue.[9]

A Systems Theoretical Conception of Organizational Communication

Definition of "Organizational Communication"

In a broad sense, the term "organizational communication" can be defined as *all* communication in and from organizations.[10] This definition includes formal communication (e.g., press releases) as well as informal communication (e.g., discussions during a coffee break). For our purpose, however, this definition is too unspecific. Instead, "organizational communication" shall be defined as *the organization of communication of the organization as a social entity toward relevant internal and external environments.* This definition refers to organization-oriented public relations (PR) theories, which conceptualize public relations as the management of communication between all societal organizations and their internal and external environments.[11] The central function of PR can be seen as the legitimation of the organization and its interests.[12] However, the term "organizational communication" is not a synonym for "public relations," but is an umbrella term. Together with PR, it includes other forms of organized communication toward internal and external environments, such as marketing, fundraising or sponsoring. Referring to the Swiss, the German, and the Austrian trade union confederations, the term "organizational communication" includes media relations, campaigning, lobbying, internal communication, and even legal advice.

Functions and Structures of Organizational Communication

To analyze the organizational communication of intermediaries in a systems theoretical perspective means to analyze, inter alia, the functions and structures of organizational communication. How, then, can we conceive the functions and structures of organizational communication?

To answer this question, we shortly examine first the structural-functionalist PR conceptions that refer to open systems theories. The structural-functionalist perspective assumes that the structures of organized communication are just a given (for instance, the structures of a sub-system "public relations"). In a second step, structural-functionalist theories attribute some special functions to these structures that are essential for the survival of the organization. Grunig and Hunt,[13] for example, conceive of public relations as a management sub-system. Referring to the structural-functionalist organization theory of Katz and Kahn,[14] as well as referring to Parsons AGIL scheme,[15] they localize this management sub-system in the adaptation and maintenance sub-system of an organization. Consequently, public relations have to fulfill the following functions: control, coordination, and regulation of the diverse sub-systems of the organization, perception of changes in the organizational environment, and the adaption of the organization to such changes, as well as keeping the balance of the organization.

The problem is that structural-functionalist theories do not ask why structures of organized communication (e.g., a PR division) exist. Neither do they ask why exactly these and not other structures exist. By obverting the line of argument, the functional-structuralist perspective of constructivist systems theory (which is focused on here) fixes this deficiency of structural-functionalist theories: in the first step, it asks about the functions that have to be fulfilled. Only in the second step does it analyze which structures are functional for this purpose. Referring to the analysis of organizational communication, we therefore first have to conceive the functions of organizational communication.

The Primary Functions of Organizational Communication

Organizations, as autonomous, self-referential closed systems, are able to communicate with their environment only by making a difference between self-reference and external reference.[16] By making this difference, organizational systems produce information about their internal and external environments. Therefore, formal organizations have to fulfill the primary function of self-observation and self-description as well as the functions of observation and description of their environment. That is to say, organizations such as trade union confederations have to observe and describe their own organizational structures (their existing positions, divisions, hierarchies, etc.), on the one hand. On the other hand, organizations have to observe and describe—more or less systematically—different potentially relevant internal and external environments, such as, for example, their members, the mass media, the political-administrative system (government, parliament, and administration) or coalition partners and competitors.

Starting from this assumption, the following essential consideration can be derived: in the course of their establishment, intermediary organizations, such as trade unions, NGOs or political parties, are creating organizational structures, which are specialized in self-observation and self-description as well as in the observation and description of the organizational environment. Here are some examples referring to the Swiss, the German, and the Austrian trade union confederations: for a systematic observation and description of the trade unions' individual members (internal environment), they collect member statistics; to observe and describe the media coverage (external environment), they use issue monitoring and press reviews; for an observation and description of the political system (external environment), they produce political monitorings; and to observe and describe their own organizational system, they produce annual reports or media releases in order to communicate organizational decisions.

Public relations (PR) are an important structural solution to fulfill the function of the observation and description of the organizational system and its environment.[17] But as the functional-structuralist perspective focuses on functional equivalents, PR is only one structural solution to the given problem, among others is market communication (advertisement, fundraising, etc.).[18] Furthermore, structural solutions can vary and change over time: the communication's division of the Swiss Trade Union Confederation (SGB) only existed since 1994. Before then, the communication duties (production of press releases and member journals, performance of campaigns, etc.) were fulfilled by the secretaries of the SGB. This example makes clear that the functions of organizational communication stayed the same, but the organizational structures having to fulfill these functions changed during the last decade. Another example is the emergence in recent years of electronic media monitorings, which fulfill the same function as traditional press reviews (systematic observation and description of the external media-environment).

Formal Structures of Organizational Communication

For Luhmann, all social systems (such as organizations, groups or societal subsystems) consist of communication. In the case of organizations—which basically consist of decisions—the preconditions for their development and reproduction are given as soon as decisions are communicated and the organizational system is closed on this operational basis.[19] "Operational closeness" means that organizations produce further decisions on the basis of existing decisions. Decisions (i.e.,

operations) are in a reciprocal relation with structures that are described as decision premises. These decisions have a regulative character for many later decisions. Consequently, the formal structures of organizational communication can
be conceived of as decision premises. Decision programs (formal structures) of
the organizational communication can be differentiated into three types, which
can be empirically observed: (1) decision programs; (2) positions and divisions;
and, (3) communication paths.[20]

Decision programs define the requirements of the factual accuracy of decisions and can be described as rules that structure the memory of the organization. They enable the organization to vary its relationships to the environment
and to decide what incidences have a causal effect on the organization. Decision
programs can be classified into input-oriented conditional programs and out-
put-oriented intentional programs. "Conditional programs" can be reduced to
the formula "if–then." When referring to organizational communication, the
observation of issues, opinions or images in the public sphere plays an important
role. An example could be an intermediary organization that uses issue monitoring for a systematic observation of media coverage. In so doing, issue monitoring
is based on a rule (conditional program) that states: "if the mass media spread
negative publicity about our organization, the communication division launches
PR actions at an early stage." "Intentional programs," on the other hand, define
the intentions of the organization as well as the preferences for the use of instruments to reach these intentions. When referring to the organizational communication of intermediary organizations, such intentions could be to better the
image of the organization, to influence the mass media or to acquire resources,
whereas the preferred instruments could be communication instruments, such
as press releases, the intranet or member magazines. The German Trade Union
Confederation (DGB), for example, launched a long-term initiative called "Initiative Trendwende" for the purpose of stopping the severe losses of members
during the last few years. In the context of this initiative, instruments of market
and opinion research as well as member-oriented services have been up-valued,
among other things.

Organizations recruit their staff of organizational communication (e.g., PR
or marketing experts) in positions that can be described as bunches of jobs.
Positions coordinate decision programs, the staff, and communication paths.
Diverse positions can build a division. Whereas small organizations such as citizens' groups or social movement organizations often do not have any specialized
positions and divisions of organizational communication at all, big, complex, and
highly formalized organizations, such as trade union confederations, have specialized divisions of PR, marketing, campaigning, etc.

The Swiss Trade Union Confederation (SGB), for example, has a spokes-
man and a division for "information and campaigns," including two editors and
one assistant. The foundation in 1994 of a communication division can be seen
as an effort to improve the coordination and integration of different forms of
internal and external communication. A similar organizational development can

be observed in the case of the German Trade Union Confederation (DGB), which in 1990 created a division for "PR, information and communication" to integrate different communication functions that were organizationally separated. Furthermore, the SGB and the DGB as well as the Austrian Trade Union Confederation (ÖGB) have recognized the importance of campaigning in the recent past and have created formal organizational structures that are specialized in fulfilling this communication duty. Whereas the ÖGB created a unit for "campaigns, projects, and target groups," the SGB and the DGB integrated campaigning into the above-mentioned communication divisions.

Finally, decision premises can regulate the *communication paths* within organizations. In this context, competencies are important; in the first instance, the competency to give orders, and, then, the competency to be heard. Communication paths arise from the competencies of the positions. According to Luhmann,[21] competencies can be differentiated into professional and hierarchical competencies. In a communication-theoretical perspective, the term "hierarchical competencies" refers to the function of an address.[22] Hereby, hierarchical competencies can be divided into line and staff organization.[23] Whereas the line organization has direct authority, the staff organization only has a supportive function. To enable professional organizational communication, it seems to be important that the correspondent positions and divisions are located closely to the executive board.[24] The term "professional competencies," on the other hand, refers to the function of professional ability. The professional competencies of the above-mentioned SGB-division "information and campaigns," for example, can be described as professional campaigning, production of member journals, and press releases, etc.

The outsourcing of certain professional competencies, such as PR, political consultancy, lobbying or public affairs, to professional consultants, public affairs agencies or specialized chambers of advocates seems to have grown in importance.[25] Referring to the SGB, DGB, and ÖGB, we can observe two divergent developments during the last 30 years: the outsourcing of certain competencies, such as editorial duties, socio-scientific research, membership promotion or graphic design, on the one hand, and a tendency to reverse the outsourcing for reasons of economy in recent years, on the other hand. Furthermore, an analysis of the coordination of organizational communication between umbrella organizations and their member organizations should be insightful. The SGB, DGB, and ÖGB, for instance, have undertaken over the last 30 years several efforts to optimize the coordination of mobilization, campaigning, membership promotion, PR, political actions or the production of information materials with their member organizations.

Issues and Interpretation Patterns

Together with formal structures in the shape of decision programs, positions, divisions, and communication paths, constructivist systems theory also enables the description of issues and interpretation patterns as structures of organizational communication. Issues and interpretation patterns can fulfill the same primary function of self-description and description of the environment:

1. On the one hand, issues and interpretation patterns form the description and interpretation of formal structures (decision premises) and processes (decisions) of the organizational system—for example, the way that the SGB, DGB, and ÖGB describe and interpret their communication instruments or existing positions and divisions of organizational communication (as efficient/inefficient, modern or technically antiquated, etc.).

2. On the other hand, issues and interpretation patterns form the description and interpretation of the organizational system's environment—for instance, the way that the SGB, DGB, and ÖGB describe and interpret environmental changes such as the losses of members (e.g., as self-inflicted or as a consequence of social change, etc.).

The latter needs some further explanations. The above-described PR conceptions, which refer to structural-functionalist systems theory, conceive the organizational environment as an objective dimension. By contrast, constructivist systems theory describes the environment as an organizational construction.[26] In this theory, it is the organizational system that defines internal or external environments as relevant or as irrelevant. And it is the organizational system that decides autonomously whether and how to observe, describe, and interpret different environments and changes within these environments respectively. This organizational construction of the environment is based on system specific processes (observations, descriptions, interpretations) and structures (issues and interpretation patterns), which were blanked out as a "black box" by structural-functionalist organization and PR theories.

In the perspective of constructivist systems theory, it seems to be fruitful to analyze and compare the description and interpretation of comparable (observed or constructed) changes in internal or external environments by intermediary organizations, such as political parties, trade unions or movement organizations. Differences concerning the examined descriptions and interpretations should be explainable (amongst others) by system specific issues and interpretation patterns that are stored in the organizational memory.

Potentially Relevant Environments of Intermediary Organizations

As has been explained above, constructivist systems theory conceives the environment as a construction of the organization and not as an objective dimension. Strictly speaking, in this theoretical perspective the relevance of different internal and external environments can only be analyzed through organizational constructions. Nevertheless, it seems to be helpful to develop an analytical framework that describes potentially relevant environments of organizations, such as pressure groups, NGOs, social movement organizations or political parties, and referring changes in these environments that could be relevant for their organizational communication. For this purpose, Streeck's conception of intermediary organizations[27] is considered as a fruitful theoretical approach.

Streeck argues that intermediary organizations have to interact with two different environments at the same time:[28] (1) with their social basis (members, supporters, sympathizers, etc.), on the one hand, which shall be called "internal environment" in the following; and, (2) with an institutional environment of the political system and external political organizations, on the other hand, which shall be called the "external environment." Both environments confront intermediary organizations with different and sometimes conflicting requests:[29]

1. In a macro perspective, the central request of the *external environment* can be described as the integration of the intermediary organization into the political system ("system integration"). In a meso perspective, intermediary organizations have to achieve external assertiveness and to influence the political decision-making process ("logic of influence"). For this purpose, intermediary organizations try to influence coalition partners as well as competitors through external communication. In the media "society," political organizations such as trade union confederations often try to mediate their interests indirectly through influencing the media coverage (using press releases, symbolic actions, demonstrations, etc.).

2. The central requests of the *internal environment,* on the other hand, can be described as the integration of the social basis (members, supporters, sympathizers, etc.) into the organizational system ("social integration"). Accordingly, intermediary organizations have to mobilize and pin down their members, supporters, and sympathizers by internal communication (internal PR, member marketing, fundraising, etc.). Furthermore, they have to meet the challenge of aggregating the diverse and sometimes conflicting interests of their social basis to reach external assertiveness.

Potentially Relevant Changes in Internal and External Environments

Some environmental changes that occurred during the last decades are suspected to have profoundly modified the general conditions of internal "social integration" and external "system integration." As a consequence, it can be assumed that these environmental changes could prompt intermediary organizations to reform their internal and external communication. The following remarks will focus on Europeanization processes of the political system and changes concerning the mass media as well as the social basis of intermediary organizations.[30]

Transnationalization and Europeanization of the Political System

In consequence of transnationalization and Europeanization processes, intermediary organizations such as political parties, pressure groups or movement organizations are forced to mediate their interests in a changed political system.[31] The emergence of a European multi-level system, which is focused on here, implicates an interdigitation of regional, national, and transnational decision-making processes.[32] On the one hand, the political-administrative system of the nation-state (government, parliament, and administration) becomes less important for the political interest mediation of intermediary organizations. On the other hand, intermediary organizations receive new chances to influence the political decision-making process on the supranational level.

Empirical studies show that political parties, associations, and social movements have adopted their external communication to the changed political context of the European multi-level system.[33] For instance, intermediary organizations try to embark on a dual strategy by representing their interests at the same time on the European level as well as on the national level, which requires a lot of resources.[34] Furthermore, complex internal coordination processes between the national and the transnational level and a professional issue management become important. In this context, the outsourcing of political communication to professional lobbying agencies is gaining in importance.[35] Certain oligarchization tendencies and a loss of influence of the social basis can be the consequence of outsourcing, as can be observed with the emergence of a newer type of NGOs.[36]

On a transnational level, the integration of organized interests within the decision and consultancy networks of the European Union is gaining in importance.[37] Since Maastricht (1993), it is an official aim of the European Union (EU) to improve the integration of organized interests within its political process. The EU-Commission, the European Parliament as well as the European Economic and Social Committee (EESC) enable diverse pressure groups and associations to mediate their political interests by consultations or hearings. Moreover, the EU provides financial support for diverse organized interests with small resources. The general conditions of the political system of the EU favor direct, conventional forms of political communication, such as lobbying or consulting. On the contrary, public-oriented forms of political communication ('pressure') such as protest, demonstrations or symbolic actions are still concentrated on the regional and national level because the European public sphere is still strongly fragmented.

Changes Concerning the Mass Media

The rise of the media "society" also brought with it an increasing tendency to mediate political interests via mass media.[38] Consequently, media relations are gaining in importance for all political actors.[39] These processes implicate an adaptation of organizational communication to the logic of the mass media (mediatization) that can be observed on the level of organizational structures (e.g., the creation of PR divisions or the professionalization of media campaigns and issue monitoring) as well as on the level of PR contents, which have to consider the values of the news, such as actuality, negativity, personalization or unexpectedness.

Furthermore, during the last decades, the western mass media have emancipated themselves from traditional intermediary organizations, such as political parties or associations and have passed through a process of economization[40] or autonomization.[41] On the one hand, these changes implicate that traditional intermediaries such as political parties or associations have lost their organs (e.g., journals of political parties). Consequently, traditional intermediaries have to professionalize their media-oriented communication (PR, paid media). On the other hand, the above-described changes implicate a change of media logic, which makes it easier for peripheral political actors such as social movements to draw the attention of the mass media by putting on symbolic actions (demonstrations, protest, sit-ins, etc.).[42] This gives new chances to peripheral political actors that do not have direct access to the political-administrative system (government, parliament, and administration) and enables them to influence the political decision-making process indirectly by influencing the public opinion via mass media. Trade unions reacted to these new chances and requirements by a professionalization of media campaigning.[43] As has already been described above, the SGB, the DGB as well as the ÖGB have created positions and divisions in the recent past that specialize in campaigning.

Changes Concerning the Social Basis

As has been described above, intermediary organizations have to integrate their social basis and their interests into the organizational system to reach external assertiveness. However, changes in the internal environment of traditional intermediary organizations, such as political parties or associations during the last decades, are suspected to have profoundly modified the general conditions of a successful "social integration." In consequence, "social integration" has become increasingly problematic and uncertain. In most European countries, intermediary organizations are confronted with losses of members and with an increasingly volatile clientele, respectively, as well as with a shrinking willingness voluntarily to engage. The reasons for these changes are seen in the individualization and in the decline of traditional social milieus during the last decades. Moreover, there is an increased competition for donators and members as a result of the pluralization of organized interests (i.e., the appearance of new intermediary organizations in the context of new social movements). Under such circumstances, it can be seen as a central challenge for intermediary organizations to mobilize (potentially new) members and to accomplish their commitment in the long-term. Therefore, a professionalization of the member and donator oriented communication (internal PR, internal marketing, fundraising, etc.) as well as the provision of "selective incentives"[44] are growing in importance. Because of the autonomization of the mass media traditional intermediary organizations, such as political parties or trade unions, cannot rely on associated media anymore to mobilize their social basis. As a result, internal media such as member journals, the intranet or newsletters gain in importance.[45]

Reactions of Autopoietic Organizational Systems to Changes in Their Environments

After the description of potentially relevant changes in the internal and external environment of intermediary organizations, the following question shall be theoretically answered: how do intermediary organizations react on such environmental changes by reforming their organizational communication?

Constructivist systems theory (together with other organization-sociological theories) focuses on the relation between organizations and their environment. Therefore, constructivist systems theory seems to be a fruitful theoretical approach in order to conceive organizational change[46] as well as to conceive the change of organizational communication (which can be seen as a particular case of organizational change) and to answer the above-mentioned question.

First, in the perspective of Luhmann's theory of autopoietic organizational systems,[47] organizational change and the change of organizational communication, respectively, can be conceived of as reforms of decision premises. In other words, intermediary organizations can decide to reform:

1. their *decision programs*—e.g., the intentions of organizational communication (recruitment of new members, influencing the public opinion, etc.) and the instruments to achieve these aims (creation of a new youth journal, starting a PR campaign, etc.);

2. their *positions and divisions* of organizational communication—e.g., the creation of a new division that has the duty to professionalize the member communication; and finally,

3. their *communication paths*—e.g., the coordination of member mobilization between a trade union confederation and its member unions.

The above-described structural-functionalist organization and PR theories assume that constant information flow from an objective environment into the organizational system, where they produce environmental pressures and force the organization to adopt its structures.[48] Therefore, in this theoretical perspective, organizations and organizational changes can be regarded as determined by the environment. At the same time, the internal structures and processes forming the organizational perception of the environment are blanked out as a "black box."

By contrast, constructivist systems theory pays a lot of attention to the system specific perception of the environment by conceiving the environment and environmental changes as a construction of the organization. Organizations are conceived as autonomous, self-referentially closed systems, which are not determined by their environment. But this does not mean that environmental changes do not have any influence on organizational changes at all. Rather, in this theoretical perspective, organizational systems can only be activated to own operations by environmental changes:[49] the perception of environmental changes is a construction of the organization, because it is the organization that decides whether and how to observe, describe, and interpret environmental irritations. Furthermore, the organization decides autonomously whether and how to reform its structures of organizational communication in reaction to perceived changes in its environment. Both the perception of environmental changes as well as the decisions to reform the structures of organizational communication recursively refers to historically grown, system-specific structures. The former refers to pre-existing interpretation patterns and issues that are stored in the organizational memory; the latter refers to pre-existing decision premises (positions, divisions, communication paths, and decision programs).

These remarks make clear that—in the perspective of constructivist systems theory—reforms of organizational communication are not determined by environmental changes. Rather, historically grown, system-specific structures, such as decision premises, issues, and interpretation patterns, shape the change of organizational communication. Therefore, it can be expected that comparable intermediary organizations, such as national trade union confederations, react differently on comparable perceived (constructed) changes in their internal and external environments, such as Europeanization or the transnationalization processes of the political system, an increased importance of the mass media for political communication, or an increasingly volatile clientele.

Outlook

In concluding this chapter, I would like to summarize the potentials of the above-described theoretical approach for the empirical research of intermediaries' organizational communication.

First, it can be summed up that this theory is suited for the analysis of all kinds of intermediary organizations, such as NGOs, social movement organizations, associations (environmental or consumers associations, trade unions, etc.), political parties, etc. The reason is that all of these organizations are confronted with comparable environmental requests, which have been described by Streeck[50] as "social integration" and "system integration." Secondly, comparisons between organizations of the same organizational field (national trade union confederations, environmental associations, political parties, etc.) should be instructive. On the one hand, the intermediaries' perception and description of similar (observed) environmental changes that modify the general conditions of internal "social integration" and external "system integration," such as changes concerning the political system, the mass media or the social basis (see above), can be compared. On the other hand, possible reforms of the intermediaries' organizational communication in reaction to the observed environmental changes can be contrasted. Referring to constructivist systems theory, differences between the perception of environmental changes as well as the differences between the reforms of organizational communication should be explainable amongst others by historically grown, systems-specific structures—decision premises on the one hand, and issues and interpretation patterns, on the other.

One possibility to study reforms of intermediaries' organizational communication as well as the reasons for these reforms in the intermediaries' description is to analyze organizational documents, such as annual reports or minutes of committees. The analysis can then focus on decisions to reform decision premises as well as on the justifications of these decisions. In so doing, it can be examined which changes in internal and external environments are picked out as central themes used to justify the reforms of organizational communication and how these environmental changes are interpreted.

Notes

1. G.F. Davis, D. McAdam, W.R. Scott, and M.N. Zald, *Social Movements and Organization Theory* (Cambridge: University Press, 2005), xiv.
2. See D. Rucht, "Öffentlichkeit als Mobilisierungsfaktor für soziale Bewegungen," in *Öffentlichkeit, öffentliche Meinung, soziale Bewegungen (= Kölner Zeitschrift für Soziologie und Sozialpsychologie, special edition 34)*, ed. F. Neidhardt (Opladen: Westdeutscher Verlag, 1994), 337–358.
3. N. Luhmann, *Organisation und Entscheidung* (Opladen, Wiesbaden: Westdeutscher Verlag, 2000).
4. See H. Willke, *Sytemtheorie I: Grundlagen: Eine Einführung in die Grundprobleme der Theorie sozialer Systeme* (6th corrected ed.), (Stuttgart: Lucius & Lucius, 2000), 51.
5. See also A.M. Theis-Berglmair.. 'Public Relations aus organisationssoziologischer Sicht," in *Handbuch der Public Relations. Wissenschaftliche Grundlagen und berufliches Handeln. Mit Lexikon*, eds. G. Bentele, R. Fröhlich, and P. Szyszka (Wiesbaden: VS Verlag für Sozialwissenschaften, 2005), 39.

6. W. Streeck, "Vielfalt und Interdependenz. Überlegungen zur Rolle von intermediären Organisationen in sich ändernden Umwelten," *Kölner Zeitschrift für Soziologie und Sozialpsychologie* 39(3) (1987): 470–495.

7. The theoretical framework that will be presented in this chapter has been developed for my Ph.D. project, which has been supported financially by the research credit of the University of Zurich from February 2007 until January 2008. See D. Lachenmeier, *Gewerkschaftskommunikation im Wandel. Eine systemtheoretische Analyse der Organisationskommunikation des Schweizerischen, Deutschen und Österreichischen Gewerkschaftsbunds 1972–2005* (Basel: edition gesowip, 2009).

8. See e.g., K. Gajewska, *Transnational Labour Solidarity: Mechanisms of Commitment to Cooperation within the European Trade Union Movement* (London: Routledge, 2009); C. Phelan, ed., *Trade Union Revitalisation: Trends and Prospects in 34 Countries* (Bern: Peter Lang, 2007); J.T. Addison and C. Schnabel, eds., *International Handbook of Trade Unions* (Cheltenham: Edward Elgar, 2003); K. Armingeon and S. Geissbühler, eds., *Gewerkschaften in der Schweiz. Herausforderungen und Optionen* (Zürich : Seismo, 2000); B. Ebbinghaus and J. Visser, *Trade Unions in Western Europe since 1945* (London: Macmillan Reference Ltd., 2000); D. Foster and P. Scott, eds., *Trade Unions in Europe: Meeting the Challenge* (Bruxelles: P.I.E. – Lang, 2000).

9. An exception amongst others is Arlt's study of the public relations of the German trade union confederation (DGB): H.-J. Arlt, *Kommunikation, Öffentlichkeit, Öffentlichkeitsarbeit. PR von gestern, PR für morgen—das Beispiel Gewerkschaft* (Opladen, Wiesbaden: Westdeutscher Verlag, 1998). See also Lachenmeier, *Gewerkschaftskommunikation im Wandel.*

10. See A.M. Theis-Berglmair, "Organisation—eine vernachlässigte Grösse in der Kommunikationswissenschaft," in *Theorien öffentlicher Kommunikation,* eds. G. Bentele and M. Rühl (München: Ölschläger, 1993), 313.

11. See O. Jarren and U. Röttger, "Public Relations aus kommunikationswissenschaftlicher Sicht," in *Handbuch der Public Relations. Wissenschaftliche Grundlagen und berufliches Handeln. Mit Lexikon,* eds. G. Bentele, R. Fröhlich, and P. Szyszka (Wiesbaden: VS Verlag für Sozialwissenschaften, 2005), 19; G. Bentele, "Grundlagen der Public Relations," in *Public Relations in Theorie und Praxis,* ed. W. Donsbach (München: Reinhard Fischer, 1997), 21–36.

12. See O. Hoffjann, *Journalismus und Public Relations. Ein Theorieentwurf der Intersystembeziehungen in sozialen Konflikten* (Wiesbaden: Westdeutscher Verlag, 2001), 138; O. Jarren and U. Röttger, "Steuerung, Reflexierung und Interpenetration: Kernelemente einer strukturationstheoretisch begründeten PR-Theorie," in *Theorien der Public Relations. Grundlagen und Perspektiven der PR-Forschung,* ed. U. Röttger (Wiesbaden: VS Verlag für Sozialwissenschaften, 2004), 25–45.

13. J.E. Grunig and T. Hunt, *Managing Public Relations* (New York: Holt, Rinehart & Winston, 1984).

14. D. Katz and R.L. Kahn, *The Social Psychology of Organizations* (New York: Wiley, 1966).

15. Parsons' AGIL scheme differentiates the following functions of social systems: (1) *Adaptation:* adaptation to changes in the environment; (2) *Goal-Attainment:* selection and attainment of goals; (3) *Integration:* integration of subsystems and elements of the system; and (4) *Latent pattern maintenance:* maintaining the stability of patterns of institutionalized culture defining the structure of the system.

16. See Luhmann, *Organisation und Entscheidung*, 72; N. Luhmann, *Soziale Systeme. Grundriss einer allgemeinen Theorie* (Frankfurt/Main: Suhrkamp, 1984), 604ff.
17. See Theis-Berglmair, "Public Relations aus organisationssoziologischer Sicht," 40f.
18. See N. Herger, *Organisationskommunikation. Beobachtung und Steuerung eines organisationalen Risikos* (Wiesbaden: VS Verlag für Sozialwissenschaften, 2004).
19. Luhmann, *Organisation und Entscheidung*, 63.
20. Ibid., 9f., 222ff.; Herger, *Organisationskommunikation*, 198ff.
21. Luhmann, *Organisation und Entscheidung*, 312.
22. Ibid., 320; Herger, *Organisationskommunikation*, 256f.
23. See Herger, *Organisationskommunikation*, 258.
24. Ibid., 259; U. Röttger, *Public Relations—Organisation und Profession. Öffentlichkeitsarbeit als Organisationsfunktion. Eine Berufsfeldstudie* (Wiesbaden: Westdeutscher Verlag, 2000), 256.
25. See M. Sebaldt and A. Straßner, *Verbände in der Bundesrepublik Deutschland. Eine Einführung* (Wiesbaden: VS Verlag für Sozialwissenschaften, 2004).
26. See e.g., Luhmann, *Organisation und Entscheidung*, 52; J. Rüegg-Stürm, *Organisation und organisationaler Wandel. Eine theoretische Erkundung aus konstruktivistischer Sicht* (Wiesbaden: Westdeutscher Verlag, 2001); K.E. Weick, *Der Prozess des Organisierens* (Frankfurt/Main: Suhrkamp, 1985).
27. Vgl. Streeck, "Vielfalt und Interdependenz."
28. Ibid., 472ff.; see also H. Backhaus-Maul and T. Olk, "Intermediäre Organisationen als Gegenstand sozialwissenschaftlicher Forschung. Theoretische Überlegungen und erste empirische Befunde am Beispiel des Aufbaus von intermediären Organisationen in den neuen Bundesländern," in *Sozialpolitik im Prozess der deutschen Vereinigung*, ed. W. Schmähl (Frankfurt/Main, New York: Campus-Verlag, 1992), 109.
29. See Streeck, "Vielfalt und Interdependenz," 489ff.; O. Jarren, A. Steiner, and D. Lachenmeier, "Entgrenzte Demokratie? Politische Interessenvermittlung im Mehrebenensystem," in *Entgrenzte Demokratie? Herausforderungen für die politische Interessenvermittlung*, eds. O. Jarren, D. Lachenmeier, and A. Steiner (Baden-Baden: Nomos, 2007), 356ff.
30. See also ibid.
31. Ibid.
32. See e.g., R. Eising and B. Kohler-Koch, "Interessenpolitik im europäischen Mehrebenensystem," in *Interessenpolitik in Europa*, eds. Eising and Kohler-Koch (Baden-Baden: Nomos, 2005), 11–75.
33. See A. Straßner and M. Sebaldt, "Die Europäisierung von Verbandsarbeit: Verbandsfunktionen, Wandlungsmuster, Konsequenzen," in Jarren et al., *Entgrenzte Demokratie?*, 123–144; A. Römmele, "Parteien als Akteure der politischen Kommunikation auf europäischer Ebene," in Jarren et al., *Entgrenzte Demokratie?*, 93–106; H. Kriesi, "Die politische Kommunikation sozialer Bewegungen," in Jarren et al., *Entgrenzte Demokratie?*, 145–161; D. della Porta and M. Caiani, "Social movements in a multilevel Europe," in Jarren et al., *Entgrenzte Demokratie?*, 163–177.
34. See Straßner and Sebaldt, "Die Europäisierung von Verbandsarbeit," 134f.; Eising and Kohler-Koch, "Interessenpolitik im europäischen Mehrebenensystem," 48; B. Kohler-Koch, T. Conzelmann, and M. Knodt, *Europäische Integration—Europäisches Regieren* (Wiesbaden: VS Verlag für Sozialwissenschaften, 2004), 241ff.

35. See Straßner and Sebaldt, "Die Europäisierung von Verbandsarbeit"; C. Lahusen, "Joining the cocktail circuit: social movement organizations at the European Union," *Mobilization: An International Journal* 9(1)(2004): 60.
36. See C. Frantz, "NGOs als transnationale Interessenvertreter und Agenda Setter," in Jarren et al., *Entgrenzte Demokratie?*, 186ff.
37. See B. Kohler-Koch and M. Jachtenfuchs, "Governance in der Europäischen Union," in *Governance—Regieren in komplexen Regelsystemen: Eine Einführung*, ed. A. Benz (Wiesbaden: VS Verlag für Sozialwissenschaften, 2004), 77–101; B. Kohler-Koch and R. Eising, *The transformation of governance in the European Union* (London: Routledge, 1999); G.F. Schuppert, ed., *The Europeanisation of Governance* (= *Schriften zur Governance-Forschung 4*) (Baden-Baden: Nomos, 2006).
38. O. Jarren and P. Donges, *Politische Kommunikation in der Mediengesellschaft. Eine Einführung*, 2nd ed. (Wiesbaden: VS Verlag für Sozialwissenschaften, 2006), 26ff.
39. See e.g., P. Donges, *Medialisierung Politischer Organisationen: Parteien in der Mediengesellschaft* (Wiesbaden: VS Verlag für Sozialwissenschaften, 2008); Kriesi, "Die politische Kommunikation sozialer Bewegungen," 151ff.; A. Ladner, "Die Rolle der Parteien in der Mediengesellschaft," in Jarren et al., *Entgrenzte Demokratie?*, 82ff.; F. Neidhardt, "Massenmedien im intermediären System moderner Demokratien," in Jarren et al., *Entgrenzte Demokratie?*, 35ff.; Römmele, "Parteien als Akteure der politischen Kommunikation auf europäischer Ebene," 94ff.
40. O. Jarren, "'Mediengesellschaft'—Risiken für die politische Kommunikation," *Aus Politik und Zeitgeschichte* 41–42(2001): 13.
41. F. Marcinkowski, *Publizistik als autopoietisches System—Politik und Massenmedien. Eine systemtheoretische Analyse* (Opladen: Westdeutscher Verlag, 1993).
42. See K. Imhof, "Politik im 'neuen' Strukturwandel der Öffentlichkeit," in *Der Begriff des Politischen* (= *Soziale Welt* 14), eds. A. Nassehi and M. Schroer (Baden-Baden: Nomos, 2003), 401–417; K. Imhof, "Eine Symbiose: Soziale Bewegungen und Medien," in *Politisches Raisonnement in der Informationsgesellschaft* (= *Reihe Mediensymposium Luzern* 2), eds. K. Imhof and P. Schulz (Zürich: Seismo, 1996), 165–186.
43. See also H.-J. Arlt and O. Jarren, "Abwehrkünstler am Werk—Über die Kampagnenfähigkeit des Deutschen Gewerkschaftsbundes," in *PR-Kampagnen. Über die Inszenierung von Öffentlichkeit*, ed. U. Röttger (Opladen: Westdeutscher Verlag, 1998), 172–193; B. Wessels, "Gewerkschaften in der Mediengesellschaft," in *Die Gewerkschaften in Politik und Gesellschaft der Bundesrepublik Deutschland. Ein Handbuch*, eds. W. Schroeder and B. Wessels (Wiesbaden: Westdeutscher Verlag, 2003), 323–341.
44. M. Olson, *Die Logik des kollektiven Handelns. Kollektivgüter und die Theorie der Gruppen* (Tübingen: Mohr, 1968).
45. See K. Armingeon, "Die politische Rolle der Verbände in modernen Demokratien. Fünf Thesen," in Jarren et al., *Entgrenzte Demokratie?*, 110ff.; Frantz, "NGOs als transnationale Interessenvertreter und Agenda Setter," 186; Ladner, "Die Rolle der Parteien in der Mediengesellschaft," 81ff.; Römmele, "Parteien als Akteure der politischen Kommunikation auf europäischer Ebene," 94ff.; Straßner and Sebaldt, "Die Europäisierung von Verbandsarbeit," 123ff.
46. See N. Luhmann, *Soziologische Aufklärung 2* (Opladen: Westdeutscher Verlag, 1975), 150ff.; Rüegg-Stürm, *Organisation und organisationaler Wandel*.

47. Luhmann, *Organisation und Entscheidung.*
48. See A.M. Theis-Berglmair, *Organisationskommunikation. Theoretische Grundlagen und empirische Forschungen,* 2nd ed. (Münster, Hamburg, and London: Lit-Verlag, 2003), 176ff.
49. See Willke, *Systemtheorie I,* 62.
50. Streeck, "Vielfalt und Interdependenz."

Part IV

Outlook for Research

The Role of Dissident-Intellectuals in the Formation of Civil Society in (Post-)Communist East-Central Europe

Mariya Ivancheva

This chapter is not going to answer the question of *what* was the role of intellectuals in the formation, transformation, or deformation of civil society in East-Central Europe in the transition from communism to post-communism. Instead, by avoiding unidirectional answers, I introduce the multiplicity of arguments voiced in the debate. I demonstrate how it split along the lines of civil society theory and practice, of pre– and post–1989 developments of civic activism in the region, and of divergent disciplinary approaches to the problem. On this basis, I suggest that the analysis of civil society as a frame of protest can be an insightful approach on *how* to research this complex question.

Contextualizing the Problem: Civil Society and Dissident-Intellectuals on Trial

Civil society—the philosophical concept that stems from the Scottish Enlightenment—undoubtedly gained a new strength in the 1980s in East-Central Europe.[1] Civil society has always been understood as a space of organized human interaction and civil activity, situated in relation to, but independent from, both state and market. In this role, it was discussed as a corporate third sector regulating the relations between the latter two (Georg W.G. Hegel); a set of mediating institutions that works to reproduce the (bourgeois) state system through fabricated consensus (Karl Marx and Antonio Gramsci); or a parallel structure of sociability emancipated and more effective in preserving the social order than the state apparatus (Thomas Paine).[2]

The rise of civil society in East-Central Europe was seen rather in the latter, anti-statist plain: initiated against repressive state-socialist regimes, the newly emerged dissident practice appeared as a genuine grassroots mobilization. The dissidents' aim was to oppose the socialist state apparatuses and to create alterna-

tive practices to what was dictated by the single party in power. "The philosophical study groups in basements and boiler rooms, the prayer meetings in church
crypts, and the unofficial trade union meetings in bars and backrooms"—an
enthusiastic account reports—"were seen as a civil society in embryo."[3] Thus,
the moral choice of the dissidents to live in constant exposure to the risk of
repression was declared in the name of free speech, human rights, and liberties.
It was viewed as a stance of unique human dignity and attracted attention and
respect among likeminded people, both home and abroad. In this process, a mutual rediscovery was taking place. Central Europe was reconceptualized by the
dissidents in its proximity to Western—as opposed to Eastern—culture;[4] hence
Hungary, Poland, and Czechoslovakia were seen as belonging to the family of
Western nation-states. At the same time, in the mirror of appreciation from the
East for the development of liberty, democracy, and the rule of law, Western
politicians, activists, and intellectuals could see their homelands as celebrated
progenitors of civil society.[5]

After the celebratory first accounts of the role of civil society in the 1980s,
studies of dissident-intellectuals and their role in its theory and practice split
into several divergent trends. Affirmative accounts praised dissidents on their
specific contribution to the Western theory of civil society. Some ascribed the
dissidents' understanding of civil society to a particular school of thought; others stressed their genuine—if not systematic—contribution to the theory of civil
society.[6] Positive comments on the dissidents' legacy in global political activism
were set against the negative analyses of their failure to contribute to the post-socialist development of a civil society.[7] The most prominent dissidents themselves
were not unanimous: whereas several shared the fascination with the civil society
ideal after 1989, the rest sounded rather disenchanted with the shortages of the
concept as it existed in the socialist era and its post-socialist realities.[8] Pessimistic
studies also reviewed the ambiguous position of former dissidents in the post-
socialist era. They were said to have helped the formation of a strong political,
instead of a civil, society. Their post–1989 political careers either followed the
track of "from *glasnost* to market," or displayed an extreme moralism. In profess-
ing the existence of one true way ahead and a single moral in politics, they were
often seen as irrelevant actors in the new political conjunctures where media
discourses claimed a multiplicity of interpretations.[9]

Recent scholarship has shown that, currently, civic organizations in the region have displayed strong "transactional" activism by mobilizing on issues of
common interest.[10] Yet, this statement came only after a wave of critical comments on the development of post-socialist civil society. Such studies find the
pressure that was put on the impoverished Warsaw Pact member states to sign
the Helsinki Final Acts (1975) by Western governments to have initiated the dis-
integration of the Eastern Bloc. While East-Central European states were forced
to obey human rights regulations under closer monitoring, private and state-
driven Western capital was poured into certain dissident projects. After 1989,

it was smoothly directed into the "portable model" of civil society, uncritically transposed from abroad into the region. However, the strong causal relationship between the mushrooming NGOs and the development of civil society assumed by democratization funds driven by US and EU sponsorship seemed wrong: civil society "barometers" detected an imperfect and "anti-political" functioning of civil society, as opposed to its old, authentic, "anti-political" form that the dissidents professed.[11] The disenchanted public mostly refused to join voluntary associations and became liable to "uncivil," anomic mobilization.[12] While the transitions were increasingly seen as a mere restructuring of power elites,[13] the momentum of civil society mass mobilization, celebrated in the beginning of the 1990s, seemed to have stopped dead.

Overcoming Methodological Dichotomies: Civil Society as a Frame

In this line of differentiation, a further disciplinary division came to play in the discussion of civil society. Whereas the theoretical and historical accounts persisted on a precise analytical definition of civil society in its relationship to the state, the practice of "measuring" civil society was appropriated by political scientists and economists. Against this background, theories from the field of contentious politics and political anthropology tried to define a researchable unit of civic activism. Their research aim was to combine theoretical and empirical approaches, and to concentrate above all on the claims that actors make in the process of social mobilization.[14]

In 1991, one of the prominent scholars of contentious politics, Sidney Tarrow, declared that the events in East-Central Europe had found researchers from the field unprepared. Tarrow outlines particular methodological biases of the field: the anti-institutional persuasion of the movements in postindustrial Western societies; the domination of the context neutral survey method; and the overemphasis on individual—as opposed to collective—actors in psychological and microeconomic theories. Instead of the overly individual resource mobilization theory, or the too globally concerned "new" social movement studies, Tarrow champions the readjustment of preexisting models and methods so that they could "aim at a moving target." The research program he offers concentrates on opportunity structure openings within declining post-socialist authoritarian regimes, but also requires the use of qualitative research methods.[15]

Tarrow's suggestive critique notwithstanding, social movement studies have scarcely been applied to the dissident movements or to their legacy in contemporary activism in East-Central Europe. On the one hand, the obscure post-socialist divide between left and right and the positioning of the dissidents toward the right side of the political spectrum was deeply problematic for scholarship originating in the 1960s from the contentious Western New Left.

On the other hand, the scarce media sources' resistance under socialism and the ostensible lack of extra-parliamentary left-wing activism made the leading "protest event analysis" approach of coding newspaper sources methodologically unfeasible.[16]

One decisive step in overcoming methodological shortages and to address frames of protest was John Glenn's book *Framing Democracy: Civil Society and Civic Activism in East-Central Europe*. Borrowing terminology from the field of contentious politics, Glenn suggests an innovative approach reconciling the dichotomy between dissidents' theory and their practice of civil society. Glenn sees civil society in a decisively new role: for him, it was a master frame of the peaceful revolutions in East-Central Europe. Glenn's interest is a classical pair-comparison in the tradition of historical sociology. He operationalizes the civil society frame within two culminating waves of protest.[17] Yet, Glenn avoids more detailed conceptual analysis and any contextually broader discussion of the civil society frame formation in East-Central Europe: an issue that could introduce extremely useful insights into the studies of contentious politics in the 1980s in the region and beyond.

Frames of interaction were conceptualized by Ervin Goffman as cognitive "schemata of interpretation," enabling individuals to "locate, perceive, identify and label" events and phenomena. In newer interpretations from the field of contentious politics, frames are seen as ordering experience and guiding action "to mobilize potential adherents and constituents, to garner bystander support, and to demobilize antagonists." Frame alignment theory can explain bottom-up mass mobilization in cases where opportunity structure openings are not present.[18] Movement actors are seen as signifying individual and collective agents, engaged in the (re)production of worlds of shared meaning, structured around issues of identity, agency, and injustice. Drawing on critical theoretical approaches, a recent "discursive tilt" in the frame alignment theory put forward the *discursive* analysis of frames. This approach displays the dynamic process of frame formation as dialogic negotiation of meaning, infused with specific power relations within a "terrain of conflict."[19]

Further Levels of Complexity: Intellectuals, (Transnational) Frames and the East-West Divide

If "civil society" is to be interpreted as a frame of collective action, eulogies of the 1989 ideal of civil society or accusations of its betrayal are of questionable relevance.[20] Frames are dynamically formed and negotiated. They often cease to exist when the aims of the campaign they mobilized are accomplished. They can also be transformed if new claims are infused into them. They can diffuse into other campaigns and contentious contexts, or, they can dissolve when facing new realities.[21]

Analyzing the civil society frame of the dissident movements, one should explore the "relations through time, relations in space, relations of power and dependency"[22] that it created. Such an interrogation would provide a deeply historical account: it will help understand how an abstract idea—civil society—used in an intellectual dialogue opened certain political opportunity structures for local and transnational activism and contributed to the process of social change in 1989 and beyond. Discursive approaches to frame analysis are sometimes seen as "normativist," "culturalist," insufficiently material and predominantly related to elite reproduction.[23] Yet, there are certain levels of complexity in the examined dissident movement from the 1980s, which suggest that such an approach is a necessary element in the analysis of civil society as a frame of collective action. On the issue of materiality, a rather ironic remark could be made: paradoxically, words counted as the most valuable resource of the opposition movements in East-Central European "post-totalitarian" regimes. This statement could be held both in political contexts where intellectual activity was severely censured (as in post–1968 Czechoslovakia, Ceausescu's Romania, and Bulgaria) and in such conjunctions where critical cultural products were tolerated as long as they did not explicitly challenge the political status quo (as in the cases of post–1956 Hungary, Yugoslavia under Tito, and, to a lesser extent, Poland). As Vaclav Havel stated,[24] regimes that claimed that their center of power coincided with the center of truth, sincerely feared words that could display alternative interpretations. Besides, dissidents were often praised for having found the importance of the power of words in changing worlds.[25]

On this basis, a serious analysis of the civil society frame formation, diffusion or dissolution would necessarily account for several levels of complexity. Firstly, it is very important to distinguish between specific features of dissident-intellectuals in East-Central Europe and critical intellectuals in Western societies. In the West, movements working within the liberal civic sphere and their intellectuals were trying to find space for activity outside the framework of the state. In Eastern Europe, belated nation-state formation and subsequent intervention of the West made intellectuals claim power on behalf of the liberation movements. They united in the struggles for national sovereignty and hoped that a state-building process would help overcome the overall "backwardness" of their own people.[26] The post-socialist era entry into power and discussions on how to rule were not a strange choice for the dissidents who remained more "rooted cosmopolitans" than "transnational activists."[27] Yet, their actions did repel the politically marginal—even if not apolitical—critical intellectuals in the West who had already developed the tradition of theorizing social change primarily from an extraparliamentary oppositional perspective.[28]

Secondly, the positions that temporally melted in 1989 into the East-Central European frame(s) of civic activism against the repressive regimes were different from country to country, and from thinker to thinker. What is nowadays called "the 1989 concept of civil society," was given different names by each one of the prominent dissidents: "anti-politics" (Gyorgy Konrad), "independent life of society" (Vaclav Havel), "parallel polis" (Vaclav Benda), "new evolutionism" (Adam Michnik), etc. This distinction was not at all nominal. Following Alan Renwick's recent analysis, one could distinguish between at least three civil society strategies vis-à-vis the state: "ignoring the state" or *anti-politics* (Vaclav Havel and Gyorgy Konrad); "engaging the state from outside" or *pressure group approach* (Polish Solidarity and a number of green movements); and "entering the state" or *political opposition* (Janos Kis and the *Beszélő* circle in Hungary).[29] To complicate this picture, one could add that in the aftermath of 1989, different aspects of the ideal were recuperated by different and controversial ideologies: the "activist" direct action against the state, the "neo-liberal" practice of democratization, and the "post-modern" analysis of civil society as an oppressive Western construct.[30]

In this light, thirdly, the transnational aspect is of crucial importance for analyzing the civil society frame. Even if the European East bore the legacy of a strong tradition of civility and associationism, civil society per se was an invention of Western modernity. While the dominating liberal theory of civil society was institutionalized in the civil sphere in Western liberal-democracies and in their globally applied practices of development and democratization,[31] left-wing thinkers and activists influenced by the re-emergence of Gramscian civil society theory turned their gaze toward grassroots mobilization of new-left movements and liberation movements in the Third World.[32] They also developed an interest in dissent behind the Iron Curtain, based on their gradual, and reluctant, realization of the illusion of Marxism put into practice.[33] By the 1980s, East-Central European dissidents' activities became visible through new channels of communication. Fostered by foundations, Western activists and Eastern European émigré-intellectuals in the West became the new target group of campaigns on issues of nuclear disarmament, human rights, and environmental policies.[34] Explicit differences and mutual reticence between Eastern and Western contexts of life and activism notwithstanding, a dialogue was built between the two sides of the Iron Curtain—the language of civil society was used to bridge this semantic gap.[35] Using this disremembered concept rediscovered by the dissidents, Western critical intellectuals praised the re-emergence of civil society in East-Central Europe. In this, they raised concerns against their own existence in centralized bureaucratic Welfare states. They bemoaned the weakening of social solidarity, autonomy, and participation under the weight of consumption, efficiency, and growth, and the apocalyptic threat of a "Doomsday" nuclear war.[36] Speaking from the tormented totalitarian context, through the recuperated idea of civil society, Eastern European dissidents were sending messages in which Western intellectuals could recognize the ideal of radical democracy: the need for an emancipated public sphere, which is independent from the state and the market and which would nurture genuine civic initiatives.

Finally, it is important to question the power relations at stake in this East-West dialogue on civil society. Speaking of civil society simply as a colonizing hegemonic concept, supplanting Western intervention in the East of Europe might be a slightly one-sided statement. The concept of civil society in the 1980s was a matter of dynamic frame negotiation: it silenced some aspects of the general concept in order to provide consensus between the involved actors, e.g., "it said nothing about distribution of wealth, ownership of the means of production, or division of division of labor."[37] In this, it is important to notice the uneven but still mutual legitimacy that this transnational communication gave to Western states as the "good" side in the Cold War. Furthermore, under the passive but persistent monitoring of Western campaigners, legitimacy was granted to Western intellectuals in their claims of global concern and to dissidents in the newly obtained rights to speak aloud. Whereas the latter were often accused of shortsightedness, the most prominent dissidents who lived "with one eye in the West,"[38] were criticized for their own locally grounded concerns. Still, the East-West divide in the power structures and struggles could not be decided as a simple unilateral equation: the interplay of agentive and structural power of any individual or collective actor remains to be examined.

In this sense, aspects of the civil society frame formation and brokerage across the Iron Curtain are still to be researched. Bodies of texts in archives, *samizdat* publications, publications in the Western press, and their smuggled copies in the East need to be examined through a more qualitatively oriented interrogation. Since the exchange was intellectual, at least as much as it was activist, it is important to interrogate the different schools of thought in their influence on particular dissident or intellectual circles, different networks through time and space, and potential mobilization of material and communicational resources. It is also crucial to see how successfully concepts were applied in the transnational dialogue in order to build trust between different contexts. Lastly, while left-wing radical activism has re-emerged in today's East-Central Europe, such networks are integrated within transnational, rather than local, contexts of contention. Despite the fact that, in their repertoires, their anti-statist claims, and lifestyles "with one eye in the West," these activists strangely continue the tradition of liberal dissidents from the 1980s. Yet the legacy of the latter is not central to the new activists' self-reflection: an issue that I believe requires further study on the adventures of the civil society frame in these post-socialist societies.

Notes

1. I use East-Central Europe as a geographical category. "Eastern Europe" could also include parts of the former Soviet Union, which are not reflected in this study. "Central Europe" mostly refers to Hungary, Czechoslovakia, and Poland (see note 4) on which the broader literature concentrates because of the visible cases of dissent, but the present study suggests methodology that would be applicable to other countries in the region as well.

2. See A. Arato and J.-L. Cohen, *Civil Society and Political Theory* (Cambridge, MA: MIT Press, 1992), and J. Keane, ed., *Civil Society and the State* (London: Verso, 1988).

3. M. Ignatief, "On Civil Society: Why Eastern Europe's Revolutions Could Succeed," *Foreign Affairs*, March/April 1995, Retrieved 8 January 2008 from http://www .foreignaffairs.org/19950301fareviewessay5029/michael-ignatieff/on-civil-society-why-eastern-europe-s-revolutions-could-succeed.html.

4. As such, Central Europe—as a term applicable to Hungary, Poland, and Czechoslovakia—entered the positive accounts in the 1980s, after the publication in the West of two articles by dissidents from the region—"Is the Dream of Central Europe Still Alive" by Hungarian writer György Konrád (1983) and "The Central European Tragedy" by Czech novelist Milan Kundera (1984).

5. An enthusiastic account see in T.G. Ash, "Does Central Europe Exist?," *NY Review of Books* 33(15) 91986). Retrieved 30 October 2007 from http://www.nybooks .com/articles/article-preview?article_id=4998 . It is interesting to note that Ash seems much less enthusiastic years later: "suddenly ten years after the changes Central Europeans have started accusing Westerners of imposing this definition on them, whereas, from the Western view point it were Czechs, Poles and Hungarians who insisted it into relevance in the late 1980s." T.G. Ash, "Conclusions," in *Between Past and Future: the Revolutions of 1989 and their Aftermath*, eds. V. Tismăneanu and S. Antohin (Budapest and New York: CEU Press, 2000), 401–402.

6. For a Lockean interpretation see Z. Rau, "Some Thoughts on Civil Society in Eastern Europe and the Lockean Contractarian Approach," *Political Studies* XXXV (1987): 573–592. For a Marxist interpretation see V. Murthy, "Civil Society in Hegel and Marx," *Rethinking Marxism*, 11(3)(1999): 36–55. For a Gramscian approach see J.A Buttigieg, "Gramsci on Civil Society," *boundary 2*, 22(3)(1995): 1–32. For the introduction of the dissident legacy in the civil society theory as a whole see J. Isaak, "The Strange Silence of Political Theory," *Political Theory*, 23(4)(1995): 636–652 and the surrounding debate in the magazine, as well as a volume studying the issues at stake in this debate in great detail, B.J. Falk, *Dilemmas of Dissidence* (New York and Budapest: CEU Press, 2003).

7. Positive comments see, e.g., in M.D. Kennedy, "Eastern Europe's Lessons for Critical Intellectuals," in *Intellectuals and Politics. Social Theory in a Changing World*, ed. C. Lemert (London: Sage, 1991), and V. Tismăneanu, "Introduction," in *The Revolutions of 1989*, ed. V. Tismăneanu (London and New York: Routledge, 1999), 1–18. For more pessimistic views on the dissident role see A. Tucker, "The Politics of Conviction: The Rise and Fall of Czech Intellectuals-Politicians," in *Intellectuals and Politics in Central Europe*, ed. A. Bozóki (Budapest and New York: CEU Press, 1998), 185–205. Also P. Kopecky and E. Barnfield, "Charting the Decline of Civil Society: Explaining the Changing Roles and Conceptions of Civil Society in East Central Europe," in *Democracy Without Borders: State and Non-State Actors in Eastern Europe, Africa and Latin America*, ed. J. Grugel (London: Routledge, 1999), 76–91.

8. E.g. A. Michnik, "Rebirth of Civil Society," in *Ideas of 1989 LSE Public Lecture Series* (1999). Retrieved 8 January 2008 from http://www.lse.ac.uk/Depts/global/ Publications/PublicLectures/PL10_TheRebirthOfCivilSociety.pdf, but G.M. Tamás "A Disquisition of Civil Society" in *Social Research* 61(2)(1994): 205–222.

9. See G. Eyal, "Anti-politics and the Spirit of Capitalism: Dissidents, Monetarists, and the Czech Transition to Capitalism," *Theory and Society,* 29(1)(2000): 50–92.

10. T. Petrova and S. Tarrow, "Transactional and Participatory Activism in the Emerging European Polity. The Puzzle of East-Central Europe," *Comparative Political Studies,* 20(10)(2006): 1–21.

11. For accounts of the donor-driven civil society in the region see e.g. K. Quigley, "Lofty Goals, Modest Results: Assisting Civil Society in Eastern Europe," in *Funding Virtue. Civil Society Aid and Democracy Promotion,* eds. M. Ottaway and T. Carothers (Washington DC: Carnegies Endowment for International Peace, 2000), 191–216. The three stages of this process—triumphalism, disillusionment, and mutual adjustment—are researched anthropologically in Poland by J.R. Wedel, *Collision and Collusion: the Strange Case of Western Aid to Eastern Europe* (New York: St Martins Press, 1998). On the "portable" model of civil society and the research on it in the anthropology of post-socialism see D. Kalb, "Afterword: Globalism and Postsocialist Prospects," in *Postsocialism: Ideals, Ideologies and Practices in Eurasia,* ed. C. Hann (London, Routledge, 1998), 317–334. On the anti-political civil society and its imperfections also T. Brannan, *From 'Antipolitics' to 'Anti-Politics': What Become of East European 'Civil Society'?,* LSE Working Paper 03(41) (2003), retrieved 2 January 2008 from www.lse.ac.uk/collections/DESTIN/pdf/WP41.pdf. See also G. Ekiert and J. Kubik, *Civil Society From Abroad: the Role of Foreign Assistance in the Democratization of Poland,* The Weatherlhead Center for International Affairs, Harvard University, Working Paper Series 00(01), 2000, retrieved 8 January 2008 from http://www.ciaonet.org/wps/kuj01/

12. E.g. M.M. Howard, *The Weakness of Civil Society in Post-Communist Europe* (Cambridge: Cambridge University Press, 2003), as well as P. Kopecky and C. Mudde, eds., *Uncivil Society? Contentious Politics in Eastern Europe* (London and New York: Routhledge, 2003).

13. E.g. A.M. Grzymala-Busse, *Redeeming the Communist Past: the Regeneration of Communist Parties in East-Central Europe* (Cambridge UK: Cambridge University Press, 2002).

14. A.T. Green, "Comparative Development of Post-communist Civil Societies," in *Europe-Asia Studies,* 54(3)(2002): 455–456.

15. Sidney Tarrow warns scholars on the decay of the protest wave of 1989, the institutionalization of dissident movements, the movement factionalism, and the decline of public involvement. He encourages methodological creativity and analysis of "handbills, manifestoes, speeches and minutes of meetings" and use of "oral accounts of … —both movements and leaders." See S. Tarrow, "Aiming at a Moving Target: Social Science and the Recent Rebellions in Eastern Europe," *PS: Political Science and Politics,* 24(1)(1991): 12–20.

16. See S. Tarrow, "Aiming at a Moving Target," 17.

17. In his text, John Glenn shows how the civil society frame was formed by the Solidarity network in Poland during the election campaign in 1989, and by the Civic Forum and Public against Violence in Czechoslovakia during the General Strike later that same year; he also reviews how the frame dissolved after these events.

18. See E. Goffman, *Frame Analysis* (1974), quoted in D.A. Snow and R.D. Benford, "Ideology, Frame Resonance and Participant Mobilization," in *From Structure to Ac-*

tion: Comparing Social Movement Research Across Cultures, eds. B. Klandermans, H. Kriesi, and S. Tarrow (London: JAI Press, 1988), 197–218. See also D.A. Snow and R.D. Benford, "Framing Processes and Social Movements: An Overview and Assessment," *Annual Review of Sociology,* 26 (2000): 611–639. On the agency-identity-injustice aspects of frame articulation, see W.A. Gamson, *Talking Politics* (Cambridge: Cambridge University Press, 1992).

19. On the discursive tilt in framing, see M.W. Steinberg, "Tilting the Frame: Considerations on Collective Action Framing from a Discursive Turn," *Theory and Society,* 27(6) (1998): 845–872. On ways of researching frames see H. Johnston, "A Methodology for Frame Analysis: From Discourse to Cognitive Schemata," in *Social Movements and Culture,* eds. H. Johnston and B. Klandermans (Minneapolis: University of Minnesota Press, 1995), 217–246.

20. I use this method in a case study in M. Ivancheva, "Civil Society as a Discursive Frame: Vaclav Havel's 'Anatomy of Reticence' as a Case Study," unpublished MA diss., Central European University, Budapest, 2007.

21. See Snow and Benford, "Framing Processes and Social Movements," 613–614.

22. D. Kalb and H. Tak, "Introduction," in *Critical Junctions: Anthropology and History Beyond the Cultural Turn,* eds. D. Kalb and H. Tak (New York: Berghahn Books, 2005), 3.

23. See M.W. Steinberg, "The Talk and Back Talk of Collective Action: A Dialogic Analysis of Repertoires of Discourse among Nineteenth-Century English Cotton Spinners," *The American Journal of Sociology,* 105(3)(1999): 738–739.

24. V. Havel, "The Power of the Powerless," in *Open Letters: Selected Writings, 1965–1990,* ed. P. Wilson (New York: Vintage Books, 1992), 125–214.

25. E.P. Thompson's Introduction in E.P. Thompson and M. Kaldor, eds., *Europe from Below: an East-West Dialogue* (Verso: London, 1990), as well as V. Havel, "Words for Words," in P. Wilson, *Open Letters: Selected Writings, 1965–1990.*

26. Z. Bauman, *On Modernity, Post-modernity and Intellectuals* (Cambridge: Polity Press, 1987).

27. For the distinction between "rooted cosmopolitans," who raise their domestic claims to higher level institutions of transnationally evolved networks of contention without shifting the scale and becoming "transnational activists" involved in a global movement, see S. Tarrow, *The New Transnational Activism* (New York: Cambridge University Press, 2005), 28–29. The current study cannot elaborate in detail on Tarrow's model describing mechanisms of contention in their transnational dimensions (global framing and internalizing contention; diffusion and modularity, and shifting scale of contention; externalizing contention and building transnational coalitions), but it would be extremely useful in any subsequent examination of aspects of the civil society frames.

28. See M.D. Kennedy, "Lessons form Eastern Europe."

29. A. Renwick, "Anti-Political or Just Anticommunist? Varieties of Dissidence in East-Central Europe, and their Implications for the Development of Political Society," *East European Politics and Societies* 20 (2)(2006): 286–318.

30. Following M. Kaldor, "The Idea of Global Civil Society," *International Affairs* 79(3)(2003): 583–593.

31. On the debates in liberal theory in the division between representative and deliberative democracy, individual rights-oriented liberalism, and communitarianism, and

between the upsurge of neoconservative critique and the defense of the welfare-state policies, see Arato and Cohen, *Civil Society and Political Theory*, 4–11.

32. See e.g., J. and J. Comaroff, "Of Revelation and Revolution," in *Anthropology of Politics: A Reader in Ethnography, Theory and Critique*, ed. V. Joan (Oxford: Blackwell, 2002), 203–213.

33. See especially F. Feher and A. Heller, *Eastern Left, Western Left* (Cambridge: Blackwell, 1987), 1–47.

34. Wedel, *Collision and Collusion*.

35. The scarce literature on this exchange shows that the Western *peaceniks'* attempts to attract activists from "the other Europe" were often far from adequate—the new language of insecurity they spoke (détente, disarmament, and peace) seemed far from the urgent issues of interest for the people surviving state socialism and who spoke the language of unfreedom: see Feher and Heller, *Eastern Left, Western Left*, 184. On the other hand, Eastern Europeans were often accused of their anti-communist views and their lack of concern for global issues beyond the region, see V. Tismăneanu, ed., *In Search for Civil Society. Independent Peace Movements in the Soviet Bloc* (London and New York: Routledge, 1990).

36. See F. Feher and A. Heller, "On Being Anti-Nuclear in Soviet Societies," in Feher and Heller, *Eastern Left, Western Left*, 161–186.

37. M.D. Kennedy, "Eastern Europe's Lessons for Critical Intellectuals."

38. On the Western-type dissidents see E.P. Thompson in P. Burke, "A Transcontinental Movement of Citizens? Strategic Debates in the 1980s Western Peace Movement," in *Transnational Moments of Change: Europe 1945, 1968, 1989*, eds. P. Kenney and G.R. Horn (Landham, MD: Rowman & Littlefield, 2004). On the qualification of dissidents as such primarily by the West, see Havel, "The Power of the Powerless."

Chapter 11

Globalization and the Transformation of National Protest Politics

An Appetizer

Swen Hutter

Introduction

Is globalization leading to a reconfiguration of political cleavage structures and mobilization in Western Europe at the beginning of the twenty-first century? And what are the specific consequences regarding protest politics? The following chapter presents key ideas of an ongoing research project* that puts globalization in a Rokkanean perspective.[1] It conceives the contemporary opening up of boundaries as a new critical juncture, which induces new structural cleavages, both within and between nation-states.[2] Using this perspective, the project tries to find novel answers to the transformation of national electoral and protest politics in a globalizing world.

Since globalization is a highly contested topic, it is essential to define it. In its broad version, globalization can be understood as a spatial widening and an intensification of regional or global economic and cultural interactions.[3] While the world has witnessed earlier phases of intensified interdependence, there is sufficient evidence to suggest that, since the 1980s, these processes have accelerated. Held et al. refer to quantitative and qualitative differences with earlier epochs, stressing particularly the "terms how globalization is organized and reproduced."[4] One of the most distinguishing factors between a nineteenth-century version and the current form is that the latter does not consolidate nation-states; on the contrary, it undermines, or rather transforms, their central power.[5] Consequently, the process of globalization is mainly conceptualized as a process of denationalization, i.e., as a process that leads to the lowering and unbundling of national boundaries.[6]

In the following section, I present four key assumptions guiding this project. Thereafter, the major results of the analyses of national electoral politics are summarized. Subsequently, I develop three theses on how protest politics might change due to the emergence of a new cleavage in the age of globalization. The theses are derived from a discussion on how claims raised in protest and electoral politics relate to each other. The concluding remarks sum up the argument and put forward further questions. As the chapter's title indicates, it only provides a first cursory view but hopefully whets the appetite for more thorough discussions that are based on empirical data.[7]

Key Assumptions: New Cleavage between Winners and Losers of Globalization

In a very dense way, the following four points highlight how globalization is expected to affect political mobilization and cleavage structures in Western Europe.

(1) The political paradox of globalization: the political consequences of globalization are diverse. A well-studied consequence is the emergence of new forms and structures of governance beyond the nation-state,[8] which create new opportunities for transnational mobilization.[9] Paradoxically, however, we assume that it occurs primarily at the national level, where the political reactions to globalization manifest themselves. The democratic rights and inclusion of citizens is still firmly tied to the nation-state, and the national level still constitutes the major context for political mobilization.[10]

(2) Winners and losers of globalization: the consequences of globalization vary between different members of a national community. In our project, we identify three mechanisms of competition that create new groups of winners and losers: economic (sectoral and international) competition, cultural competition (which is, among others, linked to massive immigration of ethnic groups who are rather distinct from the European populations[11]), and political competition (between nation-states and supra- or international political actors). In sum, the three mechanisms of competition lead to quite heterogeneous opposing groups in terms of social class, sector, education, and attachment to national communities or transnational networks. The likely winners of globalization include entrepreneurs and qualified employees in sectors open to international competition as well as cosmopolitan citizens. The losers of globalization, by contrast, include entrepreneurs and qualified employees in traditionally sheltered sectors, unqualified employees and citizens who strongly identify themselves with their national community.[12]

(3) Political potentials: the new groups of winners and losers constitute political potentials that are about the same across Western Europe.[13] Following Sartori, the translation of those potentials into politics is above all dependent on organization and mobilization by collective political actors.[14] Due to their heterogeneity, it seems to be: (a) fundamental by whom and how these political potentials are articulated and mobilized; and, (b) very unlikely that these new oppositions align with traditional structural and political cleavages.

(4) Integration-demarcation: as the above-mentioned states, we suggest that the lowering, un-, and rebundling of national boundaries paradoxically render them more salient. As they are weakened and reassessed, their political importance increases. More specifically, the destructuring of national boundaries leads to an increased salience of differences between sectors of the economy and of cultural differences, respectively, as the criteria for the distribution of resources, identity formation, and political mobilization.[15] At a general level, we therefore expect losers of globalization to seek to protect themselves through protectionist measures and through an emphasis on national boundaries and independence. Winners of globalization, by contrast, should support the opening up of boundaries and the process of international integration. The new antagonism between winners and losers of globalization is therefore referred to as a conflict between integration and demarcation.[16]

Key Results: The Transformation of National (Party) Political Spaces

Next to the key assumptions, I point out two major findings from the project's previous analysis of national political spaces: on the side of the electorate and on the side of party competition in election campaigns.

Transformed two-dimensional spaces: the study showed that national political spaces in Western Europe are still two-dimensional. A cultural and an economic dimension can be distinguished in the 1990s/early 2000s, similar to the 1970s, i.e., before and after the restructuring capacity of globalization increased. However, the meaning of the two dimensions—above all on the cultural side—has changed significantly. New conflict issues have been embedded into the existing dimensions, confirming the rise of a new conflict between integration and demarcation. In this context, one can differentiate between an open and a protectionist position on the cultural as well as the economic dimension of the political space. Regarding the cultural dimension, we observe enhanced opposition to the cultural liberalism of the new social movements, because the defense of traditional values increasingly takes on an ethnic or nationalist character. Accordingly, the newly integrated issues on the cultural dimension are immigration and European integration.[17] The two issues correspond to the cultural and political mechanisms of competition introduced above. Moreover, the cultural issues have typically acquired greater salience and structuring capacity than the economic ones at the end of the 1990s, beginning of the 2000s. On the economic side, we observe less change than expected. In other words, issues related to the opening up of national economies and their competitiveness on world markets have not entered and transformed party competition as strongly.

Repositioning of political parties: regarding the strategic repositioning of parties in the transformed political spaces, the initial thesis that the new populist radical right parties[18] are the main driving forces of change has been confirmed. Their forceful objection to cultural integration changed the party political spaces most tremendously. They have formulated a highly attractive ideological package for the "losers" of economic transformations and cultural diversity. Thereby, the populist radical right mainly mobilizes these new potentials by stressing cultural issues, i.e., resistance to immigration and European integration. In this context, the analysis indicates tripolar configurations of the major parties. The left, the moderate right, *and* the new populist radical right constitute the three main poles. In economic terms, the empirical evidence points to a substantial shift in the direction of economic liberalism in a majority of the countries. This finding once more underlines that the main changes in electoral politics are taking place on the cultural dimension of the political space.

Tentative Ideas: The Transformation of National Protest Politics

How could these ideas stimulate discussions on protest politics and social movements? First of all, it is important to once again note that one can distinguish three modes of political mobilization: political parties with their focus on the electoral arena; interest groups with their emphasis on pressure politics in and through institutions; and social movements with their reliance on protest politics.[19] Following Kitschelt, we witness an increasing differentiation between the three at the beginning of the twenty-first century.[20] This leads us straight back to the fundamental question of *by whom and how the new political potentials induced by globalization are articulated and mobilized.* In times of "fused" systems of interest mobilization and intermediation, the results of the national party political spaces would have told us a great deal about how the new cleavage leaves its imprint on protest politics. In increasingly "differentiated" systems one needs, however, to reflect on the similarities and differences of electoral and protest politics in several regards. In the following, I stress similarities and differences in *issue salience* (i.e., which dimension) and in the *positions* put forward (i.e., which side of the conflict).[21] Thus, the present perspective shifts the attention to relative shares in a research area that chiefly deals with single issue fields or movements.[22]

For my tentative ideas, I rely on three general theses on the directional nature of the relationship between the two modes of political mobilization. On a very abstract level, the three theses suggest how the claims-making in electoral politics might tell us something about the issues and positions being raised in protest politics. Recent research has made some major progress in studying the interaction between parties and social movements.[23] It is, however, still most common to assume a "simple, positive relationship."[24] This is also where my first thesis comes from. Thereafter, I introduce a counterthesis that regards protest politics as a counterweight and the terrain of so far "unheard" voices in electoral politics. Finally, I introduce a thesis that assumes different logics on the left and right.

(1) Congruence thesis: On the one hand, the congruence thesis can be derived from a very prominent reasoning in the political process approach.[25] In this context, controversy between established political actors increases the likelihood of sustained protest mobilization. Divided elites, influential allies, and shifting political alignments are all regarded as opportunities for political protest.[26] In liberal democracies, these three concepts are all closely tied to electoral politics. More specifically, if (a) parties emphasize certain issues, (b) are divided on them, (c) an influential party political ally supports a certain demand, and/or (d) electoral politics is increasingly volatile, it is more likely that similar claims give rise to protest politics. On the other hand, the comments on political (re-)alignments link the thesis to the question of how new social divides affect political mobilization in general. Due to its high restructuring capacity, one can assume that the new integration-demarcation cleavage leaves the same imprint on protest as on electoral politics at around the same time, that is, since the end of the 1980s. In the end, both dimensions and both sides of the conflict are expected to be mobilized in less institutionalized settings. In light of the above mentioned results, we should, however, see also in protest politics an increasing and higher salience of the cultural issues, above all of questions related to immigration and European integration. Furthermore, we should witness a certain return of right-wing voices that advocate cultural demarcation, because they are the main carriers of the new conflicts in electoral politics.[27]

(2) Counterweight thesis: The counterweight thesis argues against this positive-sum relationship between the two modes of political mobilization. By contrast, it expects that protest and electoral politics are inversely related to each other. Piven and Cloward are among the most forceful adherents of such a view.[28] They state that in liberal democracies, "ordinarily, defiance is first expressed in the voting booth."[29] From their perspective, electoral politics "serves to measure and register the extent of the emerging disaffection."[30] Only if their changing voting patterns have no effect, people will resort to protest mobilization.[31] This is why an issue that is already very salient and controversial in electoral politics is less likely to become a very salient goal of political protest.

As the cultural dimension changed and gained ground the most in party competition, protest politics might act as an *economic* counterweight. In other words, economic issues should flourish in the landscape of political protest since the 1990s. Looking at the positions that prevail in party competition, we see that the mainstream parties advocate a program for the winners' side; they favor economic integration. Although populist-right parties are forceful advocates of cultural demarcation, they do not as uniformly advocate protectionist positions in the economic realm. Consequently, one could expect that the losers' side, i.e., voices that criticize the economic opening up of boundaries and neoliberal reforms, preponderates in protest politics.[32]

(3) Different logics thesis: the last thesis combines the preceding ones and relates it to the specific claims put forward. Following the influential article of Offe and Wiesenthal on the two logics of collective action, it differentiates between "class conflict within political forms and class conflict about political forms."[33] Offe and Wiesenthal argue that "the relatively powerless ... will have reason to act nonindividualistically on the basis of a notion of collective identity that is both generated and presupposed by their association."[34] Actually, this leads to the same conclusion as the argument of a losers' counterweight, i.e., protest politics is the business of disadvantaged political actors favoring (economic) demarcation.[35]

For the present argument, it is probably more insightful if one stresses the historical roots and alliance partners of the mobilizing agents involved in current protest politics. Actors favouring economic demarcation or cultural integration are closely linked to the political left (i.e., "movements of the left"). In contrast, actors supporting economic integration or cultural demarcation are rooted in the political right (i.e., "movements of the right").[36] Since the end of the Second World War, the former have more or less dominated protest politics in Western Europe.[37] The protest cycle of the 1970s and early 1980s reinforced this tendency, because direct action, i.e., protest politics, was not simply part of the action repertoire, but part of the message itself of new social movements and the new left in general.[38] One can speculate that this close association between the political left and the new social movements has contributed to the rise of cultural issues in protest politics.[39] In turn, this development not only crowded out the economic ones but also led to the predominance of cultural winners' positions. In other words, the left's appeal to parts of the new middle class and its general emphasize on cultural integration undermines its appeal to the "losers of globalization" in economic terms not only in electoral but also in protest politics. At the same time, the close link between the libertarian left and direct action goes hand in hand with a close link between the populist radical right and representative democracy. Although the populist right fights for the man on the street and is highly critical of the *classe politique* and representative democracy, it mostly uses its channels and (if available) more institutionalized direct-democratic instruments to advance its claims.[40]

To sum up, the thesis of different logics suggests that cultural issues also dominate protest politics in the age of globalization. In contrast to the congruence thesis, voices *in favor* of cultural integration should be most visible and counter their opponents' rise in electoral politics. This expectation is based on the general argument that the relation between the two kinds of politics follows different logics on the left and right: even if movements of the left participate successfully in electoral competition, they continue to rely on protest politics. In contrast, movements of the right are expected to abandon it when they have a firm standing in national electoral politics.[41]

Figure 11.1 summarizes my tentative ideas. It shows how the relation between protest and electoral politics differs according to the three theses. These

Dimension	Position	Congruence thesis	Counterweight thesis	Diff. logics thesis
Cultural	Integration ("movements of the left")	+	–	+
	Demarcation ("movements of the right")	+	–	–
Economic	Integration ("movements of the right")	+	–	–
	Demarcation ("movements of the left")	+	–	+

Figure 11.1. Expected Direction of the Relationship between Protest and Electoral Politics

theses provide a simple conceptual toolkit to think about West European protest landscapes in a transforming *party* political context.

Conclusion

In a nutshell, the present chapter presented a highly speculative view on how globalization or denationalization affects national politics in Western Europe. From a Rokkanean perspective, globalization as a critical juncture induces new political potentials, which in turn can be organized and mobilized by political actors. After presenting characteristics of the new potentials and the first results on how party competition changed, I put forward three theses on the similarities and differences between the mobilization in party politics and protest politics: congruence, avantgarde, counterweight, and different logics. Of course, this is still a rather crude way to speculate about changing national protest politics in a denationalizing world. It should, however, stimulate further empirically based discussions.

Moreover, it raises many additional questions, such as: (a) what factors explain national differences (e.g., the strength of traditional cleavages, institutional and discursive opportunity structures, actors' strategies)?; (b) what alliance structures emerge between the different modes of interest mobilization on the organizational level? What role do traditional political actors (e.g., political parties and unions) play? Does the rise of a new integration-demarcation cleavage stimulate their revitalization or decline?; (c) how do the repertoires of protest change in connection with the new political potentials? Do we witness a radicalization (keyword: battle of Seattle) or an extension (keyword: political consumerism)?; (d) so far, I deliberately skipped the question of a transnationalization of protest politics. Even though there are good reasons to adhere to the political paradox of globalization, one should think about alternative conceptualization and try to incorporate the multi-level structures and dynamics of political processes in a globalizing world. Taking this into account, how do we establish appropriate research designs? Can we still opt for national comparisons or should we consider cosmopolitan alternatives?;[42] (e) and last, which methods should we use? Even though the preceding sections call for quantitative techniques that are able to cover large geographical areas and/or extensive time periods, we have a wide array of options at hand (e.g., forms of content analysis as protest event or political claim analysis, network or macro-organizational analysis, and off- or on-site surveys). In conclusion, the present small "appetizer" offers some suggestions and many more new questions on how globalization transforms national protest politics.

Notes

*   The project "Political Change in a Globalising World" is conducted by a research group at the Universities of Munich and Zurich. The German team is part of the research center SFB 536 "Reflexive Modernization." We analyze six Western European countries (Austria, Britain, France, Germany, the Netherlands, and Switzerland) from the mid 1970s to the present. This chapter draws extensively from the overall project framework. Therefore, I want to thank especially the two project leaders Edgar Grande and Hanspeter Kriesi. Detailed versions of the argument, above all concerning electoral politics, can be found in H. Kriesi et al., "Globalization and the Transformation of the National Political Space: Six European Countries Compared," *European Journal of Political Research* 45(6)(2006): 921–956, and H. Kriesi et al., *West European Politics in the Age of Globalization. Six Countries Compared* (Cambridge: Cambridge University Press, 2008).

1.   S. Rokkan, *Staat, Nation und Demokratie in Europa* (Frankfurt: Suhrkamp, 2000).

2.   For the most elaborated discussion of the cleavage concept, see S. Bartolini and P. Mair, *Identity, Competition, and Electoral Availability* (Cambridge: Cambridge University Press, 1990); and K. Deegan-Krause, "New Dimensions of Political Cleavage," in *The Oxford Handbook of Political Behavior*, eds. R.J. Dalton and H.-D. Klingemann (Oxford: Oxford University Press, 2007), 538–556.

3.   For a recent overview, see D. Zolo, *Globalisation. An Overview* (Colchester: ECPR Press, 2007).

4.   D. Held et al., *Global Transformations* (Cambridge: Polity Press, 1999), 425.

5.   C. Tilly, *Social Movements, 1768–2004* (Boulder: Paradigm, 2004), 100–101.

6.   M. Zürn, "Schwarz-Rot-Grün-Braun: Reaktionsweisen auf Denationalisierung," in *Politik der Globalisierung*, ed. U. Beck (Frankfurt: Suhrkamp, 1998), 297–330.

7.   For first empirical analyses of the Austrian and Swiss case respectively, see M. Dolezal and S. Hutter, "Konsensdemokratie unter Druck? Politischer Protest in Österreich, 1975–2005," *Austrian Journal of Political Science* 36(3)(2007): 338–352; and S. Hutter and M. Giugni, "Protest Politics in a Changing Political Context: Switzerland, 1975–2005," *Swiss Political Science Review* 15(3)(2009): 395–429.

8.   E.g., E. Grande and L.W. Pauly, *Complex Sovereignty. Reconstituting Political Authority in the 21st Century* (Toronto: University of Toronto Press, 2005).

9.   E.g., D. della Porta and S. Tarrow, eds., *Transnational Protest and Global Activism* (Lanham: Rowman & Littlefield, 2005).

10. E.g., D. Imig and S. Tarrow, "Mapping the Europeanization of Contention: Evidence from a Quantitative Data Analysis," in *Contentious Europeans: Protest and Politics in an Emerging Polity*, eds. D. Imig and S. Tarrow (Lanham: Rowman & Littlefield Publishers, 2001), 27–49.

11. "Ethnic" is meant in a large sense (including language and religious criteria). Furthermore, perceived cultural competition is not only related to *immigration* but also to the increasing opportunities for delocalizing jobs into distant, and ethnically distinct, regions of the globe.

12. The argument does not state that social inequality becomes "classless" in a globalizing world: U. Beck, *Risk Society* (London: Sage, 1992), 88. However, it goes beyond a mere understanding of gradual changes (cf. J. Goldthorpe, *On Sociology. Volume One: Critique and Program*, 2nd ed. (Stanford: Stanford University Press, 2007), ch. 5) and asks what kind of new fundamental structural changes are induced by globalization. A more detailed discussion can be found in Kriesi et al., *West European Politics in the Age of Globalization*, 4–9.

13. A latent political potential is (for the time being) a passive group with a specific interest structure due to a similar socio-structural position. A manifest political potential has already acquired a collective identity, a common goal definition, see H. Kriesi, ed., *Bewegungen in der Schweizer Politik* (Frankfurt: Campus Verlag, 1985).

14. G. Sartori, "Sociology of Parties: A Critical Review," in *The West European Party System*, ed. P. Mair (Oxford: Oxford University Press, 1990 [1968]), 150–182.

15. See B. Badie, "Le Jeu Triangulaire," in *Sociologie des Nationalismes*, ed. P. Birnbaum (Paris: Presses Universitaires de France, 1997), 447–462.

16. Integration is understood in its dual meaning of negative and positive integration, see F.W. Scharpf, *Governing in Europe: Effective and Democratic?* (London: Oxford University Press, 1999).

17. Issues related to European integration are mainly integrated into the cultural and not into the economic dimension. This means that those individuals and parties who favor cultural liberalism, European integration, and softer stances on immigration constitute the integration pole on the cultural dimension. The opposite camp is made up of those who oppose the former two issues *and* advocate a more restrictive position on migration-related questions.

18. Or their functional equivalents: transformed conservative or liberal-conservative parties. For a very comprehensive account of the populist radical right, see C. Mudde, *Populist Radical Right Parties in Europe* (Cambridge: Cambridge University Press, 2007).

19. In line with my interest in political cleavages, I focus on the two modes that are most heavily characterized by the direct participation of citizens (i.e., by mass politics): electoral and protest politics. The latter "usually denotes the deliberate and public use of protest by groups or organizations (but rarely individuals) that seek to influence a political decision or process, which they perceive as having negative [or sometimes positive] consequences for themselves, another group or society as whole." D. Rucht, "The Spread of Protest Politics," in *The Oxford Handbook of Political Behavior*, eds. R. J. Dalton and H.-D. Klingemann (Oxford: Oxford University Press, 2007), 708.

20. H. Kitschelt, "Landscape of Political Interest Intermediation. Social Movements, Interest Groups, and Parties in the Early Twenty-First Century," in *Social Movements and Democracy*, ed. P. Ibarra (New York: Palgrave Macmillan, 2003), 81–103.

21. Other important differences might refer to the general *coupling of the two arenas* and the *timing of the expected changes.* The thesis of an increasing de-coupling of protest and party politics in the age of globalization can be found in the work of Ulrich Beck (e.g., U. Beck, *The Reinvention of Politics. Rethinking Modernity in the Global Social Order* [Cambridge: Cambridge University Press, 1996]; and U. Beck, *Power in the Global Age* [Cambridge: Polity Press, 2005]). Regarding the timing, one can assume that protest politics as the more issue-specific mode of mobilization has underwent the changes induced by globalization more profoundly and at an earlier time, because the new political potentials are very heterogeneous and crosscut traditional cleavages. Therefore, established political actors, above all mainstream political parties, must find it hard to organize and incorporate them into their historically rooted programs. Following this thesis, the more peripheral political actors (e.g., niche parties *and* social movements) are the principal mobilizing agents of the new structural conflicts.

22. Of course, specific movements might often follow their own trajectory and do not necessarily reflect the more general trends that I try to deduce for more abstract issue categories. This may stem from several reasons that have to do both with factors internal to the movements and external to them. For example, certain movements have a stronger organizational structure, which allows them to keep their level of mobilization higher over time. Furthermore, some movements are more dependent on their political environment and certain critical events, which therefore renders their mobilization more likely to show pronounced ebbs and flows.

23. E.g., J. A. Goldstone, ed., *States, Parties, and Social Movements* (Cambridge: Cambridge University Press, 2003).

24. D. S. Meyer and D. C. Minkoff, "Conceptualizing Political Opportunity," *Social Forces* 82(4)(2004): 1484; see also D. della Porta and M. Diani, *Social Movements. An Introduction* (Malden, MA: Blackwell, 2006), 218; and N. van Dyke, "Protest Cycles and Party Politics. The Effects of Elite Allies and Antagonists on the Student Protest in the United States, 1930–1990," in *States, Parties, and Social Movements,* ed. J.A. Goldstone (Cambridge: Cambridge University Press, 2003), 226–245.

25. E.g., S. Tarrow, *Power in Movement. Social Movements and Contentious Politics* (Cambridge: Cambridge University Press, 1998), 76–80; and S. Tarrow, "The Phantom of the Opera: Political Parties and Social Movements of the 1960s and 1970s in Italy," in *Challenging the Political Order. New Social and Political Movements in Western Democracies,* eds. R. J. Dalton and M. Kuechler (Cambridge: Polity Press, 1990), 251–73.

26. For the still most influential summary of important features of the political context that inflence movement activities, see D. McAdam, "Conceptual Origins, Current Problems, Future Directions," in *Comparative Perspectives on Social Movements: Political Opportunities, Mobilizing Structures, and Cultural Framings,* eds. D. McAdam, J.D. McCarthy, and M.N. Zald (Cambridge: Cambridge University Press, 1996), 23–40.

27. Data on claims-making and protest events in Germany illustrate this expectation (see R. Koopmans and S. Olzak, "Discursive opportunities and the evolution of right-wing violence in Germany," *American Journal of Sociology* 110(1)(2004): 198–230; and D. Rucht, "The Changing Role of Political Protest Movements," *West European Politics* 26(4)(2003): 153–76). Longitudinal and comparative data on other coun-

tries is, however, hard to grasp (see R. Koopmans, "Explaining the rise of racist and extreme right violence in Western Europe: Grievances or opportunities?" *European Journal of Political Research* 30(2)(1996): 185–216). Our own preliminary results point to cross-national differences and stress the rather exceptional nature of the German protest landscape, see the references in note 8.

28. F.F. Piven and R.A. Cloward, *Poor People's Movements. Why They Succeed, How They Fail* (New York: Vintage Books, 1977).

29. Ibid., 15.

30. Ibid., 16.

31. Piven and Cloward base their prediction on the argument that "people have been socialized within a political culture that defines voting as the mechanism through which political change can and should properly occur" (ibid., 15). This seems slightly less convincing in supposed "movement societies."

32. The mobilization of the so-called "mouvements des sans" (e.g., unemployed, home-less people) and the global justice movement(s) might be interpreted in this way. Having said this, they pose the *social* question in a new and forceful way. According to della Porta, the global justice movement advocates the rather general "cause of justice (economic, social, political, and environmental) among and between people across the globe" (D. della Porta, "The Global Justice Movement: An Introduction," in *The Global Justice Movement. Cross-National and Transnational Perspectives*, ed. D. della Porta [Boulder: Paradigm Publishers, 2007], 6). This is why some observers highlight its trans-issue character; speaking of a "movement of movements" or of the global justice movements in the plural. Due to its heterogeneity, scholars do not only struggle to define the movement, but it is also not as easy to assign specific protest events to it (see, e.g., the different handling of the protests against the war in Iraq in the edited volume of della Porta cited above). Emphasizing its adversaries, its focus on economic issues—and on positive rather than on negative integration—becomes yet more obvious, because its "enemy is singled out as neoliberal globalization" (ibid., 16). In my opinion, this is probably the most appropriate starting point for a comparative study that wants to assess the movement's relative salience in contemporary protest politics; for the Swiss case, see Hutter and Giugni, "Protest Politics in a Changing Political Context: Switzerland, 1975–2005," 414–415.

33. C. Offe and H. Wiesenthal, "Two Logics of Collective Action: Theoretical Notes on Social Class and Organizational Form," *Political Power and Social Theory* 1(1)(1980): 94.

34. Ibid., 78.

35. The structural argument of Offe and Wiesenthal has also been criticized as depending far more on historically contingent events and processes, see W. G. Roy and R. Parker-Gwin, "How Many Logics of Collective Action?" *Theory and Society* 28(2)(1999): 203–37.

36. For a similar argument, see H. Kriesi, "Movements of the Left, Movements of the Right: Putting the Mobilization of Two New Types of Social Movements Into Political Context," in *Continuity and Change in Contemporary Capitalism*, eds. H. Kitschelt, P. Lange, G. Marks, and J.D. Stephens (Cambridge: Cambridge University Press, 1999), 398–423.

37. E.g., R. Koopmans and D. Rucht, "Social Movement Mobilization under Right and Left Governments: A Look at Four West European Countries," *WZB Discussion*

Paper (1995) FS III, 95–106; H. Kriesi, R. Levy, G. Ganguillet, and H. Zwicky, eds., *Politische Aktivierung in der Schweiz. 1945–1978* (Diessenhofen: Rüegger, 1981); and Rucht, "The Changing Role of Political Protest Movements."

38. E.g., H. Kitschelt, "Social Movements, Political Parties, and Democratic Theory," *The Annals of the American Academy of Political and Social Science,* 528(1)(1993): 13–29.

39. On the close relationship between the left and the new social movements, see H. Kriesi, et al., *New Social Movements in Western Europe. A Comparative Analysis* (Minneapolis: University of Minnesota Press, 1995). This close link is also reflected in the attitudes and protest potentials on the individual level, see, e.g., S. C. Flanagan and A.-R. Lee, "The New Politics, Cultural Wars, and the Authoritarian-Libertarian Value Change in Advanced Industrial Democracies," *Comparative Political Studies,* 36(3)(2003): 235–70.

40. E.g., P. Taggart, "Populism and the Pathology of Representative Politics," in *Democracies and the Populist Challenge,* ed. Y. Mény and Y. Surel (Basingstoke: Palgrave Macmillan, 2002), 81–98. For the moment, one can only speculate on the reasons for this "political paradox of the populist right." I reckon that it is part of a "strategy of double differentiation." The populist right leaders and followers, on the one side, try to set themselves apart from their adversary on the left and their use of "chaotic" protest activities. On the other side, they also try to set themselves apart from the extreme and neo-fascist right. The last argument is not only meant in a historical perspective, but also in a more practical way. The populist right runs the risk of being equated with its most right-extremist and racist currents if people openly advocating such ideologies take part in protest events organized or supported by populist right parties.

41. In part, this might also explain some cross-national differences, as the driving force behind the transformations in electoral politics (i.e., the populist radical right) might only be driving protest politics if it does not succeed in entering and structuring party competition; for the illustrative German case, see note 39.

42. For a cosmopolitan alternative to traditional conceptualizations, see E. Grande, "Cosmopolitan Political Science," *British Journal of Sociology* 57(1)(2006): 87–111.

Afterword

Social Movement Studies and Transnationalization

An Uneasy Relation or a Happy Start? An Afterword

Donatella della Porta

Social movement studies, as other areas of the social sciences, have been late to address phenomena of transnationalization, and are still in search of adequate methods, concepts, and theories to address them.* There are several reasons for this.

First, most scholarship has, time and again, confirmed the relevant role that national political opportunities play in influencing social movement mobilization, its dimension, duration, and forms. The modern repertoire of protest has emerged with the creation of the nation-state[1] and social movements have played an important role in the development of (national) citizenship rights.[2] So, it is at the national level that they fought for access, suffered state repression, and found alliances. Case studies as well as cross-national ones have addressed these issues in depth, remaining (as does most political sociology and political science) anchored in the nation-state. In this sense, social movement studies constituted no exception: research on political parties or interest groups shows the same pattern.

Second, and again non-exceptionally, social movement studies focused on the Western (and Northern) democracies. Here, especially since the 1980s, some tendencies toward an institutionalization (or "normalization" in a more critical language)[3] had developed and, with them, a growing formal inclusion of social movement organizations in complex systems of interest aggregations and representation. Even with cross-national differences, social movement organizations emerged as better-structured and richer in resources, but also in channels of access to national political systems. Protest appeared as a more and more conventional form of political participation in "protest societies."[4] At the same time, social movements tended to broaden their range of activity, including lobbying, institutional consultation, and even the provision of public services, contracted out by the public sector.

In the field of social movements, as in others, phenomena of transnationalization were first, not by chance, addressed within international relations and international sociology. Bringing "transnational relations back in," Thomas Risse, Kathrin Sikkink, and others had pointed at the role of environmental transnational and human right campaigns in developing international normative regimes.[5] In doing this, they innovated within their discipline by taking into account the role of non-state actors, as well as emphasizing cooperation over competition. Research on the human right regime or peace and war also stressed the emergence of international norms that challenged the vision of international politics as an anarchic system of states.

At the same time, research emerged on the development, in parallel and related to that of International Governmental Organizations (IGOs), of a population of International Non Governmental Organizations (INGOs), often in the forms of Transnational Social Movement Organizations.[6] In the last two decades, these non-governmental actors grew enormously in terms of number, membership, material resources, public resonance, and institutional access. This research also recognizes the interplay of actors at different geographical levels, going beyond disciplinary borders between internal politics and the international one. In human right campaigns, national actors, suffering repression in authoritarian regimes, found allies abroad in epistemic communities, involving IGOs, national governments, experts, and INGOs.

Focusing on the interactions between social movements and IGOs, the first studies emphasized especially the capacity of transnational social movements to adapt to the IGOs' rules of the game, with a diplomatic search for agreement over democratic accountability, discretion over transparency, and persuasion over mobilization in the street.[7] In this, they found some resonance in the more normatively oriented literature on a civil society, that tended to be seen since the beginning a *global* civil society. Stimulated by the "velvet," peaceful revolution in Central and Eastern Europe, and even before by the oppositional movements there, this approach reflected on the "taming of the social movements"[8] of the past and the potential role of a third, autonomous sphere between the state and the market.

Some time was needed before the (traditionally domestically oriented) social movement scholarship met international relations' scholars, who were studying INGOs, and normative theorists, who were reflecting on the contributions of a global civil society to cosmopolitan democracy.[9] Additionally, these encounters are still at the beginning of their relationship, with still a strong unexploited potential for cross-fertilization and mutual understanding.

Nevertheless, some first experiences at interactions developed and brought about already some innovations in social movement studies. A very first of these occasions was the Mont Pélerin (Switzerland) conference, which focused on "social movements in a globalizing world."[10] Held in June 1995, the conference involved some of the first exchanges between social movement studies and international relations. Although some time was needed before the members of the two groups started to understand each other on the use of very basic concepts (such as social movements and NGOs), the conference and ensuing volume were a useful start in the reflection about transnationalization and social movements. There were, in fact, several accomplishments that we can summarize using some main concepts in social movement research.

First, there was a reflection on multi-level opportunity structures for multi-level social movements.[11] In this sense, two main paths of transnationalization were singled out: social movements with domestic political concerns (especially in authoritarian regimes) searching for external, international allies (in what Keck and Sikkink define as the "boomerang effect"[12]); and social movements addressing their own governments, in order to influence international political decisions (in what Putnam calls double level games[13]).

A second set of contributions, in line with the attention paid to resource mobilization in social movement studies, referred to the types of resources that social movements could invest in the multi-level arenas and their (effective) strategies. On this, attention was paid to the resource exchanges between transnational social movement organizations and IGOs. Exchange of knowledge as well as a reciprocal potential legitimation was singled out as well as the potential of "vicarious activism" to sensitize the public opinion to global problems.[14] At the same time, the difficulties in protesting beyond the national borders were stressed—by looking at different data.

Third, various contributions in that volume pointed at the cognitive effects of globalization as intensification of relations beyond borders in terms of cross-national diffusion of movement frames, but also of strategies of public order control.[15] Here, as well, attention was paid to the potential for increasing exchanges, but also attention was paid on the limits upon them.

What that volume did not do, however, was to foresee the significant increase in transnational social movement activities in the years to come. The use of direct action at countersummits was yet to come, and the World social forums were not yet planned. It was not until the years of the 2000s, with the development of campaigns addressing various and diverse IGOs, that more reflections developed on the different opportunities that different international assets offered to different social movements. Such opportunities as a consensual culture as well as a reciprocal search for recognition functioned well, e.g., for the United Nations, but not for the (much more closed and hostile) international financiary institutions, such as the World Trade Organization (WTO), the International Monetary Fund (IMF), and the World Bank, which became the target of vivacious protest campaigns, such as "50 Years Is Enough," or "Our World Is Not For Sale." In fact, more recent research indicated that there are as many types of institutions at the transnational level as there are at the nation ones. Social movements that target these institutions have therefore to find specific leverage in, e.g., the unanimity rules of the WTO that makes alliances with some states particularly relevant, while the international experts and formal channels of consultation are exploited in interactions with the International Labour Organization (ILO).[16] Additionally, in recent research, IGOs emerged as complex and fragmented institutions, made of different bodies that provide external actors with differentiated opportunities. Looking at the European Union, the council, the commission, the parliament, and the courts are all targeted by social movements, but protest strategies vary with the different characteristics of these specific bodies.[17] Even more, different movements can have a more difficult or an easier life in finding access to specific (sympathetic) Directorate-Generals (DGs) in the EC, or opposing powerful DGs.[18]

Different opportunities require different strategies. If previous research had stressed, as mentioned, the taming of social movements, with a move from the street to the lobbies, recent studies rediscovered protest. In fact, going beyond the specific experiences of the parallel summits organized by the UN on environmental or women's issues, many interactions between social movements and IGOs did involve protest. With time, indeed, the frustration with the results of the more polite forms of interactions brought about the development of broader coalitions, including religious groups, unions, and social movement organizations, who combined pressures with petitions, marches, and even direct action.[19] Since Seattle, the years of the 2000s have seen an escalation of interactions between protestors and the police during the contestation of international summits.[20] Even though transnational protests remained a rare occurrence,[21] the few transnational protests (being in the forms of global days of action, countersummits or social forums) emerged as particularly "eventful" in their capacity to produce relational, cognitive, and affective effects on social movement activists and social movement organizations.[22]

Finally, at the cultural level, a global language developed, together with intensified interactions during the mentioned transnational events and a growing acknowledgment of the role and responsibilities of IGOs. Social movement activists started to present their action as part of a global justice movement, calling for global justice and global democracy. Even though the activists were still deeply rooted in the national political systems and movement families,[23] cosmopolitan activists tended to bridge the local with the global and vice versa.[24] In doing this, they are contributing to develop a transnational political system, as well as transnational identities.[25]

In this development, this volume brings still further innovation. First, with its interdisciplinary profile, it addresses empirically a question that has been ongoing throughout the debate on transnationalization: to which extent is this a new process? Already in the long-lasting debate on globalization, the question of when in history economic globalization has been more widespread is still open.[26] Research on protest events also testifies of recurrent moments of attention to international issues, which single out cycles more than trends. New transnational networks could be compared in size and breadth to the old labor movement international meetings. Also from the cultural point of view, the global focus of contemporary social movements has some precedents in the solidarity or peace movements. Although these issues are not explicitly mentioned, the mix of historical and contemporary cases covered in this volume allows for some reflections about continuities and discontinuities in social movement transnationalism over time.

Additionally, given its inclusion of Western and Eastern European countries, this volume provides a second, and equally valuable, contribution in the potential comparison in a broader space than the one usually considered by social movement studies. If, as mentioned, social movements have national roots, they are also embedded in broader geographical areas. Cross-national diffusion is easier given (structural and symbolically constructed) equivalences. Social movements themselves have constituted public spheres for communication and the exchange of knowledge (also) between the West and the East, and the North and the South. Concepts such as civil society traveled backward and forward from one area to the next (see Ivancheva's chapter), and relational and cognitive bridges were built. These moments have, however, been rare and the interaction between the East and the West (as the one between the South and the North) has been full of misunderstandings. With its empirical focus on social movements in a (broadly conceived) Europe, this volume has much to offer to a better understanding of the similarities and differences in transnationalization of social movements in the East and the West. Even though it does not take a comparative look, this volume might, however, function as a good point of departure for cross-national comparisons that go beyond the traditional intra-area ones.

In both directions, the various chapters contribute a lot of material for reflection. To give a few illustrations, several authors describe the (very different) agents (or entrepreneurs) of social movement transnationalization: from the anarchist networks after the Second World War (see Romanos' chapter) to the churches in the first wave of the peace movement (Oppenheimer's chapter), and from the Gypsy of the Diaspora during the Prague Spring (Donert's chapter) to Amnesty International (AI) in the protest against the abuse of psychiatry against political opponents in the Soviet Union (Kouki's chapter). All of these chapters are rich in reflections on the specific effects on transnational framing of the specific agents (or entrepreneurs) of transnationalization and their specific discourse (e.g., the specific anti-state appeal of the churches, or the universalizing discourse of AI). Still, in terms of the characteristics of the entrepreneurs of transnationalization, the chapters on the protest against the G8 summit in Heiligendamm in 2007 (Teune's chapter) and the comparison of the organizational structures of Attac and the Clean Clothes Campaign (Niesyto's chapter) point at the growing role of transnational communication in contemporary movements and at their growing professionalization (Lachenmeier's chapter), as well as at the internal diversity of contemporary, global movements. A third aspect of transnationalization, which the various chapters collected in this volume help to reflect upon, is the complex, multi-level environment in which it take place. Dynamic opportunities (Bosi's chapter), interaction on global and national level (Hutter's chapter), or the conditionalities imposed by IGOs on the EU (Buzogany's chapter) are all elements to take into account, as a mix of constraints and opportunities, when looking at examples of transnationalization of social movements across time and space. On all of these topics, more cross-time and cross-areas comparison is urgently needed.

Notes

*This afterword develops ideas I have presented in the preface to the second edition of *Social Movements in a Globalizing World* (New York: Macmillan, 2009).
1. C. Tilly, "Social Movements and National Politics," in *State-Making and Social Movements: Essays in History and Theory,* eds. C. Bright and S. Harding (Ann Arbor: University of Michigan Press, 1984), 297–317.
2. T.H. Marshall, *Citizenship and Social Class* (org. ed. 1950), in T.H. Marshall and T. Bottomore, *Citizenship and Social Class* (Pluto Press: London, 1992), 3–51; R. Bendix, *Nation Building and Citizenship* (New York: Wiley & Son, 1964).
3. F.F. Piven and R.A. Cloward, "Normalizing Collective Protest," in *Frontiers in Social Movement Theory,* eds. A. Morris and C. McClurg Mueller (New Haven: Yale University Press, 1992), 301–325.
4. D.S. Meyer and S. Tarrow, eds., *The Social Movement Society* (New York: Rowman & Littlefield, 1998).
5. E.g., T. Risse and K. Sikkink, eds., "The Socialization of International Human Rights Norms into Domestic Practices: Introduction," in *The Power of Human Rights International Norms and Domestic Change,* eds. T. Risse, S. Rapp, and K. Sikkink (New York: Cambridge University Press, 1999), 1–38.
6. C. Chatfield, R. Pagnucco, and J. Smith, eds., *Solidarity Beyond the State: the Dynamics of Transnational Social Movements* (Syracuse, NY: Syracuse University Press, 1996); J. Boli and G.M. Thomas, *Constructing the World Culture: International Nongovernmental Organizations since 1875* (Stanford: Stanford University Press, 1999).
7. E.g., D. della Porta and H. Kriesi, "Social Movements in a Globalizing World: an Introduction," in *Social Movements in a Globalizing World,* eds. D. della Porta, H. Kriesi, and D. Rucht (New York: Macmillan, 1999), 3–23.
8. M. Kaldor, *Global Civil Society. An Answer to War* (Cambridge: Polity Press, 2003).
9. R. Marchetti, *Global Democracy: For and Against* (London: Routledge, 2008).
10. D. della Porta, H. Kriesi, and D. Rucht, eds., *Social Movements in a Globalizing World* (New York: Macmillan, 1999).
11. Della Porta and Kriesi, "Social Movements in a Globalizing World"; F. Passy, "Supranational Political Opportunities as a Channel of Globalization of Political Conflicts: The Case of the Rights of Indigenous People," in della Porta, Kriesi, and Rucht, *Social Movements in a Globalizing World,* 148–169.
12. M.E. Keck and K. Sikkink, *Activists Beyond Borders. Advocacy Networks in International Politics,* (Ithaca and London: Cornell University Press, 1998).
13. R.D. Putnam, "Diplomacy and Domestic Politics: The Logic of Two-Level Games," *International Organization,* 42(3)(1988): 427–460.

14. See C. Lahusen, "International Campaigns in Context," in della Porta, Kriesi, and Rucht, *Social Movements in a Globalizing World,* 189–205.

15. D.A. Snow and R.D. Benford, "Alternative Types of Cross-national Diffusion in the Social Movement Arena," in della Porta, Kriesi, and Rucht, *Social Movements in a Globalizing World,* 23–39.

16. For a comparison, F. Silva, "Do Transnational Social Movements Matter? Four Case Studies Assessing the Impact of Transnational Social Movements on the Global Governance of Trade, Labour and Finance," Ph.D. diss., European University Institute, 2008.

17. L. Parks, "Social Movements and the European Union" (provisional title), Ph.D. diss., European University Institute, 2009.

18. Ibid.; also C. Ruzza, *Europe and Civil Society, Movement Coalitions and European Governance* (Manchester and New York: Manchester University Press, 2004); and R. Balme and D. Chabanet, *European Governance and Democracy. Power and protest in the EU* (Lanham: Rowman & Littlefield, 2008).

19. J. Smith, et al., *Global democracy and the World Social Forum* (Boulder: Paradigm 2007); R. Reitan, *Global Activism* (London: Routledge, 1997).

20. D. della Porta, et al., *Globalization from Below* (Minneapolis: The University of Minnesota Press, 2006); D. della Porta, A. Peterson, and H. Reiter, eds., *The Policing of Transnational Protest* (Aldershot: Ashgate, 2006).

21. See e.g., D. Imig and S. Tarrow, eds., *Contentious Europeans. Protest and Politics in an Emerging Polity* (Lanham: Rowman & Littlefield, 2001).

22. D. della Porta, "Eventful Protest, Global Conflict," *Distinktion. Scandinavian Journal of Social Theory* 17(2008): 27–56.

23. D. della Porta, ed., *The Global Justice Movement. Cross National and Transnational Perspectives* (Boulder: Paradigm, 2007).

24. D. della Porta and S. Tarrow, eds., *Transnational Protest and Global Activism* (New York: Rowman & Littlefield, 2005).

25. S. Tarrow, *The New Transnational Activism* (New York and Cambridge: Cambridge University Press, 2005); D. della Porta and M. Caiani, *Social Movements and Europe* (Oxford: Oxford University Press, 2009).

26. D. della Porta, "Globalization and Democracy," *Democratization* 12(2005): 668–685.

Bibliography

Abelló, T. and E. Olivé, "El Conflicto entre la CNT y la Familia Urales-Mont-seny en 1928. La Lucha por el Mantenimiento del Anarquismo Puro." *Estudios de Historial Social* 32–33(1985): 317–332.

Acton, T. and I. Klimová. 2001. "The International Romani Union: An East European answer to West European questions? Shifts in the focus of World Romani Congresses 1971–2000." In *Between Past and Future: the Roma of Central and Eastern Europe*, edited by W. Guy, 157–226. Hatfield: University of Hertfordshire Press.

Addison, J.T. and C. Schnabel, eds. 2003. *International Handbook of Trade Unions*. Cheltenham: Edward Elgar.

Alekseeva, L. 1985. *Soviet Dissent: Contemporary Movements for National, Religious and Human Rights*. Connecticut: Wesleyan University Press.

Allen, M.G. "Psychiatry in the United States and the USSR: a Comparison." *American Journal of Psychiatry* 130(12)(1973): 1333–1337.

Amnesty International. 1975. *Les Abus de la Psychiatre à des Fins Politiques: Rapport sur le Symposium de Genève*. Geneve: AI.

———. 1975. *Prisoners of Conscience in the USSR: Treatment and Conditions*. Chapter on "Compulsory Detention in Psychiatric Hospitals," 101–137. London: AI Publications.

———. 1976. *The Case of Leonid Plyushch*. London: AI Publications.

———. 1995. *Psychiatry: a Human Rights Perspective*. AI Index, ACT 75/003/95.

Andretta, M. et al. 2006. *Globalization from Below. Transnational Activists and Protest Networks*. Minneapolis: University of Minnesota Press.

Anheier, H.K. and H. Katz. 2006. "Network Approaches to Global Civil Society." In *Global Civil Society 2004/5*, edited by H.K. Anheier, M. Glasius, and M. Kaldor, 206–221. London: Sage.

Appelius, S. 1999. *Pazifismus in Westdeutschland. Die Deutsche Friedensgesellschaft 1945–1968*. Aachen: G. Mainz.

Arlt, H.-J. 1998. *Kommunikation, Öffentlichkeit, Öffentlichkeitsarbeit. PR von gestern, PR für morgen—das Beispiel Gewerkschaft*, Opladen. Wiesbaden: Westdeutscher Verlag.

Arlt, H.-J. and O. Jarren. 1998. "Abwehrkünstler am Werk—Über die Kampagnenfähigkeit des Deutschen Gewerkschaftsbundes." In *PR-Kampagnen. Über die Inszenierung von Öffentlichkeit*, edited by U. Röttger, 172–193. Opladen: Westdeutscher Verlag.

Armingeon, K. 2007. "Die politische Rolle der Verbände in modernen De-
mokratien. Fünf Thesen." In *Entgrenzte Demokratie? Herausforderungen für
die politische Interessenvermittlung*, edited by O. Jarren, D. Lachenmeier, and
A. Steiner, 107–122. Baden-Baden: Nomos.
Armingeon, K., and S. Geissbühler, eds. 2000. *Gewerkschaften in der Schweiz.
Herausforderungen und Optionen*. Zürich: Seismo.
Aronson, R. 2004. *Camus & Sartre: the Story of a Friendship and the Quarrel that
Ended It*. Chicago: University of Chicago Press.
Ash, T.G. "Does Central Europe Exist?" *NY Review of Books* 33(15) (1986). Retrieved 30 of October 2007 from http://www.nybooks.com/articles/article-
preview?article_id=4998.
———. 1993. *The Magic Lantern: The Revolution of '89 Witnessed in Warshaw*,
Budapest, Berlin, Prague, New York: Vintage Books.
———. 2000. "Conclusions." In *Between Past and Future: the Revolutions of
1989 and their Aftermath*, edited by V. Tismăneanu and S. Antohin, 401–
402. Budapest and New York: CEU Press.
Attac. n.d. "The Anti- Lidl Campaign, Europe-wide!" Retrieved 7 September
2006 from http://www.attac.de/lidl-kampagne/content/campaign/internat/
engl/the_anti-lidl_campaign_europe-wide.doc.
Backhaus-Maul, H. and T. Olk. 1992. "Intermediäre Organisationen als Gegenstand sozialwissenschaftlicher Forschung. Theoretische Überlegungen
und erste empirische Befunde am Beispiel des Aufbaus von intermediären
Organisationen in den neuen Bundesländern." In *Sozialpolitik im Prozess
der deutschen Vereinigung*, edited by W. Schmähl, 91–132. Frankfurt/Main,
New York: Campus-Verlag.
Badie, B. 1997. "Le Jeu Triangulaire." In *Sociologie des Nationalismes*, edited by
P. Birnbaum, 447–462. Paris: Presses Universitaires de France.
Balme, R. and D. Chabanet. 2008. *European Governance and Democracy. Power
and protest in the EU*. Lanham: Rowman & Littlefield.
Balsen, W. and K. Rössel. 1986. *Hoch die internationale Solidarität. Zur Geschichte
der Dritte Welt-Bewegung in der Bundesrepublik*. Köln: Kölner Volksblatt.
Bar, A. 1981. *La CNT en los Años Rojos. Del Sindicalismo Revolucionario al Anar-
cosindicalismo (1910–1926)*. Madrid: Akal.
Barany, Z.D. 2002. *The East European Gypsies: Regime Change, Marginality, and
Ethnopolitics*. Cambridge; New York: Cambridge University Press.
Baringhorst, S. 2005. "New Media and the Politics of Consumer Activism. Opportunities and Challenges of Euro-Asian Anti-Corporate Campaigns." Paper presented to the Workshop on *New Directions in Cultural Politic* at the
Annual Conference of the European Consortium of Political Research in
Granada, 14–19 April, 2005.
———. 2008. "Political Empowerment of Citizen Consumers—Chances and
Problems of Anti-Corporate Campaigning on the Net." In *Net Working/Net-
working: Politics on the Internet*, edited by T. Häythtis and J. Rinne, 281–
309. Tampere: Tampere University Press.

Baringhorst, S., V. Kneip, and J. Niesyto. "Anti-Corporate Campaigns—Netz-öffentlichkeit als Arena politischen Protests." *Forschungsjournal Neue Soziale Bewegungen*, 20(3)(2007): 49–60.

Barry, D., W. Butler, and G. Ginsburgs, eds. 1974. *Contemporary Soviet Law Essays in Honor of John Hazard.* The Hague: M. Nijhoff.

Bartolini, S. and P. Mair. 1990. *Identity, Competition, and Electoral Availability.* Cambridge: Cambridge University Press.

Bataille, G. 1994. *The Absence of Myth. Writings on Surrealism.* Translated by M. Richardson. London, New York: Verso.

Bauböck, R. and T. Faist, eds. 2010. *Transnationalism and Diaspora. Concepts, Theories and Methods.* Amsterdam: IMISCOE – University of Amsterdam Press.

Bauman, Z. 1987. *Legislators and Interpreters: On Modernity, Post-modernity and Intellectuals.* Cambridge: Polity Press.

Baxter, L. et al. "Discussion on the Strategy of Peoples Democracy." *New Left Review,* 55(1969): 3–19.

Beck, U. 1992. *Risk Society.* London: Sage.

Beck, U. 1996. *The Reinvention of Politics. Rethinking Modernity in the Global Social Order.* Cambridge: Cambridge University Press.

Beck, U. 2005. *Power in the Global Age.* Cambridge: Polity Press.

Belkin, G. "Writing about Their Science: American Interest in Soviet Psychiatry During the Post Stalin Cold War." *Perspectives in Biology and Medicine* 43(1), Autumn(1993): 31–46.

Bell, R.G. "Further Up the Learning Curve: NGOs from Transition to Brussels." *Environmental Politics* 13 (1)(2004): 194–215.

Bendix, R. 1964. *Nation Building and Citizenship.* New York: Wiley & Son.

Benford, R.D. "Frame Disputes within the Nuclear Disarmament Movement." *Social Forces* 71(3)(1993): 677–701.

Benford, R.D. and D. Snow. "Framing Processes and Social Movements: An Overview and Assessment." *Annual Review of Sociology* 26(1)(2000): 611–639.

Bennett, L.W. 2005. "Social Movements beyond Borders: Understanding Two Eras of Transnational Activism." In *Transnational Protest and Global Activism,* edited by D. della Porta and S. Tarrow, 203–226. New York, Oxford, and Lanham: Rowman & Littlefield.

Bentele, G. 1997. "Grundlagen der Public Relations." In *Public Relations in Theorie und Praxis,* edited by W. Donsbach, 21–36. München: Fischer.

Bergmann, U., et al., eds. 1968. *Rebellion der Studenten oder die neue Opposition.* Reinbeck bei Hamburg: Rowohlt.

Berry, D. 2002. *A History of the French Anarchist Movement, 1917–1945.* Westport, CT, London: Greenwood Press.

Beyer, W., ed. 1989. *Widerstand gegen den Krieg. Beiträge zur Geschichte der War Resisters' International/Internationale der KriegsdienstgegnerInnen.* Kassel: Weber-Zucht-Verlag.

Beyers, J. "Gaining and Seeking Access: The European Adaptation of Domestic Interest Associations." *European Journal of Political Research* 41(5)(2002): 585–612.

Billing, M., C. Condor, D. Edwards, M. Gane, D. Middleton, and A. Radley. 1988. *Ideological Dilemmas: A Social Psychology of Everyday Thinking.* London: Sage.

Bloch, S. and P. Chodoff, eds. 1981. *Psychiatric Ethics,* Oxford: Oxford University Press.

Boda, Z. and G. Scheiring. "Zöld Közpolitika-befolyásolás az Európai Unióban." *Politikatudományi Szemle* 4(2006): 41–74.

Bodemann, Y.M. "Eclipse of Memory: German Representations of Auschwitz in the Early Postwar Period." *New German Critique* 75 (Fall)(1998): 57–89.

Boli, J. and G.M. Thomas. 1999. *Constructing the World Culture: International Nongovernmental Organizations since 1875.* Stanford: Stanford University Press

Bonacker, T. and L. Schmitt. 2004. "Politischer Protest zwischen latenten Strukturen und manifesten Konflikten. Perspektiven soziologischer Protestforschung am Beispiel der (neuen) Friedensbewegung." *Mitteilungsblatt des Instituts für soziale Bewegungen* 32 (2004): 193–213.

Bonnie, R. 1996. "Introduction: the Evolution of the 1992 Law of the Russian Federation on Psychiatric Care." *Journal of Russian and Eurasian Psychiatry* 27 (1996): 69–96.

———. "Political Abuse of Psychiatry in the Soviet Union and in China, Complexities and Controversies." *The Journal of the American Academy of Psychiatry and the Law* 30 (2002): 136–142.

Boobbyer, P. 2005. *Conscience, Dissent and Reform in Soviet Russia.* London: Routledge.

Börzel, T.A. "Participation Through Law Enforcement: The Case of the European Union." *Comparative Political Studies* 39(1)(2006): 128–152.

Börzel, T.A. and T. Risse. 2003. "Conceptualising the Domestic Impact of Europe." In *The Politics of Europeanisation,* edited by K. Featherstone and C. Radaelli, 55–78. Oxford: Oxford University Press.

Börzel, T.A. and U. Sedelmeier. 2006. "The EU Dimension in European Politics." In *Developments in European Politics,* edited by P.M. Heywood, E. Jones, M. Rhodes and U. Sedelmeier, 54–70. Houndmills, Basingstoke; New York: Palgrave Macmillan.

Bosi, L. "Social Movement Participation and the 'Timing' of Involvement: the Case of the Northern Ireland Civil Rights Movement." *Research in Social Movements, Conflicts and Change,* 27 (2007): 37–61.

Bourdieu, P. 2001. *Das Politische Feld. Zur Kritik der Politischen Vernunft.* Konstanz: Universitätsverlag Konstanz.

Bozóki, A., ed. 1999. *Intellectuals and Politics in Central Europe.* Budapest and New York: CEU Press.

————. 2007. "Die Politik der Opposition im Ungarn der 1980er Jahre." In *Weltregionen im Wandel: Mittel- und Osteuropa*, edited by A. Buzogány and R. Frankenberger, 261–275. Baden-Baden: Nomos.

Bracke, M. 2007. *Which Socialism, Whose Détente? West European Communism and the Czechoslovak Crisis of 1968*. Budapest: Central European University Press.

Brannan, T. 2003. *From 'Antipolitics' to 'Anti-Politics': What Become of East European 'Civil Society'?* LSE Working Papers 03(41). Retrieved 2 January 2008 from www.lse.ac.uk/collections/DESTIN/pdf/WP41.pdf.

Bren, P. 2004. "1968 East and West. Visions of Political Change and Student Protest from across the Iron Curtain." In *Transnational Moments of Change: Europe 1945, 1968, 1989*, edited by G.-R. Horn and P. Kenney, 119–136. Lanham: Rowman and Littlefield Publishers.

Brockett, C. 1995. "A Protest-Cycle Resolution of the Repression/Popular Protest Paradox." In *Repertoires and Cycles of Collective Action*, edited by M. Traugott, 117–144. Durham: Duke University Press.

Bukovsky, V. 1978. *To Build a Castle, My Life as a Dissenter.* London: Deutsch.

Bukovsky, V. and S. Gluzman. 1975. "A Manual of Psychiatry for Dissidents." Retrieved 18 October 2007 from http://antology.igrunov.ru/authors/bukovsky/psychiatr.html.

Buzogány, A. 2009. "Romania: Europeanization in the Shadow of Forms without Substance." In *Coping with Accession: New Modes of Environmental Governance*, edited by T. Börzel, 169–181. Houndsmill: Palgrave/Macmillan.

Buzogány, A. and E. Baga. 2009. "Europa und das Gold der Karpaten. Lokale, Nationale und Transnationale Dimensionen des Bergbaukonfliktes in Rosia Montana." In *Projekte der Europäisierung. Kulturanthropologische Forschungsperspektiven*, Kulturanthropologie Notizen Bd. 78, edited by G. Welz and A. Lottermann, 43–61. Frankfurt am Main: Institut für Kulturanthropologie und Europäische Ethnologie.

Burke, P. 2004. "A Transcontinental Movement of Citizens? Strategic Debates in the 1980s Western Peace Movement." In *Transnational Moments of Change: Europe 1945, 1968, 1989*, edited by P. Kenney and G.R. Horn. Landham, MD: Rowman & Littlefield.

Buttigieg, J.A. "Gramsci on Civil Society." *boundary 2*, 22(3)(1995): 1–32.

Calvin, P. "Defining Transnationalism." *Contemporary European History*, 14(4) (2005): 421–439.

Cameron Report. 1969. *Disturbances in Northern Ireland.* Belfast: Cmd 532, HMSO.

Carmin, J. and D.B. Balser. "Selecting Repertoires of Action in Environmental Movement Organizations: An Interpretive Approach." *Organization Environment* 15 (4)(2002): 365–388.

Casanova, J. 2004. *Anarchism, the Republic, and Civil War in Spain: 1931–1939.* London: Routledge. Original ed. in Spanish, 1997.

———. 2007. *Anarquismo y Violencia Política en la España del Siglo XX*. Zaragoza: Institución Fernando el Católico.

Cassese, A. 1999. *Self-Determination of Peoples. A Legal Reappraisal*. Cambridge: Cambridge University Press.

Castells, M. 1996. *The Rise of the Network Society. The Information Age. Economy, Society and Culture*. Vol. 1. Oxford: Blackwell.

———. 2001. "Informationalism and the Network Society." Epilogue to Pekka Himanen, *The Hacker Ethic and the Spirit of Informationalism*, 155–178. New York: Random House.

———. 2001. *The Internet Galaxy: Reflections on the Internet, Business and Society*. Oxford: Oxford University Press.

Castro Alfín, D., "Palabras de Fuego. El Anticlericalismo Republicano." *Journal of Spanish Cultural Studies* 6(2)(2005): 205–225.

Cerrito, G. 1973. *Il Ruolo della Organizzazione Anarchica*. Catania: RL.

Cerutti, F. 2001. "Political Identity and Conflict." In *Identities and Conflicts. The Mediterranean*, edited by F. Cerruti and R. Ragionieri, 9–25. Basingstoke: Palgrave.

Chan, A. "Violence, Non-violence, and the Concept of Revolution in Anarchist Thought." *Anarchist Studies* 12(2)(2004): 103–123.

Chatfield, C., R. Pagnucco, and J. Smith, eds. 1996. *Solidarity Beyond the State: the Dynamics of Transnational Social Movements*. Syracuse, NY: Syracuse University Press.

Christofferson, M.S. 2006. *French Intellectuals Against the Left: The Antitotalitarian Moment of the 1970s*. New York: Berghahn Books.

Cichowski, R.A. 2007. *The European Court and Civil Society: Litigation, Mobilization and Governance*. Cambridge; New York: Cambridge University Press.

Cioc, M. 1988. *Pax Atomica: The Nuclear Defense Debate in West Germany During the Adenauer Era*. New York: Columbia University Press.

Clavin, P. "Defining Transnationalism." *Contemporary European History* 14(4) (2005): 421–439.

Clean Clothes Campaign. 2001. "Clean Clothes. International Meeting." Retrieved 7 September 2006 from http://www.cleanclothes.org/ftp/SKO_bracelonadef.pdf.

———. n.d. "FAQs. What Does the Clean Clothes Campaign Do?" Retrieved 18 September 2006 from http://www.cleanclothes.org/faq/faq02.htm.

Cmiel, K. "The Emergence of Human Rights Politics in the United States." *The Journal of American History* (Special Issue: The Nation and Beyond; Transnational Perspectives on United States History), 86(3)(1999): 1231–1250.

Cohen, D. 1989. *Soviet Psychiatry*. London: Paladin.

Cohen, J.L. and A. Arato. 1992. *Civil Society and Political Theory*. Cambridge, MA, London: MIT Press.

Collectif Ethique sur l'étiquette. N.d. "Pour le Progrès Social." Retrieved 18 September 2006 from http://www.ethique-sur-etiquette.org/index.htm.

Comaroff, J. and J. 2002. "Of Revelation and Revolution." In *Anthropology of Politics: A Reader in Ethnography, Theory and Critique,* edited by V. Joan, 203–213. Oxford: Blackwell.

Connor, W. "Self-Determination: the New Phase." *World Politics* 20(1)(1967): 30–53.

Cooper, A. 1996. *Paradoxes of Peace: German Peace Movements since 1945.* Ann Arbor: University of Michigan Press.

Crossley, N. "From Reproduction to Transformation: Social Movement Fields and the Radical Habitus." *Theory Culture Society* 20 (6)(2003): 43–68.

———. 2006. *Contesting Psychiatry: Social Movements in Mental Health.* London: Routledge.

Crowder, G. 1991. *Classical Anarchism: the Political Thought of Godwin, Proudhon, Bakunin and Kropotkin.* Oxford: Clarendon Press.

Currie, A. 2004. *All Hell Will Break Loose.* Dublin: O'Brien Press.

Curtis, R.L. and L.A. Zurcher. "Stable Resources of Protest Movements: The Multi-Organizational Field." *Social Forces* 52 (1)(1973): 53–61.

Dalton, R.J. 1994. *The Green Rainbow. Environmental Groups in Western Europe.* New Haven: Yale University Press.

Davis, G.F., D. McAdam, W.R. Scott and M.N. Zald. 2005. *Social Movements and Organization Theory.* Cambridge: University Press.

Deegan-Krause, K. 2007. "New Dimensions of Political Cleavage." In *The Oxford Handbook of Political Behavior,* edited by R.J. Dalton and H.-D. Klingeman, 538–556. Oxford: Oxford University Press.

Delacampagne, C. 2006. "The Paris School of Existentialism." In *The Columbia History of Twentieth-century French Thought,* edited by L.D. Kritzman, B.J. Reilly, and M.B. DeBevoise, 78–84. New York: Columbia University Press.

della Porta, D. 1992. "Biographies of Social Movement Activists: State of the Art and Methodological Problems." in M. Diani and R. Eyerman, *Studying Social Movements,* edited by M. Diani and R. Eyerman, 168–193. London: Sage.

———. 1995. *Social Movements, Political Violence, and the State: a Comparative Analysis of Italy and Germany.* Cambridge: Cambridge University Press.

———. "Globalization and Democracy." *Democratization* 12(2005): 668–685.

———, ed. 2007. *The Global Justice Movement. A Cross-National and Transnational Perspective.* Boulder: Paradigm.

———. 2007. "The Global Justice Movement: An Introduction." In *The Global Justice Movement. Cross-National and Transnational Perspectives,* edited by D. della Porta. Boulder: Paradigm.

———. 2008. "Eventful Protest, Global Conflict." *Distinktion. Scandinavian Journal of Social Theory* 17(2008): 27–56.

della Porta, D., M. Andretta, L. Mosca, and H. Reiter. 2006. *Globalization from Below.* Minneapolis: The University of Minnesota Press.

della Porta, D. and M. Caiani. 2006. "Europeanization From Below? Social Movements and Europe," *Mobilization: An International Quarterly* 12(1) (2007): 1–20.

———. 2007. "Social movements in a multi-level Europe." In *Entgrenzte Demokratie? Herausforderungen für die politische Interessenvermittlung*, edited by O. Jarren, D. Lachenmeier, and A. Steiner, 163–177. Baden-Baden: Nomos.

———. 2009. *Social Movements and Europe*. Oxford: Oxford University Press.

della Porta, D. and M. Diani. 2006. *Social Movements: an Introduction*, Malden, MA: Blackwell.

della Porta, D. and H. Kriesi. 1999. "Social Movements in a Globalizing World: an Introduction." In *Social Movements in a Globalizing World*, edited by D. della Porta, H. Kriesi and D. Rucht, 3–22. Basingstoke: Macmillan.

della Porta, D., H. Kriesi, and D. Rucht, eds. 1999. *Social Movements in a Globalizing World*. Basingstoke and New York: Macmillan.

della Porta, D., A. Peterson, and H. Reiter, eds. 2006. *The Policing of Transnational Protest*. Aldershot: Ashgate.

della Porta, D. and H. Reiter. 1998. *The Policing of Protest*. Minneapolis: Minnesota University Press.

della Porta, D. and S. Tarrow, eds. 2005. *Transnational Protest and Global Activism*. New York, Oxford, Lanham: Rowman & Littlefield.

Deutsch, K.W. 1953. *Nationalism and Social Communication: An Enquiry into the Foundations of Nationality*. Cambridge, MA: The MIT Press.

Diani, M. "Linking Mobilization Frames and Political Opportunities: Insights from Regional Populism in Italy." *American Sociological Review*, 61 (6)(1996): 1053–1069.

———. "The Relational Deficit of Ideologically Structured Action." *Mobilization* 5 (1)(2000): 17–24.

Dimitrova, A. "Enlargement, Institution-building and the EU's Administrative Capacity Requirement." *West European Politics* 25(4)(2002): 171–190.

Donges, P. 2005. "Medialisierung der Politik—Vorschlag einer Differenzierung." In *Mythen der Mediengesellschaft—The Media Society and its Myths*, edited by P. Rössler and F. Krotz, 321–339. Konstanz: UVK.

———. 2008. *Medialisierung Politischer Organisationen: Parteien in der Mediengesellschaft*. Wiesbaden: VS Verlag für Sozialwissenschaften.

Dolezal, M. and S. Hutter. "Konsensdemokratie unter Druck? Politischer Protest in Österreich, 1975–2005." *Austrian Journal of Political Science* 36(3)(2007): 338–352.

Donnelly, J. 2002. *Universal Human Rights in Theory and Practice*. Ithaca: Cornell University Press.

Driessen, E., S. de Boer, and H.L. Verhaar, eds. 1982. *Biographical Dictionary of the Dissidents in the Soviet Union, 1956–1975*. The Hague: Boston: M. Nijhoff.

Eagleton, T. 1991. *Ideology. An Introduction*. London & New York: Verso.

Ealham, C. 2005. *Class, Culture and Conflict in Barcelona, 1898–1937.* London: Routledge

Earl, J. 2003. "Tanks, Tear Gas, and Taxes: Toward a Theory of Movement Repression." *Sociological Theory* 21(1)(2003): 44–68.

———. "Introduction: Repression and the Social Control of Protest." *Mobilization* 11 (2) (2006): 129–143.

Ebbinghaus, B., and J. Visser. 2000. *Trade Unions in Western Europe since 1945.* London: Macmillan.

Edwards, J. 1999. *Anglo-American Relations and the Franco Question in the Early Cold War, 1945–1955.* Oxford: Clarendon Press.

Einwohner, R.L. "Opportunity, Honor, and Action in the Warsaw Ghetto Uprising of 1943." *The American Journal of Sociology* 109(3)(2003): 650–675.

Eising, R. and B. Kohler-Koch. 2005. "Interessenpolitik im europäischen Mehrebenensystem," In *Interessenpolitik in Europa,* edited by R. Eising and B. Kohler-Koch, 11–75. Baden-Baden: Nomos.

Ekiert, G. and J. Kubik. 2000. *Civil Society From Abroad: the Role of Foreign Assistance in the Democratization of Poland.* The Weatherlhead Center for International Affairs, Harvard University, Working Paper Series 00(01). Retrieved 8 January 2008 from http://www.ciaonet.org/wps/kuj01/.

Elliott, S. 1973. *Northern Ireland Parliamentary Election Results 1921–1972.* Chichester: Political Reference Publications.

Elorza, A. 1973 [1971]. "La Utopía Anarquista bajo la II República." In *La Utopía Anarquista bajo la II República,* edited by A. Elorza, 351–468. Madrid: Ayuso.

———. 1995. "Utopía y Revolución en el Movimiento Anarquista Aspañol." In *El Anarquismo Español y Sus Tradiciones Culturales,* edited by B. Hofmann, P. Joan i Tours and M. Tietz, 79–108. Madrid: Iberoamericana.

Ennis, J.G. "Fields of Action: Structure in Movements' Tactical Repertoires." *Sociological Forum* 2 (3)(1987): 520–533.

Eyal, G. "Anti-politics and the Spirit of Capitalism: Dissidents, Monetarists, and the Czech Transition to Capitalism." *Theory and Society,* 29(1)(2000): 50–92.

Falk, B.J. 2003. *The Dilemmas of Dissidence in East-Central Europe: Citizen Intellectuals and Philosopher Kings.* Budapest and New York: Central European University Press.

———. 2005. *The Dilemmas of Dissidence in East-Central Europe.* Budapest and New York: CEU Press.

Farrell, M. 1988. *Twenty Years On.* Co. Kerry Dingle: Brandon.

Faulstich, W. 1992. *Grundwissen Öffentlichkeitsarbeit: kritische Einführung in Problemfelder.* Bardowick: Wissenschaftler-Verlag.

Fedeli, U. and G. Sacchetti, eds. 2002. *Congressi e Convegni della Federazione Anarchica Italiana. Atti e documenti (1944–1995).* Pescara: Samizdat.

Feher, F. and A. Heller. 1987. *Eastern Left, Western Left: Totalitarianism, Freedom and Democracy.* Cambridge: Blackwell.

Ferenschild, S. "Zwischen Konzernkritik und Unternehmensranking. Ein-flussmöglichkeiten auf Konzerne durch eine Kampagne—das Beispiel der Clean Clothes Campaign." *Inkota Brief,* 136(2006): 12–13.

Fine, G.A. and K. Sandstrom. "Ideology in Action: A Pragmatic Approach to a Contested Concept." *Sociological Theory* 11 (1)(1993): 21–38.

Fink, C., P. Gassert, and D. Junker, eds. 1998. *1968: The World Transformed.* New York: Cambridge University Press.

Fireside, Harvey. 1979. *The Soviet Psychoprisons.* New York: Norton.

Flanagan, S.C. and A.-R. Lee. "The New Politics, Cultural Wars, and the Authoritarian-Libertarian Value Change in Advanced Industrial Democracies." *Comparative Political Studies* 36(3)(2003): 235–70.

Fontenis, G. 1990. *L'autre Communisme: Histoire Subversive du Mouvement Libertaire.* Mauléon: Acratie.

———. 2000. *Changer le Monde: Histoire du Mouvement Communiste Libertaire (1945–1977).* Toulouse: Le Coquelicot.

Foot, K. and S.M. Schneider. 2006. *Web Campaigning.* Cambridge, MA: Massachusetts Institute of Technology.

Foster, D., and P. Scott, eds. 2003. *Trade Unions in Europe: Meeting the Challenge.* Bruxelles: P.I.E. – Lang.

Foucault, M. 1961. *Histoire de la Folie a l' Age Classique.* Paris: Gallimard.

Francisco, R.A. 2005. "The Dictator's Dilemma." In *Repression and Mobilization,* edited by C. Davenport, H. Johnston, and C.M. Mueller, 58–81. Minneapolis: University of Minnesota Press.

Frantz, C. 2007. "NGOs als transnationale Interessenvertreter und Agenda Setter." In *Entgrenzte Demokratie? Herausforderungen für die politische Interessenvermittlung,* edited by O. Jarren, D. Lachenmeier, and A. Steiner, 181–197. Baden-Baden: Nomos.

Freeman, J. 1999. "A Model for Analyzing the Strategic Options of Social Movement Organizations." In *Waves of Protest: Social Movements since the Sixties,* edited by J. Freeman and V. Johnson, 221–240. Lanham: Rowman & Littlefield.

Gajewska, K. 2009. *Transnational Labour Solidarity: Mechanisms of Commitment to Cooperation within the European Trade Union Movement.* London: Routledge.

Gamson, W.A. 1975. *The Strategy of Social Protest.* Homewood: Dorsey Press.

———. 1992. *Talking Politics.* Cambridge: Cambridge University Press.

Gerhards, J. and D. Rucht. "Mesomobilization: Organizing and Framing in Two Protest Campaigns in West Germany." *The American Journal of Sociology* 98(3)(1992): 555–596.

Geyer, M. 2001. "Cold War Angst: The Case of West-German Opposition to Rearmament and Nuclear Weapons." In *The Miracle Years: A Cultural History of West Germany, 1949–1968,* edited by H. Schissler, 376–408. Princeton: Princeton University Press.

Gilcher-Holtey, I., ed. 1998. *1968. Vom Ereignis zum Gegenstand der Geschichtswissenschaft.* Göttingen: Vandenhoeck and Ruprecht.

Gilcher-Holtey, I. 2001. *Die 68er Bewegung. Deutschland, Westeuropa, USA,* München: C.H. Beck.

Giugni, M.G. 1995. "The Cross-National Diffusion of Protest." In *New Social Movements in Western Europe: A Comparative Analysis,* edited by H. Kriesi et al., 181–206. Minneapolis: University of Minnesota Press.

Glazer, P.M. "From the Old Left to the New: Radical Criticism in the 1940s." *American Quarterly* 24(5)(1972): 584–603.

Glenn, J.K., III. 2001. *Framing Democracy. Civil Society and Civic Movements in Eastern Europe.* Stanford: Stanford University Press.

Goffman, Erving. 1974. *Frame Analysis: An Essay on the Organization of the Experience.* New York: Harper Colophon.

Goldstone, J. "More Social Movements or Fewer? Beyond Political Opportunity Structures to Relational Fields." *Theory and Society,* 33 (3/4)(2004): 333–365.

Goldstone, J.A., ed. 2003. *States, Parties, and Social Movements.* Cambridge: Cambridge University Press.

Goldstone, J.A., and C. Tilly. 2001. "Threat (and Opportunity): Popular Action and State Response in the Dynamics of Contentious Action." In *Silence and Voice in the Study of Contentious Politics,* edited by R. R. Aminzade, J.A. Goldstone, D. McAdam, E.J. Perry, W.H. Sewell, S. Tarrow, and C. Tilly, 179–194. Cambridge: Cambridge University Press.

Goldthorpe, J. 2007. *On Sociology. Volume One: Critique and Program.* 2nd ed. Stanford: Stanford University Press.

Goodway, D. 2006. *Anarchist Seeds Beneath Snow: Left-Libertarian Thought and British Writers from William Morris to Colin Ward.* Liverpool: Liverpool University Press.

Gould, R.V. 1995. *Insurgent Identities: Class, Community, and Protest in Paris from 1848 to the Commune.* Chicago: University of Chicago Press.

Grabbe, H. "How Does Europeanization Affect CEE Governance? Conditionality, Diffusion and Diversity." *Journal of European Public Policy* 8(6)(2001): 1013–1031.

Graham, E. and M. Garry. "Policing, Collective Action and Social Movement Theory: The Case of the Northern Ireland Civil Rights Campaign." *British Journal of Sociology,* 51 (4)(2000): 681–699.

Grande, E. "Cosmopolitan Political Science." *British Journal of Sociology* 57(1) (2006): 87–111.

Grande, E. and L.W. Pauly. 2005. *Complex Sovereignty. Reconstituting Political Authority in the 21st Century.* Toronto: University of Toronto Press.

Green, A.T. "Comparative Development of Post-communist Civil Societies." *Europe-Asia Studies,* 54(3)(2002): 455–471.

Greschat, M. 2002. *Die evangelische Christenheit und die deutsche Geschichte nach 1945. Weichenstellungen in der Nachkriegszeit.* Stuttgart: Kohlhammer.

Greskovits, B. 1998. *The Political Economy of Protest and Patience: East European and Latin American Transformations Compared.* New York: Central European University Press.

Grewal, I. and C. Kaplan. 1994. *Scattered Hegemonies: Postmodernity and Transnational Feminist Practices.* Minneapolis: University of Minnesota Press.

Grunig, J.E., and T. Hunt. 1984. *Managing Public Relations.* New York: Holt, Rinehart & Winston.

Grzymala-Busse, A.M. 2002. *Redeeming the Communist Past: the Regeneration of Communist Parties in East-Central Europe.* Cambridge: Cambridge University Press.

Guy, W., ed. 2001. *Between Past and Future: The Roma of Central and Eastern Europe.* Hatfield: University of Hertfordshire Press.

Hajba, E. "The Rise and Fall of the Hungarian Greens." *The Journal of Communist Studies and Transitional Politics* 3(1994): 180–191.

Hallstrom, L. "Eurocratising Enlargement? EU Elites and NGO Participation in European Environmental Policy." *Environmental Politics* 13 (1)(2004): 175–196.

Hanagan, M.P., L. Page Moch, and W.T. Brake, eds. 1998. *Challenging Authority: the Historical Study of Contentious Politics.* Minneapolis: University of Minnesota Press.

Harcourt, M. and G. Wood, eds. 2004. *Trade Unions and Democracy: Strategies and Perspectives.* Manchester: Manchester University Press.

Harper, K. "'Wild Capitalism' and 'Ecocolonialism': A Tale of Two Rivers." *American Anthropologist* 107(2)(2005): 221–233.

Havel, V. 1992. "Power of the Powerless." In *Open Letters: Selected Writings, 1965–1990,* edited by P. Wilson, 125–214. New York: Vintage Books.

Heipp, G., ed. 1965. *Es geht ums Leben! Der Kampf gegen die Bombe 1945–1965. Eine Dokumentation.* Hamburg: H. Reich.

Held, D., et al. 1999. *Global Transformations.* Cambridge: Polity Press.

Herger, N. 2004. *Organisationskommunikation. Beobachtung und Steuerung eines organisationalen Risikos.* Wiesbaden: VS Verlag für Sozialwissenschaften.

Herrerín López, Á. 2004. *La CNT Durante el Franquismo. Clandestinidad y Exilio (1939–1975).* Madrid: Siglo XXI.

Herzog, D. 2005. *Sex After Fascism: Memory and Morality in Twentieth-Century Germany.* Princeton: Princeton University Press.

Hicks, B. "Setting Agendas and Shaping Activism: EU Influence on Central and Eastern European Environmental Movements." *Environmental Politics* 13 (1)(2004): 216–233.

Hilson, C. "New Social Movements: The Role of Legal Opportunity." *Journal of European Public Policy* 9 (2)(2002): 238–255.

Hirsch, F. 2005. *Empire of Nations: Ethnographic Knowledge and the Making of the Soviet Union.* Ithaca: Cornell University Press.

Hockenos, M. 2004. *A Church Divided: German Protestants Confront the Nazi Past*. Bloomington: Indiana University Press.

Hoffjann, O. 2001. *Journalismus und Public Relations. Ein Theorieentwurf der Intersystembeziehungen in sozialen Konflikten*. Wiesbaden: Westdeutscher Verlag.

Hoffmann, F.J. "From Surrealism to "The Apocalypse": A Development in Twentieth Century Irrationalism." *ELH* 15(2)(1948): 147–165.

Holl, K. 1972–1977. "Pazifismus." In *Geschichtliche Grundbegriffe: Historisches Lexikon zur politisch-sozialen Sprache in Deutschland*, 8 vols, edited by O. Brunner, W. Conze, and R. Koselleck, 782–783. Stuttgart: E. Klett Verlag.

Holl, K. and W. Wette, eds. 1981. *Pazifismus in der Weimarer Republik. Beiträge zur historischen Friedensforschung*. Paderborn: F. Schöningh Verlag.

Holzapfel, M. and K. König. "Chronik der Globalisierungsproteste." *Mittelweg 36* 6(2001): 24–34.

Hopgood. S. 2006. *Keepers of the Flame: Understanding Amnesty International*. Ithaca: Cornell University Press.

Hoppe, J. 2004. *Pražské jaro v médiích. Výběr z dobové publicistiky (Prameny k dějinám československé krize 1967–1970*. Brno: Doplněk.

Horn, G.-R. 1998. "The Changing Nature of the European Working Class: The Rise and Fall of the 'New Working Class' (France, Italy, Spain, Czechoslovakia)." In *1968: The World Transformed*, edited by C. Fink, P. Gassert, and D. Junker, 351–371. New York: Cambridge University Press.

Horn, G.-R. and P. Kenney, eds. 2004. *Transnational Moments of Change: Europe 1945, 1968, 1989*. Lanham: Rowman and Littlefield.

Horolets, A. 2005. "Pulling Europe Closer: The Strategy of Shame in Polish Press Discourse on Europe." In *Das Erbe des Beitritts: Europäisierung in Mittel- und Osteuropa*, edited by A. Kutter and V. Trappmann, 155–170. Baden-Baden: Nomos.

Horváth, S. 2005. "Pubs and 'Hooligans' in a Socialist City in Hungary: the Public Sphere and Youth in Stalintown." In *European Cities, Youth and the Public Sphere in the Twentieth Century*, edited by A. Schildt and D. Siegfried, 80–89. Aldershot: Ashgate.

Howard, M.M. 2003. *The Weakness of Civil Society in Post-Communist Europe*. Cambridge: Cambridge University Press.

Human Rights Watch and Geneva Initiative on Psychiatry. 2002. *Dangerous Minds: Political Psychiatry in China Today and Its Origins in the Mao Era*. New York: Human Rights Watch.

Hunt, L. 2007. *Inventing Human Rights. A History*. New York: W.W. Norton & Company.

Hunt, S., R.D. Benford, and D. Snow. 1994. "Marcos de Acción Colectiva y Campos de Identidad en la Construcción Social de los Movimientos." In *Los Nuevos Movimientos Sociales. De la Ideología a la Identidad*, edited by E. Laraña and J. Gusfield, 221–249. Madrid: CIS.

Hutter, S. and M. Giugni. "Protest Politics in a Changing Political Context: Switzerland, 1975–2005." *Swiss Political Science Review* 15(3)(2009): 395–429.

Ignatief, M. 1995. "On Civil Society: Why Eastern Europe's Revolutions Could Succeed," *Foreign Affairs,* March/April. Retrieved 8 January 2008 from http://www.foreignaffairs.org/19950301fareviewessay5029/michael-ignatieff/on-civil-society-why-eastern-europe-s-revolutions-could-succeed.html.

Imhof, K. 1996. "Eine Symbiose: Soziale Bewegungen und Medien." In *Politisches Raisonnement in der Informationsgesellschaft* (= *Reihe Mediensymposium Luzern* 2), edited by K. Imhof and P. Schulz, 165–186. Zürich: Seismo.

Imhof, K. 2003. "Politik im 'neuen' Strukturwandel der Öffentlichkeit." In *Der Begriff des Politischen* (= *Soziale Welt* 14), edited by A. Nassehi and M. Schroer, 401–417. Baden-Baden: Nomos.

Imig, D. and S. Tarrow. 2001. "Mapping the Europeanization of Contention: Evidence from a Quantitative Data Analysis." In *Contentious Europeans: Protest and Politics in an Emerging Polity,* edited by D. Imig and S. Tarrow, 27–49. Lanham: Rowman & Littlefield.

———, eds. 2001. *Contentious Europeans: Protest and Politics in an Emerging Polity.* Lanham: Rowman & Littlefield.

Institut für Sozialforschung. 1956. "Ideologie." In *Soziologische Exkurse,* edited by Institut für Sozialforschung, 162–181. Frankfurt am Main: Fischer.

International Association on the Political Use of Psychiatry (IAPUP). 1983. *Soviet Political Psychiatry: the Story of Opposition.* London: IAPUP.

———. 1985. *Political Abuse of Psychiatry, a List of Victims, 30 November 1975.* London: IAPUP.

Isaak. J. "The Strange Silence of Political Theory." *Political Theory,* 23(4)(1995): 636–652.

Ivancheva, M. 2007. "Civil Society as a Discursive Frame: Vaclav Havel's 'Anatomy of Reticence' as a Case Study." Unpublished MA Dissertation, Central European University, Budapest.

Jacquot, S., and C. Woll. "Usage of European Integration—Europeanisation from a Sociological Perspective." *European Integration Online Papers (EIoP)* 7(12)(2003), accessed at http://eiop.or.at/eiop/texte/2003-012a.htm.

Jarren, O. "'Mediengesellschaft'—Risiken für die politische Kommunikation." *Aus Politik und Zeitgeschichte* 41–42(2001): 10–19.

Jarren, O. and P. Donges. 2006. *Politische Kommunikation in der Mediengesellschaft. Eine Einführung.* 2nd ed. Wiesbaden: VS Verlag für Sozialwissenschaften.

Jarren, O., D. Lachenmeier, and A. Steiner, eds. 2007. *Entgrenzte Demokratie? Herausforderungen für die politische Interessenvermittlung.* Baden-Baden: Nomos.

Jarren, O. and U. Röttger. 2004. "Steuerung, Reflexierung und Interpenetration: Kernelemente einer strukturationstheoretisch begründeten PR-Theorie." In *Theorien der Public Relations. Grundlagen und Perspektiven der PR-Forschung,* edited by U. Röttger, 25–45. Wiesbaden: VS Verlag für Sozialwissenschaften.

————. 2005. "Public Relations aus kommunikationswissenschaftlicher Sicht." In *Handbuch der Public Relations. Wissenschaftliche Grundlagen und berufliches Handeln. Mit Lexikon,* edited by G. Bentele, R. Fröhlich, and P. Szyszka, 19–36. Wiesbaden: VS Verlag für Sozialwissenschaften.

Jarren, O., A. Steiner, and D. Lachenmeier. 2007. "Entgrenzte Demokratie? Politische Interessenvermittlung im Mehrebenensystem." In *Entgrenzte Demokratie? Herausforderungen für die politische Interessenvermittlung,* edited by O. Jarren, D. Lachenmeier and A. Steiner, 333–364. Baden-Baden: Nomos.

Jasper, J. 2007. *Getting Your Way.* Chicago: The University of Chicago Press.

Jaspers, K. 1957. *Die Atombombe und die Zukunft des Menschen.* München: R. Piper Verlag.

Jech, K. 2001. *Soumrak selského stavu 1945–1960.* USD: Praha.

Jenner, F.A. "The Political Misuse of Psychiatry." *British Journal of Psychiatry* 123(5)(1973): 527–530.

Johns, M. "'Do as I Say, Not as I Do': The European Union, Eastern Europe and Minority Rights." *East European Politics and Societies* 17(4)(2003): 682–699.

Johnston, H. 1995. "A Methodology for Frame Analysis: From Discourse to Cognitive Schemata." In *Social Movements and Culture,* edited by H. Johnston and B. Klandermans, 217–246. Minneapolis: University of Minnesota Press.

Johnston, H. and J.A. Noakes, eds. 2005. *Frames of Protest: Social Movements and the Framing Perspective.* Lanham, MD and Oxford: Rowman & Littlefield.

Jossin, A. 2010. "How Do Activists Experience Transnational and Protest Events? The Case of Young Global Justice Activists from Germany and France." In *The Transnational Condition: Protest Dynamics in an Entangled Europe,* edited by S. Teune, 42–63. Oxford and New York: Berghahn Books.

Judt, T. 2005. *Postwar. A History of Europe since 1945.* London: Heineman.

Juris, J.S. "Violence Performed and Imagined: Militant Action, the Black Bloc and the Mass Media in Genoa." *Critique of Anthropology* 25 (4)(2005): 413–432.

Kaelble, H., M. Kirsch, and A. Schmidt-Gernig. 2002. "Zur Entwicklung transnationaler Öffentlichkeiten und Identitäten im 20. Jahrhundert. Eine Einleitung." In *Transnationale Öffentlichkeiten und Identitäten im 20. Jahrhundert,* edited by H. Kaelble, M. Kirsch, and A. Schmidt-Gernig, 7–33. Frankfurt am Main: Campus.

Kalb, D. 1998. "Afterword: Globalism and Postsocialist Prospects." In *Postsocialism: Ideals, Ideologies and Practices in Eurasia,* edited by C. Hann, 317–334. London, Routledge.

Kalb, D. and H. Tak. 2005. "Introduction." In *Critical Junctions: Anthropology and History Beyond the Cultural Turn,* edited by D. Kalb and H. Tak. New York: Berghahn Books.

Kaldor, M. 2003. *Global Civil Society. An Answer to War.* Cambridge: Polity Press.

————. "The Idea of Global Civil Society." *International Affairs* 79(3)(2003): 583–593.

Kaldor, M. and E.P. Thompson, eds. 1991. *Europe from Below: an East-West Dialogue*. London: Verso.

Kalinová, L. 2007. *Společenské proměny v čase socialistického experimentu. K sociálním dějinám v letech 1945–1969*. Praha: Academia.

Kaminski, I.-M. 1980. *The State of Ambiguity. Studies of Gypsy Refugees*. Gothenburg: University of Gothenburg.

Kampagne für Saubere Kleidung. N.d. "Die Kampagne im Überblick." Retrieved 19 September 2006 from http://www.saubere-kleidung.de/2-fs-wir.htm.

Kantzenbach, F.W. 1993. *Politischer Protestantismus. Von den Freiheitskriegen bis zur Ära Adenauer*. Saarbrücken-Scheidt: Dadder Verlag.

Kaplan, K. 2002. *Kořeny československé reformy 1968, III–IV*. Brno: Doplněk.

Katz, D. and R.L. Kahn. 1966. *The Social Psychology of Organizations*. New York: Wiley.

Katz, E. 2006. "Human Rights Abuses in Mental Institutions Common Worldwide." *Virginia Law Journal*, 27 February. Retrieved 15 November 2007 from www.law.virginia.edu/html/news/2006_spr/perlin.htm.

Keane, J., ed.1988. *Civil Society and the State*. London: Verso.

Keck, M.E. and K. Sikkink. 1998. *Activists Beyond Borders. Advocacy Networks in International Politics*. Ithaca and London: Cornell University Press.

Kelley, J. "International Actors on the Domestic Scene: Membership Conditionality and Socialization by International Institutions." *International Organization* 58(3)(2004): 425–461.

Kennedy, M.D. 1991. "Eastern Europe's Lessons for Critical Intellectuals." In *Intellectuals and Politics. Social Theory in a Changing World*, edited by C. Lemert. London: Sage.

Kenney P. and G.R. Horn, eds. 2004. *Transnational Moments of Change: Europe 1945, 1968, 1989*. Landham, MD: Rowman & Littlefield.

Kenrick, D.S. "The World Romani Congress / April 1971." *Journal of the Gypsy Lore Society* 3(4)(1971): 101–108.

Kerényi, S., and M. Szabó. "Transnational Influences on Patterns of Mobilisation Within Environmental Movements in Hungary." *Environmental Politics* 15(5)(2006): 803–820.

Khodorovitch, T., ed. 1974. *Istoryia Boleznyi Leonida Plyushcha*. Amsterdam: Fond Imeni Gertsena.

Khodorovich, T. and Y. Orlov. 1975. "They are Turning Leonid Plyushch into a Lunatic, Why?" *Russkaya Misl*, 15 May.

Kitschelt, H. 1986. "Political Opportunity Structures and Political Protest: Anti-Nuclear Movements in Four Democracies." *British Journal of Political Science* 16 (1)(1986): 57–85.

————. "Social Movements, Political Parties, and Democratic Theory." *The Annals of the American Academy of Political and Social Science*, 528(1)(1993): 13–29.

————. 2003. "Landscape of Political Interest Intermediation. Social Movements, Interest Groups, and Parties in the Early Twenty-First Century." In *Social Movements and Democracy*, edited by P. Ibarra, 81–103. New York: Palgrave Macmillan.

Klandermans, B. "Must We Redefine Social Movements as Ideologically Structured Action?" *Mobilization* 5 (1)(2000): 25–30.

Klein, M., G. Müller, and R. Schlaga. 1978. *Politische Strömungen in der Friedensbewegung 1966-1974. Diskussionen, Auseinandersetzungen und Veränderungen in der Deutschen Friedensgesellschaft (DFG), der Internationale der Kriegsdienstgegner (IDK) und dem Verband der Kriegsdienstverweigerer (VK) bis zu deren Vereinheitlichung zur Deutschen Friedensgesellschaft/ Vereinigte Kriegsdienstgegner (DFG/VK)*. Frankfurt am Main: Verein zur Förderung Friedenspolitischer Ideen und Initiativen e.V.

Klimke, M. 2006. "Black Panther, die RAF und die Rolle der Black Panther-Solidaritätskomitees." In *Die RAF und der linke Terrorismus*, edited by W. Kraushaar, 562–582. Hamburg: Hamburger Edition.

Klimke, M. and J. Scharloth, eds. 2008. *1968 in Europe: A History of Protest and Activism, 1956–1977*. New York: Palgrave Macmillan.

Klimova-Alexander, I. 2005. *The Romani Voice in World Politics: the United Nations and Non-state Actors*. Aldershot: Ashgate.

Knapp, M. et al., eds. 2007. *Mental Health Policy and Practice across Europe: the Future Directions of Mental Health Care*. Maidenhead: Open University Press.

Knorr, R.H. 1984. *Public Relations als System-Umwelt-Interaktion*. Wiesbaden: Westdeutscher Verlag.

Koch, A.M. "Poststructuralism and the Epistemological Basis of Anarchism." *Philosophy of the Social Sciences* 23(3)(1993): 327–351.

Kohler-Koch, B. 2005. "Interessenpolitik im europäischen Mehrebenensystem." In *Interessenpolitik in Europa* (= Regieren in Europa 7), edited by R. Eising and B. Kohler-Koch, 11–75. Baden-Baden: Nomos.

Kohler-Koch, B., T. Conzelmann, and M. Knodt. 2004. *Europäische Integration— Europäisches Regieren*. Wiesbaden: VS Verlag für Sozialwissenschaften.

Kohler-Koch, B. and R. Eising. 1999. *The transformation of governance in the European Union*. London: Routledge.

Kohler-Koch, B. and M. Jachtenfuchs. 2004. "Governance in der Europäischen Union." In *Governance—Regieren in komplexen Regelsystemen: Eine Einführung*, edited by A. Benz, 77–101. Wiesbaden: VS Verlag für Sozialwissenschaften.

Kohler-Koch, B., and B. Rittberger. "Review Article: The 'Governance Turn' in EU Studies." *Journal of Common Market Studies* 44(1)(2006): 27–49.

Koopmans, R. "Explaining the rise of racist and extreme right violence in Western Europe: Grievances or opportunities?" *European Journal of Political Research* 30(2)(1996): 185–216.

————. "The Missing Link between Structure and Agency: Outline of an Evolutionary Approach to Social Movements." *Mobilization*, 10 (1) (2005): 19–33.

Koopmans, R. and D. Rucht. "Social Movement Mobilization under Right and Left Governments: A Look at Four West European Countries." *WZB Discussion Paper* (1995) FS III, 95–106.

Koopmans, R. and S. Olzak. "Discursive opportunities and the evolution of right-wing violence in Germany." *American Journal of Sociology* 110(1)(2004): 198–230.

Kopecky, P. and E. Barnfield. 1999. "Charting the Decline of Civil Society: Explaining the Changing Roles and Conceptions of Civil Society in East Central Europe." In *Democracy without Borders: State and Non-State Actors in Eastern Europe, Africa and Latin America*, edited by J. Grugel, 76–91. London: Routledge.

Kopecky, P. and C. Mudde. 2003. *Uncivil Society: Contentious Politics in Post-Communist Eastern Europe*. London and New York: Routhledge.

Kotowicz, Z. 1997. *Laing and the Paths of Anti Psychiatry*. London, New York: Routledge.

Kovach, I., and E. Kucerova. "The Project Class in Central Europe: The Czech and Hungarian Cases." *Sociologia Ruralis* 46(1)(2006): 3–21.

Kozlova, V.A. and S.V. Mironenko, eds. 2005. *Kramola: Inakomyslie v SSSR pri Khrushcheve i Brezhneve, 1953–1982 gg.: Rassekrechennye Dokumenty Verkhovnogo Suda i Prokuratury SSSR*. Moskva: Maternik.

Kriesi, H., ed. 1985. *Bewegungen in der Schweizer Politik*. Frankfurt: Campus Verlag.

———. 1999. "Movements of the Left, Movements of the Right: Putting the Mobilization of Two New Types of Social Movements Into Political Context." In *Continuity and Change in Contemporary Capitalism*, edited by H. Kitschelt et al., 398–423. Cambridge: Cambridge University Press.

———. 2007. "Die politische Kommunikation sozialer Bewegungen." In *Entgrenzte Demokratie? Herausforderungen für die politische Interessenvermittlung*, edited by O. Jarren, D. Lachenmeier, and A. Steiner, 145–161. Baden-Baden: Nomos.

Kriesi, H., A. Tresch, and M. Jochum. "Going Public in the European Union: Action Repertoires of Western European Collective Political Actors." *Comparative Political Studies* 40(1)(2007): 48–73.

Kriesi, H., R. Levy, G. Ganguillet, and H. Zwicky, eds. 1981. *Politische Aktivierung in der Schweiz. 1945–1978*. Diessenhofen: Rüegger.

Kriesi, H. et al. 1995. *New Social Movements in Western Europe. A Comparative Analysis*. Minneapolis: University of Minnesota Press.

Kriesi, H. et al. "Globalization and the Transformation of the National Political Space: Six European Countries Compared." *European Journal of Political Research* 45(6)(2006): 921–956.

Kriesi, H. et al. 2008. *West European Politics in the Age of Globalization. Six Countries Compared*. Cambridge: Cambridge University Press.

Kurlansky, M. 2004. *1968: The Year that Rocked the World.* New York: Ballantine Books.

Kurzman, C. "Structural Opportunities and Perceived Opportunities in Social-Movement Theory: Evidence from the Iranian Revolution of 1979." *American Sociological Review* 61(1)(1996): 153–170.

Lachenmeier, D. 2009. *Gewerkschaftskommunikation im Wandel. Eine systemtheoretische Analyse der Organisationskommunikation des Schweizerischen, Deutschen und Österreichischen Gewerkschaftsbunds 1972–2005.* Basel: edition gesowip.

Ladner, A. 2007. "Die Rolle der Parteien in der Mediengesellschaft." In *Entgrenzte Demokratie? Herausforderungen für die politische Interessenvermittlung,* edited by O. Jarren, D. Lachenmeier, and A. Steiner, 75–91. Baden-Baden: Nomos.

Lahusen, C. 1999. "International Campaigns in Context." In *Social Movements in a Globalizing World,* edited by D. dell Porta, H. Kriesi, and D. Rucht, 189–205. Basingstoke and New York: Macmillan.

———. "Joining the cocktail circuit: social movement organizations at the European Union." *Mobilization: An International Journal* 9(1)(2004): 55–71.

Ledesma, J.L. 2005. "La 'Santa Ira Popular' del 36: la Violencia en Guerra Civil y Revolución, entre Cultura y Política." In *Culturas y Políticas de la Violencia: España Siglo XX,* edited by R. Cruz, J. Muñoz Soro, J.L. Ledesma, and J. Rodrigo, 147–192. Madrid: Siete Mares.

Levitt, P. and S. Khagram, eds. 2007. *The Transnational Studies Reader.* London: Routledge.

Loth, W. 1988. *The Division of the World, 1941–1955.* New York: St. Martin's.

Loveman, M. "High-Risk Collective Action: Defending Human Rights in Chile, Uruguay, and Argentina." *The American Journal of Sociology* 104(2)(1998): 477–525.

Luhmann, N. 1975. *Soziologische Aufklärung 2.* Opladen: Westdeutscher Verlag.

———. 1984. *Soziale Systeme. Grundriss einer allgemeinen Theorie.* Frankfurt/Main: Suhrkamp.

———. 1988. "Organisation." In *Mikropolitik, Rationalität, Macht und Spiele in Organisationen* 2nd ed., edited by W. Küpper and G. Ortmann, 165–185. Opladen: Westdeutscher Verlag,

———. 2000. *Organisation und Entscheidung.* Opladen, Wiesbaden: Westdeutscher Verlag.

Maitron, J. 1992. *Le Mouvement Anarchiste en France.* Vol. II. Paris: Gallimard.

Marchetti, R. 2008. *Global Democracy: For and Against.* London: Routledge.

Marcinkowski, F. 1993. *Publizistik als autopoietisches System—Politik und Massenmedien. Eine systemtheoretische Analyse.* Opladen: Westdeutscher Verlag.

Marco Nadal, E. 1982. *Todos Contra Franco. La Alianza Nacional de Fuerzas Democráticas, 1944/1947.* Madrid: Queimada.

Marshall, P.H. 1992. *Demanding the Impossible: a History of Anarchism*. London: HarperCollins.

Marshall, T.H. 1992[1950]. *Citizenship and Social Class*. In T.H. Marshall and T. Bottomore, *Citizenship and Social Class*, 3–51. Pluto Press: London.

Marsilii, E.A. 2004. *Il Movimento Anarchico a Genova, 1943–1950*. Genova: Annexia.

Martin, T. 2001. *The Affirmative Action Empire: Nations and Nationalism in the Soviet Union 1923–1939*. Ithaca: Cornell University Press.

Marwell, G. and P. Oliver. 1984. "Collective Action Theory and Social Movements Research." In *Research in Social Movements, Conflict and Change 7*, edited by L. Kriesberg, 1–27. Greenwich: JAI Press.

Marwick, A. 1998. *The Sixties: Cultural Transformation in Britain, France, Italy and the United States, c. 1958–c. 1974*. Oxford: Oxford University Press.

Mastnak, T. "The Reinvention of Civil Society: Trough the Looking Glass of Democracy." *European Journal of Sociology* 46(1)(2005): 323–355.

Mathon, Y., and J.J. Marie, eds. 1976. *L'affaire Pliouchtch*. Paris: Éditions du Seuil.

Mausbach, W. "Historicizing '1968'." *Contemporary European History* 11(1) (2002): 177–187.

———. 2004. 'The Present's Past: Perspectives on Peace and Protest in Germany, 1945–1973', *Mitteilungsblatt des Instituts für soziale Bewegungen* 32, 67–98.

Mazower, M. 2000. *Dark Continent. Europe's Twentieth Century*. New York: Vintage Books.

McAdam, D. 1996. "Conceptual Origins, Current Problems, Future Directions." In *Comparative Perspectives on Social Movements: Political Opportunities, Mobilizing Structures, and Cultural Framings*, edited by D. McAdam, J.D. McCarthy, and M.N. Zald, 23–40. Cambridge: Cambridge University Press.

McAdam, D., J.D. McCarthy, and M.N. Zald, eds. 1996. *Comparative Perspectives on Social Movements: Political Opportunities, Mobilizing Structures, and Cultural Framings*. Cambridge: Cambridge University Press.

McAdam, D. and D. Rucht. "The Cross-National Diffusion of Movement Ideas." *The Annals of the American Academy of Political and Social Science* 528(1993): 56–74.

McCann. E. 1974. *War and an Irish Town*. Harmondsworth: Penguin Book.

McCarthy, J.D. and M.N. Zald. "Resource Mobilization and Social Movements: A Partial Theory." *The American Journal of Sociology* 82(1)(1977): 212–241.

McGarry J. and B. O'Leary. 1996. *The Politics of Antagonism: Understanding Northern Ireland*. London: Athlone Press.

Medvedev, Z. 1971. *Question of Madness*. London: McMillan.

Meeus, A. 1974. *White Book on the Interment of Dissenters in Soviet Mental Hospitals*. Bruxelles: Comité International pour la Defense des Droits de l' Homme en l' USSR.

Melucci, A. 1996. *Challenging Codes: Collective Action in the Information Age.* Cambridge: Cambridge University Press.

Mendelson, S.E., and J.K. Glenn. 2002. *The Power and Limits of NGOs: A Critical Look at Building Democracy in Eastern Europe and Eurasia.* New York: Columbia University Press.

Merkel, W. and H.J. Lauth. "Systemwechsel und Zivilgesellschaft: Welche Zivilgesellschaft braucht die Demokratie?" *Aus Politik und Zeitgeschichte* 42(6–7)(1998): 3–12.

Merten, K. 1992. "Begriff und Funktion von Public Relations." *prmagazin* 23(11) (1992): 35–46.

Merten, K. and J. Westerbarkey. 1994. "Public Opinion und Public Relations." In *Die Wirklichkeit der Medien,* edited by K. Merten, S. Schmidt, and S. Weischenberg, 188–211. Opladen: Westdeutscher Verlag.

Merton, R.K. "The Matthew Effect in Science: The Reward and Communication Systems of Science Are Considered." *Science* 159(3810) (1968): 56–63.

Messenger, D.A. "'Our Spanish Brother' or 'As at Plombieres'? France, the legacy of Resistance and the Spanish opposition to Franco, 1945–1948." *French History* 20(1)(2006): 52–74.

Meyer, D.S. and D.C. Minkoff. "Conceptualizing Political Opportunity." *Social Forces* 82(4)(2004): 1484.

Meyer, D.S. and S. Tarrow, eds. 1998. *The Social Movement Society.* New York: Rowman & Littlefield.

Meyer, G. 2003. "Values, Small Life Worlds and Communitarian Orientations: Ambivalent Legacies and Democratic Potentials in Post-Communist Political Culture." In *Political Culture in Post-Communist Europe. Attitudes in New Democracies,* edited by D. Pollack, J. Jacobs, O. Müller and G. Pickel, 169–181. Aldershot: Ashgate.

Micheline, I. 2004. *The History of Human Rights: From Ancient Times to Globalization.* Berkeley: University of California Press.

Michnik, A. 1999. "Rebirth of Civil Society." In *Ideas of 1989 LSE Public Lecture Series,* Retrieved 8 January 2008 from http://www.lse.ac.uk/Depts/global/Publications/PublicLectures/PL10_TheRebirthOfCivilSociety.pdf.

Miller, D. 1984. *Anarchism.* London: J.M. Dent & Sons Ltd.

Miscoiu, S. "Is There a Model for the Political Representation of the Romanian Roma?" *Sfera Politicii* (2006): 123–124, 78–89.

MLE-CNT. 1947. *Dictámenes y Resoluciones del II Congreso del MLE-CNT en Francia,* Toulouse: MLE-CNT en Francia.

Moeller, R. 2001. *War Stories: The Search for a Usable Past in the Federal Republic of Germany.* Berkeley: University of California Press.

Moyn, S. "The Genealogy of Morals." *The Nation,* 29 March 2007.

Molina, H. "Ayer, Hoy y Mañana. Relaciones entre Camus y los Libertarios Españoles: una Gran Red de Ideas, Principios y Humanismo." *Anthropos* 199 (2003): 149–154.

Molinero, C. and P. Ysàs, "La Historia Social de la Época Franquista. Una Aproximación," *Historia Social* 30(1998): 133–154.

Montseny, F. 1978. *Seis Años de Mi Vida, 1939–1945*. Barcelona: Galba.

Moore, J. "Composition and Decomposition: Contemporary Anarchist Aesthetics." *Anarchist Studies* 6(2)(1998): 113–122.

Morland, D. 1997. *Demanding the Impossible? Human Nature and Politics in Nineteenth-century Social Anarchism.* London, Washington: Cassell.

Moscow Helsinki Group. 2004. "Human Rights and Psychiatry in the Russian Federation." retrieved 12 September 2007 from http://www.mhg.ru/english/3959925.

Moyn, S. 2010. *The Last Utopia: Human Rights in History* (Cambridge: Belknap Press of Harvard University Press).

Mudde, C. 2007. *Populist Radical Right Parties in Europe.* Cambridge: Cambridge University Press.

Munro, R. 2000. 'The Soviet Case: Prelude to a Global Consensus on Psychiatry and Human Rights', retrieved November 23, 2007 from Human Rights Watch Web site http://hrw.org/reports/2002/china02/china0802-02.htm.

Murthy, V. "Civil Society in Hegel and Marx." *Rethinking Marxism,* 11(3)(1999): 36–55.

Nehring, H. 2004. "Cold War, Apocalypse and Peaceful Atoms. Interpretations of Nuclear Energy in the British and West German Anti-Nuclear Weapons Movements, 1955–1964." *Historical Social Research* 29(3)(2004): 150–170.

———. "National Internationalists: British and West German Protests against Nuclear Weapons, the Politics of Transnational Communications and the Social History of the Cold War, 1957–1964." *Contemporary European History* 14(4) (2005): 559–582.

Neidhardt, F. 2007. "Massenmedien im intermediären System moderner Demokratien." In *Entgrenzte Demokratie? Herausforderungen für die politische Interessenvermittlung,* edited by O. Jarren, D. Lachenmeier, and A. Steiner, 33–47. Baden-Baden: Nomos.

NICRA. 1978. *We Shall Overcome: The History of the Struggle for Civil Rights in Northern Ireland, 1968–1978.* Belfast: Northern Ireland Civil Right Association.

Niemöller, M. 1961. *Reden 1958–1961.* Frankfurt am Main: Stimme-Verlag.

Niemöller, M. et al. 1968. *Junge Christen befragen die Kirchen. Zwei Gespräche.* München: K. Desch Verlag.

Noakes, J.A. and H. Johnston. 2005. "Frames of Protest: A Road Map to a Perspective." In *Frames of Protest: Social Movements and the Framing Perspective,* edited by H. Johnston and J.A. Noakes, 1–29. Lanham, MD and Oxford: Rowman & Littlefield.

O'Dochartaigh, N. 2005. *From Civil Right to Armalites, Derry and the Birth of the Irish Troubles.* New York: Palgrave.

Oeffler, H.J., ed. 1977. *Martin Niemöller. Reden, Predigten, Denkanstöße 1964–1976.* Köln: Pahl-Rugenstein.

Offe, C. and H. Wiesenthal. "Two Logics of Collective Action: Theoretical Notes on Social Class and Organizational Form." *Political Power and Social Theory* 1(1)(1980): 67–115.

Oliver, P.E. and H. Johnston. 2005. "What a Good Idea! Ideologies and Frames in Social Movements Research." In *Frames of Protest: Social Movements and the Framing Perspective*, edited by H. Johnston and J.A. Noakes, 185–203. Lanham, MD, Oxford: Rowman & Littlefield.

Olson, M. 1968. *Die Logik des kollektiven Handelns. Kollektivgüter und die Theorie der Gruppen*. Tübingen: Mohr.

Oppenheimer, A. 2008. "By Any Means Necessary? West German Pacifism and the Politics of Solidarity, 1945–1974." In *Peace Movements in Western Europe, Japan and the USA during the Cold War*, edited by B. Ziemann, 41–60. Essen: Klartext.

O'Sullivan, N. 2004. *European Political Thought Since 1945*. Basingstoke, New York: Palgrave Macmillan.

Otto, K.A. 1982. *Vom Ostermarsch zur APO. Geschichte der ausserparlamentarischen Opposition in der Bundesrepublik 1960–1970*. Frankfurt am Main: Campus.

———. 1989. *APO. Die außerparlamentarische Opposition in Quellen und Dokumenten (1960–1970)*. Köln: Pahl-Rugenstein.

Parks, L. 2009. "Social Movements and the European Union" (provisional title). Ph.D. dissertation, European University Institute.

Passy, F. 1999. "Supranational Political Opportunities as a Channel of Globalization of Political Conflicts: The Case of the Rights of Indigenous People." In *Social Movements in a Globalizing World*, edited by D. della Porta, H. Kriesi, and D. Rucht, 148–169. Basingstoke and New York: Macmillan.

Patterson. H. 2002. *Ireland Since 1939*. Oxford: Oxford University Press.

Pažout, J. 2004. "Reakce československých studentů v době Pražského jara na protestní hnutí na Západě." In *Bolševismus, komunismus a radikální socialismus v Československu sv. II*, edited by Z. Karník and M. Kopeček. Praha: Dokořán.

Pecka, J., J. Belda, and J. Hoppe. 1995. *Občanská společnost 1967–1970: emancipační hnutí uvnitř Národní fronty 1967–1970*. Brno: Doplnek.

Petrova, T. and S. Tarrow. "Transactional and Participatory Activism in the Emerging European Polity. The Puzzle of East-Central Europe." *Comparative Political Studies*, 20(10)(2006): 1–21.

Phelan, C., ed. 2007. *Trade Union Revitalisation: Trends and Prospects in 34 Countries*. Bern: Peter Lang.

Pianta, M. 2001. "Parallel Summits of Global Civil Society." In *Global Civil Society 2001*, edited by H. Anheier, M. Glasius, and M. Kaldor, 169–195. Oxford: Oxford University Press.

———. 2003. "Democracy vs. Globalization. The Growth of Parallel Summits and Global Movements." In *Debating Cosmopolitics*, edited by D. Archibugi, 232–256. London and New York: Verso.

Pickvance, K. 1998. *Democracy and Environmental Movements in Eastern Europe: A Comparative Study of Hungary and Russia.* Boulder: Westview Press.

Piven, F.F. and R.A. Cloward. 1977. *Poor People's Movements. Why They Succeed, How They Fail.* New York: Vintage Books.

———. 1992. "Normalizing Collective Protest." In *Frontiers in Social Movement Theory,* edited by A. Morris and C. McClurg Mueller, 310–325. New Haven: Yale University Press.

Plyushch, L. 1976. "Preliminary Declaration by Leonid Plyushch at the Press Conference Held in Paris, 3 February 1976." In *The Case of Leonid Plyushch,* edited by M. Sapiets, P. Reddaway and C. Emerson, 143–151. London: C. Hurst.

———. 1979. *History's Carnival, a Dissident's Autobiography.* London: Collins and Harvill Press.

Podrabinek, A. 1979. *Punitive Medicine.* Ann Arbor: Karoma Publishers.

Pollack, D., and J. Wielgohs. 2004. *Dissent and Opposition in Communist Eastern Europe: Origins of Civil Society and Democratic Transition.* Aldershot: Ashgate.

Polleta, F. 2004. "Culture Is Not in Your Head." In *Rethinking Social Movements: Structure, Meaning, and Emotions,* edited by J. Goodwing and J.M., 97–110. Jasper Larham, MD: Rowman & Littlefield.

Polletta, F. and M.K. Ho. 2006. "Frames and Their Consequences." In *The Oxford Handbook of Contextual Political Studies,* edited by R.E. Gooden and C. Tilly, 187–209. Oxford: Oxford University Press.

Polletta, F. and J.M. Jasper. "Collective Identity and Social Movements." *Annual Review of Sociology* 27(1)(2001): 283–305.

Pollis, A. and P. Schwab. 1979. "Human Rights: a Western Construct with Limited Applicability." In *Human Rights: Cultural and Ideological Perspectives,* edited by A. Pollis and P. Schwab, 1–18. New York: Praeger.

Pospíšil, F. 2007. "Campaign against "Vlasatci" [long-haired people] in Communist Czechoslovakia," conference paper presented at Marie Curie Conference on European Social Movements, Zurich.

Priest, S., ed. 2001. *Jean-Paul Sartre: Basic Writings.* London, New York: Routledge.

Putnam, R.D. 1988. "Diplomacy and Domestic Politics: The Logic of Two-Level Games." *International Organization,* 42(3)(1988): 427–460.

Puxon, G. 2000. "The Romani Movement: Rebirth and the First World Romani Congress in Retrospect." In *Scholarship and the Gypsy Struggle: Commitment in Romani Studies,* edited by T. Acton and D. Kenrick, 92–113. Hatfield: University of Hertfordshire Press.

———. "Gypsies: Blacks of Eastern Europe." *The Nation,* 222 (17 April 1976): 461.

Quigley, K. 2000. "Lofty Goals, Modest Results: Assisting Civil Society in Eastern Europe." In *Funding Virtue. Civil Society Aid and Democracy Promotion,* edited by M. Ottaway, and T. Carothers, 191–216. Washington DC: Carnegies Endowment for International Peace.

Rabehl, B. 1996. "Repressive Toleranz. Der SDS und das Problem der Gewalt-freiheit." In *Gewaltfreiheit. Pazifistische Konzepte im 19. und 20. Jahrhundert,* edited by A. Gestrich, G. Niedhart, and B. Ulrich, 133–150. Münster: LIT Verlag.

Raik, K. "Bureaucratization or Strengthening of the Political?: Estonian Institutions and Integration into the European Union." *Cooperation and Conflict* 37(2)(2002): 137–156.

Rau, Z. "Some Thoughts on Civil Society in Eastern Europe and the Lockean Contractarian Approach." *Political Studies* 35(1987): 573–592.

Reddaway, P., ed. 1972. *Uncensored Russia, the Human Rights Movement in the Soviet Union, the Annotated Text of the Unofficial Moscow Journal "a Chronicle of Current Events (nos 1–11)."* New York: American Heritage Press.

Reddaway, P. and S. Bloch. 1984. *Soviet Psychiatric Abuse: the Shadow Over World Psychiatry,* London: Gollancz.

Reich, W. 1978. "Diagnosing Soviet Dissidents." *Harper's,* August, 31–37.

———. 1980. "The Force of Diagnosis, Opportune Uses of Psychiatry." *Harper's,* May, 20–32.

———. 1983. "Soviet Psychiatry." *New York Times Magazine,* 30 January, 22–30.

Reitan, R. 1997. *Global Activism.* London: Routledge.

Renwick, A. "Anti-Political or Just Anticommunist? Varieties of Dissidence in East-Central Europe, and their Implications for the Development of Political Society." *East European Politics and Societies* 20 (2)(2006): 286–318.

Richards, M. 1998. *A Time of Silence: Civil War and the Culture of Repression in Franco's Spain.* Cambridge: Cambridge University Press.

Ricoeur, P. 1997. *L'Idéologie et l'Utopie.* Paris: Éditions du Seuil.

Risse, T. and K. Sikkink, eds. 1999. "The Socialization of International Human Rights Norms into Domestic Practices: Introduction." In *The Power of Human Rights International Norms and Domestic Change,* edited by T. Risse, S. Rapp, and K. Sikkink, 1–38. New York: Cambridge University Press.

Risse-Kappen, T., ed. 1995. *Bringing Transnational Relations Back in: Non State Actors, Domestic Structures, and International Institutions.* Cambridge: Cambridge University Press.

Rokkan, S. 2000. *Staat, Nation und Demokratie in Europa.* Frankfurt: Suhrkamp.

Romanos, E. 2007. "Fernando Gómez Peláez: Crítica y Disidencia en el Movimiento Libertario en el Exilio", *Ayer* 67(3), 235-254.

Romero Maura, J. 1971. "The Spanish Case." In *Anarchism Today,* edited by D.E. Apter and J. Joll, 60–83. London, MacMillan.

Römmele, A. 2007. "Parteien als Akteure der politischen Kommunikation auf europäischer Ebene." In *Entgrenzte Demokratie? Herausforderungen für die politische Interessenvermittlung,* edited by O. Jarren, D. Lachenmeier, and A. Steiner, 93–106. Baden-Baden: Nomos.

Rose-Ackermann, S. 2005. *From Elections to Democracy. Building Accountable Government in Hungary and Poland.* Cambridge: Cambridge University Press.

Roth, R. 1994. "Lokale Bewegungsnetzwerke und Institutionalisierung von neuen sozialen Bewegungen." In *Öffentlichkeit, öffentliche Meinung, soziale Bewegungen,* edited by F. Neidhardt, 413–436. Opladen: Westdeutscher Verlag.

Röttger, U. 2000. *Public Relations – Organisation und Profession. Öffentlichkeitsarbeit als Organisationsfunktion. Eine Berufsfeldstudie.* Wiesbaden: Westdeutscher Verlag.

Roy, W.G. and R. Parker-Gwin. "How Many Logics of Collective Action?" *Theory and Society* 28(2)(1999): 203–37.

Ruane, J. and J. Todd. 1996. *The Dynamics of Conflict in Northern Ireland: Power Conflict and Emancipation.* Cambridge: Cambridge University Press.

Rucht, D. 1994. "Öffentlichkeit als Mobilisierungsfaktor für soziale Bewegungen." In *Öffentlichkeit, öffentliche Meinung, soziale Bewegungen (= Kölner Zeitschrift für Soziologie und Sozialpsychologie, special edition 34),* edited by F. Neidhardt, 337–358. Opladen: Westdeutscher Verlag.

———. 2002. "Herausforderungen für die globalisierungskritischen Bewegungen." *Forschungsjournal Neue Soziale Bewegungen* 15 (1): 16–21.

———. "The Changing Role of Political Protest Movements." *West European Politics* 26(4)(2003): 153–76.

———. 2007. "The Spread of Protest Politics." In *The Oxford Handbook of Political Behavior,* edited by R. J. Dalton and H.-D. Klingemann, 708–723. Oxford: Oxford University Press.

Rucht, D. and D. della Porta. "The Dynamics of Environmental Campaigns." *Mobilization* 7(1)(2002): 1–14.

Rucht, D. and S. Teune, eds. 2008. *Nur Clowns und Chaoten? Die G8-Proteste in Heiligendamm im Spiegel der Massenmedien.* Frankfurt am Main and New York: Campus.

Rucht, D., S. Teune, and M. Yang. 2007. "Global Justice Movements in Germany." In *The Global Justice Movement: A Crossnational and Transnational Perspective,* edited by D. della Porta, 157–183. Boulder: Paradigm.

Rüegg-Stürm, J. 2001. *Organisation und organisationaler Wandel. Eine theoretische Erkundung aus konstruktivistischer Sicht.* Wiesbaden: Westdeutscher Verlag.

Rufat, H. 2003. "En Cachette avec *L'Homme Révolté:* les Anarchistes Espagnols." In *Albert Camus et les Écritures du XX siècle,* edited by S. Brodziak, C. Chaulet-Achour, R.-B. Fonkoua, E. Fraisse, and A.-M. Lilti, 153–171. Arras: Artois Presses Université.

Rufat, R. "Homenaje en Memoria de Albert Camus (Miembro del Comité de Honor del Ateneo)." *Anthropos* 199(2003): 155–157.

Rupp, H.K. 1970. *Außerparlamentarische Opposition in der Ära Adenauer. Der Kampf gegen die Atombewaffnung in den fünfziger Jahren.* Köln: Pahl-Rugenstein.

Ruzza, C. 2004. *Europe and Civil Society, Movement Coalitions and European Governance.* Manchester and New York: Manchester University Press.

Rychlík, J. 1998. *Češi a Slováci ve 20. století. Česko-slovenské vztahy 1945–1992.* Bratislava: Academic Electronic Press.

———. 2007. *Cestování do ciziny v habsburské monarchii a v Československu: pasová, vízová a vystěhovalecká politika 1848–1989.* USD: Praha.

Sampson, S. 1996. "The Social Life of Projects: Importing Civil Society to Albania." In *Civil Society: Challenging Western Models,* edited by C.M. Hann and E. Dunn, 121–142. London: Routlege.

Sartori, G. 1990 [1968]. "The Sociology of Parties: A Critical Review." In *The West European Party System,* edited by P. Mair, 150–182. Oxford: Oxford University Press.

Scarman Tribunal. 1969. *Report of Tribunal of Violence and Civil Disturbances in Northern Ireland.* Belfast: Cmnd 566, HMSO.

Schaefer, B.C., and J. Carmin. "Scholarship on Social Movement Organizations: Classic Views and Emerging Trends." *Mobilization* 10(2)(2005): 201–212.

Scharpf, F.W. 1999. *Governing in Europe: Effective and Democratic?* London: Oxford University Press.

Scheper-Hughes, N. and A.M. Lovell, eds. 1987. *Psychiatry Inside Out: Selected Writings of Franco Basaglia.* New York: Columbia University Press.

Schildt, A. and D. Siegfried. 2006. *Between Marx and Coca-Cola. Youth Cultures in Changing European Societies, 1960–1980.* Oxford: Berghahn Books.

Schuppert, G.F., ed. 2006. *The Europeanisation of Governance* (= *Schriften zur Governance-Forschung* 4). Baden-Baden: Nomos.

Schwellnus, G. 2005. "The Adoption of Nondiscrimination and Minority Protection Rules in Romania, Hungary, and Poland." In *The Europeanization of Central and Eastern Europe,* edited by F. Schimmelfennig and U. Sedelmeier, 51–70. Ithaca: Cornell University Press.

Sebaldt, M. and A. Straßner. 2004. *Verbände in der Bundesrepublik Deutschland. Eine Einführung.* Wiesbaden: VS Verlag für Sozialwissenschaften.

Segal, B. 1976. "Involuntary Hospitalization in the USSR." In *Psychiatry and Psychology in the USSR,* edited by S. Corson and E. Corson, 267–280. New York: Plenum Press.

Siegfried, D. 1999. "Stalin und Elvis. Antikommunismus zwischen Erfahrung, Ideologie und Eigensinn." *sowi* 28 (January–March), 27–35.

Silva, F. 2008. "Do Transnational Social Movements Matter? Four Case Studies Assessing the Impact of Transnational Social Movements on the Global Governance of Trade, Labour and Finance." Ph.D. dissertation, European University Institute.

Simhandl, K. "'Western Gypsies and Travellers'-"Eastern Roma": The Creation of Political Objects by the Institutions of the European Union." *Nations and Nationalism* 12(1)(2006): 97–115.

Skalnik Leff, C. 1988. *National Conflict in Czechoslovakia. The Making and Unmaking of a State.* Princeton: Princeton University Press.

Slezkine, Y. 1994. *Arctic Mirrors: Russia and the Small Peoples of the North*. Ithaca: Cornell University Press.

Slobin, D., ed. 1966. *Handbook of Soviet Psychology: Prepared for the International Congress of Psychology, Moscow, USSR, August 4–11, 1966*. White Plains: International Arts and Science Press.

Smith, J. 2007. "Transnational Movements." In *The Blackwell Encyclopedia of Sociology*, edited by G. Ritzer, vol. x: 5060–5064. Malden, MA: Blackwell.

Smith, J. et al. 2007. *Global democracy and the World Social Forum*. Boulder: Paradigm.

Smith, J., C. Chatfield, and R. Pagnucco, eds. 1997. *Transnational Social Movements and Global Politics: Solidarity Beyond the State*. Syracuse, NY: Syracuse University Press.

Smith, M.P. and L.E. Guarnizo, eds. 1998. *Transnationalism from Below*. New Brunswick: Transaction.

Smith, T. and T.A. Olescuk. 1996. *No Asylum: State Psychiatric Repression in the Former USSR*. Basingstoke: Macmillan.

Snow, D.A. 2004. "Framing Processes, Ideology and Discursive Fields." In *The Blackwell Companion to Social Movements*, edited by D.A. Snow, S.A. Soule, and H. Kriesi, 380–412. Oxford: Blackwell Publishing.

———. 1988. "Ideology, Frame Resonance and Participant Mobilization." In *From Structure to Action: Comparing Social Movement Research Across Cultures*, edited by B. Klandermans, H. Kriesi, and S. Tarrow, 197–218. London: JAI Press.

———. 1992. "Master Frames and Cycles of Protest." In *Frontiers in Social Movement Theory*, edited by A. Morris and C. Mueller, 133–155. New Haven, CT: Yale University Press.

———. 1999. "Alternative Types of Cross-national Diffusion in the Social Movement Arena." In *Social Movements in a Globalizing World*, edited by D. della Porta, H. Kriesi, and D. Rucht, 23–39. Basingstoke and New York: Macmillan.

———. 2000. "Framing Processes and Social Movements: An Overview and Assessment." *Annual Review of Sociology*, 26(2000): 611–639.

Snow, D.A., B. Rochford, S. Worden, and R.D. Benford. "Frame Alignment Processes, Micromobilization, and Movement Participation." *American Sociological Review* 51 (4)(1986): 464–481.

Sokolová, V. 2002. "A Matter of Speaking. Racism, Gender and Social Deviance in the Politics of the 'Gypsy Question' in Communist Czechoslovakia, 1945–1989." Ph.D. Dissertation, University of Washington.

Sommier, I., et al., eds. 2008. *La Généalogie des Mouvements Antiglobalisation en Europe. Une Perspective Compare*. Paris: Karthala.

Stark, D., L. Bruszt, and B. Vedres. "Rooted Transnational Publics: Integrating Foreign Ties and Civic Activism." *Theory and Society* 35(3)(2006): 323–349.

Steinberg, M.W. "Tilting the Frame: Considerations on Collective Action Framing from a Discursive Turn." *Theory and Society*, 27(6)(1998): 845–872.

———. "The Talk and Back Talk of Collective Action: A Dialogic Analysis of Repertoires of Discourse among Nineteenth-Century English Cotton Spinners." *The American Journal of Sociology*, 105(3)(1999): 736–780.

Steir, C. 1977. *Blue Jolts, True Stories from the Cuckoo's Nest*. New York: Picador.

Stewart, M. 1997. *The Time of the Gypsies*. Boulder: Westview Press.

Stover, E. and E.O. Nightingale, eds. 1985. *The Breaking of Bodies and Minds, Torture, Psychiatric Abuse and the Health Professions*. New York: Freeman.

Straßner, A. and M. Sebaldt. 2007. "Die Europäisierung von Verbandsarbeit: Verbandsfunktionen, Wandlungsmuster, Konsequenzen." In *Entgrenzte Demokratie? Herausforderungen für die politische Interessenvermittlung*, edited by O. Jarren, D. Lachenmeier, and A. Steiner, 123–144. Baden-Baden: Nomos.

Streeck, W. "Vielfalt und Interdependenz. Überlegungen zur Rolle von intermediären Organisationen in sich ändernden Umwelten." *Kölner Zeitschrift für Soziologie und Sozialpsychologie* 39(3)(1987): 470–495.

Sumner, G.D. 1996. *Dwight Macdonald and the Politics Circle. The Challenge of Cosmopolitan Democracy*. Ithaca: Cornell University Press.

Suny, R.G. and T. Martin, eds. 2001. *A State of Nations. Empire and Nation-Making in the Age of Lenin and Stalin*. Oxford: Oxford University Press.

Suri, J. 2003. *Power and Protest: Global Revolution and the Rise of Détente*. Cambridge, MA: Harvard University Press.

———. 2004. "Remembering the Images and Emotions of 1968." *H-Net Review*. Retrieved 15 April 2008 from http://www.hnet.org/reviews/showrev .cgi?path=213331099493514.

Szasz, T. 1961. *The Myth of Mental Illness, Foundations of a Theory of Personal Conduct*. New York; Harper and Row.

Szyszka, P. 2004. "PR-Arbeit als Organisationsfunktion. Konturen eines organisationalen Theorieentwurfs zu Public Relations und Kommunikationsmanagement." In *Theorien der Public Relations. Grundlagen und Perspektiven der PR-Forschung*, edited by U. Röttger, 149–168. Wiesbaden: VS Verlag für Sozialwissenschaften, 149–168.

———. 2005. "Organisationsbezogene Ansätze." In *Handbuch der Public Relations. Wissenschaftliche Grundlagen und berufliches Handeln. Mit Lexikon*, edited G. Bentele, R. Fröhlich, and P. Szyszka, 161–176. Wiesbaden: VS Verlag für Sozialwissenschaften.

Taggart, P. 2002. "Populism and the Pathology of Representative Politics." In *Democracies and the Populist Challenge*, edited by Y. Mény and Y. Surel, 81–98. Basingstoke: Palgrave Macmillan.

Tamás, G.M. 1994. "A Disquisition of Civil Society." *Social Research* 61(2): 205–222.

Tarrow, S. 1989. *Democracy and Disorder: Protest and Politics in Italy, 1965–1975*. Oxford: Oxford University Press.

———. 1990. "The Phantom of the Opera: Political Parties and Social Movements of the 1960s and 1970s in Italy." In *Challenging the Political Order. New Social and Political Movements in Western Democracies,* edited by R. J. Dalton and M. Kuechler, 251–273. Cambridge: Polity Press.

———. "Aiming at a Moving Target: Social Science and the Recent Rebellions in Eastern Europe." *PS: Political Science and Politics,* 24(1)(1991): 12–20.

———. 1994. *Power in Movement. Social Movements, Collective Action and Politics.* Cambridge: Cambridge University Press.

———. 1998. *Power in Movement. Social Movements and Contentious Politics.* Cambridge: Cambridge University Press.

———. 2005. *The New Transnational Activism.* New York, Cambridge: Cambridge University Press.

Tarrow, S. and D. della Porta. 2005. "Transnational Processes and Social Activism: An Introduction." In *Transnational Protest and Global Activism,* edited by S. Tarrow and D. della Porta, 1–17. New York, Oxford, and Lanham: Rowman & Littlefield.

———. 2005. "Conclusion: 'Globalization,' Complex Internationalism and Transnational Contention." In *Transnational Protest and Global Activism,* edited by D. della Porta and S. Tarrow, 227–246. New York, Oxford, and Lanham: Rowman & Littlefield.

Tavera, S. 2005. *Federica Montseny.* Madrid: Temas de Hoy.

Teune, S. 2007. "A Snap-shot of Movements. Assessing Social Movement Diversity through Campaign Analysis?" Paper presented to the workshop *Campaign Analysis in a Globalizing World,* Evangelische Akademie Tutzing, 27–28 April.

———. 1993. "Organisation—eine vernachlässigte Grösse in der Kommunikationswissenschaft." In *Theorien öffentlicher Kommunikation,* edited by G. Bentele and M. Rühl, 309–313. München: Ölschläger.

———. 2003. *Organisationskommunikation. Theoretische Grundlagen und empirische Forschungen.* 2nd ed. Münster, Hamburg, and London: Lit-Verlag.

———. 2005. "Public Relations aus organisationssoziologischer Sicht." In *Handbuch der Public Relations. Wissenschaftliche Grundlagen und berufliches Handeln. Mit Lexikon,* edited by G. Bentele, R. Fröhlich, and P. Szyszka, 37–49. Wiesbaden: VS Verlag für Sozialwissenschaften.

Thornberry, P. 2001. *International Law and the Rights of Minorities.* Oxford: Oxford University Press.

Tilly, C. "Getting It Together in Burgundy, 1675–1975." *Theory and Society* 4 (4)(1977): 479–504.

———. 1984. "Social Movements and National Politics." In *State-Making and Social Movements: Essays in History and Theory,* edited by C. Bright and S. Harding, 297–317. Ann Arbor: University of Michigan Press.

———. 2002. "Political Identities in History." In *Stories, Identities, and Political Change,* edited by C. Tilly, 57–68. Oxford: Rowman & Littlefield.

———. 2004. *Social Movements, 1768–2004*. Boulder: Paradigm.

Tismăneanu, V., ed. 1990. *In Search of Civil Society. Independent Peace Movements in the Soviet Bloc*. London and New York: Routledge.

———. 1992. *Reinventing Politics: Eastern Europe from Stalin to Havel*. New York: Free Press.

———. 1999. "Introduction." In *The Revolutions of 1989*, edited by V. Tismăneanu, 1–18. London and New York: Routledge.

Touraine, A. 1968. *Le Mouvement de Mai ou le Communisme Utopique*. Paris: Editions de Seuil.

Tucker, A. 1998. "The Politics of Conviction: The Rise and Fall of Czech Intellectuals-Politicians." In *Intellectuals and Politics in Central Europe*, edited by A. Bozóki, 185–205. Budapest and New York: CEU Press.

van der Port, M. 1998. *Gypsies, Wars and other Instances of the Wild. Civilization and its Discontents in a Serbian Town*. Amsterdam: University of Amsterdam Press.

van Dyke, N. 2003. "Protest Cycles and Party Politics. The Effects of Elite Allies and Antagonists on the Student Protest in the United States, 1930–1990." In *States, Parties, and Social Movements*, edited by J.A. Goldstone, 226–245. Cambridge: Cambridge University Press.

Van Voren, R. 1983. *Political Psychiatry in the USSR*. Amsterdam: Stichting Comité Vladimir Bukovksy.

———, ed. 1989. *Soviet Psychiatric Abuse in the Gorbachev Era*. Amsterdam: IAPUP.

Vay, M., ed. 2005. *Zengő - Ökológia, Politika és Társadalmi Mozgalmak a Zengő-konfliktusban*. Budapest: Védegylet. In English as *Zengő: Ecology, Politics and Social Movements in the Zengő-conflict*.

Vega, E. "Anarquismo y Sindicalismo durante la Dictadura y la República." *Historia Social* 1(1988): 55–62.

von Unruh, F. 1961. *Wir Wollen Frieden. Die Reden und Aufrufe 1960/61*. Düsseldorf: Monitor-Verlag.

Waldinger, R. and D. Fitzgerald. "Transnationalism in Question." *American Journal of Sociology* 109 (2004): 1177–1195.

Walker, G. 2004. *A History of the Ulster Unionist Party: Protest, Pragmatism and Pessimism*. Manchester: Manchester University Press.

Ward, C. and D. Goodway. 2003. *Talking Anarchy*. Nottingham: Five Leaves Press.

Wedel, J.R. 1998. *Collision and Collusion: the Strange Case of Western Aid to Eastern Europe*. New York: St Martins Press.

Weick, K.E. 1985. *Der Prozess des Organisierens*. Frankfurt/Main: Suhrkamp.

Werkmeister, F. 1975. "Die Protestbewegung gegen den Vietnamkrieg in der Bundesrepublik Deutschland 1965–1973." D. Phil. Dissertation, Philipps-Universität Marburg/Lahn.

Wessels, B. 2000. "Verbände, Parteien und Interessenvermittlung—Erosion oder Stabilität?" In *Zur Zukunft der Demokratie. Herausforderungen im Zeitalter der Globalisierung*, edited by H.-D. Klingemann and F. Neidhardt, 27–49. Berlin: Edition Sigma.

Wessels, B. 2003. "Gewerkschaften in der Mediengesellschaft." In *Die Gewerkschaften in Politik und Gesellschaft der Bundesrepublik Deutschland. Ein Handbuch*, edited by W. Schroeder and B. Wessels, 323–341. Wiesbaden: Westdeutscher Verlag.

Westby, D.L. "Strategic Imperative, Ideology, and Frame." *Mobilization* 7(3) (2002): 287–304.

Westerbarkey, J. 1991. *Das Geheimnis. Zur funktionalen Ambivalenz von Kommunikationsstrukturen*, Opladen: Westdeutscher Verlag.

Wette, W., ed. 1999. *Pazifistische Offiziere in Deutschland 1871–1933*. Bremen: Donat.

White, S. "Making Anarchism Respectable? The Social Philosophy of Colin Ward." *Journal of Political Ideologies* 12(1)(2007): 11–28.

Wiesenthal, H. 1999. "Interessenverbände in Ostmitteleuropa. Startbedingungen und Entwicklungsprobleme." In *Systemwechsel 4. Die Rolle von Verbänden im Transformationsprozeß*, edited by W. Merkel and E. Sandschneider, 83–113. Opladen: Leske + Budrich.

Williams, K. 1997. *The Prague Spring and its aftermath. Czechoslovak politics, 1968–1970*. Cambridge: Cambridge University Press.

Willke, H. 2000. *Sytemtheorie I: Grundlagen: Eine Einführung in die Grundprobleme der Theorie sozialer Systeme*. 6th corrected ed. Stuttgart: Lucius & Lucius.

Wittner, L. 1993. *One World or None: A History of the World Nuclear Disarmament Movement Through 1953*. Stanford: Stanford University Press.

Wizner, B. 2005. "Osztok, Keverek. Cigány Programok és Roma Szervezetek Finanszírozása a Rendszerváltás Után." In *Kisebbségek Kisebbsége*, edited by J. Szalai and M. Neményi, 430–458. Budapest: Új Mandátum.

Wolin, R. 1992. *The Terms of Cultural Criticism: the Frankfurt School, Existentialism, Poststructuralism*. New York: Columbia University Press.

Woodcock, G. 1977. "Anarchism: A Historical Introduction." In *The Anarchist Reader*, edited by G. Woodcook, 11–56. Hassocks: The Harvester Press Limited.

Working Group on the Internment of Dissenters in Mental Hospitals. 1977. *Bulletin on Psychiatric Abuse in the Soviet Union*. Spring.

World Psychiatric Association. 1991. *Report by the World Psychiatric Association Team of a Visit to the Soviet Union (9–29 June 1991)*. London: Royal College of Psychiatrists.

Wortis, J. "Soviet Psychiatry." *Psychiatric News* 14(4)(1979): 12–19.

Yack, B. 1986. *The Longing for Total Revolution. Philosophic Sources of Social Discontent from Rousseau to Marx and Nietzsche*. Princeton: Princeton University Press.

Yeoh, B. and K. Willis, eds. 2003. *State/Nation/Transnation: Perspectives on Transnationalism in the Asia-Pacific.* London: Routledge.

Zald, M.N. 1996. "Culture, Ideology, and Strategic Framing." In *Comparative Perspectives on Social Movements. Political Opportunities, Mobilizing Structures, and Cultural Framing,* edited by D. McAdam, J.D. McCarthy and M.N. Zald, 261–274. Cambridge: Cambridge University Press.

———. "Ideologically Structured Action: An Enlarged Agenda for Social Movement Research." *Mobilization* 5 (1)(2000): 1–16.

Žatkuliak, J. 1996. *Federalizácia československého štátu 1968–1970 : vznik československej federácie roku 1968.* Brno: Doplněk.

Zerfass, A. 1996. *Unternehmensführung und Öffentlichkeitsarbeit. Grundlagen einer Theorie der Unternehmenskommunikation und Public Relations.* Opladen: Westdeutscher Verlag.

Zhitnikova, T. 1975. "Open Letter to A. Snezhnevsky, 7 April 1975." *Cahiers de Samizdat* 24.

Ziemann, B. "Peace Movements in Western Europe, Japan and USA since 1945: An Introduction." *Mitteilungsblatt des Instituts für soziale Bewegungen* 32 (2004): 5–19.

———. 2007. "Situating Peace Movements in the Political Culture of the Cold War. Introduction." In *Peace Movements in Western Europe, Japan and the USA during the Cold War,* edited by B. Ziemann, 11–38. Essen: Klartext.

Zimmer, A., and E. Priller, eds. 2004. *Future of Civil Society: Making Central European Nonprofit-Organizations Work.* Wiesbaden: VS Verlag für Sozialwissenschaften.

Zolo, D. 2007. *Globalisation. An Overview.* Colchester: ECPR Press.

Zürn, M. 1998. "Schwarz-Rot-Grün-Braun: Reaktionsweisen auf Denationalisierung." In *Politik der Globalisierung,* edited by U. Beck, 297–330. Frankfurt: Suhrkamp.

Notes on Contributors

Lorenzo Bosi is a Marie Curie Fellow at the European University Institute on a research project on the unfolding, development, and demise of political violence. His main research interests have been on political sociology and historical sociology, where his studies have primarily focused on social movements and political violence. He has published in several refereed journals in these fields: *Mobilization, Ricerche di Storia Politica, Research in Social Movements, Conflict and Change, Historical Sociology, The Sixties.* He is the author of a book on the Northern Ireland Civil Rights Movement that is about to be published in the Berghahn Books' "Protest, Culture and Society Series."

Aron Buzogány studied political science in Tübingen, Helsinki, Moscow, Hamburg and is a Ph.D. candidate at the Free University Berlin. In 2008–2009, he was a Max Kade Scholar and a Fox International Fellow at Yale University. Currently, he works as a researcher at the German Institute for Public Administration in Speyer, Germany. His recent publications include the edited volume of *Osteuropa. Politik, Wirtschaft und Gesellschaft* (ed. with Rolf Frankenberger, 2007) and journal articles in the *European Foreign Affairs Review, Südosteuropa, Environmental Politics, Regulation and Governance,* and *Acta Politica.*

Donatella della Porta is Professor of Sociology in the Department of Political and Social Sciences at the European University Institute. Among her recent publications are: *Social Movements and Europeanization* (with Manuela Caiani, 2009), *Another Europe* (ed., 2009), *Democracy in Social Movements* (ed., 2009), *Approaches and Methodologies in the Social Sciences* (ed. with Michael Keating, 2008), *Voices from the Valley; Voices from the Street* (with Gianni Piazza, 2008 in Berghahn Books's series "Protest, Culture and Society"), *The Global Justice Movement* (2007), *Globalization from Below* (with Massimiliano Andretta, Lorenzo Mosca and Herbert Reiter, 2006), *The Policing of Transnational Protest* (with Abby Peterson and Herbert Reiter, 2006), *Social Movements: An Introduction,* 2nd edition (with Mario Diani, 2006), and *Transnational Protest and Global Activism* (with Sidney Tarrow, 2005).

Celia Donert is a postdoctoral fellow at the Zentrum für Zeithistorische Forschung in Potsdam, having previously been a visiting fellow at research institutes in Berlin and Prague. She holds a Ph.D. in modern European history from the European University Institute in Florence, an M.A. from the School of Slavonic and East European Studies, University of London, and a B.A. from Oxford University.

Swen Hutter is a Ph.D. candidate at the Chair in Comparative Politics, University of Munich. His research interests include social movements, political parties, and public debates on Islam/Muslims in Western Europe. He is currently writing his dissertation on the transformation of protest politics in a denationalizing world. His recent publications include "Protest Politics in a Changing Political Context: Switzerland, 1975–2005" (with Marco Giugni) in *Swiss Political Science Review* 15 (2009) and "Debates over Islam in Austria, Germany, and Switzerland: Between Ethnic Citizenship, Church-state Relations, and Right-wing Populism" (with Martin Dolezal and Marc Helbling) in *West European Politics* 33 (2) (2010).

Mariya Ivancheva is a Ph.D. candidate in the Department of Sociology and Social Anthropology at the Central European University. She has published on the history and memory of socialism, dissent and its legacy, theories of elites and intellectuals, and utopian studies. She is currently doing field research on socialist intellectuals in Venezuela.

Hara Kouki is a Ph.D. candidate in the Law Department at Birkbeck College, London. She graduated in history from the University of Athens and holds a master's in film and history from the University of Kent and a master's degree in history and civilization from the European University Institute in Florence. She has co-edited The Greek Crisis and European Modernity (Palgrave, 2013). Hara has worked as an affiliated researcher with ELIAMEP (Athens, Greece) as part of the EU- funded IME research project and currently holds a Research Assistant position at the European University Institute, Robert Schuman Centre for Advanced Studies, Florence, Italy. Her research interests lie in the field of social mobilization in the post war world and she has published in academic journals, as well as in Greek and international press.

Dominik Lachenmeier received his Ph.D. at the Institute of Mass Media and Communication Research of the University of Zurich, where he has worked as a scientific assistant for several years. His main fields of research are organizational communication, political communication, as well as communication of social movements and associations. His publications include *Gewerkschaftskommunikation im Wandel* (2009), *Entgrenzte Demokratie* (ed. with Otfried Jarren and Adrian Steiner, 2007), and "Die Achtundsechziger-Bewegung zwischen etablierter und alternativer Öffentlichkei," in Martin Klimke and Joachim Scharloth, eds., *Handbuch 1968* (2007).

Johanna Niesyto is a Ph.D. student in the Department of Social Sciences at the University of Siegen, Germany. She worked as a research fellow in the project "Changing Protest and Media Cultures. Transnational Anti-Corporate Campaigns and Digital Communication," which was part of the Collaborative Research Centre "Media Upheavals" and funded by the German Research Foundation. Her field of research includes questions concerning transnational public spaces, with a focus on the Internet in general, but with particular focus on Wikipedia. She has edited the publications *Politik mit dem Einkaufswagen* (with Sigrid Baringhorst, Veronika Kneip and Anne März, 2007) and *Political Campaigning on the Web* (with Sigrid Baringhorst and Veronika Kneip, 2009).

Andrew Oppenheimer is a lecturer in the Department of History at Maastricht University, The Netherlands. He earned his Ph.D. in modern European history from the University of Chicago and is the author of "By Any Means Necessary? West German Pacifism and the Politics of Solidarity, 1945–1974," in Benjamin Ziemann, ed., *Peace Movements in Western Europe, Japan, and the USA during the Cold War* (2008).

Eduardo Romanos is a Ramón y Cajal Fellow in the Department of Sociology I at the Universidad Complutense de Madrid. He has previously worked as a postdoctoral fellow at the University of Trento and as a Juan de la Cierva Fellow at the Universidad Pública de Navarra. Eduardo received his Ph.D. in Political and Social Sciences from the European University Institute in Florence, and also holds a European Doctorate Certificate in Social History following his Marie Curie Fellow position at the University of Groningen. His work has appeared in Journal of Historical Sociology, Revista Española de Investigaciones Sociológicas, Social Movement Studies, and other scholarly journals. He is also the author of book chapters on collective action and social movements. Eduardo is currently conducting research on the Spanish indignados and the new transnational wave of mobilization.

Simon Teune works at the Social Science Research Center, Berlin. His research interests are social movements, protest, and culture. He is preparing a Ph.D. dissertation dealing with the communication strategies of global justice groups during the anti-G8 protests in Germany 2007. He is the editor of *The Transnational Condition. Protest Dynamics in an Entangled Europe*, published in Berghahn Books's series "Protest, Culture and Society."

Index

www.ingramcontent.com/pod-product-compliance
Lightning Source LLC
Chambersburg PA
CBHW060032030426
42334CB00019B/2287